HARDPRESS.NET

ISBN: 9781290809009

Published by:
HardPress Publishing
8345 NW 66TH ST #2561
MIAMI FL 33166-2626

Email: info@hardpress.net
Web: http://www.hardpress.net

# THE FASCINATING DUC DE RICHELIEU

BY THE SAME AUTHOR

Madame Récamier and her Friends
Madame de Pompadour
Madame de Montespan
Madame du Barry
Queens of the French Stage
Later Queens of the French Stage
Five Fair Sisters
Queen Margot
A Princess of Intrigue
The Women Bonapartes
A Rose of Savoy

# THE FASCINATING DUC DE RICHELIEU

LOUIS FRANÇOIS ARMAND DU PLESSIS (1696-1788)

BY

H. NOEL WILLIAMS

AUTHOR OF "THE WOMEN BONAPARTES," "A ROSE OF SAVOY"

WITH SEVENTEEN ILLUSTRATIONS



METHUEN & CO., LTD.
36 ESSEX STREET W.C.
LONDON

1910

*First Published in 1910*

TO

MY WIFE

# PREFACE

FEW names are more familiar to the student of French history in the eighteenth century than that of Louis François du Plessis, Maréchal Duc de Richelieu. Born in the year which preceded the Peace of Ryswick, he survived until the very eve of the Revolution, and commanded an inordinate share of public attention almost down to the day of his death, at the patriarchal age of ninety-two. Contemporary memoirs and correspondence are full of his adventures; when he was still scarcely more than a lad, he already enjoyed in Paris something of the fantastic renown which attached to Alcibiades in ancient Athens, while the fame of his amours and escapades had spread far beyond the frontiers of France. Spoiled child of Nature and of Fortune, handsome, debonair, witty, insinuating, magnificent, superbly brave, sublimely audacious, he dazzled the imagination of poets and historians as he dazzled the frail beauties of Paris and Versailles, and left behind him a name which will endure when those of infinitely greater and worthier men are forgotten.

The most notorious Lovelace of his age, who extended his conquests from the *coulisses* of the Opera to the steps of the throne, whom Princesses of the Blood consoled when a prisoner in the Bastille, and for the possession of whose heart titled dames contended with pistols in the alleys of the Bois de Boulogne, Richelieu's reputation for gallantry has, thanks to the *chroniques scandaleuses* of Soulavie[1] and

[1] *Mémoires du Maréchal duc de Richelieu, ouvrage composé dans le bibliothèque et sous les yeux du maréchal* (Paris, Buisson, 1790-93), 9 vols. Soulavie, who had acted as Richelieu's secretary during the closing years of the marshal's life, had undoubtedly had access to a number of original letters and other documents, and

Faur,[1] tended to overshadow his other claims to remembrance. These, however, are considerable, for he was one of the most versatile of men, and in his long and eventful life played many parts. He had a distinguished military career; he was entrusted with important diplomatic missions; he conspired with his country's enemies, and under a less mild *régime* than that of the Regency would probably have lost his head; he was the intimate friend of Voltaire, who lent him money and professed for him a boundless admiration, the confidant of Louis XV., a noted wit, a dandy of the first elegance, a redoubtable duellist, and he had a hand in nearly every Court intrigue of his time. In short, if he had been as impervious to feminine charms as the most rigid of *dévots* could have desired, his career would still afford abundant scope for the biographer.

For more than eighty years after Richelieu's death, the compilations of Soulavie and Faur remained the chief authorities on the life of the marshal. Then that charming historian François de Lescure published, in four volumes, his *Nouveaux Memoires du Maréchal duc de Richelieu*, in the form of an autobiography. So successful was the author in reproducing the atmosphere of the Court of Louis XV., that it is not uncommon

had been the recipient of many confidences. But he abused the trust reposed in him, and his book, which is intended to be a kind of satire on the old *régime*, if it contains a good deal that is true, comprises very much more that is false. An abbreviated version of it was published in Barrière's collection of French memoirs.

[1] *Vie privée du Maréchal du Richelieu, contenant ses amours et ses intrigues* (Paris, Buisson, 1791), 3 vols. This is an even more scandalous production than Soulavie's, and contains what purports to be part of a journal written by the marshal. An episode in this pretended journal—an intrigue between Richelieu and Madame Michelin, the beautiful wife of an upholsterer of the Faubourg Saint-Germain—furnished Monvel and Alexandre Duval with the subject for a play, produced at the Théâtre-Française, in 1796, with the title of *la Jeunesse de Richelieu, ou le Lovelace français*.

Richelieu, it may be mentioned, has been the subject of several other plays. In 1839, a charming comedy by Scribe's nephew Bayard and Pinel Dumanoir was produced at the Palais-Royal, under the title of *les Premières Armes de Richelieu*, in which Virginie Déjazet, who took the part of the youthful hero, secured one of her greatest triumphs. In 1899, *A Court Scandal*, an English adaptation of this comedy, appeared at the Court Theatre in London, and, nine years later, a musical version—*The Dashing Little Duke*—was produced at the Hicks Theatre, with Miss Ellaline Terriss in the part which Virginie Déjazet had so successfully created.

to find his opinions cited by English writers as those of Richelieu himself, which proves that prefaces and introductions are by no means invariably read. In some other respects, Lescure's work is much less satisfactory, since, though it makes most entertaining reading and contains much valuable information, the temptation to improve upon history has been too strong for the writer to resist, and when, as occasionally happens, the material which he so prettily embroiders will not stand the test of investigation, the reader's patience is somewhat severely tried. Thus, he devotes several pages to an account of the youthful Richelieu's experiences at the Battle of Denain, in which, we are told, the *sang-froid* which he displayed under his "baptism of fire" excited great admiration. Well, the Battle of Denain was fought on July 24, 1712, and we know, on the unimpeachable authority of Dangeau's *Journal*, that Richelieu—or Fronsac, as he was then called, his father being still alive—did not even set out to join the army of Flanders until August 2.[1] How, then, could he have been having horses killed under him on the banks of the Scheldt on July 24?

The number of important works on the social, military, and diplomatic history of the eighteenth century which have appeared since Lescure wrote have added materially to our knowledge of Richelieu, particularly in regard to his first imprisonment in the Bastille, his relations with the Regent's daughter, Mademoiselle de Valois, afterwards Duchess of Modena, his mission to Dresden, his defence of Genoa, the Minorca expedition, and his campaign of 1757 in Germany; and in introducing the marshal to English and American readers, I am able to offer them what, I venture to believe, is not only a complete, but an authentic, account of a very remarkable career.

The principal authorities, both contemporary and modern,

[1] "2 August, 1712.—The Duc de Fronsac, who came out of the Bastille six weeks ago, goes to serve in Flanders in the Musketeers and has taken leave of the King, who recommended him to be more prudent, and spoke, besides, with much kindness and consideration of the Duc de Richelieu, his father."

which I have consulted in the preparation of this volume are mentioned either in the text or the footnotes. I desire, however, to acknowledge my obligations to the following works by modern writers: the Comtesse d'Armaillé, *la Comtesse d'Egmont, fille du maréchal de Richelieu;* the Duc de Broglie, *Marie Thérèse, impératrice,* 1744–1746, and *Maurice de Saxe et le Marquis d'Argenson;* Édouard Barthélemy, *les Filles du Régent;* E. and J. de Goncourt, *Madame de Châteauroux et ses sœurs;* Lescure, *les Maîtresses du Régent;* Mary-Lafon, *les Dernières Armes de Richelieu: le Maréchal de Richelieu et Madame de Saint-Vincent;* Mr. J. B. Masson, *Madame de Tencin*; Comte Pajol, *les Guerres sous Louis XV.;* François Ravaisson, *Archives de la Bastille*, and M. Richard Waddington, *Louis XV. et le renversement des alliances*, and *la Guerre de Sept Ans.*

I must also express my thanks to the Duke of Buccleuch for his kind permission to reproduce Massé's charming miniature of Élisabeth Sophie de Lorraine, Duchesse de Richelieu, in the Montagu House Collection, and to Messrs. Harper and Brothers for their courtesy in allowing me to include several passages from my biographies of Madame de Pompadour and Madame du Barry dealing with those ladies' relations with Richelieu.

Lastly, I should like to express my appreciation of the care which has been bestowed upon the Index by Mrs. Eileen Mitchell.

H. NOEL WILLIAMS

LONDON
*March, 1910*

# CONTENTS

## CHAPTER I



## CHAPTER II

## CHAPTER III



## CHAPTER IV

## CHAPTER V



## CHAPTER VI



## CHAPTER VII

## CHAPTER XIII



## CHAPTER XIV

## CHAPTER XV



## CHAPTER XVI



## CHAPTER XVII

## CHAPTER XVIII



## CHAPTER XIX

## CHAPTER XXII



## CHAPTER XXIII

## CHAPTER XXIV



## CHAPTER XXV

# LIST OF ILLUSTRATIONS

"Si je croyais à la sorcellerie, je dirais qu'il faut que ce duc possède quelque secret surnaturel, car il n'a pas trouvé une femme qui lui ait opposé la moindre résistance ; toutes courent après lui, que c'est vraiment une honte."—*Correspondance complète de Madame, duchesse d'Orléans,* Letter of October 1, 1719.

# THE FASCINATING DUC DE RICHELIEU

## CHAPTER I

Portrait of the Duc de Fronsac (afterwards Duc de Richelieu) by Madame de Maintenon, on his first appearance at Court, at the age of fourteen—His childhood and education—He becomes the pet of all the ladies—He is married against his will to Anne Catherine de Noailles, Mlle. de Sansac—Encouraged in his follies by the Duchesse de Bourgogne, he misconstrues the princess's indulgence into a proof of her love—And pushes his presumption to the point of scandal—Letter of Madame de Maintenon to the Duc de Noailles concerning him—His father, exasperated by his conduct, demands a *lettre de cachet* from the King, and he is sent to the Bastille—His life in the Bastille—Letters of Bernaville, governor of the fortress, to Pontchartrain about him—He is visited by his wife—And by his father—He falls seriously ill of small-pox, but recovers—He is set at liberty, and sent to join the Army of Flanders.

"HE is sixteen years old, and he looks twelve. He has, for a little fellow, the prettiest figure imaginable, a handsome face, and a perfectly beautiful head. He is one of the best dancers, an excellent horseman, plays cards, loves music, and talks well. He is very deferential, very polished, has an agreeable wit, is discreet when occasion requires, and every one finds him such as I have described him." And again :

"One would like to caress him as a pretty child, and I was on the point of chucking him under the chin when he asked me to sign his marriage-contract." [1]

[1] Letters of January 11 and February 23, 1711, in Geffroy, *Madame de Maintenon d'après sa correspondance authentique.*

Thus wrote Madame de Maintenon to her friend, the Princesse des Ursins, of the Duc de Fronsac, afterwards the celebrated Maréchal Duc de Richelieu,[1] the defender of Genoa, the hero of Port-Mahon, the plunderer of Hanover, the representative of France at the Courts of Vienna and Dresden, the combatant in half a dozen famous battles, the victor in two fatal duels, the confidant of Louis XV., the correspondent of Madame de Tencin, the counsellor of Madame de Châteauroux, the enemy of Madame de Pompadour, the patron of Madame du Barry, the friend of Voltaire, the tyrant of the Comédie-Française, and the most scandalous Lovelace of a scandalous age, who extended his amorous conquests from the *coulisses* of the Opera to the steps of the throne, whom Princesses of the Blood consoled in the Bastille, and for the sake of whose *beaux yeux* great ladies contended with pistols in the alleys of the Bois de Boulogne.

Louis François Armand de Vignerot du Plessis, Duc de Fronsac, was the only son of Armand Jean de Vignerot, great-nephew of the celebrated cardinal, to whom the latter bequeathed the duchy of Richelieu and the bulk of his property, on condition that he should add the name of du Plessis to his patronymic.[2] He was born on March 16, 1696, and when, in January 1711, he made his first appearance on that stage where he was to play so prominent a part for nearly eighty years, he was only in his fifteenth year, and not sixteen, as Madame de Maintenon states.

As a child, the little duke was extremely delicate, and

[1] Other contemporaries confirm the account given by Madame de Maintenon of the impression created by the Duc de Fronsac at the Court. Dangeau writes: "Thursday 15 [January] Marly.—The King walked after dinner in the gardens. In the course of his walk he spoke to the little Duc de Fronsac, who is very much the fashion here this visit."

And, in a letter of January 28, the Marquise d'Huxelles says: "*Il* [*Fronsac*] *a été pensé fort joli à la Cour.*"

[2] Armand Jean de Vignerot was married three times: Firstly, to Anne Poussard du Vigean, widow of the Marquis de Pons, and sister of the Great Condé's inamorata, Marthe du Vigean; secondly, to Anne Marguerite d'Acigné; and, finally, in 1702, at the age of seventy-three, to Marguerite Thérèse Rouillé, widow of the Marquis de Noailles. The Duc de Fronsac was the issue of his second marriage.

"from the day of his birth struggled with death, and was enveloped and preserved in a box of cotton-wool." No one seems to have expected him to survive, and if old Fagon or some other fashionable member of the Faculty had been allowed a free hand with him, he would certainly have not. But his father distrusted doctors, and decided that with so frail a machine it was best to allow Nature to work her will. Nature showed herself eminently complaisant, and not only permitted the hope of the House of Richelieu to grow up, but endowed him with a constitution which enabled him to resist wounds, time, and the strain of a most irregular life, until he had reached the patriarchal age of ninety-two. Perhaps it would have been better for many of his contemporaries of both sexes if he had died in the box of cotton-wool, but of that the reader will presently be in a position to judge.

His education appears to have been much neglected, for his father, who had little book-learning himself, and was a very indolent old gentleman, left it entirely in the hands of a *gouverneur*, who, unhappily, was quite incompetent. Besides, the child was wilful and greatly preferred play to study, "in which he was seconded by his *gouverneur*, who, wishing to preserve his post, boasted continually of the progress of his pupil, although he made very little." [1]

Louis XIV. naturally entertained the greatest respect for the family of the great cardinal, whose iron rule had broken the power of feudalism and paved the way for his own autocratic *régime;* the Duc de Richelieu had been a good friend to Madame de Maintenon in the days when she was the widow Scarron and the extraordinary position to which she eventually attained was as yet undreamed of, and to such the old lady was always faithful. M. de Fronsac therefore entered upon his career as a courtier under exceptionally favourable auspices, and the qualities which Madame de Maintenon has described speedily made him the pet of all the ladies. The young gentleman, on his side, did not fail to take full advantage of the popularity which he enjoyed, and his precocious love-making so

[1] *Mémoires du duc de Richelieu* (*édit.* Barrière).

disquieted his venerable father that he decided to provide him with a wife without delay, and on February 12, 1711, married him to Anne Catherine de Noailles, Mlle. de Sansac, a daughter of his third wife by her previous husband.[1]

The wedding ceremony took place in the private chapel attached to the palace of Cardinal de Noailles, Archbishop of Paris, who was the bride's uncle. Mlle. de Sansac, who was some eighteen months older than her youthful consort, was "well-made, sensible and a very great heiress," but she had no pretensions to beauty. Moreover, M. de Fronsac was highly indignant at having a wife thrust upon him in this high-handed manner, and testified his resentment by treating the poor girl with the most withering disdain and indulging in numerous gallantries.

Admitted, thanks to the recommendation of Madame de Maintenon, to the little circle of the Duchesse de Bourgogne, he met with a very cordial reception from that princess, whom his amusing affectation of the tone of a man of the world greatly diverted. That she ever regarded him as anything but a feather-brained boy is extremely improbable, for in 1711 the duchess was no longer the frivolous, pleasure-loving girl who had flirted with Nangis, Maulevrier, and the Abbé de Polignac,[2] but a sensible young woman, who was beginning to realise the obligations which her position entailed and to appreciate at something like its true worth the passionate devotion which her husband entertained for her. At the same time, there can be no doubt that she showed herself very indulgent towards the follies of M. de Fronsac, who, "accustomed to meet with rather facile beauties, imagined that the kindness with which the Duchesse de Bourgogne honoured him was a proof of her love,"[3] and, in this persuasion, pushed his presumption to the point of scandal.

What precisely it was that he did is disputed. Soulavie

[1] According to Dangeau, this marriage had been resolved upon at the time when the Duc de Richelieu married Mlle. de Sansac's mother.

[2] On the flirtations of the Duchesse de Bourgogne, see the author's "A Rose of Savoy" (London, Methuen; New York, Scribners, 1909).

[3] *Vie privée du maréchal de Richelieu.*

declares that he concealed himself one fine evening beneath her Highness's bed, and, when discovered, gave as an excuse that he was anxious to hear what the ladies who attended the princess's *coucher* would say about him. But the historian Rulhière, who, at one time, acted as the duke's aide-de-camp and also claims to have been the recipient of his confidences, gives a different account of the affair:

"One day, being in attendance at the Duchesse de Bourgogne's toilette, at the moment when the men had to withdraw, to allow her to change her chemise, he concealed himself behind a screen, and was unable to resist the temptation of raising his head above it, in order to show the princess the excess of his love and of his temerity. The Dauphine, on the spur of the moment, gave a shriek. Fronsac was perceived by all the women; they all swore to him to keep the secret, and they blurted it out, without any desire to injure him, but through fear of being forestalled, each of them wishing to be the first to give information about this little episode. The King heard about it, and believed that it behoved him to punish this audacity, on account of the consequences which it might entail. He sent him to the Bastille."[1]

Whichever version is correct, it is certain that M. de Fronsac's escapade with the Duchesse de Bourgogne was not the sole cause of the disgrace into which he fell: indeed, it would appear to have been but the last of a whole bundle of peccadilloes. For, on March 22, 1711, we find Madame de Maintenon writing to the Duc de Noailles, then commanding in Spain, as follows:

"Our little prodigy, who is no longer prodigious, is going to be sent away; he is now as much blamed as he was praised during the last visit to Marly. I do not know, however, anything positive, except that he fell into a trap which was laid for him at the gaming-table. He lost twenty or thirty thousand francs at quinze, playing with a man who is believed to have had many persons at the table interested in his success. The Duc de Richelieu is of opinion that after this escapade he must

[1] Rulhière, *Anecdotes sur Richelieu, précédées d'une notice par Eugène Asse.*

send him still farther away than Flanders;[1] that the Marquis de Noailles, who is at present the object of his admiration, would keep an eye upon him under you; that he would acquire there a thorough acquaintance with his profession, and that it was very proper that he should profit by having such a cousin-germain. I thought this a very wise decision, and I trust that he will not embrace you more than reason. He is the most amiable doll that it is possible to see."[2]

However, about three weeks after this letter was written, came the adventure in the Duchesse de Bourgogne's bedchamber, which, joined to the "amiable doll's" other delinquencies, so exasperated his father that he decided that his exile to Spain would be far too light a punishment, and, on the advice apparently of Madame de Maintenon, sought an audience of the King, and demanded a *lettre de cachet* consigning his son to the Bastille.

The *lettre de cachet*, which is still in existence and bears the words "*pour correction*," was duly accorded the irate parent, who on April 22, 1711, himself conducted his young hopeful to the Bastille, "where he threatened to leave him to rot if he did not mend his ways."[3] "The Duc de Fronsac, son of the Duc de Richelieu," writes the discreet Dangeau, "having committed some fresh imprudence, his father begged the King to have him placed in the Bastille, where he now is. It is said to be the family's intention for him to remain there some time. He is so young that there is great hope that he will reform, particularly as he is very intelligent."[4]

In the closing years of the reign of Louis XIV., the famous fortress-prison in the Rue Saint-Antoine was a much less awesome place than it had been a century earlier. Then, even captives of the highest distinction were sometimes treated with great harshness, and Henri de Bourbon, Prince de Condé, when incarcerated there in 1616, was confined in a gloomy chamber,

[1] She means to the Army of Flanders.
[2] Geffroy, *Madame de Maintenon d'après sa Correspondance authentique.*
[3] *Mémoires du duc de Richelieu.*
[4] *Journal*, April 25, 1711.

the windows of which were so closely grated that scarcely a ray of light was permitted to enter, which so affected the unfortunate man's health, that when at length the windows were opened, he fainted away.[1] But with milder times had come a great change in the *régime* of the fortress; every attention was now paid to the health and comfort of the prisoners, so far as was consistent with their due security; and young gentlemen of family, like the Duc de Fronsac, undergoing a mild course of the Bastille at the request of their parents, were put to scarcely more inconvenience than if they had been condemned to detention in their own houses, with the prohibition of receiving letters or the visits of their friends. Thus, Fronsac was lodged in a fair-sized, though somewhat sparsely-furnished, room, on the second floor of the Tour de la Liberté;[2] he was allowed the services of one of his *valets de chambre;* he was permitted to take regular exercise in the inner courtyard of the fortress; a learned and pious ecclesiastic, the Abbé de Saint-Remy, who had been chosen by the King, visited him every day for the purpose of his intellectual and moral improvement, and he also had masters for languages and mathematics; his meals were served from the table of the governor, M. de Bernaville, who kept an excellent chef, and, after he had been a prisoner about a fortnight, it was arranged that he should dine and spend each afternoon at the governor's house.

"I have arranged with the Cardinal de Noailles[3] and the Duc and Duchesse de Richelieu," writes Bernaville to Pontchartrain,[4] that M. de Fronsac is to come and dine with me and

[1] For an account of the imprisonment of Condé, see the author's "A Princess of Intrigue" (London, Hutchinson; New York, Putnams, 1908).

[2] "The singular appellation had come to it from the circumstance that it had been the part of the Bastille where prisoners were lodged who enjoyed exceptionally favourable treatment, those who had the 'liberty' of walking during the day in the courtyard of the château. These prisoners were said to be 'in the liberty of the court'; the officers of the château called them the 'prisoners of the liberty,' in contradistinction to the prisoners 'in durance'; and that one of the eight towers in which they were lodged was thus, quite naturally, called the 'Tour de la Liberté.'"—Funck-Brentano, *Légendes et Archives de la Bastille.*

[3] Louis de Noailles, Archbishop of Paris (1651–1729). He was a brother of the Marquis de Noailles, the Duchesse de Richelieu's first husband, and therefore Fronsac's uncle by marriage.

[4] Louis Phélypeaux, Comte de Pontchartrain, Chancellor of France.

remain until five o'clock, when his masters of languages and mathematics will visit him. It does not appear possible that he can pass his days alone in his room without injury to his health. They are persuaded that I see no one who might set him a bad example, and I venture to believe that you have a sufficiently good opinion of me to believe that nothing happens in my presence or in that of M. de Launey,[1] either in my chamber or in our walks in the courtyard or on the bastion, which might be contrary to propriety."[2]

Notwithstanding these concessions, the young gentleman found his "translation from the bosom of pleasure and of love into the gloomy solitude of the Bastille" a sufficiently trying experience. However, he had the sense to recognise the necessity of submitting with a good grace, since any complaints or insubordination would have produced a bad effect and only have served to retard his liberation. Already an accomplished actor, he accordingly affected an air of resignation, was careful to conform to all the regulations of the fortress, and treated his gaolers from the governor downwards with the utmost courtesy, while, at the same time, he addressed letters to his father protesting his penitence and begging that he might be permitted the consolation of a visit from his wife. His petition was granted, and on May 13 Madame de Fronsac appeared, and "the fair angel who flew from Heaven to earth to set Peter free was not so radiant."[3]

"The Duc de Richelieu," writes Bernaville, "wrote to me yesterday that he had granted M. de Fronsac's request that his wife should pay him a visit in the B. [Bastille]. She came in the evening, with the intendant of the house. I received them in my apartment, where they decided to remain. The Duc de Fronsac received her very well, and expressed his gratitude to her for having so quickly obtained permission to see him." And he adds:

[1] The lieutenant of the Bastille, and grandfather of Bernard René de Launey, who was governor of the Bastille at the time of the Revolution, and was murdered on the day the fortress was taken.

[2] Letter of May 8, 1711, Ravaisson, *Archives de la Bastille*, vol. xii.

[3] *Mémoires du duc de Richelieu.*

"I have nothing, personally, but praise for his conduct towards myself and my officers. There is no one more civil or more courteous; he anticipates our wishes in every way, and no one who was ignorant of his past life, which he deplores every day, could suspect him of having committed the least fault. One can only hope that he will continue in the excellent sentiments which we now perceive in him, and the good resolutions which he is forming to lead a better life in future. I shall have the honour of rendering you an account of everything which happens concerning him, as in regard to all the rest of the B. [Bastille]."[1]

By the beginning of July, M. de Fronsac was considered to have made sufficient progress on the road to reformation to receive a visit from his father, and, after sending two of his friends "to prepare him by wise counsels to receive the paternal admonitions," the old gentleman stepped into his coach and drove down to the Bastille. The visit, we learn, passed off with much tenderness on both sides. M. de Fronsac declared that "he recognised all his faults; that he would never forget the favour which the King had done him in sending him there to make him do penance for them and repair them; that he was only too happy to be there; that he would neglect nothing which depended on him to repair them and to render himself worthy of his Majesty's kindness"; and so forth. And he ended by protesting that, so far from being impatient to quit the Bastille, "he would regard a speedy liberation as a great misfortune."[2]

Excellent actor though he was, he seems to have a little overdone his part on the present occasion. Any way, old Richelieu took him at his word, and decided that, as the Bastille cure appeared to be working such wonders, it would be a pity to interrupt it; and, in fact, it was prolonged for more than twelve months, to the profound disgust of the unfortunate patient.

In the interval, however, the prisoner came near to obtaining

[1] Bernaville to Pontchartrain, May 14, 1711.
[2] Ibid., July 8, 1711.

his release in a way which neither he nor his father had reckoned with.

On the morning of September 27, as he was dressing, he was "seized with a slight shivering," and by the evening was in a high fever. He was attended by Carlière, the doctor attached to the fortress, and Barère, the surgeon of the Musketeers, whom the Duchesse de Richelieu, on being informed of the illness of her step-son and son-in-law, brought herself to the Bastille; but, notwithstanding bleedings, purgatives, and emetics, the fever continued, and in the afternoon of the following day it was deemed advisable to send for a confessor. The divine selected was a certain Père Dolé, one of the Missionaries of Saint-Vincent de Paul, and Bernaville assures Pontchartrain that he and his penitent were "very satisfied with one another."

At night, the doctors pronounced the malady to be small-pox, and the dreaded disease soon assumed so grave a form, that in the early morning of October 3 the Holy Sacrament was administered, and received "with sentiments of piety which edified every one."[1] For several days the young duke hung between life and death, though the condition of his conscience was pronounced to be most satisfactory, which doubtless proved a great consolation to his sorrowing relatives, who were careful to remain well out of range of the contagion. But by the middle of the month he was declared to be convalescent, and on October 17 we find Bernaville writing to Pontchartrain:

"I am assured that the Duc de Fronsac is completely cured, and that he is not marked in the least. He got up yesterday, and the windows were opened, after gunpowder and all kinds of things had been burned in his room. He eats every day broths and several plates of soup, together with both wings and the breast of a large chicken, which, according to what he says, is not enough for him, for he has an excellent appetite."

In a subsequent letter, the governor informs the Minister that M. de Fronsac has received a visit from his father, who has expressed himself "very satisfied with the state of his health

[1] Letter of Bernaville to Pontchartrain, October 3, 1711.

and the condition of his mind," and that his charge receives frequent visits from his confessor, "who never leaves him without his begging him to remain longer and to return as soon as possible."

These pious sentiments, alas! vanished with the young gentleman's restoration to health, for, though he did not share the hatred of his friend Voltaire for "*l'infâme*," and held that a great noble ought to observe the ceremonies of the Church, he had no desire for a religion which would have constrained him in his pleasures.

One might have supposed that, after his son's narrow escape from death, and the evidences of contrition which he had shown, the Duc de Richelieu would have been willing to abridge his punishment; but the old gentleman would appear to have been somewhat sceptical as to the genuineness of the culprit's penitence, and it was not until the following June that he could be brought to consent to his liberation. "My father, who is here," writes Fronsac to Pontchartrain, under date June 16, "has the kindness to consent to my enlargement, and orders me to beg you to demand it of the King. I shall endeavour to render myself worthy of the favours which he has been pleased to bestow upon me, and to show that such a retreat has effected a great change in me, owing to the solid reflections which I have made. Permit me to thank you for all the obligations which I am under to you, while waiting an opportunity to do so by word of mouth."

And, in the margin of this letter, the Duc de Richelieu added:

"I am sufficiently convinced of the good dispositions of my son to join him in the request which he is making. I trust that you will be willing to do this kindness."

The Minister carried this letter to Louis XIV., and then sent it to the governor of the Bastille, with the following note in the margin:

"*Read to the King.* Since the father demands it, the King is pleased to set him at liberty, and that I should expedite the orders [of release] as soon as possible, and send them to the father, with a courteous letter from myself, to the effect that, since he [the King] only did what he desired in the first instance, now that he wishes the contrary, etc., etc.; and that moreover the King is persuaded that the son will have profited [by his sojourn in the Bastille]; and he charges me to write to the son in the same sense, and to tell him that I have read his letter to the King also. Bring me these two letters to-morrow to sign with the orders, since I wish to send them to Paris by an express."

And, three days later, Bernaville writes to Pontchartrain:

"I have just received the order which you have the goodness to send me for the Duc de Fronsac; he is remaining with us until the Duchesse de Fronsac comes to fetch him. He is very grateful for the diligence that you have had the kindness to employ in procuring his freedom, to which he is not less sensible than to freedom itself. I cannot sufficiently praise his conduct and the respect he has shown towards me while he has been here. He owes everything to your counsels, of which he stands much in need at the Court; he trusts that you will not refuse them to him."[1]

Later the same day, the Duchesse de Fronsac arrived and carried her husband off to the Hôtel de Richelieu, where, in consideration of his vows to lead an exemplary life in the future, his father promised to discharge his smaller gambling debts at once and to liquidate those more considerable by instalments.[2]

Aware that the surest means of rehabilitating himself in Louis XIV.'s estimation would be a term of foreign service, and infinitely preferring the prospect of hard fighting on the frontier to that of living at the Court or in Paris under the paternal surveillance and pretending to be devoted to a wife to whom he was more than indifferent, Fronsac solicited the King's permission to join the Army of Flanders. Thanks to the intervention of Madame de Maintenon in his favour, his request was granted, and in the first days of August he set out for

[1] Letter of June 19, 1712, *Archives de la Bastille*, vol. xii.
[2] Dangeau, *Journal*, June 26, 1712.

1712 – army

Flanders.[1] "The Duc de Fronsac, who came out of the Bastille six weeks ago," writes Dangeau, "goes to serve in Flanders in the Musketeers, and has taken leave of the King, who recommended him to be more prudent, and spoke, besides, with much kindness and consideration of the Duc de Richelieu, his father."[2]

[1] Before he left, Madame de Maintenon wrote him a letter full of good counsels, after perusing which the Duc de Richelieu informed his son that he would be "unworthy to live if he were not moved to a sincere repentance by the convincing manner in which she knew how to inspire wisdom and virtue."

[2] *Journal*, August 2, 1712.

# CHAPTER II

Desperate situation of France in the summer of 1712—Courage of Louis XIV.—Villars's brilliant victory at Denain saves the country from invasion—The Duc de Fronsac appointed aide-de-camp to Villars—He spends the following winter in Paris under the paternal surveillance, but accompanies his chief to the Rhine, in the spring of 1713—Brilliant campaign of Villars—Siege of Freiburg : Fronsac is wounded—He is chosen to convey the news of the surrender of the forts of Freiburg to the King—His reception by Louis XIV.—His conduct during the last years of the reign—He becomes Duc de Richelieu, on the death of his father, in March 1715—But finds his estates heavily mortgaged—Again in danger of the Bastille—His humble letters to Madame de Maintenon.

SELDOM in her eventful history has France been reduced to such sore straits as in the summer of 1712. "That stupendous colossus, which had overshadowed and overawed the world,"[1] exhausted by the struggle which she had been waging for more than eleven years, had at length been reduced to defending her own frontiers and repelling that scourge of invasion which she had carried with so ruthless a hand into other lands. The bones of her bravest sons lay bleaching on the fields of Ramillies, Oudenarde and Malplaquet; one by one the bastions of the great wall of Flanders—Lille, Douai, Tournai, Béthune, Saint-Venant, Aire, Le Quesnoy, Bouchain—had passed into the hands of the victorious Allies, and if Landrecies, which they were closely investing, succumbed, nothing could prevent the enemy from advancing straight upon Paris and dictating terms of peace to the monarch, who for half a century had given the law to Europe, beneath the walls of his own capital. So perilous, indeed, seemed the situation that his Ministers advised Louis XIV. to retire to Blois, but the old King

[1] Coxe, "House of Austria."

scorned to listen to such timid counsels. "If my army is beaten," said he to Villars, "I intend to go to Péronne or Saint-Quentin, assemble all the troops that are left to me, make a last effort with you, and perish together, or save the State, for never will I consent to allow the enemy to approach my capital." [1]

With his sovereign's brave words ringing in his ears, Villars set out for Flanders, and, by one of the most brilliant operations of the whole war, rescued his country from the danger which menaced her.

That redoubtable enemy of France, Prince Eugène of Savoy, who since the recall of Marlborough had commanded the Allies, had under his orders, notwithstanding the withdrawal of the English troops, an army of over 100,000 men, a force much superior to that of Villars. This army was divided into three camps: the first, under the Prince of Anhalt-Dessau, conducted the siege of Landrecies; the second, the strongest of the three, under Eugène in person, covered the operations of the investing force; and the third, under the Earl of Albemarle, which consisted entirely of Dutch troops, occupied an entrenched camp at Denain, on the Scheldt, in order to assure the communications of the besiegers with Marchiennes, a town on the Scarpe, six or seven leagues distant from Landrecies, where the Allies had established their chief magazines.

After reconnoitring the enemy's position, Villars decided that to attempt to break through the lines of the besiegers, or to give battle to the covering army, offered but a very remote chance of success, and that the only means of saving the town was to cut the investing army off from its magazines, by storming the camp at Denain. Accordingly, having induced Eugène, by a remarkably skilful feint, which deceived even his own officers who were not in the secret, to concentrate the bulk of his forces around Landrecies, in the belief that he was meditating an attack upon the lines of circumvallation, he turned sharply off for the Scheldt, crossed the river, and was marching rapidly upon Denain before his antagonist had even divined his intentions. His lieutenants suggested to Villars the advisability of deferring

[1] Maréchal de Villars, *Mémoires*.

the attack until sufficient fascines had been prepared to fill the moat which surrounded the camp. But the marshal, aware that Eugène was hastening with his whole force to the assistance of the defenders, would hear of no delay. "The bodies of the first of our people who fall will be the fascines," he replied, and at once gave orders for the assault. His apparent temerity was fully justified, for the Dutch abandoned their entrenchments and fled, after a mere semblance of resistance; and Eugène appeared on the opposite bank of the Scheldt just in time to see them driven headlong into the river, and all his plans completely ruined.

This brilliant success, which was quickly followed by the capture of Marchiennes [1] and the raising of the siege of Landrecies, was gained on July 24—that is to say, about a week before Fronsac set out for Flanders—and when he joined the army, the campaign had degenerated into a war of sieges, in which he found no opportunity for distinction. Nevertheless, he was fortunate enough to attract the favourable attention of Villars, who, recognising that the lad possessed both courage and intelligence, decided to attach him to his person, and appointed him one of his aides-de-camp.

Towards the end of the autumn, he returned to Paris, where he passed the next six months, only paying very occasional visits to the Court, since he judged it inadvisable to make a more permanent reappearance on the scene of his former exploits until he had done something to efface the memory of his "*embastillement*." He seems to have had a very dull time, for his father, who had found the liquidation of the gambling-debts which the young gentleman had contracted during his brief career as a courtier a more difficult task than he had anticipated, was in a very ill humour and kept a vigilant eye on all his actions.

Great, therefore, was his joy when he learned that the

[1] Eugène had left his mistress, a beautiful Italian, at Marchiennes, and there was much jocular speculation among the French officers as to which of them the lady would choose as the prince's successor. But, to their great chagrin, when the place surrendered, it was found that she had effected her escape and rejoined her lover.

Emperor had refused his signature to the Peace signed by the other belligerent Powers, at Utrecht, on April 11, 1713; that Villars was to be sent to the Rhine to bring his Imperial Majesty to reason, and that he had obtained permission for his little aide-de-camp to accompany him.

The campaign which followed proved another brilliant triumph for the French marshal. Although at the outset his army was considerably inferior in numbers to that of Eugène, this disadvantage was more than compensated by his superior strategy and the rapidity of his movements.

Having again deceived his adversary by a feint against the lines of Ettlingen, he burst into the Palatinate, and, marching sixteen leagues in twenty hours, occupied Speyer, after which he reduced in quick succession, Worms, Kaiserlautern, and Landau. Then, in the third week in September, he crossed the Rhine at Kehl, stormed the German lines before Freiburg, and so closely invested the town that all Eugène's efforts to raise the siege were fruitless, and on November 16 the forts which defended it capitulated. These forts, which were situated on the slope of the mountain commanding the town, were of great strength, and their reduction proved a most murderous business, a single assault in the night of October 14–15 costing the French more than 1500 killed and wounded. In this sanguinary affair no quarter was given on either side, and when the defenders had exhausted their ammunition, they loosened the stones from the ramparts and hurled them down on the heads of their assailants. One of these stones struck Fronsac on the forehead, not far from the temple, blinding him with blood and inflicting a wound of which he bore the marks all his life. He was, however, much more fortunate than one of his brother-officers, the Marquis de Laval, who had his jaw smashed to pieces, and was obliged to wear a bandage for the rest of his days, which earned him the name of Laval-*Mentonnière*. But, then, as one writer philosophically observes, the marquis had the consolation of reflecting that such a disfigurement was of little consequence, since he had passed the age for gallantry.

In this campaign young Fronsac seems to have given several

proofs of that dashing courage for which he was afterwards to become so celebrated, and he received abundant compensation for the wound he had received before Freiburg, when he was selected by his chief to bear the news of its capitulation to the King, who was then at Marly. Under date November 21, 1713, Dangeau notes in his *Journal*:

"After dinner, the Duc de Fronsac arrived. The Maréchal de Villars sends him with the news that the governor of Freiburg has surrendered the forts. . . . The King has given the Duc de Fronsac a lodging here, and he does not wish him to return [to Germany], as the army is on the point of being disbanded."

If we are to believe Soulavie, Louis XIV. was so pleased with the clear and animated account which the young duke gave of the siege, and the intelligent answers that he returned to the questions addressed to him, that, at the conclusion of the audience, he observed: "The sight of your wound effaces the memory of the *lettre de cachet* which I signed against you. Conduct yourself well, for I believe that you are destined for great things." [1]

The fall of Freiburg convinced the Emperor of the futility of continuing the struggle, and in the spring of 1714, the Treaties of Baden and Rastadt finally gave peace to Europe.

We hear very little of Fronsac during the period which intervened between his return from Germany and the death of Louis XIV. What information is forthcoming, however, shows that, notwithstanding the promises of amendment of which he had been so lavish during his sojourn in the Bastille, he was still causing his friends a good deal of trouble. Thus, in October 1714, during the annual sojourn of the Court at Fontainebleau, he and the Duc d'Aumont arranged a horse-race and made heavy wagers on the result; so heavy, indeed, Dangeau tells us, that "M. de Fronsac was advised [presumably by his father] to cancel them, and M. d'Aumont consented." [2] Some months later, we learn, that M. de Fronsac,

[1] *Mémoires du duc de Richelieu.*

[2] Dangeau, *Journal*, October 19, 1714.

deeming that he had been insulted by one of the pages of the Petite Écurie at the audience which Louis XIV. gave to the pretended Ambassador of Persia, had "taken certain steps which caused people to believe that he desired to avenge himself," and that, though he had strenuously denied the truth of this report, the Duc d'Orléans had considered it advisable to obtain from him a promise that he would do nothing to cause a breach of the peace.[1]

On May 10, 1715, Fronsac lost his father, who succumbed to an attack of apoplexy, at the age of eighty-six, and succeeded to his duchies of Richelieu and Fronsac, the seat which he occupied in the Parlement as a *pair de France*, his châteaux and estates of Richelieu, Rueil, La Ferté-Bernard, Coze, Fronsac and Lonac, and the magnificent Hôtel de Richelieu, in the Place-Royale, with its far-famed picture-gallery; while Louis XIV. allotted him the apartments in the Château of Versailles which the old duke had had, although of late years he had resided there but seldom.

Large as was this property, however, it was heavily mortgaged, for the deceased nobleman had been very extravagant in early life, and, but for the foresight of the Cardinal, it is probable that the new duke would have inherited little beyond the title. In addition to the mortgages, the estates were charged with a number of legacies and pensions, which still further depleted his coffers, and in October 1719, he found himself under the necessity of selling Rueil to the trustees of Saint-Cyr.[2]

His new dignities would not appear to have inspired the Duc de Richelieu—as we must now call him—with the discretion in which he stood so much in need, since, from two very humble letters which he addressed to Madame de Maintenon in the summer of that year, it is evident that he was again in danger of being sent to the Bastille:

"I beg you to reflect that I am but nineteen years of age,

[1] Dangeau, *Journal*, March 21, 1715.

[2] He had a short time previously sold the timber in the park to the Princesse de Conti for 500,000 livres.—Buvat.

and that it is easy to understand that age and experience are a sufficient corrective of these kind of faults. I beg you to reflect, also, that I am a poor orphan, who has no other refuge than the Court and your kindness."

And, in the second letter, he writes :

"I am in an apprehension and despair which deprives me of sleep both day and night, owing to my misfortune in having displeased the King. If I am sufficiently fortunate for him to be willing to suspend his anger or to permit me to go and throw myself at his feet, I beg you, Madame, to be so good as to inform me of it. You will restore me to life. I have received from you so many marks of kindness, that I dare to anticipate this further one, and I beg you not to doubt my sincere gratitude." [1]

[1] Cited by the Comte d'Haussonville, *la Duchesse de Bourgogne et l'Alliance savoyarde sous Louis XIV.* The original letters are in the possession of the Comte de Lesparre.

1715 Émilie is 9
Richelieu is 19

# CHAPTER III

The death of Louis XIV. followed by a violent reaction against his religious and political principles—Terrible depravity of Society under the Regency—The Duc de Richelieu adheres to the party of the Duc du Maine, and irritates the Regent by his sarcastic remarks at his expense—His proposed duel with the Chevalier de Bavière prevented by the Duc d'Orléans—Mlle. de Charolais: her personal appearance and character—She conceives a violent passion for Richelieu, and becomes his mistress—Indignation of her mother, *Madame la Duchesse*, and her brother, the Duc de Bourbon—Quarrel of the latter with Richelieu—The Comte de Gacé, believing that Richelieu has traduced the character of his wife, insults him at a *bal masqué* at the Opera—Midnight duel between the two noblemen in the Rue Saint-Thomas-du-Louvre: Richelieu seriously wounded—The Parlement of Paris, in order to humiliate the peerage, resolves to bring the combatants to trial—The peers appeal to the King—Richelieu and Gacé are sent to the Bastille—The Parlement obtains permission to prosecute, but no witnesses can be found to come forward—Ruse by which Richelieu outwits the surgeons sent to examine him by the Parlement—Mlle. de Charolais and the Princesse de Conti disguise themselves and visit the duke in the Bastille—But are eventually detected—Richelieu and Gacé are set at liberty—Death of the Duchesse de Richelieu—The Condés refuse to consent to the marriage of Mlle. de Charolais with the duke—Gallantries of Richelieu.

ON September 1, 1715, amid a general sigh of relief from his long-suffering people, Louis XIV. died, and that singular epoch in the history of France, the regency of Philippe d'Orléans, began. It was a period of violent reaction against the religious and political principles of *le Grand Monarque.* The iron hand once removed, all the living forces of the nation, so long repressed, awoke into a feverish activity. "The financiers made projects, the politicians made plans, the poets made satires"; the literary world revived; the Parlement recovered its rights of registration; the Jansenists preached

51

Habitat for Humanity®

—armande
Marie-Catherine 1685
Elisabeth-Marguerite
Marie-Gabrielle 1686
1689

early 1730s

Marquise de Thérèse

Colbert de Croissy
duchesse de St Pierre
Emilie's frequent
companion

silly, gay

up to 1735

and wrote freely once more. In every direction there was an almost frenzied leap towards what men called liberty, but which was too often only another name for license.

Nowhere, however, was the change more marked than in the private life of the upper classes. During the later years of the reign of Louis XIV., when religion—or at least a skilful affectation of it—had been the surest passport to the royal favour, even the most profligate and reckless had been constrained to some semblance of decorum. But now that austere and bigoted *régime* was no more; and the pent-up impatience of a corrupt society broke loose at once, and found relief in a veritable saturnalia of sensuality. Vice, which had for so many years scarcely dared to rear its head, stalked abroad, naked and unashamed. The Regent himself set the tone in moral depravity, and his example was followed by the Princes and Princesses of the Blood, by the bulk of the nobility, and by a considerable proportion of the wealthy middle class. "All sense of shame," wrote the old Duchesse d'Orléans, "is banished from the country."

This was the period of the scandalous orgies of the Palais-Royal, when, surrounded by the dissolute men and abandoned women in whose society he was accustomed to seek relaxation from the cares of State, the ruler of France passed his nights in revelry, gambling, and debauchery; the period when a royal princess[1] could lead a life of such shameless profligacy that when she died, at the age of twenty-four, it was impossible to find a prelate base enough to preach a funeral oration;[2] when another royal princess and an abbess,[3] to boot, was believed to be a slave to the most degrading of vices; when a future cardinal[4] was suspected of being the lover of his own sister;

[1] Marie Louise Elisabeth d'Orléans, Duchesse de Berry, eldest daughter of the Regent.

[2] *Correspondance complète de Madame, Duchesse d'Orléans*, Letter of July 20, 1719.

[3] Marie Adélaide d'Orléans, Abbess of Chelles, second daughter of the Regent. But, according to her latest biographer, M. Édouard Barthélemy, the accusations against her were quite unfounded.

[4] The Abbé, afterwards the Cardinal, de Tencin.

when a duchess and the grand-daughter of one of France's greatest warriors[1] could sit down to supper in the condition of our first parents with a party of young nobles;[2] and when two marchionesses could fight a duel in the Bois de Boulogne for the sake of a notorious libertine, who cared not a button for either of them.[3]

One might have supposed that the young Duc de Richelieu, whose gallantries, high play, and other extravagances were so soon to make him the talk of Paris, would have been a leading spirit in the group of dissolute nobles who clustered around the Regent—his "*roués*," as they were called, because, as their patron jocularly observed, they all deserved to be broken on the wheel (*la roue*). But he had been early introduced by Madame de Maintenon into the little court of the Duchesse du Maine,[4] at Sceaux, and had met with a very flattering reception from that amusing little *bas bleu* and the brilliant and witty circle over which she presided; and partly out of loyalty to his old protectress, and partly out of that spirit of opposition to constituted authority with which very young men are so often infected, he adhered to the party of the Bastards, although he did not give it any decisive proofs of his devotion until later—too late, indeed, to be of any service.

The Regent was naturally much annoyed to see the bearer of so great a name in the camp of his avowed enemies, and his irritation was not diminished by the reports which reached him of the sarcastic remarks at his expense in which M. de Richelieu was wont to indulge. When, therefore, an opportunity presented itself of letting the young gentleman feel the weight of his authority, he did not fail to take advantage of it. "The Duc d'Orléans," writes Dangeau, under date November 29, 1715, "was warned this morning that the Duc de Richelieu and the Chevalier de Bavière had quarrelled during the last few days at Chantilly, and that they had made arrangements to fight a duel

[1] The Duchesse de Retz, grand-daughter of the Maréchal de Luxembourg.

[2] *Correspondance complète de Madame, Duchesse d'Orléans*, Letter of August 6, 1722.

[3] See p. 49, *infra*.

[4] Anne Louise Bénédicte de Bourbon-Condé.

in the Bois de Boulogne,[1] where *Monsieur le Duc* was giving a grand hunting-party. He sent officers of his guard to arrest these two gentlemen, whom he caused to be brought before him, and told them that if in the course of the next ten years they had the slightest dispute, he should regard it as a consequence of this affair." He then exacted their parole, and threatened them with all kinds of pains and penalties if they broke it.

At Chantilly, where the quarrel with the Chevalier de Bavière took place, as well as at the Hôtel de Condé, Richelieu was at this time a very frequent visitor, nor was it long before the reason of his partiality for the Condé family was an open secret. The Duc de Bourbon—or *Monsieur le Duc*, as he was called—had six sisters, all of whom had inherited the good looks and intelligence of their mother.[2] The flower of the flock, however, was the third daughter, Louise Anne de Bourbon, Mlle. de Charolais, then in her twenty-first year, who was one of the prettiest women of her time. "The charms of her countenance surpassed all that the painters have been able to conceive; nothing was so beautiful as her eyes,[3] nothing so seducing as her mind. As she was the model of beauty, she was that of fashion. All the women wished to be *coiffées* and dressed as she was; but the more they sought to imitate her, the less they succeeded in being compared with her."[4]

The character of this princess was a singular compound of good and evil qualities: frank, generous, loyal, and kind-hearted, but haughty, vain, vindictive, and dissolute. In both

[1] The Chevalier de Bavière was a natural son of Maximilian II., Elector of Bavaria, by Mlle. Popel, afterwards Comtesse d'Arco. He was evidently a fire-eater, for in January 1713 we hear of him proposing to fight a duel with the Marquis de Beuseville, a colonel of cuirassiers, and of Louis XIV. sending the Maréchal de Villeroy to compel the two gentlemen to compose their differences.

[2] Louise Françoise de Bourbon, Mlle. de Nantes, second daughter of Louis XIV. and Madame de Montespan.

[3] "Amid the thousand perfections which Nature had lavished upon her, she had eyes of such wondrous beauty, that at the ball they shone through her mask and caused her always to be recognised."—Bésenval, *Mémoires*.

[4] Rulhière, *Anecdotes sur le Maréchal de Richelieu*.

LOUISE ANNE DE BOURBON-CONDÉ, MLLE. DE CHAROLAIS, IN THE HABIT OF A FRANCISCAN MONK

AFTER A PAINTING AT VERSAILLES BY AN UNKNOWN ARTIST

love and hatred she scorned half-measures; she was at once the most devoted of friends and the most implacable of enemies.

Rulhière declares that at the time when Richelieu crossed her path, Mlle. de Charolais's heart was "still in its first innocence," but, according to other writers, the young lady was already "*expérimentée*." However that may be, it is certain that she soon conceived for Richelieu a most violent passion, to which the duke, whose senses were pleased by her beauty, and whose vanity was naturally flattered by the preference of a Princess of the Blood, was not slow to respond, and that before the end of the year 1715, thanks to the facilities afforded them by a complaisant waiting-woman of her Highness, she had become his mistress.

*Madame la Duchesse*, who, by way of reparation for the irregularities of her own youth, exercised a very strict supervision over the conduct of her daughters, was exceedingly wrath on learning how she had been outwitted, and her son, the Duc de Bourbon, was also very indignant. "The Duc de Richelieu," writes Dangeau, on November 29, 1715, "has had the misfortune to quarrel with *Monsieur le Duc*, who does not wish to see him any more." The discreet chronicler refrains from enlightening us as to the cause of this quarrel, which was the prelude to a much more violent one, some four years later, of which we shall speak in due course; but it is not difficult to conjecture. However, early in the following year, an event occurred which brought about a temporary separation between M. de Richelieu and his inamorata.

The scandalous orgies over which the Regent presided found numerous imitators, who often went to far greater lengths in their disregard of decency than would have been tolerated at the Palais-Royal. In February 1716, a festive gathering took place at the hotel of the Comte de Gacé,[1] at which it was commonly reported that "things had been done worthy of the times of Heliogabalus," and that the lady of the house herself

[1] Louise Jean Baptiste de Matignon, eldest son of Charles Auguste de Poyou, Maréchal de Matignon.

had been the chief offender.[1] Now, Richelieu had been one of those present on this occasion, and, rightly or wrongly, was suspected by Gacé of having violated all the laws of hospitality, by revealing what had taken place at the house at which he had been a guest and traducing the character of his hostess, although, in point of fact, the reputation of the lady in question was already so tarnished that it would have been difficult to compromise it any further. The indignant husband vowed vengeance, and applied to one of the gutter-poets of Paris, who, for a small fee, furnished him with a biting epigram against Richelieu. Armed with this, on the night of February 17, he repaired to a masked ball at the Opera, at which he knew that the duke intended to be present, and soon perceived the object of his wrath seated in a secluded corner, making violent love to a Venetian domino, presumably Mlle. de Charolais. Approaching the pair, Gacé inquired whether M. de Richelieu had heard the latest poetical composition in his honour, which he forthwith proceeded to read, and then, turning to the lady, said : "Beautiful princess, do not listen to a mask so perfidious in love ; he will reveal everything."

White with fury, Richelieu rose, and telling Gacé that a conversation of this nature had better be continued elsewhere, and that, if he would excuse him for a few moments, he would afterwards be entirely at his service, conducted his frightened partner, who, perceiving what was in the wind, seemed on the point of swooning, to a neighbouring box, where he left her in the care of the Prince de Soubise. Then he returned to

[1] The Comtesse de Gacé, *née* Mlle. de Châteaurenaud, was a daughter of François Louis de Rousselet, Comte de Châteaurenaud. "She is a woman without intelligence," writes Mathieu Marais, "whom women of loose morals themselves despise, and who has conceived the idea that it is good style to be debauched."

The same chronicler relates that, some eighteen months later, at a supper-party given by the Marquise de Nesle, Madame de Gacé, after priming herself "with wine and all kinds of liqueurs," danced "almost naked" before the company, after which she went into the ante-chamber and gave a second performance for the benefit of the lackeys. In consequence of this exploit, her husband, "who did not mind being deceived, but objected to being made ridiculous," obtained a *lettre de cachet* and had her shut up in a convent near Paris, from which, however, she eventually escaped and had many surprising adventures.

where Gacé was standing, and, bidding him follow, left the Opera, and crossed the Rue Saint-Honoré to the Rue Saint-Thomas-du-Louvre, a quiet street, which at this hour was almost deserted. Here they stripped to their shirts, drew their swords, and in another moment a furious combat was in progress.

Aroused by the clash of steel, people soon came hurrying from the neighbouring houses, and the affray, which had begun without any witnesses, was concluded in the midst of an excited crowd of spectators. No one, however, made the least attempt to separate the combatants, though that is scarcely a matter for surprise, since both were so infuriated, that a peacemaker would have stood considerable risk of getting run through for his pains.

It must have been a singular spectacle, that midnight duel. The narrow, dimly-lit street, with its old gabled houses; the frightened faces of women peering from the windows; the throng of worthy citizens in their night-caps and dressing-gowns, hanging breathlessly on the result of every thrust; and in the centre these two young men—bearers of two of the most honoured names in France—with their tense faces and burning eyes, each intent on the death or mutilation of the other. Ever and anon, as if by common consent, they paused to take breath, and the bystanders whispered together and agreed that such a flagrant violation of the Law was a disgrace to Paris, and that it was plainly some one's duty to put a stop to it. But no one seemed at all inclined to undertake the responsibility; and so once again came the grinding of steel against steel, and the stamp of high-heeled shoes upon the slippery cobbles, and the wicked little swords flickered hither and thither quicker than the bewildered eye could follow them.

Both Richelieu and Gacé were practised swordsmen; but the latter, who was several years the elder of the two, was the stronger and the more experienced. Nor did his advantage end there, for Richelieu, who had been far from anticipating so tragic a conclusion to his evening's amusement, had probably drunk quite as much wine at the ball as was good for him.

Nevertheless, he made a gallant fight, and for a time Fortune seemed to incline to his side, as he wounded his antagonist in the arm and in two other places. The wounds, however, were but slight ones, and served only to make Gacé fight a little more cautiously; and eventually a somewhat wild thrust by Richelieu afforded him an opening, and he passed his sword right through his opponent's body, though, happily, without touching any vital part.

The young duke fell fainting into the arms of the bystanders, and was carried off to his hôtel; while Gacé, after having his wounds attended to, returned to the ball, where he remained for some time, with the object of establishing an *alibi.*

Although since the accession of Louis XIV. no less than ten edicts had been issued against duelling, which enacted that imprisonment, exile, confiscation of goods, and, in some cases, death itself should be inflicted upon those who transgressed them, they were seldom or never enforced, and if, during the last years of the late King's reign, "affairs of honour" had been of comparatively rare occurrence, this circumstance was due not to any fear of the Law, but to his Majesty's intense aversion to the practice, and the knowledge that a gentleman of combative inclinations was very coldly looked upon at Court. Even so recently as the previous November, two officers named Ferrant and Girardin, the first belonging to the Gardes-Françaises, the other to the Régiment du Roi, who had had the effrontery to settle their differences, in broad daylight, upon the terrace of the Tuileries, that is to say, within the precincts of one of the royal palaces—an offence which would have been severely visited, even in the swashbuckling times of the first Bourbon king—had escaped with the loss of their commissions, which were no doubt restored to them when the next war broke out.

In ordinary circumstances, therefore, the high rank of the combatants of the Rue Saint-Thomas-du-Louvre would have saved them from anything worse than a severe reprimand from the Regent, if the Parlement of Paris had not seen in this affair an admirable pretext for attacking its enemies, the peers.

The Parlement of Paris, it is scarcely necessary to explain, was the Supreme Court of Justice, and in no sense a legislative body, although it possessed the privilege of remonstrating against the royal edicts which it was called upon to register, and at various stages in its history strove to extend this right of remonstrance into one of veto. Its importance as a political factor varied according to the strength or weakness of the Government. Thus, during the turbulent reign of the last Valois, the early years of that of his successor, and the stormy regencies of Marie de' Medici and Anne of Austria, it had played a very prominent part; while during the latter part of the reign of Henry IV., under the iron rule of Richelieu, and the autocratic *régime* of Louis XIV., "its nails"—to borrow the great cardinal's expression—"were cut close," and it had been strictly confined to its judicial functions, its true sphere of usefulness.

However, no sooner was Louis XIV. in his grave, than the ambitions of the Parlement, encouraged by the weakness of the administration and the fact that Orléans had appealed to it to set aside the late King's will, began to revive, just as they had done seventy-two years before, when Anne of Austria had called upon that body to annul the testament of Louis XIII. and make her "Regent without conditions"; and, as a preliminary step to the assertion of more serious pretensions, the magistrates embarked upon a violent controversy with the peers, who, on special occasions, sat with them in the Grande Chambre, the tribunal in which the most important matters were decided.

This dispute, which is known as "*l'affaire du bonnet*," raged round the claim of the peers to be received by the gentlemen of the robe with uncovered heads when they took their seats in the Parlement, while they themselves remained covered. The presidents of the Parlement decided to refuse the salutation to the peers, and, further determined that, if the peers persisted in demanding it and gave their votes with their hats upon their heads, such votes should not be counted. The peers, on their side, insisted on their right to the salutation, and coupled with it a demand that no magistrate should be permitted to sit upon the same benches as themselves.

Both parties appealed to the Regent, but that prince, who saw not without secret satisfaction this rupture between two bodies whose union might be fraught with considerable danger to his own authority, excused himself from interfering; and the quarrel, which was soon complicated by other equally trivial and ridiculous matters, became every day more envenomed.

Now, when, three months before, Ferrant and Girardin had fought upon the terrace of the Tuileries, the Parlement had ignored the affair altogether, and it had been left to the Regent to punish the offenders. But the moment it learned of the affray in the Rue Saint-Thomas-du-Louvre, in which one of the combatants was a member of the peerage, it decided that such an opportunity for humiliating that haughty body, in the person of one of their number, was too good to be lost, and began to display the most ardent zeal to vindicate the outraged majesty of the Law. Accordingly, on February 27, on the specious pretext that the revival of duelling since the death of the late King called for an example, and that this example would be all the more efficacious if the offenders happened to be of exalted rank, it promulgated a decree, copies of which were served upon both Richelieu and Gacé, ordering the two nobles to surrender themselves as prisoners at the Conciergerie of the Palais de Justice within fifteen days, there to await their trial.[1]

Great was the indignation of the peers at this attack upon one of their most cherished privileges, and Richelieu addressed to the King a petition, in which he maintained that, as he was a *pair de France*, the Parlement had no jurisdiction over him, and that he could only be tried by his fellow-peers, and begged his Majesty to appoint a commission to sit in judgment upon him; while, two days later, the Archbishop of Rheims and the Bishops of Laon and Langres, on behalf of the ecclesiastical peers, and the Ducs de Sully, de la Force, de Charost, de Chaulnes, d'Uzès, de Saint-Simon, de Luxembourg, de Tresmes,

[1] Dangeau.

and d'Antin, on behalf of the temporal peerage, also presented a petition protesting against the action of the Parlement, which they declared to be a gross usurpation.

The Parlement, in support of the jurisdiction which it claimed, cited for the benefit of the King eight examples of peers having been brought to trial before it; the peers replied by enumerating fifty-six instances in which they had successfully asserted their independence of the ordinary tribunals, the earliest of which went back to somewhere about the dawn of the twelfth century. The Parlement maintained that, even supposing such exemption to be admitted, the Duc de Richelieu was none the less amenable to its authority, since he was still a minor and had not yet taken his seat in the Parlement; the peers answered that a peer by right of birth could claim the privileges of his Order, even if he were legally incapable of exercising its judicial functions. Finally, the Regent, who wished to stand well with the Parlement, whose support he required against the Maines and the Spanish party, but was unwilling to irritate the peers, fearing lest the angry magistrates might proceed to lay violent hands upon the delinquents, decided to intervene, and on March 4 Richelieu and Gacé each received a *lettre de cachet*, in which the King courteously intimated to him that "it was his intention that he should betake himself to his château of the Bastille."[1]

Since no one ever dreamed of declining the royal invitation, both young gentlemen ordered their valets to pack their valises, bade a courteous farewell to their respective consorts, neither of whom, we fear, was altogether inconsolable at the departure of her lord, wrote a tender letter to the ladies who for the moment happened to occupy the foremost place in their affections, and were driven away to the Rue Saint-Antoine.

And so, for the second time within five years, M. de Richelieu found himself an unwilling guest of his sovereign.

[1] Noblemen and officers who were sent to the Bastille were never subjected to the indignity of arrest, except in the case of high treason or some other very grave offence. They presented themselves there alone, unless they were accompanied by relatives or friends.

Although now convalescent, the young duke was still very weak, and the knowledge that it must be many days before he would be well enough to resume his usual life went far to console him for the loss of his liberty. Moreover, the authorities of the Bastille had received instructions to treat him with every possible consideration, and he enjoyed all the privileges granted him during his previous detention ; while his vanity was not a little flattered at finding that he was regarded by the Court as a sort of martyr, and that every one from the Princes of the Blood downwards was demanding permission to visit him.

Their common misfortune soon served to bring about a reconciliation between him and his late adversary, neither of whom was of a vindictive nature ; and when they met, as they frequently did at the governor's table, they consulted together as to the line of defence they should pursue ; for, notwithstanding the committal of the delinquents to the Bastille, the Parlement declined to abandon its prey.

"The Duc d'Orléans," writes Dangeau, on March 11, "gave audience after dinner to the deputies of the Parlement, who had only demanded to speak to him in reference to the affair of M. de Richelieu. The Parlement represented to him of what importance it was that this matter should be adjudicated upon, and the Duc d'Orléans assured them that he had not the least wish to avoid the adjudication, and that, during his regency, he would be, if it were possible, more severe upon duelling than the late King had been."

Encouraged by the apparent complaisance of the Regent, the Parlement, ten days later, coolly ignoring the fact that Richelieu and Gacé were now prisoners of the King, passed a second decree ordering them to surrender themselves to take their trial within fifteen days, copies of which were again sent to their respective residences.

To this Richelieu replied by a fresh appeal to the King, praying that he might be judged by his Majesty himself and his peers, or, in default of that, by a commission appointed by his Majesty, which request was backed by a second petition on behalf of the whole peerage.

The Regent, much embarrassed by the demands of the contending parties, and perceiving the necessity of taking some definite action in the matter, at length decided upon a middle course, and on May 18 authorised the Parlement to prosecute the two noblemen, who, however, were to remain in the custody of his Majesty. This, it was hoped, would pacify the magistracy, while sparing the peerage the humiliation of beholding one of their number brought to the bar of the Palais de Justice.

The Parlement, though grievously disappointed at seeing the better part of its anticipated triumph snatched from it, was none the less anxious to secure that which still remained within its reach, and deputed a counsellor named Ferrant to proceed to the Bastille and interrogate the prisoners. The nomination of M. Ferrant was certainly not a very sagacious choice, since he was a relative of one of the officers who had taken part in the duel at the Tuileries, and it was obviously to that gentleman's interest to minimise the importance of the present affair.

After subjecting Richelieu and Gacé to a lengthy examination, the worthy counsellor returned to the Palais de Justice and reported to his indignant colleagues that both nobles denied in the most positive manner that they had ever fought a duel, and expressed his opinion that the charge against them was nothing but the invention of some malicious persons, who had magnified a harmless quarrel into a bloodthirsty affray.

The magistrates, who were convinced that they had fought *à outrance*, thereupon issued notices, which they caused to be read from the pulpit of every church in Paris, calling on all and sundry who had witnessed the duel to come forward and give information, on pain of their most severe displeasure. But public sympathy was on the side of the offenders, and the good folk who dwelt in and around the Rue Saint-Thomas-du-Louvre proved to be afflicted with such astonishingly short memories that the appeal met with not a single response.

The angry magistrates, however, refused to confess themselves beaten, and since no witnesses would come forward, decreed that the prisoners should be subjected to a medical examination, to ascertain if they bore upon their persons any marks of the alleged combat. But here again discomfiture awaited them; for Gacé's hurts had long since healed, and Richelieu, getting wind of their intention, "conceived the idea of covering his wound with a light taffeta, and summoning an experienced painter to give to it a touch of colour resembling the natural skin"[1]—a ruse which was quite sufficient to deceive the complaisant eyes of the surgeons, who reported that they could discover no sign of any injury upon the person of either of the gentlemen whom they had been sent to examine.

The baffled Parlement now began to despair of ever bringing their offence home to the prisoners. Nevertheless, out of spite, rather than from any lingering hope of securing the evidence necessary for a conviction, it declined to abandon the prosecution, and they remained in the Bastille, though, as some compensation for their continued incarceration, they were allowed full liberty within the precincts of the fortress, and permitted to receive the visits of their friends.

This last concession, however, was far from satisfying M. de Richelieu, for, with the exception of his wife and mother-in-law, his visitors were all of the sterner sex, since the regulations of the Bastille did not permit of the entry of ladies other than relatives of the prisoners; and he sighed for his beloved Mlle. de Charolais, who, on her side, was in despair at the continued separation from her lover. Every time she drove past the Bastille, which we may be sure she did pretty frequently, particularly in the afternoons, when privileged captives were permitted to take the air on the terrace which overlooked the Rue Saint-Antoine, she contemplated those frowning walls which held him who possessed her heart, and racked her brains to discover some way of gaining access to the fortress.

Love is popularly supposed to laugh at locksmiths; at any rate, it did so in the present instance. Although, as we have mentioned, ladies other than relatives of the prisoners were excluded from the Bastille, exception was occasionally made in favour of charitable women who desired to visit the poorer prisoners. To two of these ministering angels, who were

[1] *Mémoires du duc de Richelieu.*

accustomed to visit the fortress together, Mlle. de Charolais repaired, poured her sorrows into their sympathetic ears, and persuaded them to allow herself and her eldest sister, the Princesse de Conti, to impersonate them. It is probable that the warders and guards had their suspicions as to the identity of the fair visitors; but a judicious distribution of the coin of the realm prevented any awkward questions being asked, and they penetrated without hindrance to the chamber of the imprisoned gallant, who received them with a joy which only a man who has been deprived for long weeks of all feminine society, save an occasional visit from an unloved wife and a mother-in-law, can realise.

Emboldened by the success of this stratagem, the ladies multiplied their pretended errands of mercy, until their frequency began to arouse the suspicions of the police, who kept a vigilant eye upon every one who entered or left the Bastille. The police communicated with the Regent, who sent orders to M. Bernaville to interrogate these two ladies who appeared to take such extraordinary interest in the welfare of those under his charge. Accordingly, one fine evening, when the princesses were leaving the fortress, they were stopped by a courteous official, who requested them to accompany him to the governor's house, where their identity was soon discovered.

After this, we need scarcely add, all communication between Mlle. de Charolais and her adorer was ruthlessly cut off, which was perhaps just as well for the latter, since the excitement which the visits of the princesses entailed had caused his wound to re-open. However, when the ladies ceased to appear, he speedily recovered his health; and there seems to have been very little amiss with him, when, on August 21, the Parlement passed a decree setting both Richelieu and Gacé at liberty "*sous caution juratoire de se représenter toutes et quand fois la cour l'ordonnera.*"[1] Their detention had lasted just five and a half months, which seems a heavy price to pay for the privilege of making holes in one another.

[1] Ravaisson, *Archives de la Bastille.*

Richelieu's release from the Bastille was followed, three months later, by his liberation from the connubial fetters. At the beginning of November, his wife was attacked by small-pox of so malignant a type that she died after an illness of two days.[1] There had been no children of the marriage ; indeed, it is probable that it had been a merely nominal tie, since Richelieu had always deeply resented the action of his family in forcing the lady upon him, and it was jocularly remarked that the duke was the husband of every wife but his own. The duchess, on her side, had accepted the situation in the spirit of a true philosopher, and appears to have found ample compensation for the loss of her conjugal rights in the society of her husband's equerry, a handsome youth of an old but impoverished family,[2] who was as devoted as his master was indifferent.

Many persons were now of opinion that Richelieu and Mlle. de Charolais would take advantage of the former's freedom to regularise a connection which was by this time the talk of Paris, and it is certain that, had the decision rested with the parties themselves, they would have lost no time in fulfilling this anticipation ; for the lady was madly in love with the duke, and the duke, if he did not altogether reciprocate the lady's passion, was keenly alive to the advantages which would accrue to him from his marriage with a Princess of the Blood. But the pride of the Condés proved an insurmountable obstacle, though *Madame* declares that their conviction that the princess would be "unhappy all her life with this utterly worthless madcap," weighed quite as much with her relatives as the inequality of rank.[3] Any way, the old Princesse de Condé, *Madame la Duchesse*, and her son, *Monsieur le Duc*, offered the most strenuous opposition to the match, and, though the amorous princess employed every possible persuasion to induce them

[1] Dangeau, *Journal*, November 7, 1716.

[2] It was still not uncommon to find impoverished gentlemen holding such posts in the households of great nobles.

[3] *Correspondance de Madame, Duchesse d'Orléans* (edit. Jæglé). Letter of March 15, 1719.

to relent, they remained inexorable. However, as we shall presently see, the lovers did not abandon all hope of ultimately gaining their end, and, in the meantime, since they were not permitted to love one another with the sanction of the Church, continued to do so without it.

It must not be supposed that Mlle. de Charolais possessed anything approaching a monopoly of the ducal affections, for the favour with which Richelieu had always been regarded by the opposite sex had been greatly increased by his duel and incarceration in the Bastille, which seems to have made a powerful appeal to ladies of romantic disposition ; while the temptation of entering the lists against a Princess of the Blood was one which comparatively few were able to resist. As for the duke, he disdained few *bonnes fortunes*, though he appears to have given the preference to those which presented the most difficulty, and the ingenuity and audacity which he and his inamoratas displayed in circumventing the vigilance of husbands and fathers have provided the scandal-loving chroniclers and letter-writers of those days with material for many a piquant page. Among several such anecdotes, we select one which is recorded by *Madame*, and which we will allow that princess to relate in her own words :

"Two young duchesses were unable to obtain a sufficiently near view of their lovers, and bethought themselves of an original expedient. They were two sisters, and had been educated at a convent some leagues from Paris. A nun belonging to this convent had just died. The ladies pretended that they were greatly distressed, and had been deeply attached to the deceased, and asked permission to pay her the last honours and to attend her funeral, which was accorded, together with much praise for the kindly feeling which had prompted them. When they arrived at the convent, they found there two strange priests, with whom no one was acquainted. They were asked who they were, and replied that they were two poor ecclesiastics who were in need of protection, and that, ascertaining that two duchesses were expected on the occasion of the funeral, they had come to solicit their patronage. The duchesses said that they should like to question them, and that, when the ceremony was over, they might come and see them in their apartment. Thither the two young priests proceeded, and remained with the ladies until the evening. The abbess thought that the audience was lasting too long, and sent to tell them to take their departure. One resisted and flew into a rage; the other only laughed. This last was the Duc de Richelieu, the other the Chevalier de Guéménée, younger son of the duke of that name. It is the gallants themselves who have related this adventure."[1]

Although Mlle. de Charolais could not but be aware of the infidelities of her lover, she appears to have laid the flattering unction to her soul that, though others might appeal to his senses, she alone possessed his heart; and such was her infatuation, that the more frequently did he transgress, the more precious did he become in her eyes. However, in the winter of 1718–1719, a much more redoubtable rival than ladies of the type of the Duchesse de Retz appeared upon the scene.

[1] *Correspondance complète de Madame, Duchesse d'Orléans.* Letter of June 11, 1717. One of the ladies—she who was enamoured of Richelieu—was the Duchesse de Retz; the other is believed to have been not her sister, but her cousin. The convent at which the incident occurred was the famous Abbey of Jouarre.

# CHAPTER IV

Mlle. de Valois, fourth daughter of the Regent, makes her appearance in Society—A *mariage manqué*—The young princess is sent to her grandmother at Saint-Cloud—Her physical and moral portrait by *Madame*—She falls violently in love with Richelieu, who discovers that to be beloved by two princesses at the same time has its inconveniences—Open rivalry between Mlles. de Charolais and de Valois—The Regent warns the duke against the possible consequences of his presumption—Richelieu carries off the prince's mistress, the actress la Souris—Mlle. Émilie consoles the Regent—A violent admirer—Extraordinary infatuation of the fair sex for Richelieu—Mesdames de Polignac and de Nesle fight a duel about him in the Bois de Boulogne—Probable secret of the duke's singular attraction for women—State of parties in France—Intrigues of the Duchesse du Maine with Spain—The Cellamare conspiracy—Richelieu conspires on his own account with Alberoni—He falls into a trap laid for him by the French Government—Warning which he receives from Mlle. de Valois—He is arrested in bed, and taken to the Bastille, for the third time.

ON January 15, 1715, there appeared in the Duc d'Orléans's box at the Opera, where a masked ball was in progress, a young girl of fourteen, who attracted a great deal of attention. The damsel in question was the future Regent's third daughter, Charlotte Aglaé d'Orléans, called Mlle. de Valois, who had a few months before been withdrawn by her father from the Abbey of Chelles, where she had been for some time *en pension* with her elder sister, Mlle. de Chartres, who was later to become the head of that institution. On March 3, she again appeared at an Opera ball—it must be admitted that Phillippe d'Orléans had singular ideas of the manner in which a young girl of fourteen should be brought up—and, a little later, attended a hunting-party at Marly, under the escort of *Madame*, who appears to have been very disappointed that her grand-daughter had not fulfilled her expectations on the score of beauty. "When she was very young," she writes, "I hoped that Mlle. de Valois would be pretty, but I have been very deceived. She has acquired a great aquiline nose, which has spoiled her. She had formerly the prettiest nose in the world. The cause of this misfortune is that she has been allowed to take snuff."

During the next couple of years, we hear nothing of Mlle. de Valois, apart from an occasional announcement by Dangeau that she had accompanied her father to the Opera, or her mother to the Comédie-Française. Beyond escorting her on these occasions, the Duc and Duchesse d'Orléans appear to have troubled themselves very little about their daughter, and to have made not the slightest attempt to shield her from the dangers to which young girls were exposed in an age in which virtue had gone altogether out of fashion and modesty was barely tolerated.

If, however, Madame d'Orléans regarded the education and moral training of the young princess as matters of small importance, she was far from indifferent to her matrimonial future. The duchess had been for some time past extremely anxious to bring about a reconciliation between the Orléans family and the little Court of Sceaux, by marrying one of her daughters to the Prince de Dombes, eldest son of her brother, the Duc du Maine, and had made great efforts to induce her second daughter, Mlle. de Chartres, to sacrifice herself on the altar of political expediency. But all her persuasions proved of no avail, Mlle. de Chartres preferring to become the bride of Heaven. The duchess, thereupon, trained her batteries upon Mlle. de Valois, and bombarded her with arguments, tears, reproaches, and threats, only to meet with an equally stubborn resistance. Nothing, the young lady declared, would induce her to marry her cousin.

Unable to triumph over her daughter's resistance, Madame d'Orléans conceived for her the most intense dislike, declared that she could not endure the sight of her, and rendered the unfortunate girl's life at the Palais-Royal perfectly miserable, by her constant reproaches. "Mlle. de Valois," writes *Madame*, under date September 6, 1718, "is not on good terms with her mother, who wished to persuade her to marry the Prince de Dombes, eldest son of the Duc du Maine. The mother is incessantly reproaching her daughter with the fact that, if she had married her nephew, the misfortune which had overtaken her brother and his son would not have happened.[1] She cannot endure the sight of her daughter, and has begged me to keep her some time with me."

Mlle. de Valois, in consequence, was installed at Saint-Cloud, where she was almost immediately asked in marriage by *Monsieur le Duc*, on behalf of his brother, the Comte de Charolais, that half-crazy prince, about whose ferocious depravity so many anecdotes are related. Mlle. de Valois would appear to have regarded the prospect not unfavourably, but her parents were of a different opinion, and declined to give their consent. No doubt, the mere fact that her daughter was well disposed towards her suitor was in itself sufficient to determine the Duchesse d'Orléans to oppose the match.

At Saint-Cloud, *Madame* had abundant opportunities of studying her grand-daughter, and the judgment she formed of both the appearance and character of that young lady was anything but favourable.

"Mlle. de Valois," she writes, "is a brunette; she has very beautiful eyes, but her nose is villainous and too big. In my opinion, she is not beautiful. There are, however, days when she is not ugly, for she has a fine complexion and a beautiful skin. When she laughs, a long tooth in her upper jaw produces a vile effect. Her figure is short and ugly; her head sunk in her shoulders; and what is worse, in my judgment, is the lack of grace that she shows in everything she does; she walks like a woman eighty years old. . . . If she were one of those persons who have no desire to please, I should not be surprised at her neglecting herself to this extent. But she loves to be thought pretty; she has some taste for the toilette, and she cannot

[1] The misfortune was the decree of August 26, 1718, which reduced the Duc du Maine and his younger brother, the Comte de Toulouse, to the rank of simple peers, and took away from the former the superintendence of the young King's education.

understand that the best toilette is graceful and distinguished manners, and that, when those are wanting, nothing can supply their place. . . . I have by no means a good opinion of her, and I do not pray for her preservation. She has no good instincts; she cares nothing at all about her mother, and very little about her father; she detests me more than the devil; she is deceitful, untruthful, and horribly coquettish; in short, she will give us all cause for mortification. I wish that she were already married and far away from here; and I should like her to be married to a foreign prince, so that one might hear no more about her."[1]

Notwithstanding the very unflattering portrait which *Madame* traces of her grand-daughter, Mlle. de Valois, at this time, seems to have been regarded by her contemporaries as a very agreeable young lady. Without being beautiful or even pretty, she pleased and attracted, since her fine eyes and her dazzling complexion went far to redeem the defects of which her grandmother speaks; she was affable and good-humoured, and, though of an extremely indolent disposition, possessed of considerable intelligence, which, had she chosen to exercise it, might have resulted in her becoming as accomplished a woman as her sister, the Abbess of Chelles.

The little sympathy which *Madame* felt for her grand-daughter did not prevent the old princess from doing what she conceived to be her duty by the girl, and during the winter of 1718–1719, she frequently escorted her to the Opera, the Comédie-Française, and to various social functions, while she also entertained a good deal at Saint-Cloud for her benefit. It was now that Mlle. de Valois seems first to have made the acquaintance of Richelieu, for whom she soon conceived a passion as ardent as that which her cousin, Mlle. de Charolais, entertained. The duke, on his side, was not the man to despise a conquest which promised to enhance so much his already great reputation as a *vainqueur de dames*, though there can be

[1] And elsewhere *Madame* writes: "Madame d'Orléans would be the most deceitful person in the world, were it not for her daughter, Mlle. de Valois. It is appalling to me to find such horrible deceitfulness in any one so young."

CHARLOTTE AGLAÉ DE BOURBON-ORLÉANS, MLLE. DE VALOIS, AFTERWARDS PRINCESS, AND LATER DUCHESS, OF MODENA

AFTER THE PAINTING BY PIERRE GOBERT AT VERSAILLES

no doubt that the young princess appealed far more strongly to his head than to his heart. Nor did he consider it at all necessary to be off with the old love before being on with the new, and, while paying his court to the daughter of the Regent, was far from neglecting the daughter of the Condés, who still remained in ignorance of a treason which was the talk of the whole Court. At length, however, she was undeceived.

The story goes that, one evening, while playing cards at Saint-Cloud, Richelieu, seeking under the table for the feet of Mlle. de Valois, between which and his own very tender communications had been established, addressed, all unwittingly, his caresses to those of her unfortunate rival, who, "though devoured by jealousy, had the patience to continue this game for a long while, in order to gauge the strength of his passion." At the conclusion of the rubber, however, she "rose like a Fury, with flashing eyes which seemed about to leap from her head, and, under the pretext of indisposition, retired to her apartments, to storm with anger and spite against Mlle. de Valois," leaving the duke much disconcerted at the consequences of his mistake, and with little desire, for that evening at least, to resume his communications with his new inamorata. What made the incident the more piquant, was that Mlle. de Valois, who did not understand that Richelieu had made a mistake, and believed that he had really intended these tokens of affection for her cousin, was even more indignant than the other. Neither of the princesses, however, testified any resentment against the duke, who was deceiving them both, but they vowed eternal enmity against one another, and showed it in the most public manner, to the great diversion of the Court.

The Regent, whose own laxity of morals did not prevent him from being extremely solicitous for the honour or, at any rate, the reputation of his daughters, was as angry as his indolent character would permit, and decided to give the audacious gallant a broad hint as to the possible consequences of his presumption. One evening, at a masked ball, having perceived Mlle. de Valois in conversation with a gentleman who was wearing a domino very closely resembling that which he knew Richelieu had assumed for the occasion, he approached and said to him: "Mask, be careful, if you do not wish to go a third time to the Bastille."

The person addressed, who was an intimate friend of Richelieu, Montconseil by name, hastened to undeceive his Royal Highness by removing his mask, upon which the prince added in a threatening tone: "Tell, then, your friend Richelieu what I have just told you, under the impression that you were he."

Partly to distract attention from his intrigue with Mlle. de Valois, and partly to avenge himself for the opposition of her father, Richelieu resolved to take away the reigning sultana of the Regent's seraglio, the actress la Souris. La Souris's amorous relations were distinctly amusing, for, while the prince was infatuated with her, she was infatuated with an impecunious young page in the service of the Duc de Luxembourg, who was, in turn, the slave of another courtesan, who was a veritable daughter of the horseleech. Thus, all the money which the Regent gave his mistress, found its way, *via* the Duc de Luxembourg's page, into the cash-box of the latter's inamorata, who must have enjoyed many a hearty laugh at the expense of his Royal Highness.

To carry out his project, Richelieu took into his confidence the famous tenor of the Opera, Thévenard,[1] and persuaded him to give a grand fête in honour of la Souris at Auteuil, where the actor had a country-house, he himself defraying the expenses. Everything was to be on the most sumptuous scale, and the Regent and a number of other distinguished persons promised to grace the proceedings with their presence.

Just as the company was rising from the dinner-table, word

[1] Gabriel Vincent Thévenard. He entered the Académie Royale de Musique in 1690, and in seven years had completely conquered the suffrages of the public and become the most fashionable singer of the Opera. His best *rôle* was perhaps that of Phinée, in the *Persée* of Lulli and Quinault, in which he excited great enthusiasm. He retired in 1730. Thévenard was not only a great singer, but a wit and a *homme à bonnes fortunes*. He also possessed a most abnormal capacity for the consumption of alcohol, "and every day swallowed considerable quantities of wine, on the specious pretext of strengthening his voice." His potations, however, do not appear to have much affected him, since he lived to the age of seventy-two.

was brought to la Souris that a nobleman of high rank desired the favour of a moment's conversation with her. The actress, who was probably not unaccustomed to requests of this nature from distinguished admirers who wished to conceal their identity, went to the door, and never returned, for, no sooner did she appear, than she was seized by two lackeys and lifted into a phaeton, the driver of which, who was, of course, none other than Richelieu, immediately whipped up his horses and drove off at full speed to Paris.

The Regent, though doubtless much irritated at seeing his mistress carried off before his eyes, deemed it wisest to conceal his vexation—perhaps he was not altogether sorry for an excuse to get rid of la Souris, of whose fidelity he was becoming suspicious—and found consolation in the arms of another star of the operatic firmament, Mlle. Émilie by name, who was "as modest and full of sentiment as her predecessor had been libertine, unfaithful, flighty, inconsequent and capricious."[1] To her he remained constant—or nearly so—for no less a period than six months, and might have done so for even longer, had not a former and desperately jealous admirer of Émilie, named Fimarçon, returned from the wars, carried her off *vi et armis*, threatened to kill her if she ever went within arm's-length of the Regent again, and so terrified the unfortunate actress, that she finally allowed him to shut her up in a convent at Charenton. The prince, fearful lest any attempt to recover his Émilie might expose her to personal violence from her infuriated lover, refrained from interfering with Fimarçon, who surrounded the convent with spies, and threatened the nuns to burn their house over their heads, if they ever permitted any one but himself to speak to the lady. About a year later, a violent assault which Fimarçon had committed upon a gentleman with whom he had quarrelled over another woman necessitated that worthy's retirement to For l'Évêque, and Émilie found herself free to leave her convent. But, by that time, new charmers had succeeded her in the affections of his Royal Highness.

[1] *Mémoires du duc de Richelieu.*

Throughout the winter of 1719, Mlles de Charolais and de Valois continued their little comedy; the one striving to win back her faithless gallant, the other to wrest him altogether from the faltering clasp of her cousin, both seemingly oblivious to the fact that Richelieu was "providing them each day with new rivals."[1] For the attentions, however fugitive, of a gentleman, who was so extraordinarily fortunate as to have two princesses contending almost openly for the possession of his heart, were regarded as a tribute to a lady's charms which no one could venture to gainsay; and citizens' wives, actresses and women of

[1] Among these rivals, were Madame de Sabran, at one time the chief sultana of the Regent's seraglio, and Madame de Guébriant, concerning whom an amusing anecdote is related:

It appears to have been Richelieu's custom to give rendezvous to his inamoratas, even to those of the highest rank, in the courts of the Palais-Royal, whither the duke would send his carriage to take them up and convey them to a little house of his in the Faubourg Saint-Antoine, where he would be waiting to receive them. One fine evening, when his carriage was waiting on this spot for Madame de Sabran, it was perceived by Madame de Guébriant, who had made use of it on many occasions. She, supposing that it was there for her, and that the note making the assignation had miscarried, entered it, upon which the coachman, who had often driven her before, concluded that he must have misunderstood the orders which his master had given him, and took the lady to the house mentioned by the duke. That nobleman was naturally much astonished and mortified at the mistake, but he was too well bred to express his surprise, and Madame de Guébriant occupied, without suspecting anything, the place which had been reserved for her rival at the supper-table.

Meanwhile, Madame de Sabran, who had been punctual to the appointed hour, was impatiently awaiting the arrival of Richelieu's carriage in the courts of the Palais-Royal; but the minutes passed, and the wheels of the ducal chariot still tarried. At length, fearing that she might be recognised if she remained any longer in a place so frequented, and transported by love and jealousy, she called a hackney-coach and was driven to the house in the Faubourg Saint-Antoine, to which she was no stranger, promising herself that she would give her lover a piece of her mind, for having exposed her to so much inconvenience.

Her indignation on learning on her arrival there that her place had been usurped by a rival can be imagined, while Madame de Guébriant was equally furious at the destruction of the pleasing illusion under which she had lain; and, as ladies in like circumstances are not accustomed to mince their language, the scene which followed was exceedingly animated, and might have occasioned a less resourceful person than M. de Richelieu considerable embarrassment. The latter, however, preserved his *sang-froid*, and taking the two exasperated rivals by the hand, made them sit down. Then, placing himself between them, he told them that it was the stupidity of his coachman that had been the cause of all the pother, and "concluded by endeavouring to prove to them that it was perfectly possible for a man to be in love with two women at the same time."

title, instead of waiting to be wooed, pursued him with a fervour and persistency which was as ridiculous as it was indecent. "If I believed in sorcery," writes *Madame*, "I should say that this duke must possess some supernatural secret, for he has never found a woman who has opposed to him the least resistance; all run after him; it is truly shameful. He is not, after all, more handsome than other men, and he is so indiscreet and fond of babbling, that he has himself declared that if an empress, beautiful as an angel, were enamoured of him and wished to pass the night with him, on condition that he should say nothing about it, he should prefer to forsake her and never see her again so long as he lived. He is a great poltroon,[1] very insolent, without heart and without soul; it revolts me to think that he is the pet of all the ladies."[2]

If we are to believe Soulavie, it was no uncommon thing for Richelieu's confidential *valet de chambre*, whose post must have been an exceedingly lucrative one, to find himself entrusted with as many as ten or a dozen letters, each inviting his master to a rendezvous for the same evening. The duke, he adds, did not take the trouble to open all these *poulets*, since most of them, particularly those of the princesses, were usually in cypher, and took some time to transcribe, but contented himself by opening that of the lady whom he wished to visit. The others he locked up in his desk, without even breaking the seals, and left them for the perusal of the historians of his time who have had access to his papers. Since his sense of honour where the opposite sex was concerned was practically non-existent, he derived a cynical amusement from making game of the passion of these foolish women, and often despatched, as though by mistake, to one whose favours he did not happen to desire the *billet doux* of some more happy rival. This procedure naturally led to bitter quarrels between the aspirants to the ducal affections, and in March 1719, one of these quarrels very nearly had a tragic termination.

[1] This, of course, is untrue, as Richelieu's courage was beyond dispute.

[2] *Correspondance complète de Madame, Duchesse d'Orléans.* Letter of October 1, 1719.

Among the countless adorers of this fortunate nobleman, none loved him with a more consuming passion than the Comtesse de Polignac,[1] a lady of Junoesque appearance, with a tall and opulent figure, raven tresses, a high colour, a bold black eye, and a ringing laugh. It is true that she had loved a great many others, and "inaugurated with the Chevalier de Bavière a series of liaisons, in which the last succeeded the first as Louis XV. succeeded Pharamond,"[2] and which included affairs with *Monsieur le Duc*, the Prince de Conti, and the son of the Turkish Ambassador;[3] but Richelieu was the idol of her heart. For some time past, however, her devotion had met with no response; the reproachful letters which she addressed to him remained unanswered, and long weary months had elapsed since his *valet de chambre* had knocked at her door. His indifference, however, did but serve to stimulate her ardour, and she continued desperately in love, and madly jealous of every lady who for a moment caught his changeful fancy.

The object of Richelieu's attentions, and consequently of Madame de Polignac's peculiar animosity, at this time was the

[1] She was the fourth and youngest daughter of the Comte de Mailly, and had married in 1709 the Comte de Polignac, a general in the Army, "who knew little besides his military *métier*, and nothing at all of the *métier* of a husband."

[2] Lescure, *Nouveaux Mémoires du duc de Richelieu.*

[3] "The disorderly and foolish life in Paris becomes each day more detestable and more horrible: every time that it thunders, I tremble for this town. Three women of quality have committed things truly frightful. They followed to Paris the Turkish Ambassador, lured away his son, made him beautifully drunk, and passed two days with this long-bearded rogue in the labyrinth [of Versailles]. I believe that no Capuchin monk would be safe with these ladies. This will give Constantinople a fine idea of Christian women and ladies of quality. The young Turk said to Madame de Polignac, one of these three ladies (he had learnt French perfectly): 'Madame, your reputation has reached Constantinople, and I see well, Madame, that they have told us the truth.' The Ambassador has been extremely annoyed by all this, and he told his son that he must keep the affair very quiet, since if it were known at Constantinople that he had got drunk and had had intercourse with Christian women, they would cut off his head. Is it not a horrible thing? . . . I do not understand why her [Madame de Polignac's] relatives and those of her husband do not take steps to put a stop to such dissolute conduct; but all sense of shame is banished from this country."—Letter of *Madame* to M. de Harling, September 27, 1720.

The *Mémoires of Maurepas* contain lengthy details concerning the scandalous adventures of this lady, who in 1732 was shut up by her relatives in a convent.

latter's sister-in-law, the Marquise de Nesle, for whom, for some reason which we are not told, she conceived so violent a hatred, that she decided that nothing but her blood could expiate the crime of having encouraged the duke, and sent her a challenge to mortal combat. The challenge was accepted in the same spirit in which it was issued, and the two ladies repaired to the rendezvous, each resolved to rid the earth of her rival. Under date March 14, 1719, Buvat writes in his *Journal:*

"The Marquise de Nesle, who is a daughter of the Duc de Mazarin, and the Marquise de Polignac, her sister-in-law, because of some jealousy which they had conceived for one another, on the subject of the Marquis d'Alincourt, second son of the Duc de Villeroy,[1] gave each other a rendezvous in the Pré-aux-Clercs, beside the Invalides. Arrived there, they alighted from their carriages, bade their people await their return, and then quickly withdrew and sat down on the grass. Then, after quarrelling and reviling one another, they rose up in fury, and, each of them drawing from her pocket a knife with which she was provided, exchanged several blows, and perhaps might have killed one another, had not their servants, perceiving this affray, rushed up and separated them. The Marquise de Nesle was wounded above the breast, and the Marquise de Polignac in the face and in several other places. They then re-entered their carriages, in order to get their wounds dressed. Subsequently, they both received an order from the King, banishing them to one of their country-houses."[2]

[1] Buvat is mistaken. That Richelieu was the cause of the affray is now undisputed.

[2] Soulavie, who says that the duel took place in the Bois de Boulogne, and not in the Pré-aux-Clercs, and that pistols were the weapons used, gives a more lengthy account of the affair, garnished with piquant details, for which, however, we leave to him the responsibility:

"After a preliminary salutation, these ladies, clothed as Amazons, each discharged a pistol. Madame de Nesle was seen to fall to the ground, and her bosom was immediately covered with blood. Madame de Polignac, proud of her victory, returned to her carriage. 'Go!' said she to her adversary. 'I will teach you to follow in the footsteps of a woman like me. If I had the perfidious one in my power, I would eat his heart, after blowing out his brains . . .' Certain curious persons, whom this novel spectacle had drawn to the spot, approached Madame de Nesle, as she lay upon the ground, and, perceiving that her bosom was covered with blood,

It may be as well to pause here for a moment to inquire what was the talisman which made this young man the idol of all the women of his time, and inspired them with so extraordinary an infatuation that they were ready to sacrifice everything to it—their happiness, their honour, nay, even their very lives. He was handsome, of course—for even his enemy *Madame* is fain to admit that he had "a very shapely figure, beautiful hair, an oval face, and very brilliant eyes"[1]—but not more so than a score of other men who could not lay claim to a tithe of his successes. He was very brave, notwithstanding what that princess says to the contrary, and, as she is again obliged to confess, he was "agreeable and did not lack intelligence."[2] But courage and agreeable manners were the common heritage of the French aristocracy, and, as for Richelieu's mental equipment, though he certainly

believed that she had received a mortal wound, and that her condition was hopeless. But, on examination, it was perceived that the blood was flowing from a scratch on the top of the shoulder, the ball having only slightly grazed Madame de Nesle. After recovering from her fright, she returned thanks to Heaven, saying that she had triumphed over her rival. These words made the bystanders, who had been much puzzled by a combat of this nature, understand that some lover was in question, and they asked Madame de Nesle if this lover were worthy of the pain she was enduring for his sake. 'Yes, yes!' exclaimed the wounded lady; 'he is worthy of an even more noble blood being shed for him.' They stopped the flow of blood with nettles crushed between two stones, bandaged the wound with some compresses, and bore her to her carriage; and when they inquired who was the fortunate mortal for whom she was shedding her blood, 'He is,' said she, 'the most amiable nobleman of the Court; I am ready to shed it for him to the last drop in my veins. All the ladies set traps for him; but I trust that the proof that I have just given him of my love will make him wholly mine. I am,' she added, 'under too much obligation to you to conceal from you his name. He is the Duc de Richelieu—yes, the Duc de Richelieu, the eldest son of Venus and Mars!'"

[1] She adds, however, as if anxious to destroy the effect of her testimony to Richelieu's good looks: "But everything in his face indicates the knave."

[2] *Correspondance complète de Madame, Duchesse d'Orléans.* Letter of April 27, 1719. In the same letter, *Madame, en revanche* for these admissions, draws a very unflattering moral portrait of the duke: "The Duc de Richelieu is an archdebauchee (*ein ertz desbeaucherter*) and a poltroon; he believes neither in God nor in his word; he has made nothing of his life and will never do anything worth doing; he is ambitious and false as the devil . . . I do not find him as pleasing as all the women who are mad about him. . . . His insolence is remarkable. He is the worst of spoiled children." Elsewhere *Madame* tells us that she calls him the gnome, "because he resembles a mischievous little demon as closely as one drop of water does another."

possessed a ready wit, his education had been far too defective to enable him to subjugate by force of intellect. We must, therefore, look elsewhere for the secret which permitted him to ruin a woman with a smile or a compliment, and rendered him more dangerous to the coquettes of those days than the flame is to the moth; and the true one is probably that given by Lescure, in his work on the mistresses of Philippe d'Orléans:

"This secret, which Soyecourt, Guiche, and Lauzun had discovered and practised together, which Richelieu had divined, thanks to the imprudences, often calumniated, of the Duchesse de Bourgogne, this formula which enabled them to remain always handsome, young, and adored, if not to be really so, I am going to reveal to you, for the shame and the punishment of the epoch which permitted it.

"*Nil mirari*, to wonder at nothing, such was the device of this hero of the boudoir, whose life was as it were the epopee of fatuity. To wonder at nothing; not in the philosophical sense of the expression, dear to the sage, but in the cynical sense. Do you wish to know why they made their way so easily in the world, all these handsome cadets of Gascony, who braved King Louis XIV. himself in his power and his amours? It was because they were surprised at nothing. Lauzun ill-treated *Mademoiselle*, the degenerate heroine of the Fronde, who began by defying Love and who ended by serving it on her knees. Rions ill-treated the tempestuous Duchesse de Berry, to continue the tradition. Richelieu did not beat any woman, but he compromised them all. He also was surprised at nothing, and that is why he triumphed. He was systematically indiscreet, calculatingly garrulous, and that is why every day some noble unfortunate, attacked by that vertigo which seizes upon the woman in the presence of every man cleverer than herself, solicited of him the honour of being dishonoured. Shocking to say! more than one woman surrendered herself, not from the intoxication of passion, but from the intoxication of pride; more than one woman ruined herself in order to be ruined by him, *and to hear it talked about*. It was as it were a competition of scandal, as a joust of immodesty. For the first time, people blushed for virtue. Richelieu did but too much to encourage this vanity singular and depraved. He possessed the great secret of his time, the most corrupt that ever existed. He made extensive use of it. In two words, do you wish to know why he was adored by all the women? It is that he despised them all."[1]

The duel between Mesdames de Nesle and de Polignac put the crown, so to speak, on the gallant reputation of M. de Richelieu; but, even while people were still busily discussing this affair, the ladies of the Court and Paris were stricken to the heart by the terrible news that the gates of the Bastille had closed upon their idol for the third time, and on this occasion for a very much more serious offence than those which had resulted in his previous incarcerations. But, to explain how this came about, we must go back to the events which preceded and followed the death of the late King.

In July 1714, Louis XIV. had issued an edict giving to his two natural sons by Madame de Montespan, the Duc du Maine and the Comte de Toulouse, the honours and position of Princes of the Blood and declaring them heirs to the throne, in case of the failure of the direct line. This edict was duly registered by the Parlement, though nearly the whole nation was shocked and scandalised; for France was the land of hereditary right and direct succession, and, however indulgent she might be to her monarch's sins, she bitterly resented an attack on her most cherished traditions. That Louis XIV., through his dislike of the Duc d'Orléans, should endeavour to treat the Crown of France as though it were his private property was regarded as an outrage.

Shortly afterwards, the King made a last will, for the purpose of regulating the regency for his great-grandson. By this testament, which was extorted from the old monarch by the persistence of Madame de Maintenon, and his Majesty's Jesuit confessor Le Tellier, Fleury, Bishop of Fréjus, was

[1] Lescure, *les Maîtresses du Régent.*

appointed the child's preceptor, Le Tellier, his confessor, and the Maréchal de Villeroy, his *gouverneur;* while the Duc du Maine was invested with the command of the Household troops and charged with the "safety, protection, and preservation of the young King." As for Orléans, who could not, of course, be passed over altogether, he was merely named President of the Council of Regency—a high-sounding title, without any real power. Thus, had the King's will been executed, all the authority would have rested with Maine, his ally Le Tellier, and the high Catholic party.

The will, however, was of no more value than that of Louis XIII. Two days after the King's death, the document was set aside by a unanimous vote of the Parlement, and Philippe d'Orléans was declared Regent, with full power to appoint the Council—a verdict which was hailed with acclamation by the great majority of the nation.

Maine, however, thanks to the restless ambition of his wife and the encouragement he received from the King of Spain, remained a force to be reckoned with; all the malcontents, all the bigots, all who regretted the old *régime*, rallied round him; and the little Court of Sceaux became the centre of countless intrigues, which had as their object the overthrow of the Regent. The latter, whom Dubois and his spies kept well informed of these proceedings, retaliated by a decree depriving Maine and Toulouse of their rights of succession to the throne and their quality of Princes of the Blood (July 1, 1717).

This decree was the prologue of the drama which precipitated the Maines into the abyss. The little duchess refused to bend before the storm, and had the imprudence to indulge in complaints and menaces. Her conduct was made the pretext for a second thunderbolt, which reduced Maine and Toulouse to the rank of simple peers, and took away from the elder brother the superintendence of the young king's education.

This fresh humiliation roused the turbulent little lady to fury. "When," said she, in 1714, in discussing the events which might happen after Louis XIV.'s death, "when one has secured the chance of succeeding to the Crown, one ought, rather than suffer it to be snatched from one, to set fire to the four corners of the kingdom." She now proceeded to do all in her power to give effect to these bold words. For some time past, through the intermediary of Çellamare, the Spanish Ambassador in Paris, she had been intriguing with Alberoni, the ambitious Minister of Philip V., who desired to assure the throne of France to his master, in the event of the death of the young King, by the removal of the Duc d'Orléans; and in the last weeks of 1718, these intrigues culminated in the plot against the Regent known to history as the Cellamare conspiracy.

The plot was discovered; and on December 29 M. and Madame du Maine were arrested and conducted, the one to the Château of Doullens, the other to the Château of Dijon; while the Abbé Brigault, the Comte de Laval, the Marquis de Pompadour, the Chevalier de Ménil, M. de Malézieu—formerly tutor to the Duc du Maine—and Mlle. de Launay (Madame de Staal), who has left us such a lively account of her experiences,[1] were sent to the Bastille. The duchess's ecclesiastical admirer, Polignac, was exiled to one of his abbeys.

The Duc de Richelieu had taken no part in the Cellamare affair, properly so-called, but early in the following year he was rash enough to engage in a little conspiracy on his own account. In February 1717, Richelieu had been selected to convey the ribbon of the Order of the Saint-Esprit to the Prince of the Asturias, eldest son of Philip V., and, though this mission, for what reason is unknown, was subsequently countermanded, it was, nevertheless, the occasion of bringing him into communication with Cellamare and Alberoni. The young duke's sympathies with the Maine faction, his personal dislike of the Regent, and the mingled ambition and levity of his character, appeared to Alberoni very promising material to work upon, and he determined to make an attempt to gain him over.

At the beginning of 1715, the Regent was informed that two of the cardinal's emissaries, the Baron von Schlieben and the

[1] Mlle. de Launay was at this time waiting-woman to the Duchesse du Maine.

Count Marini, the former a German, the latter an Italian, were passing through France, on their way to conduct some secret negotiations at the Prussian Court. He ordered both these adventurers to be arrested and placed in the Bastille. The German, who refused to betray his employer, remained there for some time; but the Italian, more subtle, offered his services to the French Government and returned to Spain.[1]

Alberoni was then seeking the means to surprise one of the French ports, and he proposed to Marini, or Marini proposed to him—it is not quite certain which—that the Italian should again make his way to France and endeavour to seduce from his allegiance the Duc de Richelieu, who was colonel of the Regiment du Roi,[2] one of the two regiments which formed the garrison of Bayonne.

Marini accordingly set out for Paris, taking with him two letters for Richelieu, one crediting the bearer to the duke,[3] the other proposing that that nobleman and the Marquis de Saillant, colonel of the other regiment in garrison at Bayonne, should facilitate the taking of that town by the troops of his Catholic Majesty.

Since Alberoni's letter to Richelieu has not been preserved,

[1] Marini received for the services he proposed to render the French Government in Spain a *gratification* of three thousand livres, and a promise that, "if he succeeded in conducting the affair successfully, he should have every reason to be satisfied with his reward" (Letter of Le Blanc, Minister for War, to Marini, February 22, 1719, in Ravaisson, *Archives de la Bastille*).

The same Archives contain a good deal of information concerning this worthy, who seems to have been a thorough rascal, and a man of the most scandalous life. In July 1726, he was sent to the Bastille, on the demand of his wife's relatives, who complained that, while he ill treated the poor lady and left her "without a sol," he was keeping two mistresses and several illegitimate children, besides allowing a pension to the husband of one of his ladyloves, to console him for the loss of his consort. In the following November, he was removed to the Îles Sainte-Marguerite, where he behaved with "a vanity, violence, and presumption which might have belonged to the arbiter of Europe." He was set at liberty in September 1728.

[2] In September 1715, Richelieu had purchased the colonelcy of the Régiment du Roi from the Duchesse de Bourgogne's former admirer, the Marquis de Nangis, for 30,000 écus (90,000 livres).—Dangeau.

[3] Here is the letter, which has been published by Lemontey, in his *Histoire de la Régence*: "The Duc de Richelieu will have the goodness to trust the bearer of this, and may place entire confidence in his executing everything with which he may wish to entrust him."

it is impossible to say what was the bribe which was sufficient to induce the heir of the great cardinal to forget that most sacred duty, unswerving devotion to which, in the face of so many dangers and difficulties, had made the greatness of his race; but it is reasonable to suppose that it must have been a very high one, and no doubt included a promise to facilitate his marriage with Mlle. de Charolais, which would have allied him with the House of Bourbon. Any way, he fell headlong into the trap prepared for him, and, never suspecting for a moment that Alberoni's letters had already been opened and read by d'Argenson,—the Lieutenant of Police—and Dubois, and afterwards carefully sealed again, decided to accept the proposals of Spain, and, with his own hand, wrote two notes to emissaries of Alberoni,[1] and a letter to the Duke of Berwick, who commanded the French troops which were then mobilising on the Spanish frontier, and whom he suspected of an intention to withdraw the Régiment du Roi from Bayonne, begging him to permit that corps to remain there until the beginning of May.[2] Finally, on March 28, he went to the Minister for War, "made a thousand protestations of devotion, and pressed him to give him permission to go and rejoin his regiment."[3]

Later on the same day, however, he received intelligence which must have caused him considerable alarm. The Regent, who was kept informed by Dubois and d'Argenson of the progress of this affair, was indiscreet enough to let fall some words at the Palais-Royal, which implied that M. de Richelieu had got

[1] *First Note.*—"Be at my house to-morrow at seven o'clock precisely. You will only have to ask for my intendant, and he will bring you to me by a staircase where none of my people will see you."

*Second Note.*—"I have received the little diamond which you have sent me by the present bearer. He will render you account of the exchange I am ready to make with you."—Lemontey.

[2] *Letter to Berwick.*—"As my regiment is one of those most ready to take the field, and, as it is about to undergo a new equipment, which it will lose entirely, if it is obliged to make any movement before that is completed, I have the honour to beg you, Monsieur, to consent to allow it to remain at Bayonne until the beginning of May, by which time the equipment will have been completed, and I beg you to believe me, etc.—The Duc de Richelieu."

[3] *Correspondance complète de Madame, Duchesse d'Orléans.* Letter of March 30, 1719.

himself into very serious trouble. Mlle. de Valois, who was informed by her mother of this, became very uneasy, and lost no time in despatching her confidential waiting-woman, Madame Pichet, to the Hôtel de Richelieu, with a letter which Soulavie has preserved for us, and of which conscientious historians will prefer to leave him the responsibility, although, as the princess's biographer, M. Edouard Barthélemy, points out, it is only fair to observe that its orthography bears a remarkable resemblance to that of the numerous letters of the lady in the Archives des Affaires Etrangères:

"As you have assured me that there could be no proof against you,[1] I do not doubt that the warning I am giving you will be useless, but, since it has appeared to me that you like to be informed of everything, I have warned you: the assembly of the Council is to consider the Spanish business. I reckon on knowing more this evening, which I will communicate to you; but what urges me to write to you, is something which has escaped my mother, who was under the impression that I knew it, and who, when she perceived that I did not, recommended me strongly to say nothing about it. I have lost not a moment in warning you of it. Write me if you are without uneasiness, for I confess that I am so no longer."[2]

The letter was followed, a few hours later, by another, in which the princess warned the duke that her father had just said publicly that he had in his possession documents which contained the most damning evidence of the plots which had been formed against him.

Richelieu had now very little doubt that he had been betrayed by Marini, and all uncertainty was removed, when at ten o'clock the following morning (March 29), while he was still in bed, Duchevron, the Provost's lieutenant, with a dozen archers, arrived at his hôtel and, scarcely giving him time to dress, conducted him to the Bastille.[3] "A letter from Alberoni to this

[1] She means in connection with the Cellamare affair.

[2] *Mémoires du duc de Richelieu.*

[3] As the Provost's officers and the archers were never requisitioned except to arrest common criminals, their employment in the case of a *pair de France* was deeply

duke [Richelieu] has been intercepted," writes *Madame*, "which renders his treason clearer than the day.[1] My son has caused him to be arrested in his bed and to be taken immediately to the Bastille. This duke will cause many tears to flow in Paris, for all the ladies are in love with him ; I do not understand why, for he is a little toad, in whom I find nothing agreeable."

resented by his brother peers, who addressed a strong remonstrance to the Regent against the insult which Dubois, to whom the execution of the affair had been entrusted, had offered to their Order.

[1] Although the Government had already made a copy of the contents of this letter before Marini carried it to Richelieu, they naturally desired to recover the original. This, however, they failed to do, for, if we are to believe the Marquis d'Argenson, eldest son of the Lieutenant of Police and the future Minister for Foreign Affairs, the duke, who kept the incriminating epistle under his pillow, contrived to tear it up and swallow it.

# CHAPTER V

Richelieu's treachery regarded as a *conspiration pour rire* rather than a serious plot—Treatment which he receives in the Bastille—Alarm of Mlles. de Charolais and de Valois at the threats of the Regent to have their common idol brought to trial for high treason—Their efforts on his behalf—Diversions of Richelieu in the Bastille—Mlle. de Valois corrupts the guards of the fortress, and the two princesses visit the duke—Indignation of *Madame* on learning the extent to which her grand-daughter has compromised herself—Her hatred of Richelieu—The Regent, alarmed at the conduct of Mlle. de Valois, determines to marry her to a foreign prince—Francesco d'Este, Prince of Modena, proposed as a husband—Mission of the Conte Salvatico to Versailles—The Regent accords his daughter the liberty of Richelieu, on condition of her consenting to wed the Prince of Modena—The duke is released from the Bastille and exiled to Conflans—His nocturnal visits to Paris necessitate his being sent to Saint-Germain-en-Laye, and subsequently to Richelieu—Aversion of Mlle. de Valois to the marriage arranged for her—Richelieu, from prudential motives, decides to break off his connection with the princess—Marriage of Mlle. de Valois—Despair of the bride at the prospect of leaving France—She falls ill from measles, which she has purposely contracted, but recovers—Her journey to Italy—Her unhappy married life—Supposed secret visit of Richelieu to Modena.

IF Richelieu's latest escapade had occurred while Louis XIV. was still on the throne, the duke would probably have paid for it with his head, as the Chevalier de Rohan did in 1674, or at least have remained a close prisoner in the Bastille for the rest of his days. Happily for him, his fate was in the hands of Dubois and the Regent, who both inclined to clemency, the one by system, the other by calculation. Happily, too, the public generally was disposed to regard the intrigue of a young "*méchant*," whose follies were the talk of every café and *cabaret* in Paris, as a subject for merriment rather than for indignation, since, according to the testimony of all his contemporaries, it was entirely unconnected with the real conspiracy, of which Sceaux was the rendezvous and the theatre.

Thus, an affair which, at first sight, appeared very grave, and likely to entail serious consequences upon its author, soon assumed a different aspect ; and, though Richelieu was at first treated with some appearance of severity and very closely interrogated by the Minister for War, Le Blanc, and d'Argenson, with the object of discovering if he had any accomplices at the Court,[1] it was not long before the rigour of his captivity was relaxed, and he was transferred from the bare and gloomy chamber in which he had been originally lodged[2] to a comfortable apartment immediately above that occupied by the Chevalier de Ménil, of whose idyll with Mlle. de Launay that lady has left us so diverting an account, and given some books, a backgammon board, and a violincello, to beguile the tedium of his enforced leisure.

These concessions he probably owed to the good offices of his feminine adorers at the Court, and more particularly to those

[1] "Although he had fallen so clumsily into the trap prepared for him, and stood convicted by his own work, Richelieu maintained silence, so long as Leblanc and d'Argenson were together ; but he made no difficulty about avowing himself guilty, when he was questioned by either of them separately. He pursued the same course with two emissaries of Alberoni, whom he always refused to see at the same time. Some false notions badly arranged in his head had persuaded him that admissions made in this way were valueless, and in this calculating inconsistency one recognises already the mixture of cunning and folly which characterised his life."—Lemontey, *Histoire de la Régence.*

[2] If we are to believe Soulavie, this chamber was "a kind of octagonal dungeon, which did not admit the light and only communicated with the outer air by means of a vent-hole. This frightful apartment was so damp, that on entering it, a mouldy smell made their hearts sink." [Richelieu, it should be mentioned, had been permitted to bring with him to the Bastille a faithful lackey, whose name, we learn from the Archives of the fortress, was Bertel, and not Rafé, as several writers have stated.] "The stones of the prison had not been able to resist the action of this humidity, and their clothes, after several hours, were penetrated with the emanations from these walls and the damp smell in the enclosed air. They found, besides, neither table, bed, books, chairs, nor armchairs, and, upon demanding them, were told that, as the Bastille was full of prisoners, all the furniture was in use." Well, the rooms on the lowest floor of the Bastille, which were known as the "cells," were quite as unpleasant places as the writer has described. [See Funck-Brentano's *Légendes de la Bastille.*] But they were never occupied by any save prisoners of the lowest class and criminals condemned to death, and it is in the highest degree improbable that a duke and peer like Richelieu would have been confined in one of them.

of Mlles. de Charolais and de Valois. No sooner did they learn of the arrest of the duke, than the two princesses, hitherto so furiously jealous of one another, agreed to forget their rivalry for the nonce, and to unite their forces for the rescue of their common idol. The Regent, much irritated, did not cease to fulminate against Richelieu, and declared that it was his intention to have him brought to trial as a State criminal, adding that the Government had sufficient evidence in its possession to cost the duke four heads, if he had them.[1]

These threats, which, it is needless to say, he had no intention of carrying into effect, threw the princesses into a terrible state of alarm, and Mlle. de Charolais, in order to spur her cousin to the most desperate exertions, actually went so far as to promise her that she would never try to see the duke again, if Mlle. de Valois succeeded in obtaining his pardon from the Regent.

That lady scarcely needed any such incitement to persuade her to move Heaven and earth on behalf of her imprisoned gallant, and she seems to have given her father a very unpleasant time of it, "quarrelling with him, demanding the duke's liberation publicly, and threatening to make a scandal, or commit some act of folly, if he were not soon released from his prison."[2] Mlle. de Charolais ably seconded her efforts, and told the Regent, who was one of her *soupirants*, that "she refused to see him, since he had sent the duke to the Bastille."[3] She also went about declaring that the Bayonne affair could never be true, "because the Duc de Richelieu, who had never concealed anything from her, had said nothing to her about it."[4]

To the despair of the two princesses, however, the Regent pretended to be inexorable, and declared that Richelieu's treason merited the scaffold, and that he was determined to bring him to trial.

The object of the ladies' solicitude seems to have been

[1] Duclos, *Mémoires pour servir à l'histoire de Louis XIV. et de Louis XV.*

[2] *Mémoires du duc de Richelieu.*

[3] *Correspondance complète de Madame, Duchesse d'Orleans.* Letter of May 19, 1719.

[4] *Ibid.*

much less disquieted as to the fate in store for him. He read the latest romances; dined twice a week with the governor; played upon his 'cello; stood at his window and sang duets with Mlle. de Launay, who was lodged in a room in the same tower,[1] and every afternoon, after making an elaborate toilette, promenaded upon the terrace of the Bastille, "when all the ladies assembled in the street to gaze at this beautiful image." [2]

Mlle. de Valois was without doubt among the ladies of whom the writer speaks, but she did not confine herself to such platonic demonstrations of sympathy. Aware that in 1716 Mlle. de Charolais had made use of a golden key to unlock the doors of Richelieu's prison, she resolved to follow her example, and Soulavie affirms that she consecrated to the corruption of the warders of the Bastille a sum of 200,000 livres, which her father had lately given her, and persuaded her cousin to reveal to her the measures which she had employed to obtain admission to the fortress. The same writer relates that the two princesses came together to see the duke, at night, "bringing with them, candles, flint and steel, sweetmeats, and plenty of banknotes, in case of need," and that Richelieu "concerted with them the answers that he should give on the morrow to the insidious questions of Le Blanc and d'Argenson."

Since the late autumn of the preceding year, Mlle. de Valois had been, as we have mentioned, living at Saint-Cloud, with her grandmother, who, however, brought her almost every day to Paris to visit the theatre or assist at some social function. The surveillance which the old princess had exercised over her charge had been but little severe, and she had treated her with great indulgence; and her wrath may therefore be imagined when she learned, as she did at the beginning of May, to what

[1] "On rising from table, as it was extremely hot, we placed ourselves at the window. The lieutenant [of the Bastille] suggested that I should sing. I began a scene from the opera of *Iphigénie*. The Duc de Richelieu, who was also at his window, sung the reply of Orestes in the same scene, which was appropriate to our situation. Maisonrouge, who thought that it was amusing me, and who perhaps wished to create a diversion, allowed us to finish the whole scene."—Madame de Staal de Launay, *Mémoires*.

[2] *Correspondance complète de Madame, Duchesse d'Orléans*. Letter of May 19, 1719.

VISITE NOCTURNE

FAITE AU DUC DE RICHELIEU, DÉTENU À LA BASTILLE, POUR LA TROISIÈME FOIS, DANS UN CACHOT, PAR DEUX PRINCESSES DU SANG DÉGUISÉES

FROM AN ENGRAVING BY LE ROY, AFTER THE DRAWING BY LE CLER

extent she had been deceived, and how hopelessly the girl had succeeded in compromising herself with "that accursed Duc de Richelieu." After a violent scene, she sent her grand-daughter back to her mother, much to the disgust of that lady, and firmly refused to receive her again; and in a letter to one of her German friends, she pours out her feelings in language "which," observes M. Barthélemy, "leaves us unfortunately very little doubt about the pranks of Mlle. de Valois." [1]

"You ask me," she writes, "what has recently caused me so much indignation. I cannot relate it in detail, but only as a whole. It is the frightful coquetry of Mlle. de Valois with that accursed Duc de Richelieu, who has shown people the letters which he has had from her, for he only loves her from motives of vanity. All the young nobles of the Court have been able to see these letters, in which she gives him rendezvous. Her mother wished me to have her back with me, which I flatly refused; but she does not cease to return to the charge, and I am horribly vexed; the human race makes me shudder. I cannot endure the idea of seeing Mlle. de Valois again, and I must do it, in order to avoid a very painful scandal. The sight of this madcap will make me ill. All this is the result of the apathy and fatuity of the mother. May God forgive her! But she has brought her girls up very badly.

"The duke [Richelieu] is audacious and full of impertinence. He knows the kindness of my son, and he takes advantage of it. If he had his deserts, he would pay for his temerity and his machinations with his head; for he has merited it three times over. I am not cruel, but I should see without shedding a tear this knave hanging on a gibbet. I am truly exasperated against him, and I detest him with all my heart." [2]

The Regent, on his side, was becoming seriously perturbed at the conduct of the young princess, since he had no desire to see another of his daughters emulating the exploits of the Duchesse de Berry, and, if he appeared to close his eyes, it

[1] *Les Filles du Régent.*

[2] *Correspondance complète de Madame, Duchesse d'Orléans.* Letter of May 13, 1719.

was in order to avoid the necessity of taking steps which would have only increased the scandal. At the same time, he was fully determined to rid himself of this "madcap" with as little delay as might be, by arranging a marriage for her with some foreign prince, and packing her off to Germany or Italy, where her peccadilloes would be her husband's affair and not his, and, as *Madame* observes, "one would no longer hear her talked about"; and at the end of the following summer, the rumour of her union with a prince from beyond the Alps began to spread at the Court, and rapidly gathered consistency.

The *parti* in question was Francesco d'Este, hereditary prince of Modena, son of Duke Rinaldo and Charlotte Félicité of Brunswick-Hanover, and was at this time twenty-two years old. *Madame*, who was not unnaturally inclined to regard any one who was desirous of taking Mlle. de Valois off her relatives' hands through rose-coloured spectacles, tells us that he was "very favourably spoken off"; that he "possessed ability and high principles," and that, though he could not be called handsome, he was "well brought up and very sensible"; but the description given of him by other contemporaries is less flattering.

It was the Marchese Ranzoni Machiavelli, the Modenese Minister at Versailles, who had first conceived the idea of this union and suggested it himself to the Regent, with whom he was on very intimate terms. That prince received the proposition very favourably, for both on political and private grounds the match was one to be desired. It would rally Modena, which of recent years had been alternately the ally of the Empire and France, definitely to the side of the latter, and, at the same time, disembarrass him in a decorous manner of a daughter whose vagaries were threatening to become a public scandal.

Machiavelli duly advised his Court of the result of his overtures, and the Conte Salvatico was deputed to proceed to France as Envoy-Extraordinary and make the formal demand for the hand of Mlle. de Valois.[1]

[1] This Salvatico caused great amusement to the French Court. He was a grotesque personage, with a long, thin face, a neck equally disproportioned, and

At the outset, Salvatico committed a mistake which came near to ruining everything, since he was so ill-advised as to address his request to the King through the medium of his Majesty's *gouverneur*, the Maréchal de Villeroy, instead of through Dubois, which so irritated that all-powerful personage that he intimated his intention of offering the most uncompromising opposition to the proposed alliance. So soon, however, as the envoy realised his mistake, he hastened to repair it, with true Italian adroitness, and begged Dubois's acceptance of five valuable paintings, among which was a work by Paul Veronese. The gift proved an effective solatium for the Minister's wounded feelings, and matters proceeded so smoothly that in a few days nothing remained but to obtain the consent of the lady.

This, as may be anticipated, proved no easy task, since the princess, more and more enamoured of Richelieu, obstinately refused to listen to any matrimonial proposition, much less to one which would entail her removal to so great a distance from her idol; and the Regent soon perceived that the only hope of persuading her to accept the Prince of Modena as a husband, and relieve the French Court of her presence, was to work upon her affection for her captive lover in such a way that she should be willing to expatriate herself for his sake.

Richelieu had now been in the Bastille for nearly five months, but, notwithstanding the representations of the Cardinal de

a most ludicrous gait, which resembled hopping rather than walking; while he bent almost double whenever he bowed to any one, and spoke the most detestable French. Notwithstanding all this, he was extremely vain and imagined himself irresistible. No sooner was he presented to Mlle. de Valois, than he became desperately enamoured of her, and the enthusiastic description of her charms which he despatched to Modena no doubt served to communicate something of his ardour to Francesco d'Este. Such was his conceit that he believed in a possible success, and more than once presented himself at the door of the princess's apartments at hours when visitors were not admitted. So far from endeavouring to conceal his passion from others, "he proclaimed it openly," writes *Madame*, "in the salons of Versailles," adding protestations which the pen of that outspoken old lady alone is able to transcribe. This comedy at first diverted Mlle. de Valois, but, after a time, she began to find it decidedly embarrassing, and when, despite sundry hints from the lady, Salvatico persisted in his unwelcome attentions, she repulsed them angrily. Thenceforth, love was transformed into hatred, and the one-time adorer into an implacable enemy.

Noailles, who declared that his nephew was in a very precarious state of health, and the entreaties and reproaches of Mlles. de Charolais and de Valois, the Regent absolutely refused to hear if his liberation. Moreover, towards the end of August, he gave the duke's friends to understand that fresh documents had recently come to light, which made the case against the prisoner even more grave than it already was.

The supposed documents had no existence save in the imagination of the Regent; but the announcement of their discovery drove the two princesses to the last extremity of despair. Upon which Orleans, perceiving that the crucial moment had arrived, played his trump card, and offered his daughter the liberty of Richelieu, on condition that she would wed the Prince of Modena.

For some days, the young princess hesitated, for the price demanded of her was a heavy one, including as it did not only the renunciation of her lover, but of her country as well—separation from Paris and the Court, beside which all the rest of the world was but an aching void. But, with all her faults, she was a generous-hearted girl, who deserved a better fate than to have bestowed her affections upon one so little capable of appreciating them; and when she recognised that her father would never yield on any other terms, and that the condition of the prisoner's health—the duke had been suffering from dysentery—was causing the doctors who attended him real anxiety, she ended by consenting.

The Regent lost no time in fulfilling his share of the bargain, and on August 30 Richelieu was liberated from the Bastille, with orders to repair to the Cardinal de Noailles's country house at Conflans, and remain there until further orders. Here is the *lettre de cachet* which he received:

"My Cousin,

"Having judged it advisable, on the advice of my uncle, the Duc d'Orléans, to permit you to leave my château of the Bastille, where you are detained in consequence of my orders, I am giving those necessary to that effect to the governor of my said château, and I am writing to you at the same time this letter, to tell you that, upon leaving my said château of the Bastille, you are to betake yourself immediately and without delay to that of Conflans-sous-Charenton, in which it is my intention that you remain, without quitting it upon any pretext whatsoever, until a fresh order from myself. And not doubting that you will conform to that which in this matter is my will, I shall not make the present longer than to pray God that He may have you in His holy and worthy keeping.

(Signed) LOUIS"

(And below) "LE BLANC"

Overjoyed at regaining his freedom, Richelieu hastened to quit his gloomy prison and to betake himself to Conflans. But he did not consider it necessary to obey the latter part of the royal command, and intelligence soon reached the Regent that, when night fell, the duke was in the habit of scaling the walls of the garden and making his way to Paris, returning, however, before his absence could be discovered, and that, on these nocturnal excursions, it was shrewdly suspected that he had paid more than one visit to Mlle. de Valois,[1] and had also been entertained by a lady who was at that moment very near his Royal Highness's heart. The consequence was that, on September 10, M. de Richelieu received a second communication from his sovereign, commanding him "to betake himself immediately to my town of Saint-Germain-en-Laye,[2] by the shortest and most direct route, where my intention is that you remain, without quitting it, until a further order from me." And the letter goes on to say that, while the duke was to have the privilege of receiving his friends and of hunting and riding

[1] If we are to believe Bésenval, the resourcefulness of the duke had enabled him to gain access to his mistress whenever he desired. "The apartments of Mlle. de Valois at the Palais-Royal," he writes, "abutted, on the side of the Rue de Richelieu, on a neighbouring house, the wall of which was merely a partition. M. de Richelieu rented this house, caused the wall corresponding to the cabinet of Mlle. de Valois to be pierced, and had a door constructed, which was hidden by a great cupboard, where the princess kept her preserves. Master of this means of approaching Mlle. de Valois, I leave you to judge if he did not constantly take advantage of it."—*Mémoires*.

[2] Richelieu had a house at Saint-Germain.

in the environs, he must not sleep away from the said town on any pretext whatsoever, and concluded by commending him to the care of God, and informing him that the sieur Dulibois, retired colonel of dragoons, had been charged to accompany him and to remain with him until recalled by his Majesty.

If the King—or rather the Regent—flattered himself that the extra distance from Paris and the appointment of the sieur Dulibois as the duke's custodian would cure that gentleman of his propensity for midnight travel, he was sadly out of his reckoning. For light carriages and swift horses are not difficult to procure, when one has a mind to pay for them, and the worthy ex-dragoon found M. de Richelieu's wine so much to his liking, that, when bedtime arrived, he was seldom in a condition to account for his own actions, let alone for those of his charge. So soon, therefore, as the duke had satisfied himself from the stentorian sounds which proceeded from Dulibois's bed-chamber, or from beneath the supper-table, where, if rumour does not lie, the gallant colonel occasionally elected to sleep off the effects of his potations, that his custodian might safely be regarded as a negligible quantity for some hours to come, he slipped out of the house, entered a phaeton which was in waiting at a little distance, and bowled merrily away to Paris.

These visits, singular to relate, escaped the observation of the police for several weeks, but at length they were discovered, with the result that, towards the end of October, the duke was exiled to Richelieu, in Poitou. He contrived, however, to maintain an active correspondence with Mlle. de Valois, in which he urged her to refuse to fulfil the promise that her father had extracted from her. In consequence, the princess who, according to *Madame*, had appeared more resigned to her fate since she had seen the ravishing toilettes which were being made for her [1] and the splendid present which her *fiancé* had sent,[2] began to evince an increasing repugnance to the marriage,

[1] Buvat says that she had sixty pairs of dresses, fifteen for each season of the year.

[2] "It is a very large and valuable jewel to wear upon the bosom, surrounded by very beautiful diamonds. The prince's portrait is in the central plaque, but it is very badly done."—(*Madame*, Letter of January 25, 1720.)

and "although her conversation was gay and animated, her eyes were always red, and one saw clearly that she passed the night in weeping."

The doleful appearance of the princess was not lost upon the public, and many were the *chansons* to which it gave rise, of which the following is an example:—

> "J'épouse un des plus petits princes,
> Maître de très-petits États,
> Et qui pour ne valent pas
> Une de nos moindres provinces.
> L'on y manqua de tout, la finance est petite.
> Quelle différence, grand Dieu !
> Entre ce triste et pauvre lieu
> Et le *riche lieu* [Richelieu] que je quitte."[1]

Richelieu would appear to have cherished the hope of persuading Mlle. de Valois to break off the match and of marrying her himself. But, after a while, he came to the conclusion that the Regent would scarcely be disposed to tolerate as a son-in-law a gentleman who had been guilty of high treason, and that the most probable result of imitating the Chevalier de Rions would be a fourth and indefinite sojourn in the Bastille, if not a still more unpleasant fate. An ardent lover might have braved even these dangers, but vanity and self-interest had counted for far more in Richelieu's liaison with the princess than sentiment; and so his letters to her grew gradually fewer and less tender, and at length ceased altogether. This no doubt explains why, towards the end of the year, Mlle. de Valois, who had since her betrothal refused to take part in any of the gaieties of the Court, reappeared at her mother's card-parties and at other social gatherings, and seemed altogether more reconciled to her approaching marriage.

The preliminaries of that event were soon completed, for, for different reasons, the relatives on both sides were at one in their desire to hasten it. On December 26, the articles of the marriage-contract, which had been sent to Modena for approval, were brought back, the Duke and his son having passed them

[1] Cited by M. Édouard Barthélemy, *les Filles du Régent.*

without any comment—a very unusual proceeding at this period—and, a few days later, Dangeau announces that the marriage has been fixed for Monday, February 12, and the departure of the bride for the following Thursday. He adds that the lady has not yet been informed of the day of her departure, "from fear of grieving her."

In point of fact, as the marriage drew nearer, Mlle. de Valois, either because Richelieu had repented of his prudent resolutions and had resumed his correspondence with her, or because of her natural reluctance to expatriate herself, began once more to reveal the aversion with which she regarded it in a manner which was apparent to every one, and which drew from *Madame* some caustic observations in regard to marriages in general and those of royal personages in particular. "This prince" [the Prince of Modena], she writes, "ought to be altogether enamoured of the portrait of his future wife; it occasions me truly great distress. Happy marriages are extremely rare, and I have seen people married for love who have afterwards come to detest each other like the devil, and who hate one another still. Happy the one who is not married! How contented should I have been, if I had been permitted not to marry and to live in celibacy! If you wish to know the true reason why princes and princesses detest one another so, it is that they are utterly worthless." [1]

However, the days of grace passed, all too swiftly for the unfortunate princess. On January 31, 1720, the marriage-contract was signed; on February 11, the betrothal ceremony took place in the King's cabinet, the Duc de Chartres, eldest son of the Regent, representing the Prince of Modena, when his Majesty presented his cousin with a magnificent collar of diamonds and pearls; and at noon on the following day, the marriage was celebrated in the chapel of the Tuileries. At its conclusion, the King, according to custom, escorted the bride to her carriage, and, addressing the coachman, said: "*À Modène.*"

[1] *Correspondance complète de Madame, Duchesse d'Orléans.* Letter of December 8, 1719.

The illness of the Duchesse de Villars, who had been chosen to accompany the princess to the frontier, necessitated the latter's departure for Italy being deferred for some days beyond the date originally fixed. This respite proved a most welcome one to her Highness, who on her wedding-day had had "more the air of a victim who was being dragged to the sacrifice than of a princess who walks to the altars of Hymen;"[1] and even *Madame*, who, as we have seen, had little sympathy for her grand-daughter was moved to pity. "I have never seen so sad a bride," she writes a week after the wedding. "For three days she has neither eaten nor slept; she spends the nights in weeping. When my son [the Regent] brought her to bid me farewell, she was not in a condition to utter a single word, so much did she weep; she could only take my hands, kiss them, and squeeze them in hers. She clasped her hands together like a person in despair. My son took her away by force, and with much emotion; he was doing as much violence to his feelings as she was."

The same day on which this letter was written, the princess was taken ill, and on the following morning the doctors pronounced her to be suffering from an attack of measles. This malady she undoubtedly owed to her obstinacy in going to Chelles, to take leave of her sister, who was herself suffering from it; and *Madame* declares that she had insisted on visiting the abbess, between whom and her younger sister there was very little love lost, in the hope of contracting the disease and thus retarding her departure, even at the risk of her life.

"When the Princess of Modena," she writes, "told me that she wished to go to Chelles to take leave of her sister, I counselled her not to do so, telling her that too short a time had elapsed since they had had small-pox in the convent; that the abbess herself was suffering from measles, and that these diseases are easily contracted. She answered: 'That is what I am seeking.' I said to her: 'Take care; one finds that sooner than something good, and often one's life is in danger.' In spite of all I did, she went there on Saturday last and

[1] Bésenval, *Mémoires*.

spent the whole day with her sister, the abbess. On Sunday, she was taken ill, and already had the symptoms of measles."

The illness of the princess, which was aggravated by her imprudence, was a somewhat serious one, and on the 25th her condition was decidedly grave. But in the night which followed she took a turn for the better, and thenceforth improved so rapidly, that two days later, to her great regret, the doctor pronounced her fit to leave her bed.

On March 10, she set out for Modena, accompanied by a veritable court, or rather a caravan, numbering over one hundred and fifty persons. But, owing to the incessant disputes over etiquette between the French and Italian members of her suite, many of which had to be referred to Versailles for settlement, and the conduct of the princess, who availed herself of every conceivable pretext for delay, the journey to Antibes, at which port she was to embark for Italy, occupied more than ten weeks, and it was not until June 3 that she arrived at Genoa, where the Modenese ladies and officials sent to receive her had been waiting since the middle of May.[1] From Genoa the princely caravan took the road to Piacenza, and was met at Reggio by the Duke of Modena and his two sons.

It would be beyond the scope of this volume to relate except very briefly the married life of this victim of the Duc de Richelieu's fascinations, who speedily discovered that the sacrifice which love had impelled her to make was an even heavier one than she had anticipated. Francesco d'Este was a plain, awkward, and morose young man, and afflicted with a timidity almost as great as that of Louis XIII., "which must have rendered him very ridiculous in the eyes of a bride for whom this word had no meaning, and who had probably nothing to learn."[2] It was not, indeed, until the Duke of Modena, who detested his elder son, instituted proceedings to set aside the prince's rights of succession in favour of his

[1] This journey, an interesting account of which will be found in M. Barthélemy's work, proved terribly expensive to the French Treasury, the sum dispensed "*pour largesses et aumônes*" alone being 27,426 livres.

[2] Barthélemy.

younger brother, on the score of impotence, that he could be prevailed upon to consummate the marriage. Thanks to the machinations of the vindictive Salvatico, who had become the relentness enemy of her who had repulsed his advances, the old duke's dislike of the husband was extended to the wife, and he treated his daughter-in-law with the greatest harshness, which was the subject of several protests from the French Government. Indeed, until the death of Duke Rinaldo, the poor princess's life appears to have been most unhappy.

Before, however, taking leave of the Princess of Modena we must say a few words concerning an anecdote related by Soulavie, which has found its way into the works of several modern writers with a weakness for the picturesque.[1]

This imaginative chronicler asserts that the romance of Richelieu and the princess did not terminate with the latter's departure for Italy, but was continued at Modena, whither, eight months later, the duke followed his expatriated inamorata, in the character of a Piedmontese hawker of books, accompanied by his equerry La Fosse, similarly disguised. On their arrival there, they stationed themselves in one of the streets of the city through which her Royal Highness was accustomed to pass on her way to hear Mass, and soon succeeded in attracting her attention. The eyes of love penetrated the disguise, and, under the pretext of examining his wares, the princess invited the duke to the palace, where "he hastened to make her forget her sorrow and her misfortunes." The author says that this rendezvous was succeeded by several others, for the princess "ardently desired to have a little image of her lover"; and he describes a very piquant interview between Richelieu and the lady's husband, who, returning sooner than was expected from the chase, had nearly surprised the pair at an exceedingly inopportune moment, but without conceiving any suspicion. Finally, the duke, who had soon grown tired of a *rôle* which obliged him to put up with a humble lodging and coarse food,

[1] Colonel Haggard, in his interesting, but not very discriminating, work "The Regent of the Roués," devotes a whole chapter to a detailed account of this adventure.

# CHAPTER VI

Richelieu restored to favour—He is elected to the Académie-Française in the place of the Marquis de Dangeau—His *discours de réception*—He takes his seat in the Parlement—Extraordinary interest which this event arouses—Continuation of his liaison with Mlle. de Charolais, which is carried on with so little attempt at concealment as to give rise to reports that they are secretly married—Duel between Richelieu and the lady's brother, *Monsieur le Duc*—Richelieu breaks off his connection with the princess—Madame d'Averne becomes mistress of the Regent *vice* Madame de Parabère—Richelieu, to be avenged upon the prince, steals away the affections of the lady.

RICHELIEU'S disgrace only lasted some three months. "The Duc de Richelieu," writes Dangeau, under date December 9, 1719, "has permission to reside in Paris; but he has not yet permission to see the King or the Duc d'Orléans."[1] On the 15th of the same month, the chronicler notes that "the Duc de Richelieu has had the honour, two days ago, to see the King and the Duc d'Orléans; thus he is in full liberty."

The exile returned to the scene of his many exploits "varnished with the importance which he had acquired from having been imprisoned for an affair of State, and with the brilliant air of a young man who owed his liberty to love,"[2] and became a greater hero than ever in the eyes of the opposite sex. For

[1] Dangeau adds that the duke had just sold the Hôtel de Richelieu, in the Place-Royale, to the Grand-Duchess of Tuscany, "who has bought it for life for the sum of 80,000 livres, and given him, besides, for two years, the house in the Place, in which she is living at present."

[2] Duclos. According to Bésenval, Richelieu had had the bad taste to attend the wedding of Mlle. de Valois, and aggravated his offence by "whispering incessantly into the ear of Mlle. de Charolais, while, at the same time, looking at the bride." "His behaviour," adds the chronicler, "revolted every one."

a while he conducted himself with comparative circumspection, and his clumsy attempt to betray his country was so soon forgotten, that, on Dangeau's death at the beginning of September 1720, the Académie-Française hastened to call to its bosom the heir of the great man who had founded it.[1]

The reception of the new "immortal" took place on the following December 12, Mlles. de Charolais, Mesdames de Gontaut, de Lambert, de Villeroy, du Deffand, de Guesbriant, de Duras, de Tencin, and other Aspasias of the time assisting at the ceremony. The Abbé Gédoyn made the complimentary speech, and eulogised Richelieu for having stood aloof from the sordid speculations which at this period had caused so many of his order to forget their rank and their dignity.[2]

This praise was not undeserved, for, whether from his natural indifference, or because he was absorbed by gallantry and ambition, and their consequences, the young duke was among the small number of great nobles who had kept their names unsullied by the mud of the Rue Quincampoix.

Richelieu's *discours de réception*, which Soulavie has preserved for us, and whose authenticity, unlike so much in the works of that sprightly historian, there seems to be no reason to doubt, consisted mainly of a fulsome panegyric of Louis XIV., which we forbear inflicting on the reader.[3] It was, however, too closely

[1] The Academy at this period, and for long afterwards, always contained a sprinkling of noblemen, who were elected without much regard to their intellectual qualifications, while many of the men of letters who graced it owed their *fauteuils* more to the favour with which they happened to be regarded in Court circles than to literary distinction. Here is the list of Richelieu's colleagues, which is a singular mixture of celebrated and obscure names: The Cardinals de Polignac and de Rohan; Caumartin, Bishop of Blois, Fleury, Bishop of Fréjus, Huet, Bishop of Avranches, Massillon, Bishop of Clermont; the Maréchaux d'Estrées and de Villars; the Ducs de Coislin and de la Force; the Marquises d'Argenson and Saint-Hilaire; the Président de Mesmes; the Abbés Bignon, Choisy, Dangeau, Dubois, Fleury, Gédoyn, Fragmer, de Roquette, and de Saint-Pierre; Boze, Campistron, Dacier, Danchet, Fontenelle, Houdart de la Motte, La Chapelle, La Loubère, La Monnoye, Malézieu, Mallet, Mangin, Massieu, Mongault, Sacy, and Valincourt.

[2] Barbier.

[3] Richelieu's education had been too much neglected for him to trust to his own unaided powers in the composition of this discourse. He therefore summoned to his assistance the witty Fontenelle, "who never neglected any opportunity of paying his court to the great," Destouches, an ex-diplomatist, who produced reams

in harmony with the spirit of the time to fail to make a favourable impression, and, indeed, seems to have been considered a masterpiece, particularly by the ladies present, so many of whom desired to offer the new Academician their felicitations in person, and, *bien entendu*, in private, that the latter, in spite of his willingness to oblige the fair, was forced to the conclusion that "there are occasions on which too much merit becomes a burden." [1]

The least action of Richelieu had now attained all the importance of a public event. What would have aroused not the smallest interest in another, attracted universal attention where he was concerned. Some three months after his reception by the Academy, the duke, who had in the interim attained his majority, took his seat on the peers' benches in the Parlement of Paris for his duchy of Richelieu, being introduced by *Monsieur le Duc*, his brother-in-law *à la main gauche*, and the Prince de Conti, whom, if rumour is to be believed, he occasionally condescended to understudy in his conjugal *rôle*. When the Duc de Brissac had been received some months before, the galleries were almost empty, but now the demand for tickets of admission threw all previous records completely into the shade. In the cafés in the neighbourhood of the Palais de Justice, so brisk a trade was done between fortunate holders who were not above making an honest louis or two in this way and the representatives of fair dames who desired to assist at the ceremony, that people imagined themselves back again in the heyday of the Mississippi "boom." From an early

of now-forgotten verse, and Campistron, whom Saint-Simon describes as "one of those dirty, starving poets who will do anything for a living." Each of these *beaux esprits* furnished the duke with a speech, from which the latter, "guided by a tact which Nature had given him," selected the passages which he considered the best, and, by reducing the learned elegancies of the writers to simple and natural language, succeeded in making the oration pass for his own work.

[1] According to Soulavie, Mlle. de Charolais, the Duchesse de Villeroy, and the Marquise de Duras each wrote to Richelieu giving him a rendezvous for the same evening! But, for the manner in which the duke rose to the occasion, and succeeded in convincing each of his fair friends that he valued her felicitations above those of all the rest of the world, we must refer the reader to the pages of the historian in question.

hour the square in front of the Palais was filled by an immense crowd, and the line of waiting carriages extended to the Rue Dauphine ; while within the temple of Themis the staircase and the galleries were choked with people, and the Ambassadors' tribune besieged by foreign ladies, who begged for admission in every tongue that is spoken from the Tagus to the Neva.

The costume of the hero of the day was worthy of the occasion. "The Duc de Richelieu, having attained the age of twenty-five years," says Mathieu Marais, "entered the Parlement. The whole of his coat, mantle, and breeches were made of a very rich stuff, which cost two hundred and sixty livres the ell. He looked like the god of Love."

The ladies present were of the same opinion as the writer, and a perfect shower of *billets doux* descended upon the duke, who found himself, in consequence, almost as much embarrassed as he had been on the occasion of his reception by the Academy.

Two years later, Richelieu was received a second time by the Parlement, for his duchy of Fronsac, and had again to make his entry under the admiring eyes of a throng of women who had been honoured by his attentions or aspired to receive them.

The expatriation of Mlle. de Valois left Mlle. de Charolais in possession of the field, for, now that her cousin was out of the way, her Highness affected to regard with sovereign contempt the numerous rivals who entered it from time to time. "It is a horrible thing," writes *Madame*, "that a princess of the blood should declare, in the face of the world, that she is amorous as a cat, and that this passion is for a knave who is beneath her in rank, whom she is unable to marry, and who is, moreover, unfaithful to her, for he has half-a-dozen other mistresses. When one tells her that, she replies : 'Good! he only has mistresses to sacrifice them to me and to relate to me what passes between them.' It is a truly frightful state of affairs."

So little attempt did the enamoured princess make to

conceal the nature of her relations with Richelieu, that reports that they had been privately married were continually being circulated in Paris, and even found their way into the foreign journals:

"15 July 1720.—I was informed to-day that Mlle. de Charolais, Princesse of the Blood, has married the Duc de Richelieu, with whom she has been in love for a long time past; that the marriage took place during the last few days in the chapel of [the château of] Vincennes; that the princess waited until she was twenty-five, having been born on 23 June 1695, and coming of age on 23 June 1720; that she sent a respectful intimation to her mother, who has always opposed this marriage, as well as the Royal Family, and that she is more pleased with having married a duke and peer, very gallant, who has an income of 50,000 écus, whom she loves, and her union with whom obliges her to remain at the Court of France, than at being a sovereign elsewhere."

"26 July 1720.—The marriage of Mlle. de Charolais and the Duc de Richelieu is confirmed."

"2 August 1720.—There is much talk (says the *Gazette de Hollande*) of the marriage between a duke and a princess, which is said to have taken place at Vincennes. The reference is to the Duc de Richelieu and the Princesse de Charolais."

"5 August 1720.—The Duc de Richelieu is with his regiment at Oléron, in Béarn. He is obliged to remain there some time. It is said that Mlle. de Charolais has informed *Madame la Princesse*, her grandmother, that she is in an interesting condition."[1]

The report of the marriage, as well as that which concerned the health of Mlle. de Charolais, were presently found to be without foundation; but both were revived some months later. "On Thursday last," writes Barbier, "the Duc de Richelieu was received [by the Parlement] as duke and peer. Every one says that he is to be married to Mlle. de Charolais, Princesse de Condé—a marriage which is bound to take place, from motives of necessity."[2]

[1] Mathieu Marais, *Journal*.

[2] Barbier, *Journal*, March 6, 1721.

The general expectation was not fulfilled, for the Condés, male and female, continued to offer the most resolute opposition to the marriage; indeed, so exasperated was *Monsieur le Duc* at the persistence of his sister and Richelieu, and the public manner in which they paraded their liaison, that, after vainly endeavouring to persuade the latter to break off the connection, or at least to conduct himself with more discretion, he forced a duel upon him.

"The Duc de Bourbon," writes Buvat, "while at a hunting-party at Chantilly, with several noblemen, compelled the Duc de Richelieu to draw his sword, saying to him: 'Richelieu, for a long time past I have had a grievance against thee, and now is the time that I must have satisfaction for it.' The astonished duke answered: 'Monseigneur, I know the respect that I owe to you, and I am not the man to fight with you.' But, finding himself pressed by the prince, he placed himself on the defensive, with the result that he wounded him with three thrusts. Then he called for assistance for the prince, who was carried to his bed, where his wounds were dressed, and on the morrow the latter admitted that he had compelled the Duc de Richelieu to draw his sword." [1]

Notwithstanding the generous action of *Monsieur le Duc* in hastening to exculpate his antagonist from all blame, a duel with the first Prince of the Blood was too serious an affair for one who had so recently quitted the Bastille to afford to regard it with complacency, and, seeing the futility of his hopes that,

[1] *Journal*, May 1721. Barbier gives the following version of the affair: "The Duc de Richelieu has been exiled during the last few days." [In a note, the chronicler states that he has been misinformed as to this.] "It is said that at Chantilly *Monsieur le Duc* withdrew into a wood, and wished to make him draw his sword, on the matter of Mlle. de Charolais, his sister. The Duc de Richelieu excused himself, on the ground that the other was a Prince of the Blood, upon which *Monsieur le Duc* threatened to kill him. The Duc de Richelieu then allowed himself to wound him in the hand, in the belief that that would be sufficient; but *Monsieur le Duc* refused to leave off there. Finally, the Duc de Richelieu wounded him in the stomach. He caused the wound to be secretly dressed immediately; and, indeed, it was reported a week ago that *Monsieur le Duc* had fallen ill at Chantilly; but this was the cause of his indisposition. Every one says that *Monsieur le Duc's* intellect has been slightly deranged for some time past. The change is not great, for he had very little before, and that of the wrong kind."

to close the mouth of scandal, the Condés would eventually withdraw their opposition to his marriage with Mlle. de Charolais, Richelieu resolved to break with that young lady, of whose adoration he was perhaps a little weary. The poor princess was of course in despair, and made many attempts to win back her lover. But the duke intimated to her, very courteously, but very firmly, that his decision was irrevocable, upon which she resigned herself to her fate and sought consolation in the society of the Duc de Melun. Of that nobleman, however, she speedily grew tired, and accordingly transferred her affections to the Chevalier de Bavière, the illegitimate sprig of royalty with whom, it will be remembered, Richelieu had once proposed to fight a duel. This second exchange of adorers gave rise to a very pretty *bon-mot*, it being observed that Mlle. de Charolais had become quite a traveller, since within the space of a couple of weeks she had journeyed from Richelieu to Melun and from Melun to Bavaria.[1]

Richelieu had returned from exile eager to be revenged upon the prince who had torn from his arms the most illustrious, if not the most cherished, of his mistresses, had compelled him to spend a spring and summer as a prisoner in the Bastille, and to languish for a further three months amid the ennui of the provinces. He did so in characteristic fashion.

The early summer of 1721 found the Regent on the look-out for a new sultana *vice* Madame de Parabère, whose infidelities were beginning to irritate even this most complaisant of lovers. Nor had he far to seek. "There is a great deal of talk," writes Mathieu Marais, whose professional duties seem to have left him abundant leisure for discussing the affairs of his neighbours, "of Madame d'Averne, the wife of an officer in the Guards, who is very beautiful, and whom the Regent desires to possess. The articles have been proposed, but are not yet accepted: a hundred thousand écus for her, a company for her husband.

[1] The *bon-mot*, however, was scarcely original, for the same remark had been made a little while before, when the Maréchale d'Estrées gave the Comte de Roussillon his *congé* and accepted the homage of Président Hénault.

PHILLIPPE, DUC D'ORLÉANS, REGENT OF FRANCE

FROM AN ENGRAVING BY CHEREAU, AFTER THE PAINTING BY SANTERRE

All this does not move her, and she is going to spend the summer at Averne, according to what she says." But he expresses his opinion that the lady's reluctance is but a diplomatic move to wring even higher terms from the enamoured prince, since there was reason to believe that the fortress had capitulated on a previous occasion. "It is a rock, but La Fontaine has said:

"'*Rocher fût-il, rochers aussi se prennent.*'"

The cynical advocate knew his world as well as La Fontaine did. Three days passed, which were spent by the Regent in completing the investment and getting his siege-artillery into position, and then Marais writes again:

"The Regent pursues his prey, and he will secure it. He has been to the house of Ariague, his treasurer, where he found Madame d'Averne and her husband, and other ladies, who were about to sup. He paid them the compliment of saying that he wished to remain with them, and would have his supper brought, which he did and delighted them thereby:

"'Et Bacchus et Cérès, de qui la compagnie
Met Venus en train bien souvent,
Furent de la cérémonie.'"

The following day, the *corbeille* was despatched to the lady, as for a marriage, the complaisant husband receiving his also, which contained a captain's commission in the Guards and the government of Navarreins, in Béarn, which the Regent had purchased for 20,000 livres from the Marquis de Louville, with double the emoluments which his predecessor had received. This concluded the business, and the prince and Madame d'Averne went off to enjoy a brief honeymoon at a country-house kindly lent them by a gentleman named Dunoyer, who had formerly adorned the Commissariat Department of the War Office and had apparently accumulated a snug little fortune out of the perquisites of his post.[1]

A rain of *chansons* descended upon the new sultana, one

[1] Marais.

of the wittiest of which began with the Virgilian hemistitch: "*Facilis descensus Averni*"; but the rain of gold which accompanied it appears to have more than consoled her for these malicious effusions. The Regent installed his enchantress in a charming house at Saint-Cloud, gave her 3,000 livres a month for the expenses of her table alone, and 100,000 livres to buy a summer outfit,[1] loaded her with jewels, and organised the most sumptuous fêtes in her honour. She drove with him in an open carriage in the park of Saint-Cloud, great care being taken to avoid *Madame*, who was, nevertheless, perfectly informed of her son's infatuation, and appeared, magnificently adorned, in the place of honour in his box at the Opera, "which had heard the last sigh of so many virtues." Great ladies vied with one another in offering her hospitality; wealth, fashion, and wit met daily in her salon; the Regent was the most generous and devoted of lovers, and she had scarcely to express a wish ere it was gratified. Never did a favourite's position appear more enviable or more secure.

Thus matters continued for several months, and then the Duc de Richelieu appeared upon the scene. Madame d'Averne had heard much of this all-conquering nobleman—who had not? She may have been among the admiring ladies who had congregated in the Rue Saint-Antoine to watch him promenading on the terrace of the Bastille; she had very probably assisted at his reception by the Academy or the Parlement, but up to this time she does not appear to have enjoyed the honour of his acquaintance. Now, however, they met frequently at fêtes and balls—so frequently, indeed, as to seem something more than a coincidence—and soon the lady began to feel quite a thrill of pleasurable excitement when M. de Richelieu levelled his lorgnette in her direction at the Opera or led her out to thread the mazes of the dance.

What need to dwell upon the sequel? How could Madame d'Averne be expected to resist him who was accounted irresistible? How could she, a mere member of the *petite noblesse*, albeit the sultana of the ruler of France, fail to be flattered by

[1] Barbier.

the homage of one over whom titled dames had been ready to fight to the death, whom Princesses of the Blood had consoled in the Bastille, and for whose sake the Regent's own daughter had made so great a sacrifice?

In June 1722, the Regent departed for Rheims, to attend the coronation of the young king, leaving Madame d'Averne, of whose fidelity he was becoming more than a little suspicious, at Versailles, where it would be possible to have her kept under closer observation than in Paris or at Saint-Cloud. His return was followed by a momentous piece of news. Marais writes:

"The return from the Coronation has not been favourable to the mistresses. The Regent told Madame d'Averne the very same day that it was not proper for her to remain at Versailles, since it was a bad example for the King; that he would be always one of her friends; that his man of affairs would be charged with hers, and that he would come and sup with her in Paris, and even pass the night at her house, if she desired, and other things which savoured of inconstancy or disgust." And he adds: "The lady is suspected of infidelity with the Duc de Richelieu, who has taken advantage of the absence of the master."

This semi-disgrace of Madame d'Averne was succeeded by an open rupture between her and the Regent, and Marais reports that the lady shows herself every day at the Opera in the company of the Duc de Richelieu and other gentlemen.

Poor Madame d'Averne soon discovered that, in exchanging her royal admirer for Richelieu, she had made a very bad bargain. A week or two of happiness, and the faithless duke began to neglect his conquest, whom, indeed, he had never valued except as a weapon wherewith to wound the Regent in his tenderest spot. It was in vain that she gave the most sumptuous fêtes, in the hope that he might be induced to attend them; it was in vain that she wrote him the most touching letters.[1] All her

[1] A number of these letters will be found in the *Vie privée du maréchal de Richelieu*, but it is doubtful if any of them are authentic. Here, however, is one which is undoubtedly genuine: "I trust that all that your ambassador has told me in your justification may be true; the manner in which you conduct yourself towards me will convince me much better. I do not know when I shall be able to see you

efforts to regain the ascendency which she flattered herself she had once possessed over him were futile, and, at length, like Mlle. Charolais and many another, she was forced to find consolation in the homage of other admirers, and the Marquis d'Alincourt, in collaboration with M. des Allures, succeeded in bringing some solace to her wounded heart.

As for the Regent, though he showed a little resentment against Richelieu, on learning that he had supplanted him in the affections of Madame d'Averne, his anger did not last long, and, perhaps being of opinion that his rupture with that lady was not altogether a matter for regret,[1] he heaped coals of fire upon the head of his successful rival, by inviting him to a supper-party at the Palais-Royal.

the earliest possible moment will be the most certain to dissipate my suspicions. I beg you as a favour not to deceive me. I know from experience that one is not master of one's heart, since I have given mine to you."—Rouen Library, Leber Collection, published by Lescure, *les Maîtresses du Regent*.

[1] According to Barbier, however, Madame d'Averne enjoyed an aftermath of favour in the spring of the following year: "The Duc d'Orléans, who has no longer a *maîtresse en titre*, still sups sometimes with Madame d'Averne. People severely censure the marquis, who was her first lover, and who has resumed the premier position, for permitting this. He is a young man who considers this as an honour."

# CHAPTER VII

Death of the Regent—Diplomatic manœuvres of Richelieu during the Ministry of the Duc de Bourbon—He is appointed Ambassador at Vienna —Review of the European situation—Career of Ripperda—The Treaties of Vienna and Hanover—Ripperda claims precedence over the Ambassador of France at the Imperial Court—Qualifications of Richelieu for this mission greater than may at first sight be supposed—His desire to make a favourable impression upon Charles VI. leads him to dissimulate his true character and to feign devotion—His letter to the Cardinal de Polignac—His discomfiture of Ripperda—Subsequent adventures of this singular personage.

ON August 10, 1723, Dubois died, and four months later (December 2) the Duc d'Orléans followed him to the grave. The Duc de Bourbon now became First Minister, under the guidance of his mistress Madame de Prie,[1] though shrewd men foresaw that *Monsieur le Duc's* tenure of office would be but a brief one, and that, when Louis XV. was a

[1] Jeanne Agnès Berthelot de Pleneuf (1698–1727), daughter of Étienne Berthelot, seigneur de Pleneuf. She was married, in 1713, to Louis, Marquis de Prie, a member of an old but impoverished family, who the same year was appointed Ambassador at Turin. On her return to France, in 1719, Madame de Prie, who is described by Saint-Simon as a beautiful, graceful, fascinating, intelligent, and well-read woman, made an abortive attempt to subjugate the Regent, but succeeded in casting her spells over the Duc de Bourbon. When *Monsieur le Duc* was appointed First Minister, she "disposed of him as a slave," and became the virtual ruler of France. She had her flatterers and her court, and Voltaire addressed to her complimentary verses and dedicated to her his comedy, *l'Indiscret.* It was she who, in 1725, played the principal part in promoting the marriage of Louis XV. and Marie Leczinska, to whom she was appointed *dame du palais.* Flushed with success and devoured by ambition, she endeavoured, some months later, to bring about the dismissal of Fleury; but the intrigue failed and proved her ruin. She left the Court and withdrew to Paris; but when, in June 1726, *Monsieur le Duc* was exiled to Chantilly, the marchioness received orders to retire to her country seat at Courbépin. Here, in October of the following year, she destroyed herself by poison, at the age of twenty-nine.

little older, his former preceptor, Fleury, Bishop of Fréjus,[1] who possessed his Majesty's fullest confidence, would certainly be called to the direction of affairs.

Richelieu, who beneath a frivolous exterior concealed much ambition, was one of those who held this conviction and shaped their course accordingly. His resignation of his pretensions to the hand of Mlle. de Charolais had speedily healed the breach between him and *Monsieur le Duc*, and, since he was one of the most assiduous of the courtiers of Madame de Prie, with whom his relations are believed to have been at one time rather more than friendly, he soon became a *persona grata* at Chantilly. At the same time, he did not neglect to ingratiate himself with the coming Mazarin, and to give him to understand that, if ever he found himself in a position to serve his interests, M. de Fréjus might count upon him. These diplomatic manœuvres did not fail of their reward, and in the early autumn of 1725, the duke learned, to his intense gratification, that he had been nominated to the post of French Ambassador at Vienna. But, before following Richelieu on this important mission, undertaken in circumstances so difficult that, having regard to the previous career of the man, it seemed almost impossible for him to escape odium or ridicule, it will be necessary to survey very briefly the European situation at this juncture.

At the beginning of December 1719, an intrigue at Madrid had undone the work which a preceding intrigue had accomplished, and the adventurous Alberoni disappeared into the obscurity from which he had emerged.

This event was the signal for one of those violent changes of policy so familiar in Spain. With Alberoni's fall, all his great

[1] André Hercule Fleury (1653–1743). Almoner to Queen Maria Theresa, 1679; almoner to Louis XIV., 1683; Abbé of la Rivoure, 1686; Bishop of Fréjus, 1678; preceptor to Louis XV., 1715; member of the Council of State, February 1723; First Minister, though without the title, June 1726; cardinal, September 1726. He must be carefully distinguished from his elder brother, the Abbé Claude Fleury (1640–1723), who was sub-preceptor, under Fénelon, to the Duc de Bourgogne and his brothers, and subsequently confessor to Louis XV. Claude Fleury was a member of the Académie Française and an ecclesiastical historian of considerable distinction in his own day.

plans for the revival of his adoped country came utterly to an end; Spain hastened to accede to the propositions of the Quadruple Alliance, and the Emperor and Philip V. agreed to recognise their respective possessions and to share definitely the *débris* of the great heritage of Charles V.

But this division, which seemed so easy on paper, was far from being so in reality, and it was in the hope of adjusting the outstanding differences between the two Powers that the Congress of Cambrai—that congress which ate and drank so much and did so little[1]—met in 1722,[2] under the mediation of England and France.

The result was calculated to astonish even the most experienced of diplomatists, for, after long months of acrimonious discussion, the plenipotentiaries of Spain and the Empire suddenly announced to the mediators, who had begun to despair of ever inducing them to come to an understanding, that they need trouble them no further, since they had decided to settle their differences directly (April 1725).

Anger, wounded vanity, and the desire for revenge had thus accomplished in a few days what eloquence, interest, and fatigue had been powerless to effect in as many months. Charles VI. was angry with England, because she had refused to guarantee the Pragmatic Sanction,[3] and had declined to sanction the establishment of the Ostend Company, while Philip V. was bitterly incensed against France, owing to the slight put upon him by the sudden and almost contemptuous breach of the

[1] Voltaire, who was at Cambrai in July 1722, wrote to Dubois that the English plenipotentiaries (Lord Polwarth and Lord Whitworth) "sent many couriers to Champagne, and few to London."

[2] "In the course of the year, delegates slowly raining in—date not fixable to a day or a month . . . More inane Congress never met in this world, nor will meet . . . spent two years in 'arguments about precedencies,' in mere beatings of the air, and wandered among the chairs till February 1724. Nor did it manage to accomplish any work whatever, even then; the most inane of Human Congresses; and memorable on that account if on no other."—Carlyle, "Frederick the Great."

[3] This Pragmatic Sanction, which was first issued in 1713, declared Charles VI.'s eldest daughter, Maria Theresa, heiress of all his dominions. From that time forward, the Emperor's whole policy was subordinated to his desire to obtain the guarantee of the European Powers to this document, which, by the irony of Fate, was to prove entirely valueless after his death.

marriage-compact which was to unite the Infanta to Louis XV., and the betrothal of the young King to Marie Leczinska, daughter of the ex-King of Poland.[1] The two Powers, for long so bitterly hostile to one another, moved thus by a common irritation, Austria against England, Spain against France, entered into a close alliance and formulated plans which threatened to set all Europe in a blaze.

The author of this *rapprochement* was one Jan Wilhelm Ripperda, another of the foreign adventurers who at this time found in Spain such a congenial field for the exercise of their talents. Born about 1680, at Groningen, of Catholic parents, Ripperda was sent abroad to be educated, and was brought up by the Jesuits, according to some writers at Boulogne, according to others, in Brabant. Love, or more probably ambition, caused him to embrace the faith of the vast majority of his countrymen, and he married a Protestant lady and entered the service of Holland, where he soon rose to prominence, and after the Treaty of Utrecht was appointed Dutch Ambassador at Madrid. Foreseeing the possibility of rapid advancement in Spain, he resigned his office, reverted to his old religion, insinuated himself into the good graces of his fellow-adventurer, Alberoni, and became the cardinal's chief adviser in matters of commerce and finance. After a time, however, he incurred the displeasure of his patron, who probably saw in him a

[1] In 1721, the Infanta Luisa Isabella, then in her fifth year, had been sent to the Court of France to be brought up until she had reached a marriageable age, when she was to become the wife of Louis XV. The little princess was installed in the apartments at Versailles formerly occupied by Maria Theresa, consort of Louis XIV., and afterwards by the Duchesse de Bourgogne, and while the Regent lived, treated as the future queen. After his death, however, *Monsieur le Duc*, fearing lest the young King should die without children, in which event the new Duc d'Orléans, whom he cordially hated, would succeed him, determined to secure an heir to the throne, even at the risk of an open breach with Philip V., that is, to send the Infanta back to Spain and marry Louis XV. to some princess who could at once make him a father. This decision was notified to the Court of Spain with a precipitation which aggravated the affront, and aroused unbounded indignation at Madrid. "In the first paroxysm of resentment," says Coxe, in his "History of the House of Austria," "the Queen tore off a bracelet ornamented with a portrait of the King of France, and trampled it under her foot; and Philip declared that Spain could never shed sufficient blood to avenge the indignity offered to his family."

potential rival, and was compelled to leave Spain. He then made his way to Austria, where Prince Eugène befriended him, and where he appears to have remained until the fall of Alberoni permitted his return to Madrid. His splendid schemes for the improvement of the finances, the increase of the army, and the extension of commerce dazzled the imagination of Philip, while, by his affected solicitude for the establishment of her sons in Italy, he succeeded in gaining the friendship and confidence of Elizabeth Farnese. It is not improbable that the policy which he now pursued had been suggested to him while residing in Vienna. Any way, he continued to urge upon the Queen that the surest means, not only of acquiring a principality in Italy for Don Carlos, but of recovering Gibraltar, was to break altogether with England and conclude a close alliance with the Emperor. His arguments fell on willing ears, and in November 1724 Ripperda set out for Vienna to negotiate the proposed alliance. He entered the city incognito, under the name of the Baron Pfaffenberg, and took up his quarters in one of the suburbs, in a house belonging to the surgeon of Charles VI., where he held secret conferences with the Grand Chancellor the Graf von Sinzendorf, and other Ministers.

The matter, however, proved far less easy to conclude than Ripperda had led his Court to believe, for, though Charles VI. was anxious to separate the two branches of the House of Bourbon and to secure Spain's guarantee to his Pragmatic Sanction, he was disinclined to pay the price demanded, and the conferences were protracted for several months. But the breach of the marriage-compact already referred to gave a great impetus to the negotiations; Philip V., who now thought only of revenge, sent orders to Ripperda to conclude, on any terms, an alliance with the Court of Vienna, and on May 30–June 1, 1725, three treaties were signed between the two Powers. By the first, the articles of the Quadruple Alliance were confirmed; Charles and Philip mutually renounced all pretensions to each other's dominions, and the latter guaranteed the Pragmatic Sanction. By the second, which was a commercial treaty, Philip engaged to open the ports of Spain to the subjects of the Emperor, sanctioned the establishment of the Ostend Company, and extended to the Hanseatic towns the same privileges of trade as were enjoyed by the English and Dutch. The third was a treaty of mutual defence, by which the Emperor promised his good offices to obtain the restitution of Gibraltar and Minorca to Spain, and the two monarchs agreed to support each other with their whole forces, if necessity arose.

In addition to these treaties, there was a secret engagement, which does not appear ever to have been committed to writing: the Emperor promised his two daughters, the Archduchesses Maria Theresa and Maria Anna, to the two sons of Philip V. by his second marriage, Don Carlos and Don Philip,[1] and agreed to co-operate by force in the recovery of Gibraltar and Minorca, and the restoration of the Pretender to the throne of Great Britain, should George I. refuse to accede to the treaties of Vienna.

So sudden and complete an understanding between two sovereigns whose rival pretensions had for so many years distracted Europe naturally aroused a great sensation, but would probably have inspired uneasiness rather than alarm, if sufficient discretion had been observed in regard to the secret engagement. But the overweening vanity of Ripperda led him to boast of the great results he had achieved, and the English and French Ambassadors were soon enabled to transmit to their respective Courts a substantially accurate account of what had been decided upon.

The secret articles were strenuously denied by Charles VI. and his Ministers, but the conduct of the two Courts left no room for doubt as to their existence; and when Spain presented her demand for the restoration of Gibraltar, Great Britain immediately commenced preparations for war.

[1] "It is not certain that Charles VI. ever seriously intended to fulfil promises which were opposed by his wife and all his German counsellors, who were at that time paving the way for the marriage of the two archduchesses to the sons of the Duke of Lorraine. At all events, he had given Spain nothing but secret promises, which he could always deny, for very positive results."—Henry Martin, *Histoire de France*, vol. xvi.

France, on her side, though less directly menaced, was scarcely less alarmed, for, even supposing that the new confederacy had no immediate designs against Alsace, French Flanders, Roussillon, or Lower Navarre, she was unable to permit the possible union of Austria and Spain, by the marriage of the Archduchess Maria Theresa to a son of Philip V. Accordingly on September 3, 1725, a defensive alliance between the two nations was signed at Hanover, and was joined by George I.'s son-in-law, Frederick William of Prussia, in return for a guarantee of his claims upon Jülich and Berg; and Europe found itself divided into two hostile camps, each of which was endeavouring to obtain as many allies as possible. Such was the position of affairs when the Duc de Richelieu set out for Vienna.

The selection of a young nobleman who enjoyed in Paris something of that fantastic renown which had attached to Alcibiades in ancient Athens, and who was believed to be tainted with the scepticism of his friend Voltaire—of whose connection with Richelieu we shall presently have occasion to speak—for an important mission to the most bigoted and decorous Court in Europe could not fail to arouse considerable surprise. Nevertheless, it was a much happier choice than may at first sight appear.

There had recently been a dispute at Vienna as to whether Ripperda or the Ambassador of France was entitled to precedence. The Dutchman, arrogant, coarse, and brutal, had publicly announced his intention to take the *pas*, boasting that, if other arguments failed, his sword or cane should decide the question. The Ambassador recently recalled, the Comte de Luc, a feeble valetudinarian, had been altogether incapable of taking up this rude challenge, and his inaction had created a bad impression at the Austrian Court; and the French Government felt that it was before all things necessary that this braggart adventurer should be taught a severe lesson and the honour of France vindicated.[1] And who better fitted to

[1] Lemontey, *Histoire de la Régence*.

undertake such a task than a man who appeared to have taken for his model the Duc d'Épernon, the audacious and insolent *mignon* of Henri III.?[1]

Nor, in other respects, was Richelieu ill-adapted for a mission which was not to call for the exercise of the highest qualities of the diplomat. For he came not to negotiate, but to observe; not to intrigue, but to conciliate; to smooth over a troubled situation by tact and courtesy; to dazzle the Viennese by the magnificence of his retinue, the lavishness of his hospitality; to insinuate himself into the good graces of those who possessed directly or indirectly political influence—in short, to prepare the ground for the seed which more experienced hands would presently sow.

And, if the young duke were but a *débutant* in diplomacy, he was an accomplished man of the world, who possessed in a high degree all the qualities which make for social success; while he had never lacked suppleness, and could, when occasion arose, dissimulate his true character with remarkable skill. Thus, aware that nothing was more calculated to make a favourable impression upon the devout Charles VI. than an assumption of piety, he resigned himself to playing the *rôle* of Tartuffe with as good a grace as he could command, and during Lent not only passed a considerable part of his time in the churches and rigorously banished meat from his table, but compelled his *entourage* to do likewise. The ennui which this unaccustomed asceticism occasioned him is pathetically depicted in a letter which he wrote at Easter 1726 to his friend the Cardinal de Polignac, at this time French Ambassador at the Vatican:

"I have led a pious life here during Lent, which has not left me a quarter of an hour to myself, and I confess that, if I had been aware of the life which an Ambassador leads here, nothing in the world would have determined me to accept this embassy, where, under the pretext of invitations and performances in chapels, the Emperor makes the Ambassadors follow him like his *valets de chambre*. There is no one except

[1] Voltaire, in one of his letters to Richelieu, speaks of "the Duc d'Épernon with whom I have seen you formerly so infected."

a Capuchin of the most robust health who could endure this life during Lent. To give your Eminence an idea of it, I have actually spent, from Palm Sunday to the Wednesday after Easter, a hundred hours in church with the Emperor. The Comte de Luc, who was here eighteen months, of which he passed nine or ten before making his official entry and the rest in being ill, has left us in ignorance of this treasury of devotion, which I have just discovered at my expense. I confess that I think that devotion desires a little more liberty, and that this unheard-of constraint, which is approved of here, and which exists in no other Court in the world, is to me an insupportable thing, and I cannot refrain from expressing to your Eminence my disgust with it."

To which the Cardinal de Polignac, who, notwithstanding his *Anti-Lucretius*—the philosophical poem in Latin which had done so much to advance his fortunes—was not perhaps quite so orthodox in his views as could be desired in a Prince of the Church, replied:

"From the picture which you have drawn of the manner in which you have fulfilled all the duties of Lent, Holy Week, and Easter, I think that I cannot do better than felicitate you on having emerged from them. Perhaps you have never done so much in your life. Imagine precisely the same thing of a cardinal at Rome. It is true that we are paid for it." [1]

But to return to the time of Richelieu's arrival in Vienna.

The new Ambassador, who had a decided weakness for display, and deemed it incumbent upon him, as the accredited representative of the greatest King in Europe, to appear in the Austrian capital with the utmost magnificence, had neglected nothing to impress the imagination of the Viennese, and had brought with him the most sumptuous equipages, a great number of gentlemen, and an immense and gorgeously-attired *valetaille*. However, notwithstanding all the splendour with which he was surrounded, Richelieu was at first very coldly received, and, to his intense chagrin, found himself regarded rather as a glorified spy than an Ambassador, for which there

[1] *Mémoires du duc de Richelieu.*

was certainly some excuse, since Ambassadors still on the sunny side of thirty were not very common, even in the third decade of the eighteenth century.

The all-important question of the relative positions of himself and Ripperda was, of course, the first to present itself and, in answer to his representations, the Grand Master of the Ceremonies informed him that, since the Baron Ripperda had been accredited to the Court of Vienna some months earlier than had the Duc de Richelieu, his Imperial Majesty was of opinion that he ought to enjoy precedence over the other.

This answer, when communicated to Versailles, greatly irritated the French Government, since, although the Comte de Luc, Richelieu's predecessor, had arrived at Vienna some time before Ripperda, the latter, on his appearance on the scene, had immediately arrogated the precedence, without the slightest protest from the Imperial Court. Richelieu, accordingly, received instructions to defer his official entry until the *pas* had been ceded to him, upon which he at once decided upon an audacious expedient to compel the insolent Dutchman to give way.

That personage, on his side, had not the smallest intention of surrendering the place which he had usurped, and, in the belief that he had nothing to fear from a young man who was just entering on his diplomatic career, determined to treat him with the haughtiness which he usually affected towards the representatives of the hostile confederation. He was soon to discover his mistake.

Early in October 1705, Charles VI. gave a reception at the palace, which was attended by the whole of the Corps Diplomatique, and, whether by accident or design, the Ambassadors of France and Spain found themselves standing side by side on the staircase leading to the throne-room. Ripperda endeavoured to pass before Richelieu ; but the latter, more active than his rival, anticipated this movement, at the same time giving the Dutchman so vigorous a push with his shoulder, that he staggered back, tripped over his sword, and fell his length upon the stairs.

The bystanders could scarcely restrain their merriment, as with perruque awry and *jabot* soiled by the contents of his gold snuff-box, which had slipped from his hands in his fall, the haughty Ripperda was assisted to his feet; while Richelieu passed on in triumph into the throne-room to salute the Emperor. The duke lost no time in following up his advantage, and that evening made a personal call at the Spanish Embassy to inquire after the health of his victim, whose fall he affected to believe had been caused by a false step or a passing faintness. The porter, who had his orders, replied that his master was in excellent health and had gone out to supper, and that he had heard nothing respecting the accident to which his Excellency referred.

Next morning, Richelieu despatched a lackey to make further inquiries, but the man returned and informed him that there was no answer.

A day or two afterwards, the duke happened to encounter the Ambassador, and expressed his astonishment that when he had not only sent, but called in person, to express his condolence and sympathy for the unfortunate accident to his Excellency of which he had been a witness, the latter's people should have disclaimed all knowledge of the occurrence. And he added that, if the affront of which he complained had been something more than an ordinary misunderstanding or a servant's oversight, he held himself entirely at his Excellency's disposition.

Ripperda, who was as pusillanimous as he was arrogant reddened, stammered some words of apology, and turned away. Shortly afterwards, he was recalled, and it is not improbable that his departure was hastened by the events which we have just related. For he did not venture to make any further attempt to dispute precedence with the audacious Frenchman, and this pacific attitude, in view of his previous rodomontades, made him cut a decidedly ridiculous figure.

A brief account of the subsequent career of this singular personage may not be without interest.

On his arrival in Madrid, Ripperda was raised to the rank

of duke, appointed Minister and Secretary of State, and vested with almost uncontrolled authority. But his triumph was of short duration, since, though he contrived for a while to retain the favour of the King and Queen, his vanity disgusted every one else, and the British Ambassador, Stanhope, reported that "he had for his inveterate enemies not only all the other Ministers, but the whole Spanish nation, to whom he had rendered himself odious beyond imagination." Finally, it became apparent that Ripperda, with a view to emboldening the Spanish Court and furthering his own advancement, had grossly exaggerated Austria's military resources, while, on the other hand, he had made promises of financial assistance to Vienna which were quite beyond the power of Spain to fulfil. The consequence was that on May 14, 1726, amid general acclamations, he was dismissed from office, with a pension of 3,000 pistoles.

Fearing the violence of the people, who were threatening to tear him to pieces, the fallen Minister fled to the British Embassy, where, either out of a desire for revenge, or in the hope of ingratiating himself with the English Cabinet, he disclosed to Stanhope the secret engagements entered into at Vienna. From this asylum, however, he was forcibly removed, in spite of the Ambassador's protests, and imprisoned in the Castle of Segovia. Here he was kept in close captivity for two years, when Fortune again smiled upon him, and, with the aid of a woman whom he had seduced and a soldier whom he had bribed, he succeeded in affecting his escape, by means of a rope-ladder, got safely across the Portuguese frontier, and made his way to Oporto, whence he sailed for England.

In England, he for a time lived in strict retirement, but subsequently rented a large house in Soho Square and displayed great magnificence. He corresponded with the Ministers and, according to Lord Mahon, "nourished a chimerical hope of becoming one of their principal colleagues";[1] but in 1731, disgusted apparently with the indifference which they showed

[1] Cited by Mahon, "History of England from the Peace of Utrecht to the Peace of Versailles," vol. ii.

towards him when once the differences with Spain had been adjusted, he passed over to Holland, and again embraced the Protestant faith.

The hopes which had prompted this new "conversion" were not, however, fulfilled, and having made the acquaintance of one Perez, a Spanish Jew, who had turned Mohammedan and acted as Moorish agent at The Hague, he decided to shake the dust of Europe off his feet, and sailed for Tangier.

Well received by the Emperor of Morocco, Muley Abdullah, he soon succeeded in securing his confidence, and having changed his religion for the fourth time, blossomed into a bashaw, under the name of Osman Pacha, and rose again to the direction of councils.

Not satisfied with political celebrity, he sought renown in the tented field, and, in response to an edict of Philip V. depriving him of his titles of duke and grandee, led an army against the Spanish possessions in Northern Africa. He gained several successes, but eventually suffered a severe defeat in an attempt to surprise Ceuta, and, on his return to Mequinez, was disgraced and thrown into prison.

An opportune revolution restored him to liberty, and he entered the service of the Bashaw of Tetuan, at which city his romantic career terminated in 1737.

# CHAPTER VIII

Public entry of Richelieu into Vienna—His audience of the Emperor and Empress—A costly banquet—Conduct of Richelieu at Vienna considered—He renders important service to Fleury in the matter of the cardinal's hat—His relations with the Countess Batthyany and the Princess von Lichtenstein—He is compromised in an affair of sorcery—Duclos's account of this matter—Richelieu is created a Chevalier of the Ordre du Saint-Esprit—He demands his recall and returns to France.

THE day which preceded Ripperda's departure from Vienna (November 7, 1726) was chosen by the Ambassador of France for his official entry; and a very imposing ceremony it must have been.

"It was on this occasion that the Duc de Richelieu displayed all the magnificence by which he loved to attract attention. Never had Ambassador appeared with such a *cortège*, for, while pleasing his own taste, he judged it necessary to impress the Court of Vienna. He had sixty-nine coaches drawn by six horses, and six others of the utmost sumptuousness, also drawn by six horses. The carriage which contained the Ambassador himself was lined on the interior and draped on the outside with crimson velvet, all covered with gold embroidery in relief, with fringes of gold; the four panels were emblazoned with the Ambassador's Arms embroidered in relief; his monogram, embroidered in the same manner, occupied the small panels at the sides; the grand panel at the back of the carriage was loaded with embroidery in relief, as was the imperial also, the velvet of which was covered with great branches of gold embroidery, likewise in relief, combining in the centre so as to form a kind of flower. The horses were bay-browns, and the harness was of crimson, covered with plates of silver gilt and Spanish lace, and aigrettes of crimson feathers wired with ornaments of gold.

"The second coach was lined and draped with blue velvet of a similar sumptuousness, embroidered with the symbols and attributes of Peace. It was drawn by dappled-grey horses, whose trappings, like the velvet of the carriage, were embroidered in gold, and who wore blue plumes wired with gold ornaments.

"The third carriage was of green velvet embroidered and fringed with gold; the imperial was surmounted by ornaments of bronze gilt; the horses light bay, with green velvet trappings and green plumes with gold decorations.

"The fourth carriage was of yellow velvet, with embroideries and fringes of silver; on the imperial were allegorical figures representing Prudence, Secrecy, etc.; and it was drawn by black Italian horses, with trappings of the same coloured velvet as the carriage, covered with plates and embroideries of silver, and yellow plumes.

"Of the two remaining coaches, one was of grey velvet embroidered with gold, with horses, trappings, and plumes to match; the other of rose velvet embroidered with silver, with sorrel horses and rose trappings, with plates and embroideries of silver, and plumes of the same colour."[1]

The number and gorgeousness of the *entourage* was in keeping with that of the equipages. Six running-footmen, wearing coats of red velvet entirely covered with silver lace, and waistcoats and breeches of cloth of silver, walked at the head of each coach. Fifty footmen in liveries of scarlet cloth galooned with silver and purple silk, and hats embroidered with silver lace and adorned with white plumes, and carrying silver swords, walked by the side of the horses or at the doors of the coaches, and kept back the crowd, being assisted in that task by twelve *heiduques*, who from time to time scattered money amongst the people. The *cortège* was closed by twelve mounted pages dressed in red velvet embroidered with silver.

The rest of the Ambassador's Household was in proportion: governor of the pages, assistant-governor, equerry, assistant equerries, porters, and postilions. These last, to the number of twenty-four, were on horseback, each leading a second horse.

[1] *Mémoires du duc de Richelieu.*

This imposing procession formed in the Landstrasse suburb, and, entering the city by the Italian Gate, wended its way in solemn state to the San Johannstrasse, in which the French Legation was situated. The streets, the windows, the balconies, and even the roofs of the houses, were thronged with spectators, who were unanimously of opinion that the pageant presented to them completely eclipsed in magnificence anything of the kind which Vienna had witnessed for many a long year.

As for the populace, its enthusiasm knew no bounds, for, with the object of winning the suffrages of the people and giving an example of the wealth and generosity of France, Richelieu had conceived a happy idea. "The horses of the duke's carriage and the saddle and led-horses were shod with silver shoes. These were divided in two, and only held together by a very small nail, in such fashion, that, on the way, all the horses cast their shoes, and the populace was able to share their spoils."

The following day, on which the Ambassador had his public audience of the Emperor, the Empress, and the Empress-Dowager, Amelia, was marked by the same ostentation. The duke appeared in the magnificent costume which was worn by the peers of France when they attended the Parlement, and, later in the day, gave a sumptuous banquet, at which covers were laid for five hundred persons, champagne and other costly wines flowed in rivulets, and the tables groaned beneath every imaginable delicacy.

Nor were the distinguished guests to whom formal invitations had been issued the only persons to partake of the ambassadorial hospitality, for, as soon as the last of them had retired, Richelieu ordered the doors to be thrown open, and the populace admitted to dispose of the remains of the feast. An immense crowd at once poured in, and fell upon the unaccustomed dainties with such goodwill, that in a surprisingly short space of time nothing remained but gnawed bones and empty bottles. Unfortunately, these humble guests did not confine their attentions to the edibles and liquors, and a considerable portion of the Ambassador's plate and cutlery was missing in the morning.

However, Richelieu had the consolation of reflecting that, if he had had to pay a high price for his popularity, he had succeeded in establishing it upon a firm basis.

The disgrace of *Monsieur le Duc* and Madame de Prie, early in the summer of the following year, and the rise of Fleury to power, occasioned Richelieu no surprise; indeed, according to Lemontey, he had shown so remarkably an intelligent appreciation of events, that "before crossing the Rhine on his way to Vienna, he had already betrayed his benefactors, and, in a correspondence conducted with the greatest secrecy, revealed to the King's preceptor the smallest details of his mission." [1]

The part played by "*l'Ambassadeur Fanfarinet*," as the wits of Paris named our youthful diplomatist, in the tortuous negotiations which finally culminated, in 1729, in the Congress of Soissons and the settlement of the points at issue between the allies of Vienna and Hanover, has remained obscure. But, though Soulavie declares that he laboured from twelve to fifteen hours a day, and frequently passed the whole night in writing long despatches to Versailles, and claims that the conclusion of the treaty was largely due to his "industry, consummate tact, and insinuating spirit," [2] it is probable that it was a very subordinate *rôle* indeed, and confined to communicating to the Austrian Court the views of his Government.

On the other hand, Lemontey's assertion that Richelieu's conduct after the departure of Ripperda—whose somewhat abrupt termination of his mission, however, he ascribes to his discomfiture at the duke's hands—was that of a "presumptuous novice," and that he "failed everywhere and fell constantly into the snares which he endeavoured to lay for others," is not confirmed by any other historian. It should also be observed that when in 1726 the Ambassador, finding that the magnificent state and lavish hospitality which he felt obliged to maintâin were, in the absence of the promised financial assistance from his Court, involving him in serious embarrassment, threatened to demand his recall, Fleury hastened to soothe his ruffled feelings by a conciliatory letter, and that his mission

[1] *Histoire de la Régence.*

[2] *Mémoires du duc de Richelieu.*

was continued until the end of 1728. If Richelieu had really been guilty of the presumption and rashness which Lemontey attributes to him, it is scarcely likely that the French Government would have been willing to retain his services for so long, or that, on his return, Fleury would have treated him with marked favour.

Fleury, however, had reasons of his own for being grateful to Richelieu, for, however insignificant the *rôle* which the duke had filled in the peace negotiations, he had undoubtedly rendered the Minister important service in the matter of the cardinal's hat, which was bestowed upon him in September 1726. In an affair of this kind, an Ambassador who had rendered himself personally popular was naturally able to do a great deal, and Richelieu, as we have seen, had neglected nothing to secure the goodwill of the Imperial Court.

If we are to believe the memoirs of the time, the aged Minister owed his elevation to the Roman purple in part to feminine support, for the good fortune in love which Richelieu had enjoyed in France had not abandoned him in Germany, and, having gained the favour of the Countess Batthyany,[1]

[1] The Countess Batthyany was not the only *grande dame* with whom Richelieu succeeded in ingratiating himself during his residence in Vienna. Another distinguished conquest was the Princess von Lichtenstein, who belonged to the moderate party at the Court, that is to say, to the party opposed to the alliance with Spain and war with France, and who is said to have furnished him with some valuable information concerning the intentions of the Austrian Government. In connection with this intrigue, partly sentimental and partly political, Soulavie relates an amusing anecdote:

From fear of compromising the princess and exciting the suspicions of the Austrian Ministers, it was Richelieu's habit to visit her unaccompanied, very plainly dressed, and on foot, and to be admitted into her palace by a private door, which was opened at a prearranged signal. One night, when he had gone out as usual in this disguise, he happened to meet, not far from the princess's house, three of his own lackeys, in a rather hilarious condition, who, perceiving a man, whom they took to be an ordinary citizen, evidently very desirous of escaping observation, proceeded, in that spirit of mischief which inebriation often begets, to follow him. The duke endeavoured to shake them off, but without success, and when, on reaching the princess's door, he found that they were still at his heels, he lost his temper and struck one of the men with his cane. The fellow, smarting with the pain, immediately began to shout out that the servants of the Ambassador of France were being insulted; a crowd quickly assembled; the watch came hurrying up, and Richelieu, in order to avoid being arrested, was obliged to reveal his identity to the astonished bystanders and the terrified lackeys.

mistress of Prince Eugène, he was able, through this channel, to secure the Emperor's nomination for his patron.

It was certainly well for Richelieu that he had placed the now all-powerful Fleury under a personal obligation, for towards the close of his mission to Vienna he was concerned in an affair which might have been followed by very unpleasant consequences, if the Minister had not intervened to protect him.

"A very scandalous rumour has been circulated concerning M. de Richelieu, Ambassador at Vienna," writes Barbier, in July 1728. "It is said that he has always had a liking for chemistry, magic, and such-like extraordinary sciences; that he formed a friendship with a nobleman of the Emperor's Court who had the same taste; that they brought two Franciscans to a country-house, where they made them say a Mass, and that, after the consecration, the wafers were given to two he-goats, one white, and the other black, with the intention of seeing the devil; that the Papal Nuncio, having received warning, surprised them, and has sent the Franciscans to the Inquisition, while the Emperor has written to the King. In point of fact, the *Gazette* has announced the appointment by the Emperor of a commission to arrest and punish persons who committed sacrileges, which proves that there was some truth in it. However, this story was general in Paris, where it is now said that M. de Richelieu had no part in it." [1]

Duclos gives a different and much more circumstantial account of this affair, from which it would appear that a crime more serious in the eyes of the Law than sacrilege had been committed.

According to him, there was residing at this time in Vienna, one of those impostors who live on the credulity of those who believe in magic and such-like absurdities. "This personage persuaded Richelieu and two of his friends, who shared his curiosity concerning the occult sciences, the Abbé von Sinzendorf, son of the Grand Chancellor, and the Comte de Westerloo, a Flemish nobleman, who commanded the Halberdiers of the Emperor's Guard, that, with the assistance of

[1] *Journal.*

the devil, he could procure for them whatever they most desired."[1]

"The rendezvous, for the evocation of the devil, was a quarry near Vienna, to which they proceeded at night. It was summer, and the incantations were so long that the day was beginning to break, when the quarrymen, who were on their way to their work, heard such piercing cries that they came running up, and found a man dressed as an Armenian, bathed in blood and at his last gasp. It was apparently the pretended magician, whom these gentlemen, as barbarous as they were credulous, and ashamed of having been so, had just immolated in their vexation."

The quarrymen, fearing to be taken for accomplices, hurried back to the city and gave information to the police. The latter soon discovered the names of the parties concerned, but, since they happened to be of such exalted station, contented themselves by informing the Grand Chancellor.

The Chancellor was naturally much perturbed, though, strangely enough, it was not the legal, but the ecclesiastical, aspect of the matter which troubled him. That his son, in a fit of anger, should have run a miserable magician, who had duped him, through the body, supposing him to have been the culprit, was, in his Excellency's opinion, a mere peccadillo, but that he should be implicated in an affair of sorcery was a very serious business indeed, since he had lately purchased for the young gentleman, from the Abbé Strickland,[2] the Polish nomination

[1] Duclos adds that Richelieu's desire was "the key to the heart of princes, since he already possessed that of women."

[2] Thomas John Francis Strickland, son of the Right Hon. Sir Thomas Strickland, of Sizergh, Westmoreland. He was born about the year 1679, brought up in France, and graduated at Douay. On the accession of George I., he endeavoured to effect a reconciliation between the English Catholics and the new dynasty, and his efforts in this direction were rewarded by the rich Abbey of Saint-Pierre de Préaux, in Normandy, to which he was presented by the Regent, at the request of Lord Stair, the British Ambassador in Paris. In 1727, he became Bishop of Namur, where he restored and enlarged the episcopal palace. During his later years, he resided for some time in Rome, as agent of the British Government, and was sent by the Emperor Charles VI. on a secret mission to England. He died in 1740. Strickland was an extremely able man, but, according to Lord Hervey, "famous for his dissolute manners wherever he went"; and it was probaby the fear that this might prove

to the cardinalate, which that singular clerical adventurer had obtained some years before from Stanislaus Leczinski. Rome, he knew, could stomach a good deal where highborn candidates for the purple were concerned, but the mere suspicion of the crime of magic would infallibly ruin his son's prospects.

The Chancellor, Duclos continues, made heroic endeavours to hush up this ugly affair, but, fearing that his own influence might be insufficient to avert the scandal which he had so much reason to dread, wrote to Fleury to invite his co-operation. The cardinal, on learning that Richelieu was also compromised, willingly lent his aid; but, notwithstanding the combined efforts of the two Ministers, rumours of what had occurred began to get about and even penetrated to the Vatican.

The Chancellor and Fleury thereupon decided to send a memoir to the Pope, in which the adventure was represented as a mere indiscretion of young men, which calumny was grossly exaggerating, but for which, however, they requested an absolution *ad cautelam*.

An absolution was very easily obtained in those days when demanded by a powerful Minister; and it was sent without hesitation and given in private to both the Abbé Sinzendorf and Richelieu, of whom the former not long afterwards obtained his cardinal's hat; "while, to dissipate all suspicion, the duke was included in the next promotion to the Ordre du Saint-Esprit, with permission to wear the insignia before his reception."

The third culprit, the Comte de Westerloo, having neither a Minister for his father nor a cardinal for his patron, was not included in the papal indulgence. Since the affair had become known, it was deemed necessary to make an example; and the unfortunate nobleman was deprived of his office and banished to Flanders, where he was condemned to pass the rest of his life.[1]

Such is the account furnished by Duclos, which we give

an obstacle to his elevation to the cardinalate which led him to dispose of his nomination.

[1] Duclos, *Œuvres*, vol. vi.

with all reserve, since the Historiographer Royal's weakness for exaggeration is well known. Any way, he is quite incorrect in attributing Richelieu's promotion to the Ordre du Saint-Esprit, three years before he was eligible to receive this coveted honour,[1] to a desire "to dissipate all suspicion," for the very good reason that the duke's nomination preceded by several months his adventure in the quarry: to be more precise, the *cordon bleu* reached Vienna at the end of January 1728; the eventful *séance* seems to have taken place in the latter part of the following June.

In the autumn, Richelieu, who was becoming heartily tired of Vienna and the monotonous and decorous life which his official position exacted, demanded his recall, and, as a settlement of the European imbroglio was now in sight, and the presence of an Ambassador at the Imperial Court was no longer necessary,[2] his request was granted. He arrived in Paris at the end of December, and on New Year's Day worthily inaugurated his return to his favourite theatre, by his solemn reception as a Chevalier of the Ordre du Saint-Esprit.

[1] The Ordre du Saint-Esprit in France corresponded to that of the Garter in England. By the statutes of the Order, no one could be created a chevalier until he had attained the age of thirty-five.

[2] The French Court was also much mortified by the conduct of Charles VI., who had recalled his Ambassador at Versailles three years before, and had not troubled to replace him.

# CHAPTER IX

Financial embarrassments of Richelieu after his return from Vienna—His friendship with Voltaire—Madame de Tencin—Her extraordinary career—Her relations with Richelieu—She advises the duke to rehabilitate his fortunes, by joining her in providing the King with a mistress who will be willing to govern him through them—Louis XV. and Marie Leczinska—Growing indifference of the King to his consort—Plots to "awaken" the King—Madame de Mailly, the candidate of Madame de Tencin for the post of *maîtresse en titre*—Richelieu supports the pretensions of Madame de Portail, who, however, fails to make more than a passing impression upon the royal heart—The duke, in disgust, goes to Germany, in search of military glory—His magnificent *entourage*.

THE *cordon bleu* was practically the only recompense which Richelieu received for his services in Vienna; and, greatly as this distinction was coveted, we are inclined to think that there were moments when the duke would very willingly have exchanged it for some less honourable, but more substantial, form of reward. For the immense expenditure which his three years' residence in Vienna had entailed had made serious inroads into a fortune already crippled by extravagance and high play, and he found himself so pressed for money, that he was compelled to have recourse to the generosity of his friends, and, on one occasion, even to accept a rouleau of louis which a feminine admirer, pitying the indigent condition of her Adonis, had sent him, in token of sympathy.

Among those who placed their purses at his disposal was Voltaire, who seems to have been in the habit of accommodating his noble friend in this manner for the greater part of his life. He and Richelieu, who was two years the poet's junior, had been fellow-students together at the College of Louis-le-Grand;[1] but

[1] In the *Commentaire historique*, Voltaire relates that he was presented to Richelieu during a visit to the Château de Villars. "But," writes Henri Beaune,

their acquaintance there seems to have been of the slightest, and they did not become at all intimate until after the former's first successes in the literary world. Then, however, they met frequently at the country-houses of the Duc de Sully, the Maréchal de Villars, Lord Bolingbroke, the Duc de Brancas, and other noblemen, where the young poet was ever a welcome guest; and a firm friendship was soon established between them, which endured until Voltaire's death in 1778.

It is probable that self-interest counted for not a little in an intimacy between two men so widely different in character, at least in its early stages. Voltaire had an inimitable gift for flattery, as well as for ridicule, and to a vain man like Richelieu his homage was as agreeable as his enmity was to be dreaded; while to an author whose views were constantly bringing him into collision with constituted authority there were times when the friendship of a duke and peer might prove very useful.

One must admit, however, that, during the Regency, Richelieu's friendship so far from being of use to Voltaire, proved decidedly the reverse, and shortly after the duke was committed to the Bastille in the spring of 1719, the Government requested the poet to spend a few months in the seclusion of the country.

In the autumn, when Richelieu, having been set at liberty, was exiled to the estate from which he took his title, Voltaire joined him there; and during the next few years we find the two friends visiting several places together. Thus, when, in the spring of 1724, after the failure of *Mariamne*, Voltaire went to the waters of Forges to endeavour to forget his disappointment and recruit his health, Richelieu accompanied him, and in August 1729 they went together to Plombières.

Close, however, as was this friendship, it was not untroubled by storms. The *grand seigneur* was often imperious, as he felt he had a right to be; the poet was occasionally

in his interesting work, *Voltaire au Collège*, "it is certain that they were already acquainted. Young Fronsac's father was the client of Voltaire's, and, with the Duchesse de Saint-Simon, had even stood sponsors to Armand Arouet."

inclined to be impertinent. A haughty gesture from the one, a biting witticism from the other—and they were not on speaking terms for weeks or even months. One such quarrel seems to have taken place in the autumn of 1731, since we find Voltaire writing to his friend Thiériot:

"I esteem him [Richelieu] too much to believe that he can have spoken to you with an air of displeasure, as though I had failed in what I owe to him. I owe him nothing save friendship, and not subjection, and if he required that, I should no longer owe him anything. I counsel you not to see him again, if you expect to receive from him, in my name, reproaches which would resemble a reprimand, since it would become him very ill to make them, or me to endure them."[1]

In spite of this dignified protest, it would appear that the equality to which Voltaire pretended was not always respected, and though, as M. Beaune observes, "the poet may very well have imagined that the flattering language which he almost invariably employs in his letters to the duke was inspired by personal admiration rather than by respect for rank, one feels that his pen, so free when he wishes, is not completely at its ease, and that between the two friends there always exists, thin, and transparent, that ice of etiquette which the soft and penetrating warmth of college life had failed to melt."

The relations of Richelieu with Voltaire, though not without considerable interest, are of far less importance than his connection with another person who enjoyed at this time almost as much celebrity as the author of the *Henriade* and *Zaïre*. This was the famous—or infamous—Madame de Tencin, one of the most remarkable of the many remarkable women who have assisted to make the eighteenth century an epoch of unrivalled interest to the student of French Society.

Claude Alexandrine Guérin de Tencin was born at Grenoble in 1681, being the daughter of Antoine Guérin, seigneur de Tencin, *president à mortier* of the Parlement of Grenoble. She was educated at the convent of the Dominican nuns of Montfleury, where, in 1696, she took the veil, in obedience to

[1] Letter of September 11, 1731, cited by M. Henri Beaune, *Voltaire au Collège*.

the wishes of her parents, but with the firm resolution to divest herself of it at the earliest possible moment. How she succeeded has furnished material for several romantic conjectures, though it has never been fully explained ; but, any way, she found it no easy task, since it was not until 1714 that a Bull of Secularisation was accorded her. Madame de Tencin—she was styled "Madame" in virtue of her office of canoness of the chapter of Neuville-en-Bresse—had not waited for the papal permission to free herself from her vows, and having, about 1712, joined her brother Pierre, the future Cardinal de Tencin, in Paris, she opened a salon, where her wit and beauty soon drew around her a crowd of admirers, and embarked on a career of gallantry and intrigue.

Her love-affairs were, for the most part, conducted on strictly business principles, for a more cold and calculating woman it would have been difficult to find.[1] Nevertheless, she did not lack "protectors," among whom may be mentioned the Regent, Cardinal Dubois, the Lieutenant of Police, d'Argenson, Fontenelle, and two Englishmen, Lord Bolingbroke and the poet-diplomatist, Matthew Prior. By another lover, the Chevalier Destouches—sometimes confounded with the poet of that name—with whom she formed a liaison which Sainte-Beuve describes as "*l'une des plus étroites et des plus tendres de sa vie*," she had, in November 1717, a son, whom, the day after his birth, she deposited upon the steps of the little church of Saint-Jean-le-Rond, where he was found and adopted by a kind-hearted glazier, the father afterwards making him a small allowance, but without acknowledging the paternity. This child was d'Alembert, the Encyclopædist.

The last liaison of Madame de Tencin had a tragic issue. On April 6, 1726, a member of the Grand Conseil named La Fresnais shot himself through the heart in her house, leaving behind him, in the hands of a notary, a document in which he made serious charges against his mistress. This affair created

[1] Talking one day with the poet Fontenelle, she laid her hand upon his heart, and observed with a smile : "It is not a heart that you have there ; it is all brain, as in the head." She might with even more justice have said the same of her own.

MADAME DE TENCIN

FROM AN ENGRAVING IN THE BIBLIOTHÈQUE NATIONALE

a great sensation, and Madame de Tencin was arrested and taken to the Bastille, where she remained for three months.[1]

After this unpleasant experience, the lady decided to renounce gallantry—it was certainly time, since she had reached her forty-sixth year—and to occupy herself with intrigue and literature. The advancement of her brother, whose relations with her were commonly believed to have been rather more than fraternal, was henceforth the great object of her life, while her salon in the Rue Saint-Honoré became the most brilliant literary resort in the capital—the "ante-chamber of the Académie Française"—to which Fontenelle, Montesquieu, Marivaux, Helvétius, Duclos, Piron, Marmontel, d'Argental, Pont-de-Veyle, Lords Bolingbroke and Chesterfield, and other distinguished men were constant visitors. "She called them her beasts, her menagerie, and used to present each of them, by way of a New Year's gift, with two ells of velvet, to make himself a pair of breeches, to which they responded by presents of the same kind, accompanied by verses." Judging from some of these verses which have been preserved, the tone of the menagerie's conversation must have been decidedly unconventional.

It was during this second period of her life that Madame de Tencin composed the romances which have assured her an honourable place among the women of letters of the eighteenth century: *les Mémoires du Comte de Comminges*, *le Siège de Calais*, and *les Malheurs de l'Amour*. Published anonymously, they were ascribed, while she lived, to her nephew d'Argental and Pont-de-Veyle; but after her death in December 1747, her friends and principally Montesquieu, whose genius Madame de Tencin had been one of the first to appreciate, proved that she was the author.

Richelieu and Madame de Tencin were old friends. There had been a time, indeed, when they had been something more; but, though the lady soon ceased to be the duke's mistress, she

[1] Voltaire was undergoing his second *embastillement* at the same time. "We were like Pyramus and Thisbé," he writes, "only we did not kiss each other through the chink in the wall."

remained his Egeria, whose judgment in "affairs" he esteemed as highly as did her "beasts" her opinion in literary matters.

It was therefore only to be expected that when on his return from Vienna Richelieu found himself in financial straits, he should have repaired to the Rue Saint-Honoré, to take counsel with Madame de Tencin as to the best means of filling his depleted coffers.

The lady received him cordially, for the duke was not only a great nobleman, but a shrewd man of the world, who, being, like herself, quite untrammelled by scruples, might prove a valuable coadjutor in a scheme which she was even then maturing. Having listened to his tale of distress, she hastened to express her sympathy with his disappointment at the very inadequate recognition which his patriotic sacrifices at Vienna had met with from an ungrateful country. In the time of the late King, said she, not only the *cordon bleu*, but a lucrative government or some other equally desirable post would have been his reward, for *le Grand Monarque* would never have allowed one of his subjects—and that subject the bearer of the name of Richelieu —to half-ruin himself in his sovereign's service. But *autres temps, autres mœurs*, and those who wish to succeed must perforce accommodate themselves to the change and seek fortune elsewhere than in war or diplomacy. With a feeble, indolent voluptuary, such as Louis XV. promised to become, honourable services would count for little or nothing; the only road to advancement would be the favour of women, since the King would certainly allow himself to be dominated absolutely by any woman who once succeeded in acquiring influence over him. Let Richelieu join forces with her to provide his Majesty with a mistress of their own choosing, preferably one who would be willing to govern her royal lover through them. Then the ball would be at their feet. Such was the advice of Madame de Tencin, and, whatever else we may think of it, it was undoubtedly sound.

For the young King had long since tired of a consort who was seven years his senior, and who, though virtuous and amiable, possessed neither beauty nor charm. For a few months after their marriage he had been quite a devoted husband, had compared Marie Leczinska to Queen Blanche, the mother of Saint-Louis, and had said to those who called his attention to the beauty of some lady of the Court: "I find the Queen still more beautiful."

Then came the abortive attempt of *Monsieur le Duc* and Madame de Prie to procure the disgrace of Fleury, with which Marie Leczinska, out of complaisance for those who had brought about her marriage, was so ill-advised as to associate herself; and from that time Louis, who had never felt any real tenderness for his wife and was entirely under the domination of his former preceptor, began to treat her with increasing indifference. It is true that, restrained by his excessive timidity when in the company of women, and by that morbid dread of the consequences of sin which caused him in after years to dismiss his mistresses whenever he imagined himself on his death-bed, he remained materially faithful to the Queen for some years—a period which was marked by the birth of two sons and several daughters. But, all the while, the latter's natural coldness of temperament, which increased as she grew older, her excessive and often inopportune piety, her entire lack of sympathy with her young husband's tastes and pursuits, and "the thousand *enfantillages* by which she irritated the nerves of this nervous King"[1] were slowly but surely destroying what little affection her husband still retained for her; and at the time at which we have now arrived Louis had already had, or was believed to have had, some passing gallantries; and it was obvious that the moment when his Majesty would definitely emancipate himself from the conjugal fetters would not be long delayed.

To precipitate that hour was the ardent desire of all the dissolute and greedy courtiers who had sneered at what they were pleased to call their sovereign's "bourgeois life," and

[1] Among these *enfantillages*, may be mentioned an overpowering dread of ghosts, which necessitated her always keeping within call a *femme de chambre*, whose hand she might hold during her paroxysms of superstitious terror, and a passionate affection for a lapdog, which slept in her room, and to feed and caress which she rose several times during the night.

several conspiracies were set on foot to "awaken" the King and secure the elevation of various facile beauties to the coveted post of *maîtresse en titre*, which had now been without an occupant for nearly half a century.

The Court became a veritable hotbed of intrigue and conspiracy. Almost every day the King's name was coupled with that of some noble dame or other. Some said that Mlle. de Charolais would bear away the prize; others the Comtesse de Toulouse. Half the *dames du palais*, whose official duties naturally provided them with exceptional facilities for attracting the favourable attention of their sovereign: Mesdames de Gontaut, the Maréchale de Villars, the Duchesses de Tallard, de Béthune, and d'Épernon, and the Comtesse de Mailly, were in turn the object of suspicion and envy.

This last lady was the candidate of the clique which had Madame de Tencin for its guiding spirit, and to which she had invited Richelieu's adhesion. The eldest of the five daughters of Louis II., Marquise de Nesle—four of whom were to attain such unenviable celebrity[1]—and of Armande de la Porte-Mazarin, one of the heroines of the duel described in a previous chapter, she was born in the same year as Louis XV., and married, at the age of sixteen, to her cousin, Louis Alexandre de Mailly-Rubempré, Comte de Mailly, a worthless individual, and so poor that, according to the expression of a contemporary, it was the marriage of hunger and thirst.[2]

Childless and neglected by her husband, Madame de Mailly had already had an intrigue with the Marquis de Puisieux, afterwards Minister for Foreign Affairs, when, on the death of her mother in October 1729, she succeeded to her post of *dame*

[1] The other sisters were:

Pauline Félicité, born in 1712; married in 1740 to the Comte de Vintimille; died in 1741.

Diane Adélaide, born in 1714; married in 1742 to the Duc de Lauraguais; died in 1769.

Hortense Félicité, born in 1715; married in 1739 to the Marquis de Flavacourt; date of death unknown, but was still living in 1797.

Marie Anne, born in 1717; married in 1734 to the Marquis de la Tournelle; died in 1744.

[2] Marquis d'Argenson, *Mémoires*.

*du palais*, not altogether to the gratification of poor Marie Leczinska, who liked to believe that the reputation of her ladies-in-waiting was as spotless as her own.

Madame de Mailly was not beautiful, nor even, strictly speaking, pretty. But she had a graceful figure, sparkling black eyes, "and the finest leg that was to be seen at Court." [1] She knew, too, how to make the most of what charms she possessed, and was noted for her exquisite taste in dress, which her rivals in vain attempted to imitate; while she was both amiable and amusing. Any way, she pleased the King and, after a while, the observant courtiers began to remark that his Majesty blushed whenever her name was mentioned.[2]

Given a little skilful manœuvring on the part of those who hoped to profit by her "elevation," it seemed to be only a question of time for the proud position of *maîtresse déclarée* to be hers; and it therefore seems strange that Richelieu should not have enrolled himself among her supporters. But, by some caprice, which can only be explained by a disinclination to share the spoils of victory with others, instead of associating himself in the designs of Madame de Tencin, he decided to thwart them and to endeavour to fix the choice of the King upon a candidate of his own. The lady whom he put forward was Madame de Portail, wife of the First President of the Parlement of Paris, a very pretty woman, though her charms were somewhat discounted by a "deformity of the neck." Having suborned the King's confidential *valets de chambre*, Bachelier and Lebel, an interview was arranged, which passed off so well that his Majesty begged for a second rendezvous. But before the evening arrived, Louis, who still attached considerable importance to *les convenances*,

[1] *Mémoires du duc de Richelieu.*

[2] *Mémoires du duc de Luynes.* Soulavie places the beginning of the King's liaison with Madame de Mailly in 1732, but the Duc de Luynes, writing on December 8, 1744, says that it began in 1733, and he is probably correct: "I was informed only a few days ago that the intercourse of the King with Madame de Mailly dated from 1733, and I learned it in a way which admits of no doubt, and no one had any suspicion of it at that time." The affair, indeed, was kept so secret that the Marquis d'Argenson, generally well informed, makes it date from 1736, and it was not until a visit of the Court to Compiègne in July 1738 that the lady was publicly acknowledged.

thought it prudent to institute certain inquiries into Madame la Président's past history, and, learning that she was coquettish, malicious, and a little inclined to boast about her distinguished admirers, decided not to see her again, and sent the Marquis de Lugeac to make his excuses. Madame de Portail received a pension of 2,000 écus, by way of compensation for her blighted hopes; but Richelieu, of course, got nothing, and, in high disgust, he determined to turn his back upon the Court for a time, and, the War of the Polish Succession having just broken out, went off to Germany, in search of military glory (October 1733).

Although the duke was still deeply in debt, his financial embarrassments did not prevent him from surrounding himself with a magnificence more suited to a monarch making a progress through his dominions than a simple colonel of infantry [1] going on a campaign. "The Duc de Richelieu, formerly Ambassador at Vienna, who is not even a general officer," writes Barbier, "has seventy-six sumpter-mules, thirty horses for himself alone, and a great number of lackeys, and he has caused tents to be made on the model of those of the King." And he adds: "The general officers who are rich are taking with them scullions and pantry-boys, as though it was to celebrate some fête; and those who are not equally rich are ruining themselves, and making it quite impossible for them to sustain several campaigns." [2]

[1] Richelieu was now colonel of the regiment which bore his name. It was an old corps, having been raised in 1595.

[2] *Journal*, October 14, 1733.

# CHAPTER X

Richelieu proposes for the hand of Mlle. de Guise—His suit, at first rejected by her family, is eventually successful, owing to the intervention of Voltaire—The poet's letter to Cideville—His *Épithalame à Madame de Richelieu*—The marriage takes place at Montjeu (April 7, 1734)—Refusal of the bride's cousins, the Princes de Lixin and de Pons, to attend the wedding and sign the contract—Richelieu rejoins the army—Philipsburg invested by the French—Richelieu having been grossly insulted by the Prince de Lixin, kills him in a duel in the trenches—Fall of Philipsburg and return of the duke to France—Anger of his wife's relatives, who decline to hold any communication either with him or Madame de Richelieu—Their married life—Their children—The duke is appointed Lieutenant-General of Languedoc—Duel between him and the Baron von Pentenrieder behind the Hôtel des Invalides, in which the latter is killed and Richelieu seriously wounded—Voltaire visits the duke on his sick-bed, and makes him a loan of 40,000 livres—Difficulties with which Richelieu has to contend in Languedoc—His skilful conduct—He is joined by his wife—Birth of their daughter, the future Comtesse d'Egmont—Death of Madame de Richelieu.

RICHELIEU did not find any glory awaiting him in Germany, for it was too late to accomplish much that year, and the French had to content themselves with the capture of Kehl. When the army went into winter quarters, he returned to Paris, hoping for better fortune when hostilities should be resumed in the spring.[1] But before he again beheld the waters of the Rhine, an important event in his life had taken place. To the astonishment of himself, as much as to that of his friends, after a widowhood of eighteen years, he married again.

And what was still more surprising, was that he—this cold, cynical *roué*, who regarded women as but the playthings of an idle hour, to be cajoled, caressed, and thrown aside as his

[1] He had, however, been raised to the rank of brigadier.

humour dictated, or as useful pawns in the game of ambition—married for love! Yes, for love, or at least that sentiment, confined for once within the limits of the conscience—if M. de Richelieu can be said to have possessed a conscience—was his principal motive, though it is probable that ambition counted for something.

For the lady of his choice was a daughter of the younger branch of the princely House of Lorraine—that famous family of Guise, whose genius and audacity had once been the talk of Europe, and who, though no longer foremost in the battle-field and the council-chamber, and, indeed, fallen somewhat from their high estate, never for a moment forgot that the blood of the defender of Metz and of the hero of the League ran in their veins.

Élisabeth Sophie de Lorraine, Mlle. de Guise, was the younger of the two daughters of Anne Marie Joseph de Lorraine, Prince de Guise, Comte d'Harcourt, and Marquis de Neufburg, and of Marie Christine de Casville, Marquise de Montjeu. Her elder sister was already married, having become the wife of the Duc d'Albret. The Princesse de Guise had recently died, and the girl was at this time living very quietly with her widowed father at the Hôtel de Guise, in the precincts of the Temple, only going out to attend Mass, accompanied by her *gouvernante* and followed by an equerry.

Élisabeth was not strictly beautiful, at least her beauty, the Duc de Luynes tells us, consisted rather in the sweetness of her expression than in the regularity of her features, but she had "large black eyes, full of fire,"[1] a perfect shape, and a graceful carriage. Altogether, she must have been very pleasant to look upon, particularly in the extremely becoming mourning habiliments of that period; and Richelieu, meeting her one day, fell in love at first sight, and lost no time in asking her hand in marriage. His suit was at first rejected, for the Guises looked down upon a man whose ancestors had been simple country-gentlemen, when theirs had been commanding armies and governing kings; and the House of

[1] Voltaire, *Épithalame à Madame de Richelieu.*

Lorraine declared with one voice that it regarded such a marriage as a *mésalliance.*

The lady herself, however, was far from sharing the views of her relatives, and gently yet firmly represented that it was her wish to wed the duke. "Every one was astonished," says the Comtesse d'Armaillé, in her charming monograph on the Comtesse d'Egmont, "for this chaste and pious creature seemed born to marry some grave, austere man, religious like herself. But who does not know the fascination of certain contrasts and the attraction of forbidden fruit? These two beings so different pleased and suited each other." [1]

In no way daunted by his first rebuff, Richelieu returned to the charge, this time supported by the King and *Monsieur le Duc.* But, if we are to believe Voltaire, it was neither of these illustrious persons, but he himself, a close friend of the Prince de Guise, as well as of Richelieu, who wrested the paternal consent from the teeth of the haughty Lorraines, a task which was no doubt greatly facilitated by the fact that the duke consented to take his bride without a *dot.* Not content with this, the versatile poet, remembering that he was a notary's son, must needs draw up the marriage-contract, after which he started for the Château of Montjeu, the Prince de Guise's country-seat, where the wedding was to take place, feeling that he had done his duty by all concerned.

"My dear friend," he writes to Cideville, "I am leaving to witness a marriage which I have just made. I had long ago conceived the idea of marrying the Duc de Richelieu to Mlle. de Guise. I have concluded this affair like an intrigue in a play. The *denoûment* is about to take place at Montjeu, near Autun. Poets are more accustomed to composing epithalamia than contracts. However, I have drawn up the contract, so I shall probably not write any verses."

Nevertheless, the temptation to immortalise the happy event, which was celebrated in the chapel of the Château of Montjeu, on April 7, 1734,[2] proved too great for him to resist,

[1] Comtesse d'Armaillé, *la Comtesse d'Egmont, fille du maréchal de Richelieu.*

[2] Among the wedding-guests, it is interesting to note, was Émilie de Breteuil,

and he duly composed an *Épithalame à Madame de Richelieu* which, we fear, must have brought a blush to the lady's cheek :

> "Un prêtre, un oui, trois mots latins
> À jamais fixent vos destins ;
> Et le célébrant d'un village
> Dans la chapelle de Montjeu,
> Très-chrétiennement vous engage
> À coucher avec Richelieu,
> Avec Richelieu, ce volage,
> Qui va jurer par ce saint nœud
> D'être toujours fidèle et sage.
> Nous nous en défions un peu,
> Et vous grands yeux noirs, pleins de feu,
> Nous rassurent bien davantage
> Que les serments qu'il fait à Dieu," etc., etc.

A little incident somewhat marred the harmony of the occasion. Two of the Lorraine princes, cousins of the bride, the Prince de Lixin[1] and his brother the Prince de Pons,[2] "who set small store by Richelieu's character and still less by his nobility,"[3] showed their disapproval of the marriage by declining to appear at it and sign the contract. Their refusal, though it caused some embarrassment to both sides, was not regarded as of much importance ; but, in point of fact, it deeply offended Richelieu, and was the beginning of a mutual antipathy between himself and the two princes, which culminated, two months later, in a tragedy which cast a gloom over the happiness of the newly-wedded pair.

The honeymoon only lasted a week, at the end of which

Marquise du Châtelet, lately Richelieu's mistress, soon to become Voltaire's "divine Émilie."

[1] Henri Jacques de Lorraine. He was Grand Master of the Duke of Lorraine's Household, but resided in France and held the rank of brigadier of cavalry in the army.

[2] Charles Louis de Lorraine.

[3] That is to say, to the Vignerots' claim to nobility, which was disputed. "Since he uses the name Vignerot," writes Barbier, "and people of condition assert that that does not make him even a gentleman, they [the Princes de Lixin and de Pons] believed that the Prince de Guise was dishonouring them, and refused to sign the marriage-contract." It should be borne in mind that Richelieu's father was only related to the great cardinal on the distaff side, and assumed the name of Du Plessis-Richelieu in accordance with the terms of his uncle's will.

ÉLISABETH SOPHIE DE LORRAINE, DUCHESSE DE RICHELIEU

FROM THE MINIATURE BY JEAN-BAPTISTE MASSÉ IN THE MONTAGU HOUSE COLLECTION

Richelieu was compelled to tear himself from the arms of his weeping bride and set out for Germany to rejoin the army. Voltaire, however, remained at Montjeu till the beginning of May, and doubtless did what he could to console the poor lady, by chanting the praises of her absent lord. Then he started for Champagne to visit the Du Châtelets at their country-seat at Cirey, thus fortunately escaping from the clutches of the myrmidons of the Lieutenant of Police, who, five days after his departure, arrived at Montjeu, with a warrant for his arrest and committal to the Bastille.[1]

On his arrival at the front, Richelieu found the French army under Berwick advancing on Philipsburg, the key of that part of the Rhine country, whose capture would enable it to push forward into the very heart of Germany. During the winter the Imperialists had constructed strong lines at Ettlingen,[2] a little place not far from Carlsruhe, between Kehl and Philipsburg. But, by a skilful manœuvre, Berwick succeeded in turning them, upon which the Duke of Würtemberg, who commanded the defending force, abandoned his position and hastily retreated to Heilbronn, where he resigned his command to Prince Eugène, who had recently arrived from Vienna, leaving the French to invest Philipsburg at their leisure.

Now, as ill-luck would have it, the Prince de Lixin and his brother were both serving in the Army of the Rhine, and, moreover, were attached to the same division to which Richelieu belonged. For some weeks they appear to have been prudent enough to keep apart, but on the evening of June 2, they were all three invited, together with a number of other officers, to a supper-party which the Prince de Conti was giving in celebration of his birthday.

[1] This was on account of his *Lettres anglaises*, which, quite unknown to him, had been published in Paris on April 24, with his name on the title-page, and had made a great sensation.

[2] "These entrenchments, made after the fashion of the Turks, consisted of big trees set zigzag (*en échiquier*), twisted together by the branches; the whole about five fathoms thick."—Maréchal de Noailles, *Mémoires*, cited by Carlyle, "Frederick the Great."

It happened that that day Richelieu had been in command of a detachment working in the trenches, and his duties had detained him there until some time beyond the hour at which M. de Conti's guests were to assemble. Thinking, very naturally, that, as the prince was one of his oldest friends, and as a soldier's supper is not a Court banquet, he might safely dispense with ceremony, he did not trouble to return to his quarters to change his uniform, but presented himself just as he was, covered from head to foot with the dust of the trenches.

Conti and all his guests readily accepted the duke's apologies for his somewhat unkempt appearance, with the single exception of the Prince de Lixin, who observed, in a contemptuous tone, that it seemed that, notwithstanding M. de Richelieu's admission into his family, a good deal of dirt still clung to him.

In those days, so gross an affront could meet with but one reply, and, though Richelieu's friends endeavoured to pacify him, for duels between officers on active service were rigorously forbidden and severely punished, he insisted on receiving immediate satisfaction.

Lixin, on his side, was more than willing to oblige him; indeed, it is probable that his insulting words were uttered with the deliberate intention to provoke the hot-tempered duke to a duel; and the two noblemen, each accompanied by a lackey bearing a lantern, and followed by several officers, who vainly endeavoured to persuade them to renounce their purpose, made their way to a deserted spot at the extremity of the trenches, where they might settle their differences without fear of interference from the Provost's guard.

Since the night was dark and the lanterns did not give sufficient light, the lackeys were ordered to replace them by torches. Immediately one of the enemy's batteries opened fire upon the party, and the duel began to the accompaniment of a storm of shot and shell.

Both combatants were evenly matched, for the Prince de Lixin was a noted swordsman. The first exchanges, indeed, were in his favour, and he wounded Richelieu in the thigh, upon which the officers present endeavoured to stop the fight, protesting that honour was satisfied, and that, if they remained there much longer, not a man of them would be left alive, as the German gunners were now beginning to find the range, and one of the lackeys had already been hit.

The duke, however, insisted on continuing the combat, and, after being again wounded, this time in the shoulder, he ran his sword right through his opponent's body, close to the heart. The unfortunate man sank to the ground, and expired almost immediately.

Every effort was made by those present to hush up this deplorable affair, and it was at first represented that Lixin had been killed by a shot from the enemy's battery, which, as we have seen, might very well have happened;[1] but in a few days the truth leaked out. By that time, however, what was supposed to have happened to the prince had actually happened to Berwick, and his successor, the Marquis d'Asfeld, learning of the provocation which Richelieu had received, took a very lenient view of his offence, and contented himself with a reprimand.

It was believed at first that Berwick's death would end the campaign, as Turenne's had ruined that of 1675, and that the French would raise the siege and retreat across the Rhine. But, owing to the feeble support which he received from the Princes of the Empire, who regarded the war chiefly as an Austrian affair, Eugène found himself unable to profit by it, and on July 18 Philipsburg surrendered. With its fall the Rhine campaign closed, and Richelieu, who had suffered at the hands of the enemy as well as at those of the unfortunate Lixin, returned to France to enjoy some much-needed repose.

[1] Such was the report which reached Paris, for Barbier writes in his *Journal:* "The 2nd of this month, the Prince de Lixin, of the House of Lorraine, took into his head to enter the trenches, although he had received no orders to do so, he being, as a matter of fact, a brigadier of cavalry. In the evening, as he was leaving the trenches, he was struck by a musket-ball, which pierced his arm and traversed his body, and from which he died half an hour afterwards. It is sad that imprudence, bravery, or curiosity should have cost a prince of this name his life."

His duel, he discovered, had added considerably to his already high reputation for courage, but, on the other hand, had embittered the Guises against him to such a degree, that they refused to hold any communication with the duke or his wife. The Prince de Pons, indeed, went even farther than this, and declined to attend any social function at which Richelieu was expected to be present—an action which was sometimes the cause of a good deal of embarrassment to other people, as the following incident related by the Duc de Luynes will show:

"June 3, 1637.—On May 30, M. de la Mina,[1] on account of its being the Feast of St. Ferdinand, gave a supper to a number of ladies and some men. Madame de Luynes and I were present. The invitations were in the name of Madame de la Mina. There were a great many games of brelan, quadrille, and piquet. A large table accommodated seventeen ladies and six men, and at a smaller one sat five ladies and eight men. The cause of the ladies being thus separated was a little embarrassment that arose. M. de la Mina only learned the previous day, at eleven o'clock in the evening, that the Duc de Richelieu and the Prince de Pons had reasons for not meeting in the same place. Both were invited, and also Madame de Pons and Madame de Richelieu. M. de la Mina was very upset and very uneasy at this circumstance; but his thoughtfulness atoned for it. M. and Madame de Pons played cards in one room, M. and Madame de Richelieu in another; M. and Madame de Richelieu were at the little table, M. and Madame de Pons at the big one. I have been told that a similar embarrassment arose at a repast at M. de Stainville's, where both M. de Pons and M. de Richelieu were present."[2]

It was fortunate for the young wife that the intense affection which she had early conceived for Richelieu was proof against this unhappy estrangement from all her relations, otherwise her married life would have been a very sad one, for her health was delicate, she had nothing in common with the duke's gay friends, and the duke himself, though really attached to his

[1] The Marquis de las Minas, the Spanish Ambassador.

[2] *Mémoires du duc de Luynes.*

wife, was far too wedded to pleasure to renounce it, and his escapades, which, to do him justice, he appears to have made heroic efforts to conceal from her, must have caused her great distress.

Three children were born to them: two sons, one of whom died in infancy, while the other, the Duc de Fronsac, lived to become almost as notorious a libertine as his father, though, as he lacked the latter's powers of fascination, his exploits were mostly confined to the *demi-monde*; and a daughter, the future Comtesse d'Egmont, the friend of Gustavus III. of Sweden, one of the most interesting figures of the second half of the eighteenth century.[1]

Richelieu, it will be remembered, had received nothing with his wife, and the increased expenditure which his marriage necessarily entailed—for he insisted on maintaining an establishment mounted on a quasi-royal footing—added to the heavy costs incurred in a lawsuit, plunged him once more into serious financial difficulties. In these circumstances, he decided to quit the Court and Paris for a time, and begged Fleury to obtain from the King an appointment for him in the provinces.

His application was successful, and on March 31, 1738, he was nominated one of the three lieutenant-generals of the King in Languedoc,[2] to which, according to the so-called *Mémoires* of Maurepas, the cardinal added a present of 100,000 livres, which he had recently won at cards off the Duc de la Trémoille. As, however, the three lieutenant-generals held the Estates of the province in turn, and Richelieu's was not until the following year, he remained for the present in Paris, and beguiled the time by a love-affair with a certain Madame de la Martelière, the pretty wife of a revenue farmer, "who appeared to him unworthy of such a treasure," and by yet another "affair of honour," which, like that which had preceded it, ended fatally for his antagonist.

[1] Sophie Jeanne Armande Élisabeth Septimanie de Vignerot du Plessis, born March 1, 1740; married February 10, 1756, to the Comte d'Egmont; died October 14, 1773.

[2] Six months earlier, Richelieu had been promoted to the rank of *maréchal de camp*.

During his residence in Vienna, Richelieu had quarrelled with a German nobleman, a certain Baron von Pentenrieder; but the duke's official position had, of course, debarred them from settling their differences in the way in fashion with gentlemen at this period. However, in the autumn of 1738, Pentenrieder happened to find himself in Paris, and met the ex-Ambassador. Now there was no longer any obstacle to their meeting, and a pretended quarrel over a woman was followed by a ferocious duel behind the Hôtel des Invalides.

It was a veritable combat of David and Goliath, for the baron was a gigantic creature, "*grand et fort comme un buffle*"; but victory, as in that historic encounter, was not decided by thew and sinew.

Nevertheless, Pentenrieder's great strength, joined to the German method of fencing, which was not only probably strange to Richelieu, but gave a great advantage to a tall man, rendered him a formidable opponent, and he succeeded in breaking down the duke's guard and wounding him severely in the side. Though bleeding profusely, the Frenchman continued the combat, and, as the baron, believing victory assured, rushed in for the *coup de grâce*, met him with a furious *riposte*, which stretched his huge antagonist dying at his feet.

This fatal affray was Richelieu's last appearance upon the "field of honour," and henceforth his sword was never unsheathed save in his country's service. He had, however, already done enough in this direction to earn for himself the reputation of being one of the most redoubtable duellists of his time, though it is only fair to remark that this celebrity had been achieved rather against his will, for, as we have seen, in three at least of his four encounters, he was not the aggressor, one, indeed—that with *Monsieur le Duc* at Chantilly—being literally forced upon him.

The duke's wound, though not in itself dangerous, was a serious one for a man of forty-two, whose constitution was already impaired by excesses of all kinds; and it was at first feared that, even if he recovered, his health would be permanently affected. But, though he suffered considerable pain for some little time, in a few months he was as well and as active as ever.

It was while he lay upon his sick-bed, and the doctors were shaking their heads and declaring that if M. le Duc were ever able to leave it again, he might consider himself singularly fortunate, that Voltaire came to condole with him and to offer him a loan of 40,000 livres. The poet was himself in indifferent health at the time, and observed, with a sigh, as he handed over the money, which Richelieu, needless to mention, had thankfully accepted, that he very much feared that he should not long benefit by the interest which was to be paid him. The interview between the two friends, each of whom imagined himself in a moribund condition, is distinctly amusing, in view of the fact that the one died at eighty-four and the other at ninety-two.

So soon as he was well enough to travel, Richelieu set out for Montpellier, the capital of Languedoc, which the lieutenants-general of the province, of course, made their headquarters during their term of office. On his arrival there, he found himself called upon to face serious difficulties. Ever since the Reformation, Languedoc had been a stronghold of Protestantism, and the embers of the terrible religious strife of which it had been the scene in bygone days still smouldered, and of late had even been threatening to burst into flame. The Estates, too, which a century before had dared to assert their independence against the iron rule of the man whose name the new lieutenant-general bore, and had been a thorn in the side of successive governments, had in their last session been unpleasantly insistent for the redress of their grievances. They were about to reassemble, and would be duly asked to vote supplies; but, in their present state of feeling, it seemed very improbable that the money would be forthcoming.

It was a difficult situation with which to contend, and one entirely without experience in dealing with sectarian bitterness and the pretensions of provincial assemblies might well have been pardoned if he had been found wanting. The versatile duke, however, confounded those who had criticised his appointment, by the display of unexpected qualities. By turns dignified and supple, conciliating and firm, he pacified, temporarily at least, the contending religious factions, and, by specious arguments and generous promises, persuaded the reluctant Estates to vote the money required. The news of his unexpected success reached Versailles at a moment when the harassed Government had almost abandoned hope, and Fleury congratulated himself on the fortunate result of what the Minister's enemies had doubtless stigmatised as a "job" of the most flagrant kind.

Madame de Richelieu had not accompanied the duke to Montpellier. She was ill at the time, and mourning the loss of her second son, who had recently died. However, the separation from her dear Richelieu soon proved insupportable—he was certainly not the kind of husband whom a loving wife would care to allow very long out of her sight—and, a few weeks later, she followed him, having first taken upon herself the responsibility of dismissing the ruinous swarm of gorgeous menials whom he insisted upon keeping, however hard pressed for money he might happen to be, and of letting their hôtel in the Place-Royale to the Neapolitan Ambassador. It was well that she did so, for, in order to ingratiate himself with those whom he governed, Richelieu found it necessary to entertain on a princely scale, and even occasionally to resort to still more costly methods of securing their good-will, for certain prominent members of the Estates were not averse to the lieutenant-general's appreciation of their services taking a very practical form.

However, the death of the Prince de Guise, which occurred not long after his daughter had left Paris, came to relieve the financial situation, which was threatening to become more serious than ever; and, for the first time for many years, the duke found himself comparatively free from debt.

Poor Madame de Richelieu did not live long to benefit by this improvement in their fortunes. She had been suffering for some time past from a chest affection, hereditary in her family, which the long journey from Paris to Montpellier appears to have aggravated. On March 1, the future Comtesse d'Egmont was born, and received among other names that of Septimanie, in honour of the province,[1] the deputies of the Estates acting as sponsors;[2] and this otherwise happy event made demands upon her strength which she was in no condition to support.

After the birth of her little daughter, indeed, the poor duchess's health declined rapidly, and when, in the following summer, Richelieu, at her earnest request, brought her back to Paris, the end was very near. It came, in fact, on August 3, at the Hôtel de Guise, which had been bequeathed to her by her father.

The Duc de Luynes has left a touching account of her last moments, in which all her thoughts were for her husband.

"Compiègne, 3 August 1740.—We were informed to-day of the death of Madame de Richelieu. She had been ill for a long time from a chest complaint. The journey to Montpellier, where she gave birth to a daughter, was the beginning of this illness; or, at any rate, greatly augmented it. . . . She was of a very amiable disposition and had a pleasant face; and she had always entertained the most tender affection for M. de Richelieu, of which in her last illness she gave him yet another proof. After she had made her confession to Père Ségaud, Jesuit, M. de Richelieu inquired if she were satisfied with him, upon which she pressed his hand and said: 'Assuredly, for he has not forbidden me to love you.' The day that she died, feeling, at five o'clock in the morning, that she was at the point of death, she asked for M. de Richelieu, who at that moment was in the room, and told him that all her desire had been to die in his arms. And, with these words, she made a last effort to embrace him and expired."

[1] The ancient march or duchy of Septimanie was a fief appertaining directly to the Crown of France. The name of Septimanie came to it, it is said, from the seven principal towns of this part of Narbonnese Gaul: Narbonne, Agde, Béziers, Magnelonne, Carcassonne, Elme, and Lodève. Another tradition attributes it to the establishment of a colony of Roman soldiers belonging to the seventh legion.—Comtesse d'Armaillé, *la Comtesse d'Egmont*.

[2] In one of her letters to Gustavus III. of Sweden, the Comtesse d'Egmont says that she was the first girl in France who had ever had the deputies of the Estates for sponsors.

# CHAPTER XI

Grief of Richelieu at the death of his wife—Decline of the favour of Madame de Mailly—Richelieu and Madame de Tencin determine to replace her by a friend of her own, and select as their candidate, Marie Anne de Mailly-Nesle, Marquise de la Tournelle—Madame de la Tournelle and her sister, Madame de Flavacourt, are installed at the Court—Alarm of Fleury at the ascendency of Richelieu over Louis XV.'s mind—Unsuccessful efforts of the cardinal and Maurepas to prevent Madame de la Tournelle being appointed *dame du palais* to the Queen—Richelieu persuades Madame de Mailly to resign her post of *dame du palais* in favour of Madame de Flavacourt, and thus to throw away her only safeguard against the ingratitude of the King.

SO far as his shallow and selfish nature permitted, Richelieu had reciprocated his wife's passionate devotion, and he appears to have been genuinely affected by her premature death. He imposed upon himself a longer and more severe mourning than custom enjoined, and, not a little to the surprise of his friends, who had supposed that, now that his financial difficulties had been, temporarily at least, surmounted, the pleasures of Court and capital would prove an irresistible attraction, divided his time for the next eleven months between the Château de Richelieu and his official duties in Languedoc. About the middle of July 1741, however, he re-appeared at Versailles, and we find his name included among the favoured courtiers who received commands to accompany the King on a visit to Choisy.[1]

The closing months of that year found the Court once more on the tip-toe of expectation, for it was apparent to all that the days of Madame de Mailly's favour were numbered. The King was growing weary of a mistress whom he had had for nearly

[1] *Mémoires du duc de Luynes.*

ten years, who had never been beautiful, and who was no longer young. That she loved him for himself alone—Louis at this period, it must be remembered, was one of the handsomest princes of his time[1]—and was so disinterested that she cost him "less than an Opera-girl would cost a banker," counted for nothing in his eyes: indeed, they were, if anything, additional reasons for discarding her, since Louis XV. was one of those men whose passion is stimulated and kept alive by a suspicion of indifference, and who appraise women at the value which they set upon themselves.

Already he had given her a rival in the person of one of her sisters, Pauline Félicité de Nesle, two years younger than herself, with whom, from fear of losing her lover altogether, she had weakly submitted to share his affections. Pauline Félicité, having had the misfortune to become *enceinte*, the King, to save appearances, married her to a complaisant nobleman, the Marquis de Vintimille, a grand-nephew of the Archbishop of Paris, that venerable prelate bestowing the Church's blessing on the pair without the least compunction. The new marchioness died suddenly a few months later (September 9, 1741), after giving birth to a son—the Comte du Luc—who, in after years, bore such a striking resemblance to the King, that his Majesty became visibly embarrassed whenever he encountered him, and he was dubbed the "*demi-Louis*."

The monarch, who appears to have seen in the untimely demise of Madame de Vintimille a judgment from Heaven upon his sins, was "in the most terrible grief, sobbing and choking."[2] Madame de Mailly wept with him and sought to console him; but Louis, though, by way of penance, he remained faithful to her for a short time,[3] needed other consolations, which she could no longer give him.

[1] "He had the finest head in the world, and he carried it with equal dignity and grace. No painter, however skilful, has succeeded in rendering the expression of that splendid head when the monarch turned to look kindly at any one."—Casanova, *Mémoires*.

[2] Marquis d'Argenson, *Mémoires*.

[3] "The King turns to devotion since the death of Madame de Vintimille. In the limited society to which he confines himself nothing is spoken of but religion. . . His Majesty intends to live with Madame de Mailly as the Duc de Bourbon

There were, however, far too many who possessed the youth and beauty which the poor lady lacked, and asked nothing better than to place them at their sovereign's disposal, for his Majesty to remain long disconsolate; and once more the Court became a hotbed of conspiracy.

To Madame de Tencin, who, though she never appeared at Versailles, being, indeed, an object of Louis XV.'s particular aversion, often manipulated the wires which set the puppets of the Court dancing, the reign of Madame de Mailly had proved a bitter disappointment. Not only had the latter, even in the heyday of her favour, asked nothing for herself—a squandering of opportunities which, though it provoked her contempt, she might have pardoned—but she had asked nothing, or next to nothing, for her friends: nothing for those who had worked and schemed to raise her to the proud position she occupied. And this the disappointed Madame de Tencin could not forgive. A hundred times, indeed, did she curse the hour when she had been so ill-advised as to employ her unrivalled powers of intrigue on behalf of a sentimental fool, who seemed perfectly content so long as she was permitted to adore the Master; and the moment she recognised that the star of Madame de Mailly was on the wane, she began to look about for a successor who would better serve her own and her brother's interests.

Once more she invited the co-operation of Richelieu; and this time the duke did not refuse, for Madame de Mailly had had the misfortune to make of him an implacable enemy.

Although prior to his departure for Languedoc in 1739, Richelieu had not been one of the King's intimate friends, he had several times been invited to the supper-parties in the *petits appartements*—those luxurious repasts at which his Majesty unbent, etiquette was relaxed, and every one was permitted to speak without restraint, and even to rally their royal host. His handsome face—at forty-two the duke did not look a day more

lived with Madame d'Egmont, as a friend, with hardly any sexual intercourse, and that only by accident, then quick to confession. . . ."—D'Argenson, November 21, 1741.

LOUISE JULIE DE MAILLY-NESLE, COMTESSE DE MAILLY

AFTER THE PAINTING BY NATTIER

than thirty—the elegance of his dress, his unflagging gaiety, his ready wit, his insinuating manners, and his reputation for courage and gallantry, which rendered him equally redoubtable to men and to women—all combined to make upon the King a very favourable impression. Mlle. de Charolais, however, who at this period exercised considerable influence over Madame de Mailly, and had never forgiven Richelieu's defection, notwithstanding the latter's efforts to conciliate her, thereupon made it her business to represent to the favourite the danger of allowing too near the King an ambitious and profligate man, who might secure the first place in his Majesty's confidence and encourage him to follow his example.

Madame de Mailly, greatly alarmed, at once determined to do everything in her power to oppose the duke's growing credit; and, aided by her friends, set to work to prejudice the King against him. Their efforts were successful, and Louis not only ceased to invite Richelieu to his *petits soupers*, but treated him with marked coldness. This check to his hopes of advancement was no doubt partly responsible for that nobleman's resolution to seek employment at a distance from the Court, and for his avoidance of Paris and Versailles during the year which followed his wife's death. But, with the vanishing influence of the favourite, the prejudices which she had created in his Majesty's mind vanished also, and Richelieu reappeared at the royal supper-table, bitterly incensed against Madame de Mailly and determined to drive her away and replace her by a woman in whose friendship he might be able to repose the fullest confidence.

Accordingly, he entered into a close alliance with Madame de Tencin for the overthrow of the favourite—favourite now by courtesy alone, since the King was no longer able to dissemble the ennui which the lady occasioned him, though, from force of habit, he continued to visit her and to give her the place of honour at his supper-parties.

The two skilful intriguers passed in review all the possible candidates for Madame de Mailly's post, carefully weighed the chances of each, and calculated the probable measure of docility and gratitude they might expect in return for their support.

This one, they agreed, was both beautiful and amiable, and could be trusted, in the event of her success, to do her best to further their interests; but she was vapid and silly, and, though the King might be her slave for a time, in three months he would be bored to death. That one was clever and amusing, and likewise their very good friend; but she was scarcely young or pretty enough to hold her place against the assaults of youth and beauty, even if they contrived to secure it for her. Another possessed all the qualifications necessary to both capture and retain the royal affections, and, once firmly seated in the saddle, would guide the feeble monarch whither she willed. But she could not be relied upon, so far as they themselves were concerned. She would be prodigal of promises, effusive in her gratitude, so long as she needed their assistance; but when she was able to dispense with it, she might prove to be possessed of an inconveniently short memory. And they did not intend to leave anything to chance.

The matter was, indeed, one which called for the most careful consideration, and for some time Richelieu and his ally were unable to arrive at any definite decision. But at length, fearful lest, if they delayed any longer, they might find themselves forestalled, they selected as their candidate a woman who possessed the advantage of having already attracted the favourable notice of the King. The lady of their choice was yet another of those sisters de Nesle who possessed such a singular fascination for Louis XV.—the youngest of the batch, Marie Anne by name.

Marie Anne, who was at this time in her twenty-fifth year, had married, at the age of seventeen, the Marquis de la Tournelle, a pious and estimable young man, who loved her to distraction, but whom, if we are to believe the gossip of the time, she compelled to endure the tortures of Tantalus, until, in November 1740, death came to his relief. Madame de la Tournelle had been presented at Court at the end of January 1739, at the same time as her sister, Hortense Félicité, who married a few months later the Marquis de Flavacourt, but we hear little about her until the spring of the following year. Then the King, visiting the Duc d'Antin, at his château of Petit-Bourg, had his attention drawn to the lady. "*Mon Dieu! qu'elle est belle!*" he exclaimed, and shortly afterwards Madame de la Tournelle began to appear at the suppers in the *petits appartements.* However, as Madame de Vintimille happened to be at that time in possession of the royal heart—or rather the greater portion of it—and was inclined to be jealous, the invitations soon ceased, and after the death of her husband in the following November, Madame de la Tournelle went to live with her aunt, the Duchesse de Mazarin, who had brought her up, at the Hôtel Mazarin in Paris, and, except on the occasion of a masked ball given in the Dauphin's apartments on Shrove Tuesday, 1742, at which she assisted in the costume of a Chinese lady, the Court would not appear to have seen her again for nearly two years.

Some contemporary writers represent Madame de la Tournelle as being at this period in very poor circumstances, but this was not the case; and the real motive which led her to take up her residence with Madame de Mazarin was probably the hope that her aunt, who was wealthy and in indifferent health, might be prevailed upon to leave her a considerable part of her fortune. In this she was disappointed, and when, in September 1742, the duchess died, she left the whole of her property to the Marquis de la Vrillière, her son by her first husband, and the Comte de Maurepas, her nephew, Minister of the Marine.[1] These two noblemen, incensed against Madame de la Tournelle, owing to the efforts they suspected her of having made to divert her aunt's fortune in her own direction, promptly turned both her and her sister, Madame de Flavacourt, who, during the absence of her husband with his regiment, had also found a home at the Hôtel Mazarin, out of the house, scarcely giving them time to put

[1] Jean Fréderic Phélypeaux, Comte de Maurepas (1701–1781). He was the son of Jérôme de Pontchartrain, Secretary of State for the Marine and the King's Household, and grandson of the Chancellor of that name. In 1715, on the resignation of his father, who had secured for him the reversion of his post, he became Minister of Marine, at the age of fourteen, though the Marquis de la Vrillière, whose daughter he subsequently married, discharged his duties for the next four years.

together their belongings. Hence the bitter enmity which Madame de la Tournelle always entertained for Maurepas.

Soulavie relates that Madame de Flavacourt, who was a resourceful young woman, hit upon a singular expedient to bring her homeless condition to the notice of the Court. She set out for Versailles, hired a sedan-chair, and had herself carried into the middle of the Cour Royale, where she told the porters to set her down, remove the poles, and take their departure. Then she waited calmly until a nobleman of her acquaintance, the Duc de Gesvres, came up and inquired what she was doing there. She told him, and the astonished duke hurried off to inform the King, who was so amused that he at once gave the two sisters a lodging in the palace.

Unfortunately, the truth is less romantic. Madame de Mazarin, who, since the "elevation" of Madame de Mailly, had declined to have anything to do with that lady, yielding to the exhortations of her confessor, was reconciled to her niece on her death-bed, when she commended Mesdames de la Tournelle and de Flavacourt to her care. The favourite, who was the most kind-hearted and unsuspicious of women, readily promised to do everything possible for her sisters, lent her own apartment to Madame de Flavacourt, and begged the King to accord one to her youngest sister. As no apartment happened to be vacant at that moment, it was feared that Madame de la Tournelle would have to wait, when Richelieu, who was already maturing his plans, suggested to the King that she should be given that of the Bishop of Rennes, who was then in his diocese and likely to remain there some months, until another could be found for her. This apartment was situated in the Cour des Ministres, near the Cour des Princes.

The death of the Duchesse de Mazarin having created a vacancy among the *dames du palais* of the Queen, Madame de la Tournelle went to Fleury and asked for the post, and Madame de Mailly warmly supported her demand.[1]

[1] The Duchesse de Mazarin had been *dame d'atour* to Marie Leczinska; the Maréchale de Villars now succeeded her, and the latter's place as *dame du palais* had to be filled.

The old cardinal was very embarrassed. He had closed his eyes to the first liaison of his former pupil, and had appeared to regard with complacency the elevation of Madame de Mailly, whose regard for Louis he knew to be disinterested, who never attempted to interfere in affairs of State, and who, indeed, was so little in his way that it was actually rumoured that the Minister had himself put her forward, in order to save the young monarch from falling a victim to some greedy or ambitious woman. But when to Madame de Mailly was joined Madame de Vintimille, and Louis began to show signs of a desire to embark upon a career of libertinage, he became very uneasy, and he saw with alarm the growing ascendency which Richelieu was beginning to exercise over the King's mind. For since his return to Court in the summer of the previous year, Richelieu's progress in the royal favour had been very rapid. He was continually being invited to the *petits soupers*; he was invariably among the favoured few who accompanied the King on his visits to Choisy or Saint-Léger; his Majesty conversed with him longer and more frequently than with any one, and, when in his company, was observed to lose that air of boredom and indifference with which he generally received the attempts of his courtiers to interest or divert him, and to become almost gay and animated. It was but too evident that this debonair, witty, audacious, profligate nobleman possessed an invincible attraction for the King; that he was becoming his unconscious ideal or—as his Eminence probably termed it—his evil genius. And what would be the fate of the feeble, invertebrate monarch in the hands of such a man, who would not hesitate to drag him to the lowest depths of degradation, if, by so doing, he might rise himself to power and influence? The old Minister who, to do him justice, was sincerely attached to his master, shuddered at the prospect which rose before him.

That Richelieu fully intended to exploit Madame de la Tournelle for his own purposes, if the smallest opportunity were afforded him, the Cardinal did not for a moment doubt, for he was aware of the very suspicious interest he had taken in the lady's installation at Versailles. He knew, too, that the King was already half in love with the new arrival, and that he had made the death of Madame de Mazarin the pretext for writing her a letter in which he had inserted "something tender and affectionate";[1] and he foresaw that the appointment of Madame de la Tournelle to the post of *dame du palais* would mean the triumph of Richelieu and his allies the Tencins, since the impressionable prince would not long be able to resist the daily attacks which the marchioness's duties about the Queen's person would enable her to make upon him.

Nor was he concerned solely for the welfare of his sovereign. Hitherto the King's mistresses had occasioned him little personal anxiety. Madame de Mailly had left affairs of State severely alone, while Madame de Vintimille had been summoned to another world before she had had time to become really dangerous. But this new aspirant to the royal favour might be ambitious or greedy, and, any way, Richelieu and the Tencins were both. The cardinal saw his authority and his coffers in serious jeopardy.

The aged Minister did what he could to avert, or at any rate to postpone, the impending catastrophe. For nearly a week he abstained from saying a word to the King of Madame de la Tournelle's application for the post of *dame du palais*. Then one day, Louis, acting probably on a hint from Richelieu, inquired what had been the object of the visit which he had heard that the marchioness had paid his Eminence. His Eminence was obliged to admit that it had reference to the vacancy among the Queen's ladies, and that he was about to ask if it were the King's wish that Madame de la Tournelle's name should be placed on the list of those who were soliciting this honour. "Yes, I have spoken about it to the Queen," answered the King, and when, a day or two later, Fleury presented the list of candidates to his Majesty, with the observation that the name of La Tournelle was the last upon it, Louis took up a pencil, erased her name, wrote it at the head of the list, and, throwing the paper back to the cardinal, said, in a more imperious tone than he had ever used to his

[1] D'Argenson.

former preceptor: "The Queen is informed, and wishes her to have the place." The cardinal, though much chagrined, refused to abandon hope, and, in conjunction with Maurepas, who had as much cause as himself to fear the influence which Madame de la Tournelle and the Richelieu party might acquire over the King's mind, set to work to discover some obstacle which might prevent the nomination of this dangerous young woman, without his appearing to be opposed to the wishes of his Majesty.

After an exhaustive search among the papers in their respective offices, the two Ministers unearthed a letter written by the Marquis de Tessé, wherein he reminded the cardinal that, three years before, he had promised the next vacancy among the *dames du palais* to a certain Madame de Saulx. Armed with this, Maurepas went to the Queen, who is said to have loved him "as a son"—a rather singular comparison, seeing that the Minister was the elder of the two—and persuaded the poor woman, who, at the instance of her husband, had just demanded the place for Madame de la Tournelle, to write a letter declaring that, if the King left her free to choose her new lady-in-waiting, she gave the preference to Madame de Saulx.

The King, however, did not leave her the choice, and on September 20, 1742, the nomination of Madame de la Tournelle was formally announced; and the Queen, who, a day or two before, had sent a message to that lady to express her regret at being obliged to yield to the superior claims of Madame de Saulx, now found herself under the necessity of despatching her *dame d'honneur* to announce to her the news of her appointment.

The same day, the Court learned, to its profound astonishment, that, without demanding any compensation whatever, Madame de Mailly had resigned her post of *dame du palais*, with the salary and privileges attached to it, in favour of Madame de Flavacourt, This generous act, which was quite beyond the comprehension of the selfish and calculating courtiers, and was, indeed, to prove a species of suicide, was the work of

Richelieu. Having succeeded in ingratiating himself with the poor lady, who possessed all the virtues of a dupe, the astute nobleman had drawn such a touching picture of the gratitude of this sister, who had no *locus standi* at the Court, if she were to surrender to her her post, and of the admiration which the King would entertain for a mistress capable of such generosity and nobility of soul, that he had experienced little difficulty in persuading her to this fatal step.

His object, which was, of course, perfectly clear to those who, like Fleury and Maurepas, had already divined the game he was playing, was as follows:

Richelieu knew that Madame de la Tournelle was a very proud woman, who would certainly not tolerate even the suspicion of a divided empire, and that, unless her eldest sister were not only discarded by the King, but banished from the Court, she would refuse to take her place in the royal affections. But, so long as Madame de Mailly retained her post as *dame du palais* to the Queen, Louis XV. could not well order her to leave the Court, except for some really grave offence, since her official position protected her. It was, therefore, of the utmost importance to lure her into casting aside her only safeguard against the King's ingratitude.

Madame de Mailly's friends made great efforts to persuade her to withdraw her resignation, but the favourite persisted in her resolution; and on September 21 the Court saw her, accompanied by Mesdames de la Tournelle and de Flavacourt, going to thank the King and Queen for what their Majesties had done for them.

## CHAPTER XII

The King hopelessly enamoured of Madame de la Tournelle, who, however, declines to respond to the royal advances, being herself in love with Richelieu's nephew, the Duc d'Agénois—Ruse by which Richelieu succeeds in putting an end to this affair—Diplomatic conduct of Madame de la Tournelle—Richelieu persuades Louis XV. that Madame de la Tournelle will remain obdurate so long as her elder sister remains at Court—Madame de Mailly leaves Versailles for Paris, and receives orders not to return—Madame de la Tournelle formulates her terms of surrender—Her letter to Richelieu—Visit of the King to Choisy—Means by which Madame de la Tournelle seeks to inflame his Majesty's passion and persuade him to accord the "brilliant conditions" she demands—Return of Richelieu from Flanders—Madame de la Tournelle, having secured the acceptance of her terms, surrenders—Departure of Richelieu for Languedoc—His travelling-carriage—Fate of Madame de Mailly.

SO far, Richelieu and his confederates had every reason to congratulate themselves on the success of their odious schemes. Madame de la Tournelle was installed at the Court; she had obtained a post which brought her into daily contact with the King, and the only obstacle to the banishment of Madame de Mailly, whenever his Majesty should be pleased to desire it, had been removed.

But, though much had been done, much more remained to be accomplished. In the first place, the admiration which Louis already entertained for Madame de la Tournelle must be transformed into an ardent passion; in the second, Madame de la Tournelle must be persuaded to accept the King's propositions, when he should be prepared to make them, to assure which it would first be necessary to cure her of a most unfortunate infatuation, which, by the irony of Fate, she had been so foolish as to conceive for Richelieu's nephew, the fascinating

Duc d'Agénois;[1] and, in the third, Madame de Mailly must be not only discarded but banished from the Court.

The first task was not difficult; in fact, it was fatally easy. With good reason had Louis XV. exclaimed when he saw Madame de la Tournelle that spring day at Petit-Bourg: "*Mon Dieu! qu'elle est belle!*" Her beauty was, indeed, incontestable; a complexion of lilies and roses, beautiful blue eyes, a pretty mouth, a charming smile, rippling masses of blonde hair, a perfect shape, and a graceful and dignified carriage. In a week, she had become a regular guest at the *petits soupers;* in a fortnight, the King was hopelessly enamoured, and thought only of possessing this peerless creature.

Then Richelieu turned his attention to Madame de la Tournelle, and painted for her an alluring picture of the power and influence which she would enjoy as the favourite of the King. His Majesty, he told her, was ready to fall at her feet; all he required was a little encouragement.

The lady, however, declined to give it. She was intensely ambitious and very far from insensible to the advantages which the exalted position which his Majesty was apparently so anxious to offer her would bring with it; but she was sincerely attached to d'Agénois, and not yet prepared to surrender him, even for a King. She told herself that the Court was no place for sentiment, when it ran counter to interest, and endeavoured to put him out of her thoughts; but somehow the young man continued to occupy them.

Richelieu, however, came to her aid. He sent his inconvenient nephew to Languedoc, where a lady of disturbing beauty was instructed to lay siege to his heart, a great position in Paris being promised her in the event of success. The provinces offered but few diversions in those days to the gilded youth of Versailles, and the unsuspicious d'Agénois, thinking it a pity to refuse so agreeable a means of passing the time as this

[1] Emmanuel Armand de Vignerot du Plessis-Richelieu (1720-1782), son of Armand Louis de Vignerot du Plessis-Richelieu, Duc d'Aiguillon. Under this title, to which he succeeded on the death of his father in 1750, he played an important, if not very creditable, part during the last years of Louis XV.'s reign, and became Minister for Foreign Affairs in June 1771.

affair promised, fell into the trap which his uncle had so skilfully baited for him, and wrote his inamorata a number of very tender epistles. These the fair Languedoçienne despatched to Richelieu, who carried them in triumph to the King, who, in his turn, laid them before Madame de la Tournelle, with some jesting observation about the fidelity of the handsome d'Agénois; and the lady, indignant at her lover's perfidy, soon ceased to think anything more about him, except to get back the letters which he had had from her.

Nevertheless, she still pretended not to understand the somewhat timid advances that his Majesty made her, and remained distant, cold, and almost haughty. Louis was in despair, and implored Richelieu to intercede for him. But the duke replied that his Majesty had been under a complete misapprehension in supposing that Madame de la Tournelle was one of those ladies who would be ready to fall into his arms on the slightest provocation; that she was a woman of an altogether different stamp—one who required to be wooed and conquered; that this was a kind of conquest which the King's generals would be unable to make for him, and that he very much feared that, unless his Majesty took his courage in both hands and did his wooing in person, she would never be his.[1]

As the result of this conversation, Louis grew a trifle bolder, ogled the object of his desires bravely at the *petits soupers*, and even went the length of paying her evening visits in the company of Richelieu. But, though the ice showed some signs of giving way, the hoped-for thaw was evidently still a long way off.

Then Richelieu told the impatient monarch that there was an obstacle in the way of his happiness, the removal of which, however, was entirely in his own hands. This obstacle, it is needless to say, was Madame de Mailly, the faithful mistress whose affection for her royal lover was proof against all his coldness and all his neglect, who asked only to be allowed to adore him. As long, said the duke, as Madame de Mailly

[1] *Mémoires du duchesse de Brancas*, cited by E. and J. de Goncourt, *la Duchesse de Châteauroux et ses sœurs*.

remained at Versailles, as long as the least doubt existed that the connection had not been definitely severed, so long would the King sigh in vain for Madame de la Tournelle. But let him publicly discard the elder sister, let him order her to withdraw from Court, and, if he (Richelieu) knew anything of women, the younger would very speedily capitulate. For a little time, Louis hesitated. Bad as he was, he was not yet entirely without sense of shame, not yet wholly indifferent to what his subjects might say of him; and he knew that Madame de Mailly's conduct since her elevation had won her the reluctant esteem even of those who had most deplored her fall. Moreover, if he had long ceased to love her, he was still, in his selfish way, attached to her. A creature of habit—no man was ever more so—he liked to see about him faces to which he had grown accustomed; he liked to know that there was a woman near at hand who was used to his ways, who was ever ready to lend a sympathetic ear to his troubles, in whose presence he need never feel awkward or constrained. For these reasons, although he was only too willing to discard Madame de Mailly as a mistress, he wished to keep her as a friend.

But Richelieu knew that his candidate was not the woman to be satisfied with half-measures; besides which, he bore Madame de Mailly a grudge, and was determined, like Shylock, to feed it fat. Nothing, he told the King, but the disgrace of her predecessor in his affections would persuade Madame de la Tournelle to listen to his Majesty's propositions. In vain Louis pleaded that his royal word that all was at an end between him and Madame de Mailly, and that henceforth she would be to him nothing but a friend, ought to be enough even for this imperious beauty. Richelieu shrugged his shoulders, spread out his hands, expressed deep regret that the lady should prove so very exacting, but declared his conviction that she meant what she said.

And so poor Madame de Mailly had to go. On October 23, Richelieu set out to join the army of Flanders, leaving Madame de Tencin to complete the work which he had begun; at seven o'clock in the evening of November 3, Madame de Mailly quitted Versailles, "dismissed a little more harshly than an Opera-girl,"[1] and withdrew to Paris, where the Comtesse de Toulouse had placed part of her hôtel at her disposal.

"Great news!" writes d'Argenson, two days later, "the King has dismissed Madame de Mailly, in order to take her sister, Madame de la Tournelle. This was done with a harshness difficult to understand in a most Christian Majesty; it is the sister who has driven the sister away; and this third sister taken for mistress makes people believe that Madame de Vintimille was mistress also, which seems to prove that we have a vicious master."

They certainly had, though d'Argenson is in error in supposing that Madame de la Tournelle had already surrendered to the King. "The King," writes the Duc de Luynes, "continues to go every evening to see Madame de la Tournelle, and stays there two or three hours. He goes there, according to what people say, alone, and with a long peruke over his *papillotes*, and a cloak. We are assured, however, that there is nothing settled. It appears that she would not be annoyed if one spoke to him of all this; people pretend that she demands brilliant conditions, which the King is very reluctant to accord; but he is extremely enamoured."[2]

These brilliant conditions were the position of *maîtresse déclarée*, on the same footing as Madame de Montespan; a settled income sufficient to enable her to maintain that dignity and secure her against any reverse of fortune; the privilege,

[1] This is not quite correct. Madame de Mailly was not ordered by Louis XV. to leave Versailles. She did so voluntarily, having been persuaded by Madame de la Tournelle, who pretended to be greatly grieved and embarrassed at the transference of the royal affections from her sister to herself, and by other false friends, that her departure would rekindle the King's love for her; and, in fact, Louis, on taking leave of her, said: "Till Monday." (The day she left was a Saturday.) But the following day the King sent orders to her not to return to Court.

"Madame de Mailly is still in Paris," writes the Duc de Luynes on the Tuesday; "the King's carriage which conveyed her thither is still there. The King writes to her almost every day, and she replies; but it is believed that it is to order her to remain in Paris, and it is thought that this is the first condition which Madame de la Tournelle has exacted." *Cf.* the letter of Madame de la Tournelle to Richelieu, p. 148, *infra*.

[2] *Mémoires*, November 6, 1742.

when she happened to be in need of money, of drawing bills upon the Treasury; letters patent raising her to the rank of duchess, and the legitimation of her children, if she had any. Such were the terms on which the lady would condescend to accept the love of the King; but, first of all, she required a positive assurance that Madame de Mailly's dismissal was a final one, and that she would never again pass the portals of the palace where she had once reigned almost as Queen.

And here is a letter which she wrote to Richelieu a few days after her sister's departure from Versailles—a letter wherein the woman paints, so to speak, a full-length portrait of herself, and which for cynicism, ingratitude, and absolute heartlessness, it would indeed be difficult to equal. For which reasons, it merits to be given at length:

"I have shown the King your letters, which diverted him; he assured me that he never told Madame de Mailly that it was you who had managed the affair, but only that he had acquainted you with the fact, and that you had accompanied him on his visits to me. You can well believe that a great many stories will be afloat. You have only to maintain always that you had no knowledge of the affair until it was far advanced; this will also be convenient for me. I do not wish to have the appearance of having sought for this advantage, nor my friends for me, as we neither of us thought of it.

"Assuredly Meuse[1] will have told you of all the trouble which I have had to make Madame de Mailly pack off (*déguerpir*); at length, I got him [the King] to write that she was not to return unless invited. You think, perhaps, that the affair is concluded? Not at all; the fact is that he [the King] is overcome with grief, that he never writes me a letter without speaking to me about her, and that he begs me to make her come back, saying that he will not *approach* her, but that he asks to be allowed to see her occasionally. I have at this

[1] Henri Louis de Choiseul, Marquis de Meuse. He was an intimate friend of Richelieu, and a great favourite of Louis XV., and played a prominent part in this shameful affair.

moment received a letter from him, in which he says that, if I refuse him, I shall shortly be relieved both of her and of him, meaning apparently that they will both die of grief. As it would never suit me that she should return, *I intend to hold out.* As *I have entered into no engagement*, at which, I admit to you, that I am very pleased, he will have to decide between her and me. I foresee, dear uncle, that all this will give me much pain. So long as the Cardinal [Fleury] lives, I shall never be able to do anything I like. This has inspired me with a desire to take the old scoundrel into my interests, by going to see him. This appearance of confidence might perhaps gain him over to my side. It deserves reflection. As you may conceive, every one is on the watch, and all eyes are turned upon the King and myself. As for the Queen, you may well understand that she glares at me like a dog; it is the law of the game. I am going to tell you the ladies who are going to Choisy: Mlle. de la Roche-sur-Yon, Mesdames de Luynes, de Chevreuse, d'Antin, de Flavacourt, and your very humble servant. He did not even dare to go to Choisy; it is I who told him that I wished it. No one will lodge in the apartment of Madame de Mailly; I shall be in that which is called yours, that is to say, if M. du Bordage[1] has any intelligence, for the King will give him no orders on the subject. He [the King] must have written to you that *the business between us is settled* because he tells me in his letter of this morning to undeceive you. It is true that, when he wrote to you, he counted that it would be for this evening; but I have raised some difficulties as to execution, of which I do not repent."[2]

On November 12, Louis went to Choisy, and Madame de la Tournelle was one of those who accompanied him. On arriving there, she was allotted the bedchamber of *Mademoiselle*, on the second story of the château and adjoining that of Madame de Mailly, which was known as the "*chambre bleue*," because it was

[1] René Amaury de Montbourcher, Marquis du Bordage. He was, at this time, fulfilling the duties of governor of Choisy, during the absence of the Comte de Coigny on active service.

[2] E. and J. de Goncourt, *la Duchesse de Châteauroux et ses sœurs*.

upholstered and decorated entirely in blue and white. The "*chambre bleue*," which remained unoccupied during this visit, communicated with the King's bedchamber on the floor below by a private staircase, which enabled his Majesty to have access to it without being observed. This arrangement did not suit the plan of the marchioness, which was to inflame the passion of the King by an affectation of indifference, in order that she might the more easily persuade him to accede to her terms.

At supper, according to the Duc de Luynes, who was one of those present, Madame de Tournelle "wore a slightly embarrassed air and scarcely spoke at all"; and, so soon as the company rose from table, approached the Duchesse de Chevreuse, who, as the youngest lady of the party, had been given a small room on the floor above her own, drew her into a corner, and asked her if she would exchange rooms with her, as she was "unable to endure large apartments." The duchess replied that she would exchange rooms very willingly, if the King expressed a desire for her to do so, but that otherwise she felt bound to remain where she was, and, though she was assured by Madame de la Tournelle and her friend and confidant, the Marquis de Meuse, that the King would approve of the exchange, she persisted in declaring that it was impossible for her to consent without knowing his Majesty's intentions.[1]

That night, when all the château had retired to rest, the King ascended the private staircase, with the intention of paying his fair guest a surprise visit. But he found her door securely bolted, and, though he scratched gently for some time, it remained closed to him.

Next morning, Madame de la Tournelle, with the object of still further piquing her royal admirer, persuaded Du Bordage to cause the doors of the ante-chamber leading from the "*chambre bleue*" to her own room to be locked, which put an effectual stop to further nocturnal excursions on the part of his Majesty, since to gain the apartment of his beloved, it would have been necessary for him to pass through that of the Duc d'Antin, or along the balcony of Madame de Flavacourt's room.

[1] *Mémoires du duc de Luynes*, November 17, 1742.

Madame de la Tournelle did not fail to communicate what had passed at Choisy to her counsellor-in-chief, Richelieu, who, fearing lest the policy that she was pursuing might have the opposite effect to that intended, and, instead of forcing the King to agree to her conditions, cause him to abandon the pursuit in despair, deemed it necessary to write her a sharp letter of remonstrance. To which the lady replied:

"Versailles, Tuesday, 3 a.m.

"I am not surprised, my dear uncle, at your anger, since I expected it; I do not think it, however, too reasonable, and I fail to see where is the folly which I have committed in courteously declining the little visit. All that can make me repent of it, is that it will increase the desire that he has. That is all I fear. The letter that you have sent me is very beautiful, even too much so. I shall not write it[1] . . . and then it would have the appearance of great eagerness, which, in truth, I do not desire. Try to come and see me; it is absolutely necessary. Good night, I shall tell you nothing more, since I am so sleepy that I can no longer hold my pen. I am, however, sufficiently awake to understand that you would be for surrendering at once. What is amusing, is that you consider it very extraordinary that others should not be altogether so ready. For myself, I felicitate myself upon it, and I am perfectly satisfied with my position. I do not bring so much ardour into this affair as you do, and I am prospering in it.

"Be at ease, dear uncle; all will go well, though not as you would wish it. I am very sorry, but that is impossible for me. Adieu, dear uncle. I deserve that you should have a few caresses for me, considering my fashion of thinking of you. Above everything, have the appearance of knowing nothing, since he [the King] recommends to me an inviolable secrecy."[2]

Richelieu returned from Flanders on November 16, by

[1] This, according to the Goncourts, proves that Richelieu composed the letters which Madame de la Tournelle wrote to the King.

[2] Autograph letter of the Duchesse de Châteauroux, Leber Collection, Bibliothèque de Rouen, published by E. and J. de Goncourt.

which time his astute confederate, by alternately encouraging and repulsing the royal suit, had driven the amorous monarch almost to distraction, and was fast reducing him to a condition of the most abject docility. On the evening of the duke's arrival, he supped with Madame de la Tournelle, and "they had long conversations both before and after supper." [1] In these conversations it was apparently agreed that the lady should continue to keep the King at a distance for some time longer, since it was not until a third visit to Choisy, whither his Majesty preceded on December 9, that, the terms of the capitulation having been settled to her entire satisfaction, she finally surrendered.

"On Sunday," writes the Duc de Luynes, "the King, while in his coach on the way to Choisy, drew from his pocket a snuff-box, which he immediately replaced. On the morrow, this snuff-box was discovered under the pillow of Madame de la Tournelle. She showed it in the morning to M. de Meuse." [2]

Three days later, at nine o'clock in the evening, Richelieu, his work accomplished, started for Languedòc, to preside over the meeting of the Estates. His travelling-carriage was the *dernier cri* in luxury, and contained a regular bedroom and a miniature kitchen, in which three dishes could be prepared at the same time. As the triumph of Madame de la Tournelle meant the triumph of her "dear uncle" likewise, all the courtiers staying at Choisy considered it their duty to assist at his departure. The duke, having undressed in the château, descended the steps in a *robe de chambre*, ordered a warming-pan to be passed through his bed, and then entered the carriage, and settled himself between the sheets before the eyes of the admiring throng, telling his servants to wake him at Lyons.[3]

On December 19, the new *maîtresse en titre*, supremely indifferent to the rain of chansons which was descending upon

[1] Luynes.

[2] Luynes. On this visit, Madame de la Tournelle occupied the "*chambre bleue.*"

[3] Luynes.

her,[1] showed herself at the Opera in a superb toilette, as though anxious to advertise to all Paris the infatuation of the King. By Christmas, she had removed to the new apartment which had been prepared for her, which was that formerly belonging to the Maréchal de Coigny, and wrote to Richelieu that "it suited her very well, and that she was passing there very pleasant days."

As for the deposed favourite, after being at first lodged in an apartment at the Tuilleries, "very depressing and very cold," the King purchased for her a house in the Rue Saint-Thomas-du-Louvre. "It was pointed out to her, some days ago," writes Luynes, "that the house which she was going to occupy was a very gloomy one. She replied that that mattered not at all to her, and that if the King had ordered her to inhabit a prison, it would have been all the same."[2] Following the example of Louise de la Vallière, she sought consolation in religion, and, falling under the influence of the Dominican preacher Père Renaud, "flung herself into a great and estimable devotion."[2] Henceforth until her death Madame de Mailly devoted her whole time and income[3] to good works, reserving for herself scarcely sufficient to procure the bare necessaries of life.

[1] One of these prophesied that it would soon be the turn of the remaining sisters to enjoy the royal favour :

"L'une est presque en oubli, l'autre presque en poussière ;
Le troisième est en pied ; la quatrième attend
Pour faire place à la dernière.
Choisir une famille entière,
Est-ce être infidèle ou constant ?"

[2] Marquis d'Argenson, *Mémoires*.

[3] Louis XV. gave her a pension of 20,000 livres, in addition to one of 12,000 livres which she already had. He also, after some demur, paid her personal debts, which amounted to a very large sum, though most of them had been incurred in entertaining him. He did not therefore treat her so shabbily as some historians have stated.

# CHAPTER XIII

Death of Fleury—Efforts of Richelieu and Madame de Tencin to raise the Cardinal de Tencin to the vacant position of First Minister foiled by Maurepas—Semi-disgrace of Richelieu—Sagacious conduct of Madame de la Tournelle—Impatience of Richelieu and Madame de Tencin at the delay in the realisation of their ambitions—The favourite created Duchesse de Châteauroux—The fifth of the sisters de Nesle, Diane Adélaïde, Duchesse de Lauraguais, appears at Court—Her appearance and character—Her suspicious relations with the King—Skill of Madame de Châteauroux in maintaining her hold upon Louis XV.'s affections—Richelieu distinguishes himself at Dettingen—The King accords him the *premières entrées*—He is appointed First Gentleman of the Chamber—The Régiment de Septimanie—Triumph of the Richelieu-Tencin-Châteauroux coalition—Visit of Frederick the Great's secret envoy Rothenburg to Richelieu—New treaty between France and Prussia—Louis XV. persuaded by Madame de Châteauroux to take the nominal command of the Army of Flanders—Departure of the King for Flanders.

ON January 29, 1743, old Fleury passed away, in his ninetieth year, having clung tenaciously to the reins of power to the very last. For this moment Richelieu and Madame de Tencin had long been preparing, in the hope of raising the lady's brother, who, having blossomed into a cardinal in February 1739, had been appointed a Minister of State in the previous August, to the vacant position of First Minister, and of procuring the disgrace of Maurepas, who had himself designs on his late Eminence's shoes and was the chief obstacle in the path of their ambition. It is quite possible that, with the aid of Madame de la Tournelle, they might have succeeded, if the Minister of Marine, who suspected their intentions, had not had the good fortune to intercept one of the letters which Richelieu addressed almost every day to the favourite, outlining the policy which she was to pursue. In this letter the duke laid down, as one of the conditions of his maintaining Madame de la Tournelle in the exalted position which he had secured for her, the dismissal of the majority of the persons attached to the King. The contents of this epistle were duly communicated to Louis XV., who was highly indignant with Richelieu, and for some little time the duke found himself in a species of disgrace. He was, to his intense disgust, passed over in the next promotion of *maréchaux de camp* to the rank of lieutenant-general; he was not recalled to the Court till the following April, and, when he did return, his request to be allowed to exchange his post in Languedoc for that of governor of Montpellier was refused, or rather ignored.

Madame de la Tournelle, too, found herself involved, to some extent, in the King's resentment against her ally; that is to say, his Majesty forebore to speak of affairs of importance before her, and seemed to be very much on his guard. Altogether, it appeared that, however great might be Louis's affection for his new mistress, he did not intend to permit her to exercise any appreciable influence, and that M. de Richelieu had been a little too sanguine when he had predicted, some months before, that "soon the person who penetrated into the ante-chamber of Madame de la Tournelle would enjoy more consideration than he who, at that moment, was conversing with Madame de Mailly." [1]

The sagacity and tact of the favourite saved the situation. Almost from the moment of her installation she had comprehended that one of the most singular traits in the character of Louis XV. was what the Marquis d'Argenson calls "his dislike of being penetrated," and that he strongly objected to being questioned, even by those whom he had admitted to his intimacy. Weak and indolent as he was, no one would be more easily ruled by a strong and resolute will; but, at the same time, no one would more deeply resent any ostensible attempt to influence him. He who knows not how to dissemble, knows not how to reign had been old Fleury's favourite

[1] *Mémoires du duc de Luynes*, April 20, 1743.

maxim, and he had governed the King and France for seventeen years. If she desired to govern, too, she saw that she must dissemble likewise. And so, to the great disappointment of Richelieu and Madame de Tencin, this imperious, ambitious, and enterprising woman, though hungering for power as a starving man hungers for bread, for many months held aloof from politics, and declined to side with any of the contending Ministers who allowed the armies of France to be driven out of Germany, and her fleets to be swept from the seas, the while they wrangled with and intrigued against one another.[1]

This delay in the realisation of the great hopes they had based on the elevation of Madame de la Tournelle was not at all to the taste of her two principal allies, and Madame de Tencin, in her letters to Richelieu, cannot contain her impatience.

"The King," she writes, "is very attentive to Madame de la Tournelle, who, however, does not obtain any remarkable favour. It is said that she is proud, and does not wish to ask for anything. She is a woman who appears to possess energy, and I believe that, for her interests and ours, it would be very essential that she should form a close connection with my brother. She does not take any side. I am very sorry that you cannot be always here to make her decide upon something."[2]

The favourite was, however, determined to play her own game, and not to be dictated to by Madame de Tencin, whom she regarded as "an extravagant woman," who "saw everything in a microscope." She perceived that she had only to wait her time, and the power and influence she desired would assuredly be hers, for Louis XV., who, in feeble imitation of *le Grand Monarque*, had, after the death of Fleury, announced

[1] "Everything is going from bad to worse, my dear duke," she writes to Richelieu, "although you [the Army of Germany] are fighting like brave men, here, in response to your bravery, we cabal; each one accuses another, and would like to overthrow him, in order to take his place."—*Lettres de la duchesse de Châteauroux au duc de Richelieu.*

[2] *Lettres de Madame de Tencin au duc de Richelieu*, Paris, 1806.

his intention of being his own Prime Minister, had speedily begun to feel the reins of State too heavy for his indolent hands, and would ere long be only too ready to hand them over to one who commanded his entire confidence. And that person she was resolved should be herself.

That she had accurately gauged the situation was soon apparent. In a few weeks, the indolent monarch, who was so absolutely indifferent to the duties of his exalted position that he "only attended the meetings of the Council as a matter of form, signed everything that was put before him, and in every case inclined to the course which promised the least trouble,"[1] came of his own accord to his mistress to lament to her the ennui which affairs of State occasioned him, and to seek her advice. In a few months, he had begun, almost insensibly, to act upon it, for the lady had had the art to divine the personal predilections and prejudices of her royal lover, and upon these she based her policy.

And so slowly but surely her influence increased, and when, at the end of October 1743, Louis XV., notwithstanding the opposition of Maurepas, created her Duchesse de Châteauroux, the Court recognised that a new force had arisen, which even the most favoured Ministers would have to take very seriously into account.

In the meanwhile, the fifth of the sisters de Nesle, Diane Adélaïde, had made her appearance upon the stage of Versailles, where she had already begun to play a very prominent part. This lady, who was at that time known as Mlle. de Montcarvel, had been brought to Court towards the end of the previous year and married to the Duc de Lauraguais, eldest son of the Duc de Brancas. Richelieu had had too large a share in bringing about this match for his motives not to be suspected, and it was the general opinion that, since the de Nesle women seemed to be predestined for the royal love, the duke was protecting himself against the chance of the new arrival one day succeeding her sisters.

[1] Letters of Madame de Tencin to Richelieu, June 22 and August 1, 1743.

By no stretch of imagination could the Duchesse de Lauraguais be pronounced a beauty; in fact, she was distinctly plain, with a figure which made up in circumference what it lacked in height—"*un bon fauteuil*" is the description given of her by the Duc de Luynes. But she was possessed of a ready, if somewhat coarse, wit and an imperturbable good-humour, against which even the ennui of Louis XV. was not proof. Soon the Court saw "*la grosse réjouie*"—as the Marquis de Meuse had baptized her—high in favour and an indispensable guest at the *petits soupers*, and gossip declared, with, it would appear, only too much reason, that his Majesty, not satisfied with the pleasure he derived from the lady's company at these repasts, occasionally invited her to return after the party had dispersed. It added that the favourite had prudently decided to ignore what was going on, so long as she preserved her influence, while Madame de Lauraguais did everything possible to conceal from her sister's knowledge the private audiences with which the King honoured her.

But, whatever may have been Louis XV.'s relations with the elder sister, and there can be very little doubt that, in this instance, rumour did not lie, they had no effect upon the position of Madame de Châteauroux, as we must now call the favourite. For never did favourite comprehend better the character of the man with whom she had to deal. Instead of allowing the King to suppose that the condescension was on his side, she gave him very clearly to understand that she considered the reverse to be the case. She spared him none of the torments of uncertainty which ordinary lovers are called upon to endure, and, if at times she could be all tenderness and sympathy, at others her coldness and indifference were such that he was in mortal terror lest she intended to leave him. She knew, too, how to excite his jealousy, without, however, ever allowing herself to be compromised, and, to show him that, although she was the mistress of a king, she was not insensible to the admiration of lesser men. Finally, she taught him that what he had looked upon as a right, was a favour—nay, a priceless boon—to be accorded or withheld

"LE POINT DU JOUR" (MARIE ANNE DE MAILLY-NESLE, DUCHESSE DE CHÂTEAUROUX)

FROM THE PAINTING BY NATTIER IN THE COLLECTION OF LIONEL PHILLIPS, ESQ.

as the humour took her; and many a time she allowed him to tap unheeded at her chamber-door. By these means she guarded his passion from satiety and kept the flame burning bright; for he could never be sure of her for a moment, and, with some, uncertainty is the breath of love. Years afterwards, when Madame de Pompadour questioned him concerning her predecessors in his affections, he told her that Madame de Châteauroux was the only one whom he had really loved.

And he spoke the truth.

Still hankering after the glory which had, up to the present, eluded his pursuit, though it is only fair to say that he had invariably made the most of the few opportunities for distinction which Fortune had vouchsafed him, Richelieu, in the spring of 1743, joined the army of the Maréchal de Noailles, operating between the Rhine and the Main, and took part in the Battle of Dettingen.

In this celebrated engagement, in which the rashness of the Duc de Gramont ruined the well-laid plans of his uncle, and converted an almost certain victory into a disastrous defeat, Richelieu displayed a courage which was applauded by the whole army, and went some way at least to redeem the despicable part which he had lately played at the Court.

The last day of October saw him once more at Versailles, where, three weeks later, the King accorded to him the coveted *premières entrées*. This mark of the royal favour was only an earnest of a much greater one, which, however, he owed not to his valour on the stricken field, but to the services which he had rendered his sovereign in a very different capacity, and the gratitude which those services had inspired in both Louis and Madame de Châteauroux.

Among the nobles who had fallen at Dettingen, was the Duc de Rochechouart, one of the four First Gentlemen of the Chamber.[1] Rochechouart had left a little son, four years of age, for whom he had secured the reversion of his office; but

[1] The other three First Gentlemen were the Ducs de Fleury, de Gesvres, and de la Trémoille.

on December 18, 1743 the child died. Several candidates immediately presented themselves, each of whom could adduce more or less substantial reasons why the post should be accorded him. The Duc de Saint-Aignan could point to the fact that both his father and brother had possessed it; that he had lost by the death of the Duc de Berry his place as First Gentleman of the Chamber to that prince; that he had served in many campaigns and had shed his blood for his Majesty; that he had been his Majesty's representative for four years at Madrid and for ten at Rome, and, finally, that "his affairs were greatly deranged." The Duc de Châtillon, the Dauphin's *gouverneur*, could urge that that prince would soon be of age, when his duties would terminate, and his handsome salary with them, and that it was only just that his services in the education of his Royal Highness should be suitably recompensed. The Duc de Luxembourg pretended that the King, during the favour of Madame de Mailly, had given him a written promise, or, at any rate, something which could be construed into a promise, that he should be given the first vacancy. The Duc de la Trémoille was of opinion that, as he himself was a First Gentleman of the Chamber, his Majesty could not do better than appoint his son one also.[1]

The chances of the various candidates were eagerly discussed, but the best informed of the quidnuncs were of opinion that M. de Richelieu had claims far superior, in the royal eyes at least, to those of his competitors, and that the honour of removing his Majesty's boots and serving him at table would certainly be his.

They were right, and on December 27 Luynes writes in his journal:

"We were informed yesterday, after the *coucher* of the King, that the post of First Gentleman of the Chamber had been given to the Duc de Richelieu, who is at present holding the Estates of Languedoc, at Montpellier. The King had certainly made his decision immediately after the death of the little Duc de la Rochechouart; and the reason why the favour

[1] *Mémoires du duc de Luynes*, December 23, 1743.

was not announced for several days, is that his Majesty did not wish M. de Richelieu to learn the news except by the courier whom he has sent to him, and who only started on the 24th." [1]

And so Richelieu found himself preferred to the Saint-Aignans, the Châtillons, the Luxembourgs, and the La Trémoilles, and in possession of a post which gave its occupant the privilege of access to the King at any hour and assured him great influence at the Court. Early in February, he returned to Versailles, and on the 14th of the month took the oath on assuming his new duties. The same morning, he waited on the King at his *lever*, and a week later served him for the first time at table.[2]

Before leaving Languedoc, Richelieu had rendered a real service to the King. The popularity which he enjoyed with the Estates—a popularity which had been enhanced by his espousing their cause in one of their periodical quarrels with the Parlement of Toulouse—had enabled him to persuade them to raise and equip a regiment of dragoons which was to be maintained at the expense of the province. The colonelcy of the new corps, which was subsequently named the Régiment de Septimanie, was given by Louis XV. to Richelieu's little son, the Duc de Fronsac, the Marquis de Nogaret being appointed to command it until the duke was old enough to take his place at its head.[3]

The early spring of 1744 found the Châteauroux-Richelieu-Tencin coalition triumphant at Versailles—not quite so triumphant as it intended to be a little later, when the ship of State should have weathered the storm, and certain prominent members of the crew, Maurepas, needless to say, amongst them, might be conveniently dropped overboard ; but still sufficiently to cause their enemies serious anxiety, and to bring some very flattering

[1] Faure, in his *Vie privée du maréchal de Richelieu*, asserts that he had seen the letter written by Louis XV., in which he said that the "Princess" [Madame de Châteauroux] had demanded the post for him.

[2] On the 16th, he had accompanied the King and "the three sisters" to la Muette, where there was a good deal of high play, "at which M. de Richelieu, who is in good luck, as admits of no doubt, won largely."

[3] *Mémoires du duc de Luynes*, February 22, 1744.

testimony to the influence they wielded from a high foreign quarter.

When, in March, Frederick the Great sent the Graf von Rothenburg to Paris, it was to Richelieu that the secret envoy first addressed himself, and it was the Cardinal de Tencin, who, under the direction of the duke and the favourite, drew up the terms of the new treaty between Potsdam and Versailles, which was to create so fortunate a diversion on the Rhine and permit Louis XV. to make with a tranquil mind his military promenade to Flanders.

For, whatever their faults, the members of the confederacy did not lack energy and enterprise; indeed, as Carlyle himself admits, in comparison with some of the King's Ministers, they were quite able persons. As the letters of Madame de Tencin to Richelieu prove, both she and her brother were fully alive to the hideous incompetence which had characterised the conduct of the war, both by land and sea, and believed that the surest road to the power which they aspired to monopolise was by persuading Louis XV. to take the field in person and place himself at the head of armies. "It is not," writes she, "that, between ourselves, he is fit to command a company of grenadiers, but his presence will do much. The people love their King through habit, and will be overjoyed to see him take a step which will have been suggested to him. His troops will do their duty better, and the generals will not dare to fail so openly in theirs. In fact, this idea appears to me excellent, and it is the only way to continue the war with less disadvantage. The King, whatever he may be, is for the soldiers and the people what the Ark of the Covenant was for the Hebrews; his presence alone foretells success." [1]

And the success of the campaign would certainly be followed by the complete triumph of the writer and her allies, for Louis, flattered by victories which the sycophants who surrounded him would attribute to his genius, would henceforth place his entire confidence in those who had had the wit to point out to him

[1] Madame de Tencin to Richelieu, July 24, 1743, *Lettres de Madame de Tencin au duc de Richelieu*, Paris, 1806.

the path to glory. This scheme found a zealous supporter in Madame de Châteauroux, "who possessed that natural loftiness of sentiment which sometimes survives the fall of moral principles in energetic minds."[1] Since the King had made her a Montespan, she thought that it would be a fine thing to make him a Louis XIV., and she accordingly lost no opportunity of urging him to earn the applause of his subjects and the admiration of Europe by appearing at the head of his army.

Her task was no easy one, for the apathetic monarch could be obstinate enough when it was a question of displaying the smallest degree of activity, and he offered a stubborn resistance. "You are killing me with all this energy," he exclaimed plaintively one day, when his mistress was striving to arouse in him some sense of the responsibilities of his position. "So much the better," was the reply; "we must have the resurrection of a king." She did resuscitate him, in fact, since she was the first woman who had succeeded in inspiring Louis with something beyond the intoxication of the senses; and at a quarter past three on the morning of May 4, 1744, the King left Versailles to take the nominal command of the army destined for the conquest of Flanders.

[1] Henri Martin, *Histoire de France.*

# CHAPTER XIV

Fall of Amelot, Minister for Foreign Affairs, engineered by the coalition in conjunction with Rothenburg—Nomination of Madame de Châteauroux to be *Surintendante* of the Household of the Dauphine-elect—Mesdames de Châteauroux and de Lauraguais follow the King to Flanders—Unfortunate impression created by the arrival of his Majesty's fair friends at Lille—"Madame Enroux"—Louis XV. sets out with the army for Alsace, taking the ladies with him—Madame de Châteauroux falls ill at Rheims, but soon recovers, and joins the King at Metz—Cabal formed by Maurepas against the favourite—A wooden gallery constructed at Metz, to connect the royal quarters with those of the duchesses, creates a grave scandal—Serious illness of the King—Mesdames de Châteauroux and de Lauraguais install themselves at the royal bedside, and Richelieu refuses to admit the grand officers of the Crown and the Princes of the Blood to the sick-room—The Comte de Clermont forces his way in—Interview between Richelieu and the favourite, and the King's confessor, Père Pérusseau—The King growing worse, the Bishop of Soissons enjoins him to confess—Dismissal of Mesdames de Châteauroux and de Lauraguais insisted on as a condition of absolution being accorded—Conduct of the Bishop of Soissons—Flight of the ladies from Metz—Recovery of Louis XV. after his life has been despaired of—Richelieu exiles himself to Basle, where he intrigues for the restoration of Madame de Châteauroux—His memoir to the King—Louis XV. returns to Versailles, and Madame de Châteauroux is recalled—Her death.

THE departure of Louis XV. for Flanders had been preceded by two notable triumphs for the favourite and her friends. The first was the dismissal of Amelot, the Minister for Foreign Affairs, a passive instrument of their chief enemy, which, as the delighted Madame de Tencin expressed it, was "to put out one of Maurepas's eyes." The pretext for the dismissal of Amelot was his failure to inform the King of the existence of certain letters, written by Frederick of Prussia to Louis XV. previous to his desertion of his allies in Bohemia in 1742, which had been received by Fleury, who had suppressed them and forbidden Amelot to speak of them. What purported to be copies of these letters were shown to the King by Rothenburg, who intimated that his master had been greatly irritated by not receiving a reply from his Majesty. There can be no doubt that the business had been arranged between the envoy and the favourite's party, who had demanded as the price of their support the dismissal of Amelot, and that the so-called copies differed very materially from the original letters; but Louis XV.'s vanity was deeply wounded, and, at the instigation of Madame de Châteauroux, who declared that an impediment in his speech from which the Minister suffered always caused her great annoyance, he promptly informed him that he had no further need of his services.

It was rumoured that Richelieu was to succeed him, and no doubt that personage considered that he had every qualification for the post. But the favourite having inspired the King with a desire to emulate his brother of Prussia, his Majesty announced that he intended henceforth to conduct his Foreign Affairs himself. He did so, in fact, for a week or two, with the assistance of Du Theil, the *introducteur* of the Ambassadors; but was soon glad to relinquish them into the hands of the Comte d'Argenson, pending the appointment of his elder brother, the marquis, in the following November.[1]

The second triumph was the nomination of Madame Châteauroux to be *Surintendante* of the Household of the Dauphine-elect[2]—a post which had been specially created for her benefit. The Duchesse de Lauraguais was appointed *dame d'atour* and most of the ladies-in-waiting were selected from among the friends and *protegées* of the favourite. Never, in fact, had the credit of Madame de Châteauroux stood higher; never had

[1] The two d'Argensons must be carefully distinguished. The elder brother, René Louis de Voyer de Paulmy, Marquis d'Argenson, the author of the famous *Mémoires*, was Minister for Foreign Affairs from November 1744 to January 1747; the younger, Marc René de Voyer de Paulmy, Comte d'Argenson, became Secretary of State for War in 1743, and held that office until February 1757.

[2] The Infanta Maria Theresa, daughter of Philip V. of Spain, and Elizabeth Farnese. She was married to the Dauphin in February 1745, and died on June 22, 1746.

the position of the Richelieu-Tencin party seemed so strong, as on the day when, amid the acclamations of Court and people, Louis XV. set out for Flanders.

Richelieu, whom the King had appointed one of his aides-de-camp, and who, at the beginning of June, was promoted to the rank of lieutenant-general, accompanied his Majesty ; Mesdames de Châteauroux and de Lauraguais—"*les vivandières*," as Madame de Mailly sarcastically named them—followed, after a discreet interval.

The favourite had been strongly advised by her friend, the Maréchal de Noailles, to renounce her intention of following the King to the wars, as such a course was contrary to all precedent and "would not be conformable to her true interests." It was, of course, the fact that Mesdames de la Vallière and de Montespan had both followed Louis XIV. in his campaigns, but they had gone in attendance upon the Queen, and passed most of the time that *le Grand Monarque* was winning what he imagined to be glory with her Majesty in some town on the frontier, and Louis XV. had decided to leave his long-suffering consort behind, "since the expense prevented him from taking her with him."[1] "I cannot prevent myself from telling you," writes the old courtier, "that both the King and yourself must have some plausible reason to give, to justify in the eyes of the public the course which you propose to take."

However, Madame de Châteauroux was too much afraid of leaving her royal lover exposed to the machinations of her enemies, and Louis XV. was too anxious to have the lady with him, for them to find this prudent counsel palatable ; and Richelieu and the Tencins, learning that Maurepas was urging the King to leave the duchess behind, scented danger, and decided that, come what may, his Majesty must not be separated from his mistress. And so precedent and public opinion were alike disregarded, and on June 11 the favourite and her under-study rejoined the King at Lille, and were lodged in a house adjoining that of the governor, where Louis XV. had taken up his quarters.

[1] Luynes.

Up to this moment Louis had been extremely popular, both with the army and the people, for he could play the King in public excellently well when he cared to take the trouble. The appearance of the two duchesses upon the scene, however, produced a most unfortunate impression. The Flemings were scandalized, d'Argenson tells us, and when, two hours after the ladies' arrival, the barracks caught fire, they declared that it was a manifestation of the celestial anger. As for the troops, who were neither prudish nor superstitious, they appear to have regarded the presence of his Majesty's fair friends as an insult to their enforced celibacy, and the soldiers of the Swiss Guards might be heard singing beneath the windows of the favourite a song which some years before had been very popular in Paris:

> "Ah! madame Enroux,
> Je deviendrai fou,
> Si je ne vous baise."

This refrain was soon caught up by the townsfolk, who, not having the same need for circumspection as the soldiers, did not hesitate to substitute "*belle Châteauroux*" for "Madame Enroux."[1]

The opinion of Paris was as unfavourable as that of the provinces and the army; and, as the King, the ladies, and even Richelieu himself deemed it prudent to make a pretence of surrendering to so universal a condemnation, Louis reluctantly separated from Madame de Châteauroux and went off to the siege of Ypres.

On June 25, Ypres shared the fate which had already befallen Courtrai, Menin, and other places, and the King, after making a sort of triumphal progress through the principal towns of Flanders, rejoined his mistress at Dunkerque. There, however, the alarming news was received that Prince Charles of Lorraine at the head of an army of 63,000 men had completely outmanœuvred the old Maréchal de Coigny, crossed the Rhine at four different points, and was overrunning Alsace. Upon this, the King announced his intention

[1] Marquis d'Argenson, *Mémoires*.

of going in person to repel the invaders of his realm, and, having detached Maurice de Saxe with 45,000 men to secure their recent conquests and hold the feeble forces of the Allies in check, marched southwards with Noailles and the main body of the army, leaving most of his baggage behind, but taking the two duchesses with him (July 19).

In every town at which the King halted, the Grand Maréchal des Logis, the Comte de la Suze, who preceded the army, had orders to secure a house for the reception of Madame de Châteauroux adjoining that of the King and to open communications between her apartment and his Majesty's;[1] and the people were thus afforded the edifying spectacle of their King living with his mistress with scarcely any attempt at concealment.

At Rheims, the favourite fell ill of an "*ébullition*," which the courtiers maliciously attributed to remorse at the news that her old lover d'Agénois had been dangerously wounded in Italy. "His Majesty could speak of nothing else but the malady of Madame de Châteauroux, except where he should bury her, and what kind of tomb he should erect to her memory."[2]

The "*ébullition*" of his mistress detained the King for a day at Rheims, when he pushed on to Châlons, and thence to Metz, where he was soon joined by Madame de Châteauroux, whose cure had no doubt been precipitated by his departure and the knowledge that no one but Richelieu and Meuse stood between his Majesty and the machinations of a very formidable cabal, which had been recently formed against her by her arch-enemy Maurepas.

When Louis XV. set out for Flanders, Maurepas had requested permission to follow him; but the favourite and her friends had persuaded the King that the dockyards and fortifications on the coast of Provence were in a condition which demanded immediate attention, and the Minister of Marine had been sent thither on a tour of inspection, which, it

[1] "The workmen were seen piercing the walls, and every one knew for what purpose."—*Vie privée de Louis XV.*

[2] Marquis d'Argenson, *Mémoires.*

was hoped, would keep him employed for some months. However, Maurepas was a gentleman of infinite resource, at least where his own interests were concerned—about his administration of the Navy the less said the better—and, travelling night and day, he completed his tour in a surprisingly short space of time, and, to the intense chagrin of Madame de Châteauroux and Richelieu, joined the King at Dunkerque.

Here he immediately began to intrigue actively against the favourite, and swept into his net, among a number of more or less distinguished persons, the Ducs de Chartres,[1] de Bouillon,[2] and de La Rochefoucauld,[3] and the austere James Fitz-James, Bishop of Soissons, First Almoner to Louis XV.,[4] who was particularly horrified by the presence of the King's mistress in the camp. The object of the cabal seems to have been to give as much publicity as possible to his Majesty's "goings on," in order to inflame popular resentment against him, bring home to him the enormity of his conduct, and thus cause the downfall of the favourite.

At Metz, the scandal reached its height, for M. de la Suze, with the laudable intention of concealing his master's visits to the duchesses from the vulgar gaze, caused a wooden gallery to be constructed, to connect the royal lodging with the Abbey of Saint-Arnould, three streets away, where Madame de Châteauroux and her sister were quartered. This arrangement greatly scandalized the people, since "its purpose was very obvious." [5]

However, the good people of Metz soon had something more serious to talk about, for, on the morning of Saturday,

[1] Louis Philippe d'Orléans, eldest son of the Duc d'Orléans, first Prince of the Blood.

[2] Charles Godefroy de la Tour d'Auvergne, Grand Chamberlain.

[3] Alexander de la Rochefoucauld, Grand Master of the Wardrobe.

[4] He was the son of the Duke of Berwick, most of whose dignities he had renounced in order to enter the priesthood. As head of his family, he had retained, however, the title of Duc de Fitz-James. He was a rigid Jansenist and the author of several theological works.

[5] "The prior of Saint-Arnould was the only person who thought differently. He piously believed that it was a proof of the King's devotion, to enable him to come under cover into his house, and thence to the church."—Luynes.

August 8, after a day spent in visiting the fortifications under a blazing sun, and a night of wine, love, and song, his Most Christian Majesty awoke in a high fever,[1] which offered so stubborn a resistance to all the bleedings, purgings, and emetics to which his physicians had recourse, that they soon became seriously alarmed.

Then began an extraordinary scene, which, however, was to have its parallel thirty years later, when Louis XV. lay on what proved to be his death-bed, and wherein one of the chief actors in the drama of Metz was again to play a prominent *rôle*.[2]

From the moment when the King was taken ill, Richelieu and the two duchesses established themselves at his bedside, where, taking advantage of his office of First Gentleman of the Chamber, which gave him absolute control over his Majesty's domestics, the duke, for four days, refused to permit any one but the doctors, La Peyronie [3] and Chicoyneau, and the *valets de chambre* and aides-de-camp,[4] all of whom belonged to the party of the favourite, to approach the sick man. The Princes of the Blood [5] and the grand officers of the Crown were admitted at the hour of Mass, but ordered to withdraw immediately the service was over.

Acting upon Richelieu's instructions, La Peyronie and Chicoyneau concealed the gravity of the King's illness from the anxious courtiers, and, in response to the demands of the princes for a public consultation, declared that there was not the smallest cause for alarm. At their consultations, Richelieu alone assisted, and, though it was the undoubted privilege of Bouillon, as Grand Chamberlain, to be present, he was rigorously

[1] "After the supper, the Duc de Richelieu shut the King up with the two sisters. This was the cause of the fever and the headache."—Barbier.

[2] See p. 300 *et seq.*, *infra*.

[3] François Gigot de la Peyronie, First Surgeon to the King.

[4] The King's aides-de-camp were the Prince de Soubise, the Ducs de Richelieu, de Boufflers, de Luxembourg, d'Ayen, d'Aumont, and Picquigny, and the Marquis de Meuse.

[5] The Princes of the Blood at Metz were the Duc de Chartres, the Comte de Clermont, and the Duc de Penthièvre, but the latter was ill and unable to leave his quarters.

excluded. The grand officers complained bitterly of not being allowed to discharge their functions, and the princes were equally indignant at the duke's refusal to admit them to the sick-room, which their rank entitled them to enter. But the cool effrontery of Richelieu was proof against all their expostulations; and when, on the 12th, they represented to Madame de Châteauroux that propriety and custom both required that they should be admitted, the lady replied that, "if these two principles were adhered to, she herself would not have the right of remaining in the King's chamber."

Upon this, the Comte de Clermont, who was something of a favourite with his royal cousin, forced his way into the room and, going up to the bed, told the King that "he could not believe that it was his Majesty's intention that the Princes of the Blood who were at Metz should be deprived of the satisfaction of learning news of him themselves; that they had no desire that their presence should incommode him, but only to have the liberty of entering for a few moments, and that, to prove that, for his own part, he had no other object, he would withdraw at once." The King, so far from resenting Clermont's boldness, bade him remain, and the customary order was re-established.

The great object of the enemies of the favourite and Richelieu was to induce the King to make his confession, for, in that case, his *directeur*, Pere Pérusseau, albeit a Jesuit of the most subtle kind, would scarcely dare to grant him absolution, unless he were first to dismiss his mistress. Madame de Châteauroux and the duke, aware of this, sent for Pérusseau, and had a long conference with him in a little room adjoining the King's bedchamber, with the object of gaining him over to their side.

The unfortunate Jesuit found himself in a terrible position. If he failed to obtain the dismissal of the favourite, and the King died, he would be driven with ignominy from the Court—that wretched Jansenist of a Bishop of Soissons would see to that; if he did his duty, and the King recovered, his disgrace was equally certain. There he stood, trembling in every limb, like a traveller who has lost his way among the mountains, and finds himself at dead of night upon a narrow path with a bottomless abyss on either hand. Perhaps, said he, the King would take a turn for the better, and confession would not be necessary; perhaps, even if he did confess, he would say nothing about Madame la Duchesse, in which case, he (Pérusseau) should certainly not touch upon so delicate a subject, since, for his part, he did not for one moment believe that there had been anything criminal in her relations with his Majesty. Then he tried to escape, but Richelieu, barring his retreat, begged him to have done with "ifs" and "perhapses" and give them a definite assurance that Madame de Châteauroux should be sent away without scandal. Pérusseau, however, refused to commit himself: to the cajolery of the favourite, the threats of Richelieu, he was alike impervious; and at last they had to let him go.

This interview seems to have taken place on Tuesday the 11th, on which day La Peyronie had felt compelled to admit to the Bishop of Soissons that his Majesty's condition was serious. The following morning, after Mass, the bishop spoke to the King and urged him very strongly to unburden his soul. "The only response of the King was that he was weak, that his head ached terribly, and that he would have a great many things to confess," which we can well believe. M. de Soissons rejoined that, if that were so, he could at any rate make a beginning that day and conclude on the morrow. His Majesty did not appear to see the force of this, but a little incident which occurred later in the day showed that the prelate's words had struck home.

"Madame de Châteauroux being near the King's bed, he took her hand and kissed it. Then, pushing her away, he said to her 'Ah! princess (his pet name for his mistress), I believe that I am in a bad state.' She wished to embrace him; but he refused, saying to her: 'We must part.' To which it is said that she responded very well and in a very proper manner." [1]

The King passed a very bad night, and, though he was bled at seven o'clock the next morning, this operation afforded him

[1] *Mémoires du duc de Luynes*, August 18, 1744.

LOUIS XV

FROM THE PAINTING BY LOUIS MICHEL VAN LOO IN THE BOWES MUSEUM, BARNARD CASTLE

no relief, and during Mass, which was celebrated in the sick-room, he called the Duc de Bouillon, and told him to summon Père Pérusseau.[1] The crucial moment had arrived.

Richelieu and the two duchesses retired into the little cabinet in which the interview with the confessor had taken place two days before, there to await the inevitable *dénoûment*.

It came quickly, and dramatically. The door was flung open; the Bishop of Soissons appeared upon the threshold, and, in a voice which shook the rafters, cried out: "The King commands you, Mesdames, to retire from his presence immediately!" Pérusseau, with the eye of his ecclesiastical superior upon him, had not dared to shirk his duty, and had told his Majesty that it was impossible for him to grant him absolution, unless the duchesses were first dismissed. Louis, with the fear of death and hell heavy upon him, had consented, and banished them fifty leagues from the Court.

Madame de Châteauroux, far greater in her disgrace than she had ever been in her prosperity, received her sentence with an unmoved countenance, and, followed by her sister, immediately quitted the room and the house, and returned to the Abbey of Saint-Arnould, where Richelieu had advised them to remain and await developments. The duke himself proceeded to the ante-chamber, where a violent altercation was in progress between the two factions. His enemies turned fiercely upon him, vowing that, if the King died, he should answer for it with his head; but he laughed at their threats, telling them that the storm would pass and the two sisters return more powerful and more triumphant than ever.

The disgraced ladies were not permitted to remain many hours in Metz. That evening, shortly before Louis XV. was to receive the Viaticum, M. de Soissons was informed that Madame de Châteauroux was still at the Abbey of Saint-Arnould, upon which the implacable prelate requested the Bishop of Metz, with whom he had been acting in concert throughout this affair, to give instructions that the consecrated

[1] "*Mon Bouillon, mon Bouillon, je me meurs, le père Pérusseau, vite le père Pérusseau!*"—Luynes.

elements were not to leave the church "until the cause of so much scandal had ceased to profane the palace and the town." Then he went to the King and told him that "all the laws of the Church and the canons strictly forbade the bringing of the Viaticum while the *concubine* still remained in the town"; and obliged the unfortunate monarch to issue orders for the immediate departure of the ladies.

This departure was attended by considerable personal danger, for the news that the Holy Sacrament had been forbidden to the King, so long as Madame de Châteauroux remained in Metz, had got abroad—very probably, M. de Soissons intended that it should—and enlisted in the cause of the Church the passions of the populace, already inflamed against the favourite. Such, indeed, was the fury of the people that the Maréchal de Belle-Isle, who was governor of Metz, fearing that, if they did not start without a moment's delay, they might be roughly handled, lent the duchesses two of his own carriages, which happened to be ready. In these, with drawn blinds and guarded by an escort of soldiers, they left the town, followed all through the streets and far into the country by an enraged mob, who heaped the grossest insults upon the woman to whom the monarch whose peril they were deploring was indebted for the one flash of manly activity which he had shown throughout his worthless reign. In every village through which they passed similar scenes were enacted; indeed, but for the resolute attitude of the soldiers who guarded them, they would inevitably have been torn to pieces. At length they reached Paris, and entered the city unnoticed, amid those almost frenzied lamentations which Voltaire has so graphically described for us.

After the departure of the sisters was known, M. de Soissons, in his capacity of First Almoner,[1] administered the Holy Sacrament to the King. The next morning, the 14th, as there was no improvement in his Majesty's condition, he received Extreme Unction, from the same hands, but not

[1] This duty belonged, of course, to the Grand Almoner, the Cardinal de Rohan; but he was at Strasbourg.

until the bishop had extracted from him an order that Madame de Châteauroux, who had stopped some leagues from Metz to await events, should continue her journey immediately; and had summoned the Princes of the Blood and the grand officers and told them that "the King asked pardon for the scandal which he had caused, and the bad example which he had given, and that it was his Majesty's intention that Madame de Châteauroux should not remain near the Dauphine." To which declaration the King added: "Nor her sister."[1]

One knows what followed: The summoning of the princes and grand officers to the royal bedside to take part in the prayers for the dying; the universal belief that every hour would be Louis XV.'s last; the rescue of the King from the very jaws of death by the retired army-surgeon Moncerveau; the sudden transformation of Paris from a city of mourning into one of frenzied rejoicing—"a vast enclosure full of madmen";[2] the arrival of the Queen at Metz; the edifying reconciliation between the royal pair, and all the virtuous resolutions, which returning health were soon to dissipate.

While they lasted, however, the friends of the fallen favourite had a somewhat anxious time, and Richelieu, who, with the rest of the King's aides-de-camp, with the exception of Meuse and Luxembourg—who was ill—had received orders to leave Metz and rejoin the Army of the Rhine, deemed it prudent, so soon as his military duties permitted, to retire to Basle. From this retreat he recommenced his intrigues, corresponding incessantly with Madame de Châteauroux and the Tencins, and working for the re-establishment of the mistress with all the zeal which comes from the assurance of a speedy success. Having first taken the precaution to gauge the sentiments of Louis XV., by means of Tencin and Noailles, he addressed to him a skilfully-worded memoir concerning the affair of Metz, in which he justified his own conduct, accused the enemies of Madame de Châteauroux and himself of having

[1] *Mémoires du duc de Luynes*, August 26, 1744.
[2] D'Angerville, *Vie privée de Louis XV.*

shamelessly exploited the remorse of a sick man for the furtherance of their own selfish and ambitious ends, and did not scruple to hint that the astonishment of "*ces messieurs*" at his Majesty's happy recovery had been equalled by their vexation.

This memoir, which Madame de Châteauroux, to whom it was first submitted, found "*comique et très-bonne*,"[1] was not without its effect upon the King. Being now completely restored to health, his Majesty, like the devil in the old proverb, had soon forgotten his vows of amendment, and was hungering for a sight of his mistress; while he would have been more than human had he failed to resent the public humiliation by which the arrogant Bishop of Soissons had compelled him to purchase the Sacraments of the Church. The magnificent reception which he received on his return to France after the fall of Freiburg removed his last lingering scruples. "Glorious" and "well-beloved," he found in "his glory" and in the "love of his people" an encouragement to brave scandal. At the dinner at the Hôtel de Ville on November 15, 1744, to which the municipality of Paris entertained him, he inquired of the Prince de Dombes, governor of Languedoc, and of Bernage, the intendant of that province, when they considered that Richelieu, who had gone to hold the Estates at Montpellier, would be likely to conclude his official duties and be at liberty to return to Court. It was evident that Richelieu's brief disgrace was at an end, and that his return to favour presaged that of an even more important person.[2]

[1] Letter of Madame de Châteauroux to Richelieu, October 18, 1744, cited by E. and J. de Goncourt, *la Duchesse de Châteauroux et ses sœurs*.

[2] *Mémoires du duc de Luynes*, November 16, 1744. The Goncourts and several other writers, following Soulavie, speak of an interview which took place between Louis XV. and Madame de Châteauroux at the latter's house in the Rue de Bac, in Paris, on the night of the King's return to Versailles, to which he went escorted by Richelieu. That there was such a meeting is quite possible, but not that Richelieu was present at it, since, as we have just seen, he was then at Montpellier, nor did he return to Court until Christmas Eve, three weeks after the death of Madame de Châteauroux. On Christmas Day, the Duc de Luynes writes: "M. de Richelieu arrived yesterday in the evening, and saw the King, probably in private before his *coucher*; for it is certain that when the King returned from chapel, he shut himself up. The Queen did not know the hour of Mass for to-day; she sent to ask him, and was told that the King could not be disturbed."

In point of fact, ten days later (November 25), when the Council rose, Louis XV. drew Maurepas aside and ordered him to proceed to Paris, to Madame de Châteauroux's house in the Rue du Bac, and inform that lady that "the King was very annoyed at all that had happened at Metz, and at the indecency with which she had been treated; that he begged her to forget it, and that, to give her a proof of it, he trusted that both she and her sister would be willing to return and resume possession of their apartments at Versailles; that he would give them, on all occasions, proofs of his protection, esteem, and friendship, and that he restored to them their posts."[1]

The selection of Maurepas to convey to Madame de Châteauroux her formal recall to Court—a commission which was naturally extremely distasteful to the Minister in question—was by way of punishment for the prominent part he had taken in the intrigue which had led to her disgrace. It was the only punishment which he received, for, though the lady had demanded his dismissal from office and banishment from Court, Louis XV. could not bring himself to accord it, since Maurepas's wit was accustomed to relieve the tedium of the Council. Nevertheless, Madame de Châteauroux secured a sufficiently brilliant reparation for what she called the "affront of Metz" by the exile of the Bishop of Soissons, the Ducs de Bouillon and de la Rochefoucauld, and several other members of the hostile cabal.[2]

Nothing now remained for the victorious favourite save to return to Versailles and resume her interrupted reign; but she was never again to behold the scene of her former triumphs. Always a delicate woman, the violent agitations of the past four months had proved too much for her strength. Even when she received her recall, the hand of death was already upon her; two days later, she was in the grip of a violent fever, and at

[1] *Mémoires du duc de Luynes*, November 27, 1744. Letter of Madame de Châteauroux to the Duchesse de Lauraguais, November 25, 1744.

[2] Père Pérusseau was not exiled; but the King kept him in a state of mortal terror for some time, by announcing that it was his intention to disgrace him.

seven o'clock in the morning of December 8, she died, at the age of twenty-seven, after terrible sufferings.

In that short agony, the imposing edifice which Richelieu and the Tencins had so patiently constructed crumbled to dust. Richelieu, it is true, continued to enjoy the favour of the King—a favour of which even the hostility of Madame de Pompadour was powerless to deprive him—but it was as the confidant of his amours, the witty companion of the supper-table, not as the director of his policy, the trusted adviser of the council-chamber. All his ambitious hopes lay buried in the vault of the chapel of Saint-Michel at Saint-Sulpice which held the mortal remains of the Duchesse de Châteauroux.

# CHAPTER XV

Richelieu accompanies Louis XV. to Flanders—The Allied army, under the Duke of Cumberland, advances to the relief of Tournai—Skilful dispositions of Maurice de Saxe—Battle of Fontenoy—Part played by Richelieu in the engagement considered—He attempts, aided by Voltaire and the Marquis d'Argenson, to exaggerate his own services at the expense of Saxe—Voltaire's *Poème de Fontenoi*—General irritation in the Army of Flanders against the duke—The Dauphin's letter to his wife—Richelieu's name practically omitted from the official report of the battle drawn up by the Minister for War and Saxe—Voltaire in prose (*Siècle de Louis XV.*) attributes to the duke the part which he has already assigned to him in verse—Opinions of other historians on this question.

ON Sunday, May 2, a courier from Maurice de Saxe arrived at Versailles, with the news that on the night of April 30–May 1, the trenches had been opened before Tournai; and at a little after seven o'clock on the morning of the 6th, Louis XV. and the Dauphin, accompanied by *Monsieur le Premier*[1] d'Ayen, Richelieu, and three other nobles set out for Flanders.[2]

At Douai, which was reached on the following day, the King received dispatches from Saxe announcing that the Allied army, under the Duke of Cumberland, was advancing to the relief of Tournai, and that a general engagement was inevitable, upon which he sent orders to the garrisons of Douai and Valenciennes to reinforce the investing army, and, hastening on, arrived at the French camp early in the forenoon of the 8th.[3] Three days later the Battle of Fontenoy was fought.

[1] Henri Camille, Marquis de Béringhen, First Equerry to the King.

[2] Luynes.

[3] Louis XV. passed the night of the 8th at the Château of Pont-à-Chin, at the northern extremity of the French lines, but on the following day he removed to the Château of Calonne between Tournai and Anthoin.

Saxe was so ill with dropsy that he was unable to mount his horse and had to be carried about in a wicker litter, but, if his body were racked with pain, his mind was as vigorous as ever. Foreseeing that the Allies would advance by the Mons road, he had chosen for the arena of this memorable action a cultivated plain, sloping gently upwards from the Scheldt, which was traversed by the highway about five miles to the south-west of Tournai.

Here he took up an exceedingly strong position upon the crest of the rising ground, with the village of Anthoin and the river on his right, the hamlet of Fontenoy and a narrow valley protecting his centre, and his left covered by a dense wood known as the Bois de Barré. The passage of the Scheldt, and a retreat in the event of disaster, were secured by fortified bridges thrown across the river at Calonne and Vaulx in his rear, and by a reserve of the Household troops.

In spite of the indignant protests of most of his officers, who hotly maintained that Frenchmen were fully equal to dealing with their foes in the open field, Saxe resolved to convert his already formidable position into one which might well bid defiance to the boldest assailant. He accordingly erected five redoubts: three on the ridge between Fontenoy and Anthoin, and two on the edge of the Bois de Barré, facing Fontenoy, that nearest the village being called the Redoubt d'Eu, owing to its being held by a battalion of the regiment of that name. Both the villages of Anthoin and Fontenoy were strongly fortified and garrisoned, and abbatis constructed in the Bois de Barré; while, in addition to the numerous artillery which defended this improvised citadel, a battery of six 12-pounders was stationed on the western bank of the Scheldt opposite Anthoin, to play upon the left flank of any force advancing in that direction.

Impregnable as this position seemed to the French officers, it might have been still further strengthened by the construction of a sixth redoubt between the Redoubt d'Eu and Fontenoy. As it was, this part of Saxe's line was unprotected by any earthworks, the marshal being of opinion that it was sufficiently defended by the picked troops which he had stationed there, the broken nature of the ground, and the terrible cross-fire to which any troops who attempted to force a passage at that point would be exposed.

The expected attack was not long delayed. On the evening of the 9th, Cumberland arrived at Brussoel, within sight of Saxe's army. On the 10th, having driven the French out of the village of Vezon, which they had occupied as an advanced post, he reconnoitred their lines, in company with the Prince of Waldeck, who commanded the Dutch, and the Austrian veteran, Marshal Königseck, and, daunted neither by the strong position nor the superior numbers of the enemy, resolved to attack on the morrow. It was decided that the Dutch and Austrians were to assail the French centre and right, the Dutch concentrating upon Fontenoy, while the British and Hanoverians attacked the French left between that village and the Bois de Barré.

What student of the military history of the eighteenth century is not familiar with the main incidents of that fateful day? How, at five o'clock on the morning of May 11, the advance of the Allies began, to the accompaniment of a heavy artillery-fire from the batteries on either side, which mortally wounded General Campbell, the leader of the British cavalry, and the Duc de Gramont, the gallant but headstrong young officer whose rashness had lost the French the Battle of Dettingen. How Brigadier Ingoldsby was sent to storm the Redoubt d'Eu, as a preliminary to the general attack upon the French left, but failed entirely, owing, as he subsequently alleged, to the contradictory orders which he received. How the Dutch and Austrians, appalled by the fire from the entrenchments in front, and by that from the 12-pounder battery on the farther bank of the Scheldt, which took them in flank as they advanced against Fontenoy and Anthoin, shrunk back under cover of some earthworks which they had prudently thrown up the night before, and could not be prevailed upon to move forward again. How Cumberland then placed himself at the head of the British infantry and a few Hanoverian battalions, and led them, in column, with shouldered arms and slow and measured step as though on parade, through the deadly cross-fire of the French batteries, straight against the one weak point in the enemy's line. How that heroic column advanced, "strewing the sward behind it with scarlet, like some mass of red blossoms that floats down a lazy stream, and sheds its petals as it goes,"[1] until it was within fifty paces of the French. How Lord Charles Hay, of the First Guards, stepped forth from the ranks, doffed his hat, and drank with much courtesy to the health of the Gardes Françaises, at the same time expressing a hope that they "would wait for the English to-day, and not swim the Scheldt as they had swum the Main at Dettingen." How there burst from the serried British ranks "such a torrent of deadly and continuous fire as was rarely seen before or since."[2] How Saxe hurled infantry, then cavalry, and then infantry again, upon the column, only to see them beaten back with frightful slaughter.[3] How the British, "girdled with insupportable fire," advanced until they were three hundred paces within the French lines, and the day seemed won, so that most of the French generals entreated the King to take shelter with the Dauphin behind the Scheldt, while there was yet time, which, however, Louis, who had shown commendable coolness and courage throughout the day, refused to do. How, as a last resource, four cannon which had been placed on the road to the bridge of Calonne, to protect the retreat of the King and Dauphin, if the day should go against the French, were brought to bear upon the front of the column, at a distance scarcely exceeding forty paces, shearing gaps through it from end to end, after which the Irish Brigade, part of which had been kept in reserve, and the Régiments de Normandie et des Vaisseaux, led by Marshal Löwendahl, fiercely assailed its right flank, while the Household cavalry, the Gendarmerie and the Carabiniers, led by Richelieu, Biron, and d'Estrées, fell, sword in hand, upon its centre. And,

[1] Fortescue, "History of the British Army."

[2] Carlyle, "Frederick the Great."

[3] According to d'Espagnac (*Histoire du Maréchal de Saxe*), the Régiment du Roi had 460 men laid low by a single volley.

MAURICE, COMTE DE SAXE, MARSHAL OF FRANCE

FROM AN ENGRAVING BY J. G. WILL, AFTER THE PAINTING BY HYACINTHE RIGAUD

finally, how the heroic battalions, exhausted by their tremendous exertions, cannonaded both in front and flank, and surrounded on all sides by superior numbers, wavered and fell back as steadily as they had advanced, blasting with a last withering discharge the Carabiniers and the Régiment de Noailles, who made a furious onslaught on their rear as they faced about.[1]

As excellent and exhaustive accounts of the Battle of Fontenoy are to be found in many histories, both English and French,[2] we shall not add anything to the brief description given above, but confine ourselves to endeavouring to determine the part which Richelieu played in the engagement.

That Richelieu greatly distinguished himself is generally admitted: indeed, he was one of those who received the special thanks of Louis XV. after the battle. It was he who acted as the King's chief aide-de-camp, and we can well believe that something of the superb courage which he invariably showed in the hour of danger communicated itself to his royal master and helped to retain Louis on the field, even when Saxe himself had begged him to retire. It was he who proposed that the Irish Brigade and the Régiments de Normandie and des Vaisseaux should be thrown upon the right flank of the British column.[3] It was he who carried to the Household cavalry, the Gendarmerie, and the Carabiniers the order to charge, and who led those splendid squadrons in their furious onslaught against the British centre.[4]

History, however, would more willingly render justice to

[1] The Régiment de Noailles was almost annihilated; the Carabiniers lost twenty-seven officers killed and wounded.

[2] The best English accounts of the battle are those given by the Hon. J. W. Fortescue, in his "History of the British Army," vol. ii., and by Mr. F. H. Skrine, in his "Fontenoy and the War of the Austrian Succession"; the best on the French side will be found in Comte Pajol's monumental work, *les Guerres sous Louis XV.*, d'Espagnac's *Histoire du Maréchal de Saxe*, and in *Marie Thérèse, impératrice*, by the late Duc de Broglie. The Duc de Broglie's account has also been published separately, under the title of *la Journée de Fontenoy*, illustrated by some very charming etchings by Lalauze. The most picturesque descriptions are, of course, those of Carlyle ("Frederick the Great," vol. vi.) and Voltaire (*Siècle de Louis XV.*).

[3] The Duc de Broglie, *Marie Thérèse, impératrice*.

[4] *Relation envoyée de M. de Vezannes*, *Mémoires du duc de Luynes*, vol. vi.

the incontestable services which Richelieu rendered during that memorable day, if the duke, aided by Voltaire and the Marquis d'Argenson—now Minister for Foreign Affairs and on anything but cordial terms with Maurice de Saxe—had not endeavoured to exaggerate his own merits at the expense of the real victor, and maintained that it was he alone who had arrested the flight of the King; who had conceived the happy idea of bringing the four cannon to bear upon the enemy's front, and following up the effect of their fire by a general charge upon the wavering column; who, in a word, had saved the army, the King, and the kingdom from irremediable disaster.

The natural irritation of Saxe and his brother-officers at Richelieu's pretensions was sensibly increased by the publication of Voltaire's *Poème de Fontenoi,* of which more than 20,000 copies are said to have been sold in a single day. In this effusion, whereof a rather inaccurate account of the battle sent him by the Marquis d'Argenson had furnished the materials, Voltaire consecrates some ten or twelve verses to the glorification of his friend and "his hero" while the exploits of Saxe and of the King himself are each dismissed in four or five:

> "Richelieu, qu'en tous lieux emporte son courage,
> Ardent, mais éclairé, vif à la fois et sage.
> Favori de l'Amour, de Minerve, et de Mars,
> Richelieu vous appelle ; il n'est plus de hasard.
> Il vous appelle ; il voit d'un œil prudent et ferme
> Des succès ennemis et la cause et le terme ;
> Il vole, et sa vertu secondant son grand cœur,
> Il vous marque la place où vous serez vainqueur."

"It would have been impossible," observes the Duc de Broglie, "to state in clearer terms, and under a thinner poetic veil, that all was lost without Richelieu, and that by him also all had been saved." [1]

For a time, Richelieu was the most unpopular man in the Army of Flanders, and even the phlegmatic King was moved to anger against him. "M. de Richelieu," writes the Duc de

[1] *Marie Thérèse, impératrice.*

Luynes, "no longer appears to have any credit, and it may even be said that he is not on good terms with any one. Although he conducted himself well in the battle, people are of opinion that Voltaire has said too much about him, and those to whom the success of this great day are really due must have appeared wounded by these excessive praises." [1]

To make matters worse, copies of a letter written by the Dauphin to his wife were circulated in the army, in which that prince, who was well known to have little love for Richelieu, relating the only incident of the day which he had witnessed personally—the final charge—spoke, with all the natural enthusiasm of youth for valorous deeds, of the conduct of the duke.

The affair appeared sufficiently serious, for Louis XV., who had judged the facts with more deliberation, to believe it his duty to interfere, in order that public opinion might be no longer led astray, and, having asked to see his son's letter, he gave strict orders that it was not to be circulated or even spoken of. The too enthusiastic admirers of Richelieu then comprehended the necessity of reserve; and Voltaire, who was too late to correct the mistake he had committed, had the mortification to see the success of his poem compromised by that excess of zeal which, at the Court, was a fault not easily pardoned, and was compelled to digest as best he might the storm of mordant satires which his precipitation had brought upon him.

The unpleasantness which had been aroused, however, did not end there. The Comte d'Argenson, the Minister for War, who had been present at Fontenoy, was naturally charged by the King to draw up the official account of the battle, which he did in concert with Maurice de Saxe. Now the count detested Richelieu, of whose insolence towards him in his official capacity he had had more than once to complain,[2] and

[1] *Mémoires*, May 17, 1745.

[2] "M. d'Argenson (of the Ministry for War) is on no better terms than the others with M. de Richelieu. This detail has been sent me by a very well-informed person on the spot."—Luynes, May 1, 1745.

his relations with his elder brother of the Foreign Office, who supported the duke, were just then very strained indeed; while the marshal was naturally exasperated by the endeavours of Richelieu and his friends to deprive him of his laurels. The consequence was that, in the report which they composed, the name of Richelieu hardly figured at all, and of the really brilliant services he had rendered in the concluding stage of the battle no mention whatever was made. This, as the Duc de Broglie observes, was to repair one injustice by another; and it is not surprising to learn that, some years later, Richelieu having become a marshal of France, while Saxe was dead and d'Argenson in exile, persuaded the Marquis de Paulmy, the then Minister for War, to add a note at the end of the despatch rectifying the omission of his predecessor.[1]

About the same time, Voltaire, now free from all constraint, resumed in prose the subject which he had developed in verse, and, in his *Siècle de Louis XV.*, stooped so low as to falsify history in the interests of "his hero":

"The battle appeared hopelessly lost. . . . The English column seemed to be mistress of the field. . . . The success of a last attack was uncertain. The Maréchal de Saxe, who saw that victory or defeat depended entirely on this last attack, thought of preparing a safe retreat; he despatched a secret order to the Comte de la Mark to evacuate Anthoin and to march towards the bridge of Calonne, to cover this retreat, in the event of a final disaster. . . . The success of the day was, at that moment, despaired of.

"A rather tumultuous council of war was held around the King, who was urged on behalf of the General (Saxe),[2] and in the name of France, not to expose himself further.

"The Duc de Richelieu, lieutenant-general, who was serving

[1] Duc de Broglie, *Marie Thérèse, impératrice.*

[2] This is incorrect. When the column was nearing the French lines, it is true that Saxe had begged the King to retire by the bridge of Calonne; but after the British had penetrated them, he energetically opposed his retreat, on the ground that it could not fail to have a disastrous moral effect upon the troops, and might even be the signal for a general stampede, in which case his Majesty and the Dauphin would be in considerable danger.

in the capacity of aide-de-camp to the King, arrived at this moment. He had come from reconnoitring the column near Fontenoy. Having thus galloped about on all sides without being wounded, he presented himself all breathless, sword in hand, and covered with dust. 'What news do you bring?' said the Maréchal de Noailles to him; 'what is your advice?' 'My news,' said the Duc de Richelieu, 'is that the battle is won, if you desire to win it, and my advice is that four cannon be immediately brought up against the front of the column; and that, while this artillery is causing it to waver, the Household cavalry and the other troops will surround it. We must fall upon it like foragers.' The King was the first to approve of this plan."

Voltaire's account had been wholly or partially accepted by several historians who wrote in the earlier or middle part of the last century, notably by Stanhope, Coxe, and Carlyle;[1] while Michelet, on the authority of so discredited a chronicler as Soulavie, depicts Louis XV. and Saxe himself as stricken with terror, the one for himself, the other for his master, and thinking only of flight, when Richelieu, like a *deus ex machinâ*, appears upon the scene, and saves them, in spite of themselves. Later writers, however, are, in general, far more just to the great captain to whom the glory undoubtedly belongs, though the controversy cannot be regarded as ended.

[1] "Duc de Richelieu, famous blackguard man, gallops up to the Maréchal, gallops rapidly from Maréchal to King, suggesting: 'Were cannon brought *ahead* of this close deep column, might they not shear it into beautiful destruction, and then a general charge be made?' So counsels Richelieu." Carlyle, however, adds: "It is said that the Jacobite Irishman, Count Lally of the Irish Brigade, was the prime author of this notion—a man of tragic notoriety in time coming"; and several contemporary accounts give the credit of the proposal concerning the cannon to that gallant and ill-fated Irishman. Others name Saxe himself; while a note preserved in the Archives of the Ministry of War states that the suggestion came from a captain of the Régiment de Touraine, named Isnard, who was rewarded with the Cross of Saint-Louis. In the opinion of the Duc de Broglie, the advisability of bringing up the four cannon, which, while they remained in the position in which they had been placed, were of no use whatever, except to cover the retreat of the King, and directing their fire against the front of the victorious British column, was sufficiently obvious to have occurred to several persons at the same time, each of whom may well have honestly believed that the idea originated with him: and his supposition is probably correct.

# CHAPTER XVI

Mortification of Richelieu at the installation of Madame de Pompadour as *maîtresse en titre*—His conduct towards the new favourite—"His credit diminishing"—Efforts of the Jacobites to procure assistance from France—Prince Charles Edward lands in Scotland—The French Government resolve to send an expedition to England, and the command is entrusted to Richelieu—The secrecy and promptitude essential to the success of the undertaking are observed neither by the duke nor the Government—Richelieu arrives at Dunkerque, but the favourable moment is lost, and bad weather and the presence of the British fleet prevent the embarkation of the French troops—The duke demands a *congé* and returns to Versailles—The success of the enterprise is recognised as hopeless—Death of the Dauphine, the Infanta Maria Theresa—Marie Josèph de Saxe, daughter of Augustus III., Elector of Saxony and King of Poland, selected as the second wife of the Dauphine—Richelieu chosen to proceed to Dresden as Ambassador Extraordinary to make the formal demand for the princess's hand—Efforts of the Saxon Court to prevent his nomination—Views of Brühl and the Marquis d'Argenson—The petard of Maurice de Saxe—Richelieu's secret mission—His arrival at Dresden—The marriage—The duke exceeds the instructions he has received from d'Argenson, and thus contributes to the fall of that Minister.

RICHELIEU had other causes of mortification at this time besides the refusal of Louis XV. and the army to recognise in him the real victor of Fontenoy. Early in July, he learned, to his profound chagrin, that the astute Madame d'Étioles, whose tender relations with his Majesty he had at first regarded as a mere *galanterie*, had been ennobled under the name of the Marquise de Pompadour, and that, when the King returned to Versailles, she would undoubtedly be installed there as *maîtresse en titre*.[1] It was vexatious enough that the King should take unto himself a

[1] For the details of this affair, see the author's "Madame de Pompadour" (London: Harpers, New York: Scribners, 1902).

mistress not of his selection, but the knowledge that, ever since the death of Madame de Châteauroux, he had been making heroic efforts to awaken the bereaved monarch to the charms of two most suitable candidates for the vacant place in his affections, to wit, the widowed Duchesse de Rochechouart and the pretty wife of the rich financier La Popelinière—of which latter lady more anon—and that all his pains had been wasted, was a cruel mortification.[1]

Three courses were open to him when, early in September, he returned with the King to Versailles: to endeavour to ingratiate himself with the new favourite, as Voltaire and Madame de Tencin were already doing; to join the powerful party which, headed by Maurepàs, was moving Heaven and earth to procure the downfall of the *petite bourgeoise* who had dared to thrust herself into a position which had always been regarded as the peculiar appanage of the nobility, or to remain neutral.

After mature reflection, he decided to take the middle course, at any rate for a time. Pride forbade him to sue for favours where, if he had shown his usual prescience, he might have dictated terms, as he had done in the case of Madame de Châteauroux, and he was also a little dubious if the lady would be able to retain her position in the face of such violent opposition. On the other hand, he had no desire to co-operate with Maurepas, whom he cordially hated, and did not see that he had anything to gain by assisting to overthrow the new mistress

[1] If we are to believe the gossip of the time, his Majesty had not required any one to awaken him to the charms of his deceased favourite's sister, Madame de Flavacourt, "a pretty brunette with beautiful eyes," to whom, according to the Duc de Luynes, he had, some time before his expedition to Flanders, shown so much attention, that Madame de Châteauroux became seriously alarmed, and insisted on her being banished from the *petits appartements*. Soulavie asserts that, after the death of Madame de Châteauroux, Louis determined to install Madame de Flavacourt in her place, and charged Richelieu to negotiate the affair. "There was no kind of persuasion which the Duc de Richelieu did not employ to induce her to yield; but the beautiful and virtuous Flavacourt replied in these terms: 'That is all, then, M. de Richelieu? . . . Well! I prefer the esteem of my contemporaries.'" Such a sentiment would have done the speaker infinite honour, had it not subsequently transpired that her husband, who was of an excessively jealous disposition, had threatened to kill her the moment he had reason to suspect her fidelity.

unless he could be certain of replacing her by a creature of his own. He was aware, moreover, that opposition to a monarch's choice, while the royal passion is still at a high temperature, is always a dangerous game to play, and, in times past, had ruined more than one promising career. It would therefore be more politic to hold aloof until he saw which way the wind was likely to blow, and could trim his sails to catch it. If Madame de Pompadour's reign seemed likely to be a long one, he could rally to her side; if he perceived that her favour was on the wane, he could throw in his lot with her enemies, and look about for a suitable successor.

Unfortunately for himself, this skilful opportunist had greatly underrated the abilities of the new favourite, who was even more astute than he was himself, and who had been fully enlightened by the few friends whom she had at the Court as to the manœuvres which had followed the death of her predecessor. Since the duke did not seem inclined to respond to her friendly overtures, she decided to regard him as an enemy; and in November 1745 the Duc de Luynes notes that "M. de Richelieu appears to stand rather moderately with Madame de Pompadour, and it is believed that his credit with the King has diminished."

As was his habit when matters were not going well with him at Court, Richelieu turned to his profession for consolation, and, since there was no fighting to be done on the Continent until the resumption of hostilities in the following spring, decided to seek glory beyond the sea.

Ever since the death of Fleury, the hopes of the Jacobites for French assistance in an attempt to re-establish the Stuarts by force of arms had been steadily reviving. The attachment of the Cardinal de Tencin to the exiled House; the bitter feeling between France and England engendered by the progress of the war; and the obvious advantage to the former of diverting the attention of her hereditary enemy from Continental affairs—all seemed to indicate that the intervention which they had so often sought in vain would not much longer be withheld. Nor were they disappointed. In the autumn of

1743, thanks mainly to the efforts of Tencin, an expedition, commanded by Prince Charles Edward Stuart—the "Young Pretender"—and Saxe, embarked at Dunkerque and actually sailed as far as Dungeness. There, however, it was dispersed by a violent storm, which caused the total loss of several of the transports, with all the men on board, wrecked others, and obliged the remainder to put back to Dunkerque, in a sadly damaged condition.

After this fiasco, all Charles's efforts to obtain assistance from the French Government proved unavailing, and he, therefore, resolved to proceed to Scotland and make his attempt with the aid of his British adherents only. The news of the Battle of Fontenoy decided him to put his romantic project into execution with as little delay as possible; on July 2, he sailed from Saint-Nazaire, at the mouth of the Loire, and on the 25th of the same month, landed at Loch-nan-Uamh, between Moidart and Strisaig, with seven companions.

For several months the French Government sent the bold invaders no help beyond small supplies of arms and money, some of which were intercepted by the English cruisers; but about the beginning of November, encouraged by the reports of Charles's triumphant progress, it yielded to the appeals of his partisans in France, which redoubled as the prince advanced southwards, and active preparations for the despatch of a force to his assistance were begun at Dunkerque.

A landing on the Scotch coast was at first contemplated, but the Jacobites urged that a descent upon the south coast of England, in the neighbourhood of Plymouth, promised far greater results. The appearance of a French army there, they assured the Government, would be the signal for a general rising of the adherents of the Stuart cause in the southern counties, and the invaders could then advance towards London and effect their junction with the prince's troops.

There was, according to these enthusiasts, only one obstacle to the complete success of the undertaking—the possibility of the British fleet getting wind of their intention and appearing in time to prevent the disembarkation. But this they proposed

to overcome by employing only merchant-vessels and a few corsairs, which might slip across the Channel under cover of the darkness, and land a force of eight or ten thousand men and the necessary artillery before the morning revealed their presence.

Richelieu's vanity had been deeply wounded by the refusal of the Ministry for War to recognise his services at Fontenoy, and he had publicly announced that he had no longer any desire to become a marshal of France, since that distinction had evidently ceased to be the reward of merit. Great, therefore, was the general surprise when it became known that the duke had been offered and had accepted the command of the "Army of England," the more so that the enmity existing between him and Maurepas, who, as Minister of Marine, had been charged with the fitting-out of the expedition, was a matter of common knowledge.

If we are to believe Voltaire, however, the Jacobites in France had "demanded for the chief of this enterprise the Duc de Richelieu, who, judging by the services rendered on the day of Fontenoy, and by the reputation which he enjoyed in Europe, was more capable than any one of conducting with ardour this bold and delicate affair";[1] and certainly the undertaking was of a nature to appeal to the duke's adventurous instincts. As for Maurepas, who might have been expected to offer strenuous opposition to his enemy's appointment, since he appears to have been anything but sanguine regarding the result of the expedition, he probably believed that it was far more likely to lead to an English prison or a watery grave than to the marshal's *bâton*, and was therefore naturally reluctant to stand in the way of possibilities so eminently desirable from his own point of view. Nevertheless, he took the precaution of insisting that all arrangements between himself and the duke relative to the transport of the troops should be committed to writing, "in order that M. de Richelieu might not be able to accuse him of having failed in the promises which he had given him."[2]

[1] *Siècle de Louis XV.*

[2] *Mémoires du duc de Luynes*, November 18, 1745.

On December 23, Richelieu, who was to be followed by Henry, Duke of York, younger brother of Charles Edward, Lord Clare, and the Prince de Montauban, set out for Ghent, to confer with Maurice de Saxe, before proceeding to Dunkerque, "where," says Luynes, "it is supposed that he will embark immediately for England."[1] Nothing, we are told, had been neglected which might contribute to the success of the expedition, not even the versatile pen of Voltaire, who, at the request of the Marquis d'Argenson, had been employed in the composition of a most eloquent and persuasive proclamation on behalf of Charles Edward, in which the King of France declared that although he felt it his duty to intervene on behalf of a prince so worthy to sit upon the throne of his ancestors, it was his intention to respect the rights of the English nation.

It is quite possible that the enterprise might have been attended with some measure of success, that is to say, that Richelieu might have contrived to evade the British fleet, which was then engaged in blockading Ostend, and have effected a landing in England, if secrecy and promptitude had been employed. Neither of these conditions, however, were fulfilled. The duke, faithful to his habits of boasting and ostentation, gave far too much publicity to his preparations for their object to remain unknown to any one. He attached to his person a numerous staff, bragged of the glory which awaited him beyond the seas, and actually permitted his officers to go in uniform to take leave of their friends at the Court and in Paris, as they did when they set out in April for a campaign in Flanders.[2]

Then the Government, in order to ensure a sufficient number of transports, proceeded to requisition every merchant-vessel which lay in the Channel ports, thus causing a suspension of commerce which would have been alone sufficient to put England on her guard.

However, if the expedition had been able to get under way so soon as its commander reached Dunkerque, the passage might still have been made in safety; but, owing to some misunderstanding, the artillery had not arrived. "Yesterday," wrote

[1] *Mémoires du duc de Luynes*, December 24. [2] Marquis d'Argenson, *Mémoires*.

Richelieu to the Comte d'Argenson, "the wind was favourable, and, if my artillery had arrived, I should have crossed over to England with all the facility imaginable."

By the time the artillery had put in an appearance, the advance-guard of the British fleet had also arrived upon the scene.

"It was hoped," writes Luynes, on January 6, 1746, "that the embarkation would have taken place on the 31st or the 1st, and with so much more facility, since it was known that the English fleet was blockading Ostend. But we begin to fear greatly that the embarkation may be, at least, much delayed, because one or two English ships have appeared off Calais, and we have no ships-of-war to convoy our transports. M. de Richelieu sent a courier, two or three days ago, with intelligence that, as a French corsair, which was convoying some of our transports from Dunkerque to Calais, had been captured by two English corsairs after a rather long combat, he believed that it was very important to set sail at the earliest possible moment, and that he was going to start with the ships which were in readiness. However, it is certain that they have not yet started."

The embarkation had been prevented by bad weather and by the appearance of more than thirty British ships, and by January 5 the general, who had set out for Dunkerque with so much confidence, was in despair: "I know not what to do, if the wind does not change and some miracle does not operate in our favour, as you can see by the particulars of our situation." And he adds, in reference no doubt to the *chansons* which were circulating in Paris at his expense: "I believe that those who have great military talents are no more sheltered from ridicule than those who have less." [1]

Needless to relate, no miracle came to his relief, and the expedition remained inactive at Dunkerque throughout the whole of January, whilst Richelieu, more and more disgusted at the ridiculous fiasco in which his indiscretions had involved him,

[1] Despatches to the Comte d'Argenson, cited by the Duc de Broglie, *Maurice de Saxe et le Marquis d'Argenson*.

racked his brains to discover some means of releasing himself from a command which he now bitterly regretted ever having been led to accept. As he did not venture to advise that the enterprise should be definitely abandoned, he proposed that the port of departure and the point where the expedition was to endeavour to effect a landing should both be altered; and when the Government, as he expected, declined to entertain his suggestion, wrote to the Minister for War declaring that he threw all the responsibility of the failure of the expedition upon him and his colleagues: "It is not I who formed the project of carrying assistance to England. . . . But, having been chosen to command the troops which were to be sent, I believed it to be my duty to do everything possible to ensure success. . . . The Duke of York and his party will have nothing to reproach me with."

At length, towards the middle of February, he became, or pretended to be, ill, and demanded permission to return to Court, where, coolly ignoring his own share in the matter, he attributed all the blame to the delays and indiscretion of the Ministries of War and the Marine. Paris, however, took a different view of the affair, and greeted the duke with a broadside of *chansons*, one of which compared him to a spaniel who had gone to fetch a *bâton* from the other side of a river, but had not been able to summon up sufficient courage even to venture into the water.[1]

After the return of Richelieu, the expedition, though not officially countermanded, was practically abandoned, and when two isolated attempts made by the Duc de Fitz-James to land small bodies of troops at isolated spots on the English coast

[1] Another ran as follows:

"Quand je vis partir l'Excellence
De Richelieu,
Je prévis la mauvaise chance.
Hélas! mon Dieu!
Ce pilote ignore les vents
De l'Angleterre:
Il ne sait qu'embarquer les gens
Pour l'île de Cythère."

The ostensible reasons were the great expense which the reception of an Ambassador Extraordinary would entail, and the wish to spare the *amour-propre* of the Marquis des Issarts, who considered that the negotiations for the marriage ought to be left in his hands. But the real motive was a much deeper one, which requires a word of explanation.

The Marquis d'Argenson, the friend of Richelieu and Voltaire, who had succeeded Amelot as Minister for Foreign Affairs in France, was a statesman of the school of Richelieu and Mazarin, the keynote of whose foreign policy had been the humbling of Austria through the support of the smaller German States; and to this end he desired to bring about a *rapprochement* between Prussia and Saxony. Brühl, on the other hand, who regarded Frederick the Great with the bitterest hatred, had no desire for such an understanding, but dreamed of being the mediator between Louis XV. and Maria Theresa, and of drawing France into a coalition against Prussia. The arrival of an Ambassador Extraordinary from the King of France on a mission of concord and peace would have been an excellent opportunity for renewing the attempt at mediation which he had already made at the time of the Peace of Dresden at the beginning of 1646; but the Ambassador selected was a friend of d'Argenson, and he was, moreover, informed that Frederick the Great had, through Voltaire, expressed a desire to meet the celebrated Duc de Richelieu, whose amours, duels, and courage on the battlefield had procured him a European reputation, and that the duke intended to visit Berlin on his way to Dresden. Now, if Richelieu went to Berlin, it was not improbable that he might be charged by Frederick, with the consent of d'Argenson, with proposals for a *rapprochement* between Prussia and Saxony, which would place the Court of Dresden in a very embarrassing position, and postpone indefinitely Brühl's scheme of bringing about a reconciliation between France and Austria.

Brühl was well aware that the great obstacle to this reconciliation was the Marquis d'Argenson, for, so long as that Minister continued to direct the foreign policy of France, he would insist on terms of peace so humiliating to Austria as to destroy all hope of an eventual alliance between the two Powers. To procure the dismissal of the marquis was, therefore, an indispensable preliminary to the success of his plans.

Although d'Argenson had many enemies at the French Court, including Madame de Pompadour and the brothers Pâris—the Rothschilds of those days—who were desirous of replacing the upright Minister by a creature of their own, his task would have proved one of great difficulty, had he not found a powerful ally in Maurice de Saxe. The marshal, who shared Brühl's views with regard to an eventual alliance between France, Saxony, and Austria, which he believed would be of great advantage to both the country of his birth and that of his adoption, and was animated by personal hostility to d'Argenson, perceived that not only the Minister for Foreign Affairs, but his brother at the War Office, against whom he had also causes of complaint, might be got rid of, if Louis XV. could be brought to believe that they stood in the way of peace with Austria.

On November 27, Brühl wrote to Saxe as follows:

"If you adopt our manner of viewing the situation; if you believe with us that it is time to make peace, the surest means to arrive at it would be a confidential and previous arrangement between France and Austria. Saxony would be too happy to offer her good offices to that end; but it would be above all things of urgent importance to get rid of the brothers d'Argenson, at any rate of the elder, the Minister for Foreign Affairs; for the too pronounced sympathies which this statesman shows for Prussia are little relished at Vienna, and they accuse his false system of preventing accommodation."[1]

On December 10, the marshal replied:

"The d'Argensons are tottering. He of the Foreign Office is so boorish that the King is ashamed of it. . . .[2] People are beginning to suspect MM. d'Argenson of having no sincere

[1] Published by Comte Vitzhum d'Eckstaedt, *Maurice, Comte de Saxe.*

[2] The courtiers called the Marquis d'Argenson, on account of his careless dress, awkward manners, and slow speech, "d'Argenson *la bête.*"

desire to make peace. It is a bomb. If one lays a match to it, they will be blown up; for all the kingdom desires peace, the King, the Court, and the clergy."

The marshal and Loss had done everything in their power to prevent the despatch of Richelieu to Dresden, but their representations came too late, Louis XV. having confirmed the duke's appointment as Ambassador Extraordinary so soon as he received an affirmative answer to his letter to Augustus III. They had succeeded, however, in preventing the dreaded Berlin visit,[1] by representing to d'Argenson that it might give offence to his Polish Majesty; and had followed it by a far more important success.

This was to secure permission for Richelieu to seek the good offices of the Court of Dresden in order to bring about peace between France and Austria.

The Marquis d'Argenson had only consented with a very bad grace, and with many misgivings, to this proposal, and there can be no doubt that he would have offered it the most strenuous opposition, save for the fear that it might confirm the suspicions that he had no sincere desire for peace with which his enemies had already succeeded in inspiring the King. As it was, the instructions which he gave to Richelieu were such as to render the negotiation altogether futile, since he was well aware that the haughty Maria Theresa would never consent even to consider such terms. However, if to d'Argenson the duke's commission was nothing but a vain formality, it was regarded very differently by Brühl and Maurice de Saxe.

[1] Frederick, in a letter to Voltaire, expressed his regret at the news that Richelieu had been obliged to abandon his intended visit to Berlin, and spoke of the duke in terms so flattering, that it is very evident that he hoped, sooner or later, to find an opportunity of exploiting him:

"I am very vexed that the Duc de Richelieu is not coming to Berlin. He has the reputation of uniting better than any other man in France the talents of mind and of learning to the charm and illusion of politics. He is the model the most advantageous to the French nation which his master can have chosen for this embassy; a man of every country, citizen of all places, and who will have in every age the same suffrages which France and all Europe accord him. I am accustomed to dispense with many of the pleasures of life; and I shall, therefore, support more easily being deprived of the agreeable company of which the gazettes have announced the arrival."

VOLTAIRE

FROM AN ENGRAVING BY LEGUAY, AFTER THE PAINTING BY LA TOUR

On December 9, Richelieu set out for Dresden, accompanied by the Marquis de Paulmy, son of the Marquis d'Argenson, who, on the disgrace of his uncle, ten years later, succeeded him as Minister for War, Lally-Tollendal, and a suite which numbered over eighty persons, his departure being celebrated by Voltaire in verses which it is to be hoped served to console him, in some degree, for the *chansons* which had greeted his return from Dunkerque:

> "Très magnifique ambassadeur,
> De votre petite maison
> A tant de belles destinée,
> Vous allez chez le roi saxon
> Rendre hommage au dieu d'hyménée.
> Vous, cet aimable Richelieu
> Qui, né pour un autre mystère,
> Avez souvent battu ce dieu
> Avec les armes de son frère.
> Revenez cher à tous les deux,
> Ramenez la paix avec eux
> Ainsi que vous eûtes la gloire,
> Aux campagnes de Fontenoy,
> De ramener aux pieds du roi
> Les étendards de la victoire."

"And, making use of a simile which only poetic license is able to excuse, he compares the gallant Richelieu, become the official witness of a marriage, to those women of easy morals, 'who on certain days in their existence feel the need of regularising their condition in this world by a legitimate alliance.'"[1]

Richelieu's arrival at Dresden had been announced for the 20th; but the roads were in such a shocking condition, that it was not until the evening of Christmas Day that he reached the Saxon capital, to the great relief of his hosts, who had begun to fear that the Ambassador and all his suite had been carried off by one of the roving bands of Croats and Pandours who invested the country, who would have had scanty respect for the passports and safe-conducts which Loss had procured from Vienna, few of them, indeed, being able to read.

Richelieu was lodged in one of the royal palaces, which

[1] Duc de Broglie, *Maurice de Saxe et le Marquis d'Argenson.*

occupied the site where the Saxon Chambers now stand, and which he describes in one of his despatches as "*le plus beau palais du monde*," and "received with a magnificence and a distinction so great, that he was scarcely able to express how much the King ought to be sensible to the singular honours which his Polish Majesty desired to pay his Ambassador." He was graciously pleased to approve of the Dauphine-elect. "I have found her really charming," he writes to Maurice de Saxe. "It is not, however, that she is in any way a beauty: a large nose, full fresh lips, the brightest and the most intelligent eyes in the world, and, finally, I assure you that if there were such women at the Opera, there would be a crush sufficient to raise the prices of admission."

On New Year's Day 1747, the marriage-contract was signed by Brühl, on behalf of Saxony, and by Richelieu and Des Issarts, on behalf of France. On the 7th, at half-past ten o'clock in the morning, the two Ambassadors had their solemn audience to make the formal demand for the princess's hand. The evening of the same day, Richelieu, who neglected nothing to dazzle both Court and town by his magnificence, gave a sumptuous fête, at which handfuls of money were thrown among the people, while from fountains which he had caused to be constructed in several of the streets and squares of the city flowed streams of red and white wine. On the 10th, the marriage by procuration was celebrated by the Papal Nuncio, the Electoral Prince representing the Dauphin, and was followed by a dinner—a Gargantuan feast of one hundred and forty-three dishes, exclusive of those reserved for their Majesties. In the evening, there was a State ball, the feature of which was the famous *danse aux flambeaux*,[1] of which Louis XV. afterwards demanded a full description from the Maréchal de Saxe, with the intention of introducing it at Versailles.

[1] "The *danse aux flambeaux*," writes Vitzhum, to whom we are indebted for the above details, "was a march or procession which was executed to the sound of trumpets and tymbals. The most exalted personages opened the march, walking two and two, holding torches in their hands; and the *fiancée* made the round of the room with each of her parents in turn. The ceremony concluded with a minuet, which Marie Josèphe danced with the King, her father."

The three days which followed were devoted to fêtes and rejoicings, and on the 14th, the princess who was destined to become the mother of three French kings set out on her journey to France, accompanied by so enormous a suite that no less than two hundred and forty-eight horses were required to transport it.

Let us now speak of the second and secret part of Richelieu's mission.

On the morrow of his arrival at Dresden, the duke had waited upon Brühl and informed him that "the King of France, strengthened by a boundless confidence in the justice and equity of the King of Poland, desired that his Majesty should charge himself with the task of bringing about, by his good offices, an arrangement between the Courts of France and Austria."

Brühl replied that the King of Saxony would most willingly undertake the part of mediator, but that the terms which Richelieu had mentioned were too vague to permit any hope of a definite understanding being arrived at, and that he desired to have his Most Christian Majesty's "last word" upon the matter, which meant that he considered that the terms which d'Argenson was willing to allow Saxony to offer Austria stood no chance of acceptance at Vienna, and that he wished him to abate his demands. And he adds: "We shall not abuse this confidence, but shall make use of it at Vienna, without mentioning from what quarter the overtures come. We shall represent them, on the contrary, as coming from us, as a plan of accommodation that, in the interests of Europe, Saxony was proposing, in order to bring about an understanding, hitherto impossible, neither party being willing to be the first to speak."

Now, Richelieu knew very well that he already had the "last word," if not of Louis XV., certainly of the Marquis d'Argenson, and that, by consenting to what Brühl proposed, he was not only exceeding his instructions, but placing the Minister whose friend he was—or pretended to be—in a very dangerous position, since, if the latter refused to abate demands which the mediating party held to be unreasonable, his enemies would be able to denounce him as an enemy to peace. But, flattered by the consideration with which the astute Brühl—who had been instructed of his little weaknesses—treated him, and ambitious to play a prominent part in an affair so important, he yielded and wrote to d'Argenson to demand more precise instructions, urging him strongly not to render the proposed negotiation futile, by declining to make any concessions to Austrian pride.

Richelieu's courier reached Versailles on January 3, bearing not only the Ambassador's despatch, but a letter from Brühl to Maurice de Saxe, who had returned from Flanders a few days before, informing him of the result of his interview with the duke, and containing this significant sentence: "I hope that, since your Excellency compares the negotiation for an accommodation to a petard, that he will be willing to charge and light it himself, while I shall endeavour to provide him with the materials necessary to secure the end which we have in view."

The "materials" speedily arrived, in the shape of another letter from Brühl stating that the Saxon Ambassador at Vienna had had an audience of Maria Theresa, that the Empress had absolutely declined even to consider the terms proposed, and had expressed her opinion that the brothers d'Argenson were insuperable obstacles to any accommodation between France and Austria.

After an unsuccessful attempt to induce d'Argenson to recede from the position which he had taken up, the marshal fired his petard, by handing Brühl's letter to Louis XV.; and on January 10, the Minister who, either by his virtues or his faults, had been unfortunate enough to incur at the same time the resentments of the Courts of Madrid,[1] Dresden, and Vienna, of Maurice de Saxe, the Maréchal de Noailles, Madame de Pompadour, and the brothers Pâris, received his dismissal.

[1] The Court of Madrid was incensed against d'Argenson by his refusal to countenance the proposed marriage between the Dauphin and his deceased wife's younger sister, the Infanta Antonia, but its resentment had been purposely exaggerated by the Maréchal de Noailles, the late French Ambassador in Spain.

Thus did the vanity and ambition of Richelieu contribute to the fall of the most able and upright statesman whom France possessed from the death of Fleury to the rise of Turgot, and pave the way for the "lame peace" of Aix-la-Chapelle, and for that fatal alliance with Austria which involved France in the disasters of the Seven Years' War.

# CHAPTER XVII

Course of the war in Italy—Success of the Bourbon forces in the campaign of 1745—Reverses of the following year—Genoa surrenders to the Austrians—Invasion of Provence—Revolt of Genoa against the Imperialists, who are compelled to evacuate the city—Retreat of the Austro-Piedmontese army from Provence—Genoa again invested—French troops under the Duc de Boufflers are despatched to its assistance, and the Austrians are compelled to raise the siege—Death of Boufflers—Richelieu chosen to succeed him—He is *chansonné* by the Parisians—His reception at Genoa—His speech to the Senate—Failure of his attempt on Campo-Freddo—Capture of Varaggio and repulse of the Austrians at Voltri—Expedition against Savona—Richelieu decides to give battle to Browne—Dishonourable action of the Austrian general—Termination of hostilities in Italy—Honours paid to Richelieu by the Genoese—He is created a marshal of France by Louis XV.—His conduct of the operations considered—Fulsome flattery of the new marshal by Voltaire.

IN the Flemish campaign of 1746, the French, taking full advantage of the withdrawal of the greater part of the British troops to oppose the Pretender, followed up their successes of the previous year; Brussels, Mechlin, Louvain, Antwerp, Mons, Charleroi, and Namur were in turn besieged and taken; Prince Charles of Lorraine was completely defeated by Maurice de Saxe at Raucoux, and the campaign closed with the whole of the Austrian Netherlands, with the exception of Luxembourg and Limburg, in the possession of France.

Very different was the course of events in Italy. In 1745 the Bourbons had been everywhere successful. In May of that year, the Treaty of Aranjuez assured to them the active co-operation of the Republic of Genoa, which, disgusted by the Treaty of Worms, whereby Maria Theresa had ceded the marquisate of Finale to the King of Sardinia, declared war against that sovereign and agreed to bring 18,000 men into the field. The combined forces of France, Spain, Naples, and Genoa were now in a position to take the offensive, for the struggle with Frederick in Germany tied the hands of Maria Theresa and prevented her sending any reinforcements to Italy; Tortona, Piacenza, Parma, and Pavia successively surrendered to them; Charles Emmanuel was defeated by the Spaniards under the Count de Gages in his camp at Bassignano (September 28), and on December 19, Don Philip entered Milan.

But the conclusion of the Treaty of Dresden with Frederick in January 1746 enabled the Empress-Queen to turn her attention to Italian affairs, and the 30,000 Austrian veterans whom she despatched to the peninsula gave the Imperialists and Piedmontese a numerical superiority which completely altered the position of affairs. Don Philip hurriedly quitted Milan, in the midst of his carnival gaieties, and retired to Pavia; one after another the towns captured in the previous campaign were recovered, and a signal victory gained by Lichtenstein at Piacenza over the united forces of France and Spain (June 16) secured their ascendency.

On July 9, Philip V. of Spain died, and was succeeded by Ferdinand VI., his second son by his first wife, Maria Luisa of Savoy. Ferdinand had little sympathy with the ambitious projects of his step-mother, Elizabeth Farnese, and, though he sent assurances of his determination to carry on the war with vigour to Louis XV., one of his first acts was to supersede the energetic Gages by Las Minas, with orders to retreat to Nice. Maillebois, who commanded the French, instead of attempting to defend Genoa, as the promises given by France to that republic should have obliged him to do, decided to retreat likewise; and the combined army fell back along the coast of Liguria, and did not halt until it had crossed the Var.

The retreat of the French and Spaniards left the Genoese at the mercy of the Austrians and Piedmontese; Charles Emmanuel occupied Finale and the Riviera di Ponente; the Imperialists took Novi, Voltaggio, and Gavi, and seized the pass of the Bochetta; while a British squadron blockaded the part by sea. Thus shut up on every side, the Genoese found themselves compelled to capitulate, practically at the discretion of the conquerors, who proceeded to impose the most humiliating terms upon the unfortunate inhabitants. The city was to be delivered to the Empress-Queen, with all the artillery and warlike stores of the republic; the garrison were to surrender themselves prisoners of war; the Doge and six senators were to proceed to Vienna, to implore the forgiveness of Maria Theresa for having presumed to take up arms against her,[1] and four other senators were to be delivered as hostages for the fulfilment of the articles of capitulation.

After the surrender of Genoa, Charles Emmanuel and Lichtenstein, with some 40,000 Austrians and Piedmontese, crossed the Var and invested Antibes, which was also bombarded by a British squadron. As the Spaniards had separated from their allies in order to defend Savoy, and the expected reinforcements from Flanders had not yet arrived, Belle-Isle, who had succeeded Maillebois in command of the *débris* of the French army, now reduced to 11,000 men, was unable to offer any opposition to the invaders. He retreated to within a few miles of Toulon, and half of Provence was abandoned to the fury of the Croats and Pandours.

Events in Genoa, however, prevented the Austro-Piedmontese army from taking advantage of the almost defenceless condition of South-Eastern France.

On September 5, in accordance with the terms of the capitulation, the Marchese di Botta, with a force of 15,000 men, had taken possession of the city in the name of Maria Theresa. Botta, who was himself a Genoese by birth, seems to have hated his fellow-countryman with all the bitterness of a renegade, and, from the moment of his entry, treated the inhabitants as though they had been subjects in revolt against their legitimate sovereign, and loaded them with every species of indignity and

1 It will be remembered that a similar humiliation had been inflicted on Genoa by Louis XIV. in 1685. *Le Grand Monarque*, however, had been satisfied with four senators instead of six.

oppression. Not only did he exact enormous contributions, amounting in less than three months to over 24,000,000 florins, and force them to provide free quarters and maintenance for the army of occupation, but he banished a number of the nobles, and suffered his troops to commit the most brutal excesses among the citizens and the peasantry of the surrounding country.

At length, the patience of the Genoese was exhausted. On December 5, as the Austrians were removing the heavy artillery of the city, with the intention of transporting it to Provence and employing it against Toulon, some soldiers endeavoured to force the passers-by to harness themselves to a mortar, the carriage of which had broken down. A lad of fifteen threw a stone; a volley of similar missiles followed, and the soldiers beat a hasty retreat.

It was the signal for revolt. During the night, the populace rose as one man, and, after five days of murderous street-fighting, Botta was compelled to evacuate the city, with the loss of fully one-third of his force.

In freeing itself, Genoa liberated Provence. The Austro-Piedmontese, deprived of their siege-artillery and of the supplies which they drew from Genoa, recognised the futility of attempting the reduction of Toulon, and when, shortly afterwards, the expected reinforcements from Flanders reached Belle-Isle, they abandoned the siege of Antibes and fell back into Piedmont.

In the spring, the Cabinet of Vienna, exasperated by the loss of Genoa, determined to make great efforts for its recovery. Maria Theresa issued a manifesto in which the Genoese were declared rebels and subjected to all the penalties of treason, and, two months after the evacuation of Provence, an Austrian corps forced the passage of the Apennines, and invested the city on the land side, while the British ships blockaded the port. In the meanwhile, however, France, now fully alive to the importance of succouring her courageous ally, had despatched to the assistance of the citizens arms, engineers, and troops, and a brave and able general, in the person of the Duc de Boufflers, a son of the gallant old marshal who had so heroically defended Lille in 1708.[1]

Thanks to the energy of Boufflers and the devotion of the Genoese, the defence was conducted with the utmost spirit, and almost every day sorties were made against the advance-posts of the investing army, which little by little was compelled to give ground. At length, towards the middle of July, the approach of Belle-Isle and Las Minas, who had occupied the county of Nice early in June, and were now advancing on Piedmont, compelled the Austrians to raise the siege, though they still remained in occupation of the greater part of the territory of the republic.

Boufflers did not live to witness the liberation of the city which he had so ably defended, as he succumbed on July 2 to an attack of small-pox. The Senate of Genoa, to do honour to his memory, inserted his name and that of his family among the nobles of the republic, and erected a handsome mausoleum over his grave.

Though saved from immediate danger, the situation of Genoa remained extremely precarious, for the Austrians were still in possession of the eastern part of the republic from Campo-Freddo to Novi and Gavi, while the King of Sardinia occupied Finale and Savona on the western coast, and the other ports were blockaded by the British cruisers. The sluggishness of the Spaniards, whose army, the French declared, was "of no more use than if it had been made of pasteboard," paralysed the energies of Belle-Isle, and the attempts of his younger brother, the Chevalier de Belle-Isle, to descend upon Piedmont, by forcing a passage through the Valley of Susa, had ended in a sanguinary reverse and the death of that officer. It was obvious that, unless the Spaniards could be brought to co-operate energetically with their allies, Genoa would have to sustain a second siege, and it was therefore of great importance to replace Boufflers by a general who

[1] Joseph Marie, Duc de Boufflers, born in 1706. He had served with distinction in Bohemia, on the Rhine, and in Flanders, and had reached the rank of lieutenant-general and been appointed aide-de-camp to Louis XV.

would command the confidence of both the troops and the citizens.

After some delay, it was resolved to offer the post to Richelieu, who, whatever might be thought of his military talents, possessed the twofold qualification of inspiring the soldiers under him with his own dauntless courage and of rendering himself popular wherever he went.

After his return from Dresden, there seems to have been some idea of again employing the duke in a diplomatic capacity, either at the Congress of Breda or at some foreign Court; and at the beginning of April Luynes reports that "for the last three weeks or thereabouts M. de Richelieu has had several conversations with the King in private and has worked with M. de Puisieux.[1] However, nothing came of these conferences, and at the end of May Richelieu accompanied Louis XV. to Flanders, and was present at the victory of Lauffeld (July 2), where, however, no opportunity for distinction presented itself. Eager for another chance of gaining his marshal's *bâton*, the duke gladly accepted the command at Genoa, and in the latter part of September he embarked at Villefranche, and, having had the good fortune to escape the British cruisers, landed at Genoa on the 27th, with reinforcements which raised the strength of the auxiliary corps to over 15,000 men, of whom 3,000 were Spaniards under the Count of Carcedo.

Richelieu's selection met with anything but universal approbation in Paris, which had not forgotten the Dunkerque fiasco. The *chansonniers* found him too old and too dandified, and proceeded to pour upon him a stream of ridicule.

> "Le rejeton de Vignerot
> Vient de s'embarquer sur les eaux,
> Pour porter à la République,
> Au nom du Roi, pour tout secours,
> Un vieille médaille antique,
> Qui parmi nous n'a plus de cours.

---

[1] The Marquis de Puisieux, who had succeeded the Marquis d'Argenson as Minister for Foreign Affairs.

C'est le doyen des freluquets,
Le patron des colifichets,
C'est le grand prêtre de la lune,
C'est un gentilhomme du Roi,
Dont la race n'est pas commune,
Et qui vaut presque Villeroy."[1]

*En revanche*, he met with a great reception at Genoa, "where the most sanguine expectations were conceived from his presence, not only as being a nobleman of great merit, but likewise a favourite of the King his Sovereign." Enthusiastic crowds lined the streets as he made his way to the magnificent Palazzo Balbi, in the Rue Carioli, which had been assigned him as a residence, and everywhere the highest honours were paid him.

The first act of the new general was to proceed in solemn state to the Senate, and to deliver an harangue, in which he assured them that no object was more near to the heart of the most Christian King than the liberation of the illustrious Republic of Genoa from the yoke of Austria, and that, as for himself, he should spare no endeavour to emulate the services which his predecessor, the Duc de Boufflers, whose loss they so much deplored, had rendered to the common cause.

The Doge replied, expressing the deep gratitude which he and all present felt towards the King of France. "He likewise thanked the Duc de Richelieu, assuring him that His Most Christian Majesty could have done them no greater honour, or given them a more convincing proof of his concern for the safety of the Republic, than by sending them so able a general, and one whom he so dearly loved."[2]

After this exchange of compliments, Richelieu turned his attention to the prosecution of the war. On October 3, he made an exhaustive inspection of the defences, and of the principal positions occupied by the enemy during the recent investment, and ordered several new outworks to be constructed

[1] Francois de Neuville, Maréchal de Villeroy, one of the most unfortunate of French generals.

[2] Buonamici, *Commentarii de Bello Italico* (English translation, 1755).

with all possible despatch, so that they might be completed before the Austrians could resume the siege.

Aware of the importance of animating the courage of the troops and the Genoese by an early success, the duke, having done everything that he considered necessary for the security of the city, decided to assume the aggressive and to dislodge the enemy from Campo-Freddo, a mountain village on the eastern frontier of the republic, which the Austrians had strongly fortified and garrisoned, and from which they constantly threatened the Genoese posts in the Apennines. On October 14, the Allies advanced on Campo-Freddo in four columns, led by the Chevalier Chauvelin,[1] Carcedo, the Marquis de Guénaut, and Madame de Châteauroux's old admirer, the Duc d'Agénois ;[2] while, the following day, Richelieu with two other divisions set out for Marcharotto, in order to bar the road by which the Austrian general Nadasti, who lay at Voltaggio with the main body of the Imperialists, must advance to the relief of the garrison.

After a sharp skirmish at Ronciglione, the Austrian advance-posts were driven in and the investment of Campo-Freddo successfully completed; and the place would have been speedily reduced to submission if the siege-artillery which was required could have been brought up from Genoa. But the peasantry, less patriotic than the citizens, had not responded to the appeal of their Government to repair the roads, which continuous rain had rendered almost impassable for heavy vehicles; while intelligence was received that Nadasti and the Piedmontese governor of Savona were both preparing to advance in strong force to the relief of the place. In these

[1] He was a nephew of the former *Garde des Sceaux* of that name, and had commanded the garrison of Genoa since the death of Boufflers. Luynes describes him as "an officer of distinguished merit, who, besides possessing all the talents that one can desire in a soldier, is very amiable in society." Just before Richelieu's arrival, he had made a dash into Montferrato, and captured "nine officers, a quantity of cattle and other beasts, horses, mules, sugar, tobacco, and soap."

[2] The fascinating d'Agénois had been somewhat unfortunate in Italy. He had been severely wounded in the attack on the Château Dauphin in the summer of 1744, and in the autumn of the preceding year had been taken prisoner by the Piedmontese at Asti.

circumstances, Richelieu had no alternative but to raise the siege and fall back to Genoa—a movement which was effected without loss.

The remainder of the year passed without any incident of importance, but at the beginning of 1748, Richelieu, having in the interim received considerable reinforcements from both France and Spain, again assumed the aggressive. On January 5, a detachment sent by him under Roquépine, a nephew by marriage of the Duc de Boufflers, captured Varaggio by a *coup de main* and took 400 Piedmontese prisoners, while, shortly afterwards, Massa shared the same fate.

The following month an affair occurred which served to raise still further the spirit of the defenders of Genoa. On February 17, Nadasti made a sudden attack in considerable force upon the post of Voltri, between Genoa and Savona, which was held by a detachment under the Marquis de Monti. Richelieu, however, hurried up from Genoa to his support, and, after some fierce fighting, the Austrians were repulsed with heavy loss.

Encouraged by these successes and by the arrival of further reinforcements from France, which reached him towards the middle of March, Richelieu determined to make an attempt upon Savona. This city not only contained an immense quantity of arms, ammunition, and stores of all kinds, the loss of which would be a severe blow to the enemy, but its capture, by preventing the British fleet from anchoring in the neighbouring roadstead of Vadi, would assure to the Genoese and their allies the possession of the whole of the Western Riviera as far as the River Var.

Relying on the great strength of the defences and the presence of the British fleet, the Piedmontese had placed but a very slender garrison in Savona, and had left the citadel almost unguarded. This fact was duly communicated to Richelieu by certain of the citizens, who bore no goodwill to their new masters, owing to the rigorous treatment to which they had been subjected, and they likewise informed him that there was "a part in the ramparts on the side of the sea extremely

LOUIS FRANÇOIS ARMAND DU PLESSIS, MARÉCHAL DUC DE RICHELIEU

FROM THE STATUE BY PIGALLE IN THE LOUVRE

convenient for surprising the foe, as being full of rents sufficient to let men enter by, and, what was no less advantageous, a thick bush of ivy covered the wall, so that it seemed next to impossible to discover the stratagem." [1]

On receiving this intelligence, the duke immediately decided to make a simultaneous attack upon the town by sea and land. His plan was that, under cover of night, d'Agénois with some 3,000 men was to proceed to Savona by sea, and, while part of his force diverted the attention of the defenders by a feigned attack upon the opposite side of the town, the rest would enter by the breach of which we have spoken, and, with the assistance of the citizens, overpower the garrison. In the meanwhile, he himself with the main body of the army would advance upon Savona by the coast-road, and take advantage of the general confusion caused by the surprise of the town to storm the citadel, which was situated just outside the walls.

In order that the enemy might conceive no suspicion as to what was intended, Richelieu proceeded to Sestri di Levante, where he began assembling troops, as though in preparation for a movement against the Austrian posts to the eastward of Genoa. However, early on March 26, he sent orders to d'Agénois to be in readiness to embark by the evening, impressing upon him the importance of using all possible despatch, so that he might reach Savona before daybreak revealed his presence. He himself hastened to Voltri, where Chauvelin had already assembled seven battalions, and marched at once on Savona by the coast-road, followed, after a short interval, by the remainder of the army.

Unfortunately for the success of this daring and well-conceived enterprise, either owing to the remissness of those responsible for the collection of the transports, or to the fact that Richelieu, fearful lest any inkling of his design should reach Savona, had not allowed them sufficient time in which to make their preparations, it was nearly midnight before d'Agénois's troops had all embarked, whereas Richelieu had

[1] Buonamici, *Commentarii de Bello Italico* (English translation, 1755).

given orders that they were to sail as soon as darkness fell. Moreover, the weather, which when they left Genoa had been all that could be desired, changed towards morning, and a heavy sea greatly impeded their progress. The consequence was that the day had already broken when they arrived off Savona, and the enemy discovered the whole affair.

Notwithstanding the failure of his intended surprise, d'Agénois determined to attempt by force what he was unable to affect by stratagem, and accordingly landed between the villages of Celli and Abisolla, burned the enemy's magazines which he found in the neighbourhood, and occupied all the eminences which overlooked the town.

Meanwhile, Richelieu, advancing by the coast-road, had captured in succession the outlying defences of the city, thè astonished Piedmontese abandoning them without firing a shot and retiring in disorder to Savona, and had come within sight of the ramparts. The investment of the town was completed without opposition, but, recognising the impossibility of carrying the place without siege-artillery and the danger of the Austrians breaking in upon his communications, Richelieu reluctantly decided to abandon the enterprise, and on the evening of the 27th gave the order to retreat.

During April further reinforcements from France and Spain reached Genoa, and Richelieu found himself in command of thirty-five battalions, of which three-fourths were French. These reinforcements were much needed, for on April 26 Marshal Browne had arrived at Parma, with orders to assume the offensive in vigorous fashion, and towards the end of May he began to advance against Genoa, at the head of 40,000 men, nearly all of whom were veteran soldiers. Richelieu decided to give him battle, and, leaving nine battalions under Chauvelin at Genoa, marched to meet the Austrians, and took up a very strong position, in an entrenched camp on the heights above Sestri di Levante.

A general engagement seemed imminent, when, on June 10, the duke received a despatch from the Comte d'Argenson informing him that the Court of Vienna had acceded to the preliminaries of peace on May 26, and the Court of Turin on the 31st, and that the cessation of hostilities in Italy had been fixed for the middle of June. He at once despatched by a drummer a copy of the preliminary treaty, which the Minister for War had enclosed, to Browne, and, at the same time, sent an officer with a letter to the Austrian general, pointing out that, as only a few days remained before the date on which hostilities were to cease in Italy, he sincerely trusted that he would be willing to conclude an immediate armistice, in order to avert useless bloodshed.

Browne returned a favourable answer, and suggested that each army should appoint an officer to regulate the armistice. But scarcely had the negotiations begun, when the Austrians suddenly issued from their camp and made a furious attack on the advance-posts of the unsuspecting Allies. Browne, less solicitous for his military honour than for conquering at any price, had seen in Richelieu's proposal only an opportunity of surprising him, and of occupying as much Genoese territory as possible before the time when the suspension of arms would have to be observed; and he had not hesitated to seize it. He gained, however, nothing by this gross breach of faith, for his troops were driven back with heavy loss, while an attack by Nadasti on the right wing of the Allies met with no better success; and the two armies were still occupying the same positions when the 15th arrived and hostilities of necessity terminated.[1]

In October, the Peace of Aix-le-Chapelle put an end to the war, and re-established the courageous Genoese in all their former possessions.

They did not prove ungrateful to those who had assisted them in their hour of need. On the proclamation of peace, an extraordinary meeting of the Senate was convened, and a decree passed creating Richelieu, d'Agénois, and Ahumada—the commander of the Spanish troops—and their posterity nobles of Genoa, with the privilege of joining the Arms of the Genoese

[1] Pajol, *les Guerres sous Louis XV.*; Oudart de Bréquigny, *les Révolutions de Gênes*; Buonamici, *Commentarii de Bello Italico* (English translation).

Republic to those of their own families; while it was also determined that a statue of Richelieu, bearing the inscription "*Liberator Patriae*," should be erected in the hall of the Senate. Palavicini, the Envoy Extraordinary of the republic at Versailles, had already received instructions to solicit for the duke a marshal's *bâton*, and the news that Louis XV. had acceded to the request, and that Richelieu had at last secured the coveted distinction which had so long eluded him, reached Genoa at the very moment when he was about to proceed to the Senate to return thanks for the honours which had been bestowed upon him.

On the whole, these honours were not undeserved, though certainly the description "*Liberator Patriae*" would have been more applicable to the ill-fated Boufflers than to Richelieu, who had, for the most part, only reaped where his predecessor had sown. However, if he had displayed no great military talents, he had shown an abundance of activity, while his courage and unconquerable optimism must have had an excellent effect both upon his own troops and the Genoese, with whom he seems to have made himself immensely popular. Several of his undertakings were well conceived and successfully executed, and if the enterprises against Campo-Freddo and Savona failed, they were due to circumstances for which he was only partially responsible.

The distinctions accorded to Richelieu would certainly have been better received by his countrymen, if Voltaire had not seen in them an opportunity for another of those fulsome eulogies which only served to bring ridicule upon both the writer and his friend:

"Je le verrai cette statue
Qui Gêne élève justement
Au héros qui l'a défendue.
*Votre grand-oncle, moins brillant,*
*Vit sa gloire moins étendue;*
Il serait jaloux à la vue
De cet unique monument."

Could flattery possibly go farther?

# CHAPTER XVIII

M. and Madame de la Popelinière—Story of their marriage—Its unhappiness—La Popelinière informed by anonymous letters that his wife is receiving clandestine visits from the Maréchal de Richelieu—The secret of the chimney—Attempt of Maurice de Saxe to reconcile La Popelinière to his wife—Madame de la Popelinière compelled by her husband to leave his house—Her sad fate—Triumph of Madame de Pompadour—Antagonism of Richelieu to the favourite—The Théâtre des Petits Appartements—The marshal forbids the musicians of the King's Chamber to perform there without his sanction—Indignation of Madame de Pompadour—Tact of Louis XV.—Reconciliation between the marchioness and the marshal—Richelieu as an orator—Disgrace of Maurepas—Richelieu's part in this affair considered—Revival of his ambitious hopes—The Marquis d'Argenson prophesies that the marshal will become Prime Minister—But the opposition of Madame de Pompadour proves an insurmountable obstacle—The favourite proposes a marriage between her daughter, Alexandrine d'Étioles, and Richelieu's son, the Duc de Fronsac—Diplomatic reply of the marshal.

RICHELIEU left Genoa at the end of October 1748, and, after proceeding to Montpellier to hold the Estates, reached Versailles on November 25, where his military successes were soon forgotten in a new scandal, which greatly diverted both Court and town, though it proved a very serious matter for one of the parties concerned.

In the Rue de Richelieu, opposite the Bibliothèque du Roi, there lived a wealthy revenue-farmer named La Popelinière. This La Popelinière had a very pretty and charming wife, daughter of the celebrated actor Deshayes—or Dancourt, as he was known on the stage—whom he had married under somewhat unusual circumstances. The lady had at first been his mistress, but, being desirous of inducing the financier to regularise their connection, obtained an introduction to Madame de Tencin, who, she knew, possessed, through her brother the cardinal, considerable influence over old Fleury, and, assuming the character of an artless young girl, complained that La Popelinière, after betraying her by the hope of marriage, now refused to perform his promise.

Madame de Tencin, who was good-natured enough when no sacrifice on her part was required, and liked to show her power, agreed to assist her. "La Popelinière shall perform his promise," said she. "But do not tell him you have seen me; dissemble with him."

Mlle. Deshayes did dissemble, and La Popelinière suspected nothing of what was in the wind until the moment arrived when the farms of the revenue were to be let anew, and he waited on Fleury to solicit the renewal of his lease. "Who is Mlle. Deshayes?" said the cardinal to him. "She is a young person whom I have taken charge of," replied the financier; and he then began to extol her intelligence, her charming manners, and her excellent education. "I am very pleased," replied the Minister drily, "to hear you say so much good of her. It is in accord with what everybody tells me, and the King, therefore, intends to give your place to whoever shall marry her. It is quite just that, after betraying her, you should leave her as her marriage-portion the fortune which, in consequence of your promise, she had a right to expect from yourself."

La Popelinière attempted to deny that he had ever promised the lady marriage; but the cardinal, "to whom Mlle. Deshayes had been represented as an interesting victim of seduction, and La Popelinière as one of those men who laugh at the promises by which they have surprised the artless credulity of innocence,"[1] was inexorable. "You have ruined her," said he; "were it not for you, she would still be innocent. You must atone for the injury. Such is the advice I give you, and, unless you follow it without delay, I can do nothing for you."

Recognising that he must either marry the lady or lose his place, the revenue-farmer chose the less disagreeable alternative; and the following day Mlle. Deshayes became Madame de la Popelinière.

[1] Marmontel, *Mémoires*.

So long as he could delude himself with the idea of being loved, La Popelinière, who was a good-hearted man and genuinely attached to and proud of his pretty and clever wife, was happy enough. His balls and supper-parties were the talk of Paris, and his hôtel in the Rue de Richelieu and his country house at Passy became the rendezvous of some of the most brilliant intellectual society of the day, where might be met Rameau, Marmontel, Vaucanson, the mechanician, Latour, Carle Vanloo, and other persons distinguished in literature, art, and science.

But his happiness was of very brief duration. Madame de la Popelinière, to use Marmontel's expression, "had taken her flight." "Carried into a vortex where he could not follow her, she went without him to evening entertainments; and people took an ill-natured pleasure in informing him, by anonymous letters, that he was laughed at by that brilliant court which his wife kept at his house." [1]

Soon the anonymous epistles took a more serious turn, and assured him that he had a successful rival, who visited madame both in Paris and at Passy. Thereupon he began to watch his wife and to set others to spy upon her, night and day. This, however, was done so maladroitly, that the lady speedily discovered that she was under surveillance, and did not fail to let her husband perceive what she thought of his conduct.

Marmontel, who, at the urgent request of the revenue-farmer, had gone to live with the La Popelinières, draws a pathetic picture of their luxurious house, "where arts, talents, and elegant pleasure seemed to have taken up their abode, but where this abundance of all the means of happiness was poisoned by distrust and fear, by dismal suspicion and gloomy chagrin."

"I wish," he continues, "you had seen this couple sitting opposite to each other at table; the mournful silence of the husband, the cold and haughty indignation of the wife; the care with which they avoided each other's eyes, and the gloomy manner in which they met, particularly before their servants;

[1] Marmontel, *Mémoires*.

the effort which it cost them to address a few words to each other, and the dry and harsh tone in which they answered. It is difficult to conceive how two beings so entirely alienated could live under the same roof; but she was determined not to leave his house; while, in the eyes of the world and of justice, he had no right to expel her."

An opportunity of doing so eventually arrived. Towards the end of December 1748—that is to say, shortly after Richelieu's return from Genoa—La Popelinière received fresh anonymous letters, which informed him that his wife received that hero every night in her apartments. Since the fidelity of the concierge was above suspicion, it was obvious that, if the accusation were true, the marshal must be gaining access to the lady by some secret passage unknown to him. He accordingly resolved to take advantage of his wife's absence at a review which Maurice de Saxe was holding in the Plaine des Sablons on December 28, and to make a thorough investigation of her apartments, with the object of discovering whether it was possible for a man to be introduced into them.

But we will allow Marmontel to relate the result in his own words:

"He was assisted in his search by Vaucanson and Balot, the latter a low attorney, shrewd and penetrating. As for Vaucanson, his intelligence was wholly confined to his art; take him out of mechanics, and no one could be more ignorant or stupid. On examining the apartments of Madame de la Popelinière, Balot remarked that there was a carpet laid in the closet where her harpsichord stood, yet that in the chimney of this room there were neither wood, ashes, nor fire-irons, though the weather was cold, and every one had fires. By inference, he thought of striking the back of the chimney with his cane; it gave forth a hollow sound.

"Vaucanson then approached, and discovered that it was mounted on hinges, and so perfectly joined to the lining on the sides, that the junction was scarcely perceptible.

"'Ah, Monsieur,' exclaimed he, turning to La Popelinière, 'what a beautiful work do I see! What excellent workman has done this? The plate is moveable—it opens; but the hinges are so nicely done. What a clever fellow must that be!' 'What, Monsieur,' said La Popelinière, turning pale; 'you are sure, then, that this plate opens?' 'Sure, Monsieur—I see it!' replied Vaucanson, transported with admiration and delight; 'nothing can be more wonderful.' 'And pray what have I to do with your wonders? We came here, forsooth, to admire!' 'Ah, Monsieur, one very seldom meets with such workmen. I certainly have some who are very good, but none that——'

"'Enough of your workmen,' interrupted La Popelinière; 'but send me one who can force this plate.' 'It is a thousand pities,' said Vaucanson, 'to break such a masterpiece.'

"Behind the plate an opening, made in the partition-wall, was closed by a panel, which, in the adjoining house, was concealed by a mirror. This opened at will, and gave the clandestine tenant of the neighbouring apartment free access into the music-room."[1]

This tenant was, of course, Richelieu, who had rented the adjoining house for the express purpose of facilitating his interviews with his inamorata. His liaison with Madame de la Popelinière appears to have begun two or three years before, and to have been conducted with such discretion that no one had even suspected it, with the exception of a confidential *femme de chambre* of the lady. Some little time before Richelieu left for Genoa, this woman had quitted Madame de la Popelinière's service, and, according to Barbier, her mistress had promised her a pension of 600 livres to ensure her secrecy. However, during the duke's absence in Italy, Madame de la Popelinière, having presumably turned for consolation elsewhere, repented of her promise, and imprudently refused to pay the pension. The ex-*femme de chambre* determined to be revenged, and, having discovered on Richelieu's return that the intrigue had been resumed, wrote the anonymous letters which put the injured husband on the alert.[2]

The unhappy La Popelinière, furious at this convincing

[1] Marmontel, *Mémoires*. [2] Barbier, *Journal*.

proof of his wife's infidelity, thought only of getting rid of her as soon as possible, and, sending for a notary, had a document certifying his discovery and his dishonour drawn up on the spot.

Madame de la Popelinière, all unconscious of the storm which was impending, was still at the review, when a faithful lackey of hers came to warn her of what was going on at home. She waited until the review was over, and then sought out Saxe and Löwendahl, both of whom were intimate personal friends, and begged them to accompany her back to Paris and endeavour to pacify her husband.

The two marshals willingly agreed to do what they could; and Löwendahl returned with her at once to Paris. On reaching the Rue de Richelieu, however, she was refused admission, and Löwendahl would not take it upon himself to force the door. Madame de la Popelinière then drove back to find Saxe. "All I ask," said she, "is that you procure me access to my own house and an interview with my husband; by so doing you will save me." The marshal took her into his own carriage, and when they came to the house, he himself alighted and knocked. The concierge, half-opening the door, was beginning to tell him that he had strict orders to admit no one, when the marshal interrupted him. "Do you know who I am?" said he imperiously. "Learn that no door can be shut against me. Enter, Madame, into your own house." Saying which, he gave the lady his hand, and they went in together.

La Popelinière, in a great rage, came to meet them and began to upbraid his wife at the top of his voice. "My good friend," said the marshal, "why do you make all this disturbance? Why do you exhibit your quarrels in public? Be assured you will get nothing but ridicule by all this. Do you not see that your enemies are seeking to foment dissension between you? Do not be their dupe. Listen to your wife, who will justify herself completely, and who desires only to live with you in a proper manner." Then, having recommended decorum and peace, he took his departure.

Left alone with the exasperated financier, Madame de la

Popelinière essayed to defend herself, boldly declaring that the secret door was a criminal invention of their enemies to ruin her with her husband. "I was too happy with you," said she, "and this happiness has stirred up envy against me. Anonymous letters have not been sufficient; proofs have been needed, and this detestable invention has been contrived. . . . I contributed to the happiness of a man whose intelligence, whose talents, and whose honourable rank in society, are a torment to the envious. It is you whom they desire to render both ridiculous and miserable. Yes, this is the motive of the anonymous libels which you are receiving every day; this the hoped-for success of the palpable snare which is now laid for you." Then, throwing herself at his feet, she exclaimed: "Ah! Monsieur, restore to me your esteem, your confidence, nay, I venture to say it, your affection, and my love shall avenge both myself and you for the injury done us by our common enemies."

But all her eloquence, all her entreaties, were in vain. La Popelinière remained inflexible, and coldly told her that he had decided that she must leave his house, and that nothing could change his resolution. If she withdrew without further disturbance, he would provide for her; but if she obliged him to employ force, he would give her nothing.

Madame de la Popelinière left the house. Her husband made her a small allowance, which appears to have been supplemented by another from Richelieu, and, after residing for a short time with her mother, Madame Deshayes, she took a lodging in the Rue Ventadour, where she died, some years later, from cancer, abandoned by that gay society which once had flattered her so much, but which ignored her now that she was reduced to comparative poverty.

"While she was wasting away in the most cruel sufferings," writes Marmontel, "the Maréchal de Richelieu sought elsewhere for amusement, but failed not, *en passant*, to pay her a few polite attentions. Accordingly, after his death, every one observed, 'The Maréchal de Richelieu has really behaved admirably! He continued to visit her till the very last moment.'"

And the chronicler adds :

"It was to be loved in this manner that a woman, who, by virtuous conduct, might, in her own house, have enjoyed the public esteem and the pleasures of a happy and respected life, had sacrificed her repose, her virtue, her fortune, and every enjoyment. And what gives a still more dismal view of this frenzy of vanity, is that neither her heart nor her senses were much concerned in it. However lively her imagination, Madame de la Popèliniere was extremely cold, but she was ruined, like many others, by thinking that a duke, celebrated in the annals of gallantry, would be a glorious conquest." [1]

On his return from Italy, Richelieu had found Madame de Pompadour all-powerful. Not only had she conciliated many of her former enemies and surrounded herself with a powerful party at the Court, but, by her really extraordinary power of pleasing, by her unrivalled skill in inventing new diversions and imparting novelty to old, and in keeping by these means the bored King continually entertained and amused, she had succeeded in establishing the most complete ascendency over her royal lover.

People stood on the staircase outside her apartments awaiting the hour of her toilette, just as they thronged the ante-chambers of the Ministers ; even the foreign Ambassadors, by the King's express desire, paid their court to her as they did to the Queen. Her household at Versailles numbered between fifty and sixty persons, who drew in salaries over 42,000 livres. She possessed in Crécy and La Celle two of the most charming country houses in France, and a magnificent mansion—a veritable palace of enchantment—was in course of erection on the slope overlooking the Seine between Sèvres and Meudon. Her father—old Poisson, the absconding clerk, who had once been sentenced to be broken on the wheel—had been ennobled [2] and presented with the *seigneurie* of Marigny, in Brie, the rent-roll

[1] *Mémoires.*

[2] In the preamble of his patent of nobility, he was declared to have been the victim of a most deplorable miscarriage of justice.

of which amounted to nearly 8,000 livres; her brother, Abel Poisson, had been created Marquis de Vandières,[1] and appointed to the *capitainerie* of Grenelle,[2] which Louis XV. had purchased for him; and people talked of a great marriage for him and also for the favourite's little daughter by M. d'Étioles, Alexandrine.

The triumph of Madame de Pompadour gave the greatest umbrage to Richelieu, who had never forgiven her for having secured the place which he had intended for a nominee of his own. To oust her from it was, for the time being at any rate, impossible, but, strong in the favour of the King, he could not resist the temptation to harass and annoy her whenever an opportunity presented itself. Few men were more adept in the art of making themselves intolerable to the objects of their aversion, while maintaining towards them an attitude of perfect friendliness, and this art Richelieu practised unsparingly against the favourite. At the King's supper-parties and at the marchioness's own, to which, in deference to Louis's wishes, she was compelled to invite him, he would sometimes exasperate her almost beyond endurance by his familiarity; at others he would adopt a patronising tone towards her, which was even more galling. In vain did she beg the King to exclude him; but Louis could not make up his mind to do without one whose cynical wit and entertaining anecdotes contributed so much to his amusement, besides which the marshal was a dangerous person for even a king to offend. And so he merely shrugged his shoulders and replied: "You do not know M. de Richelieu. If you send him out by the door, he will return by the chimney"; the remark about the chimney being, of course, an allusion to the La Popelinière adventure.[3]

[1] This title the wits of the Court forthwith converted into *the Marquis d'Avant-hier* (the marquis of the day before yesterday). In 1757, the *seigneurie* of Marigny was created into a marquisate in his favour, and he was henceforth known as the Marquis de Marigny.

[2] In 1749, he was given the reversion of the post of Director-General of the Board of Works, an office which included the supervision of the academies and art collections of France.

[3] D'Argenson, *Mémoires*.

At length, Richelieu, gathering boldness through impunity, ventured to attack Madame de Pompadour in her holy of holies, the Théâtre des Petits Appartements. This theatre, all the actors and actresses belonging to which were prominent members of the Court, had been founded by Madame de Pompadour, for the amusement of the King, in the winter of 1746–1747, the first play performed being Molière's *Tartuffe*, in which the favourite took the part of Dorine.

Until the autumn of 1748 the performances took place in a gallery adjoining the Cabinet des Médailles, which had been transformed into a perfectly-appointed little theatre. But the plays were presented here under two serious disadvantages. In the first place, the theatre was too small to accommodate more than a handful of spectators, and, in the second, the stage was so far away from the auditorium, that the majority of the actors had considerable difficulty in making themselves heard. To remedy these defects, advantage was taken of the annual autumn visit of the Court to Fontainebleau to construct an entirely new theatre, which was fitted up in the cage of the Ambassadors' Staircase, and is described by Luynes as a "masterpiece of mechanism, which could be set up in twenty-four hours, and taken to pieces in fourteen." [1]

Now, the First Gentlemen of the Chamber, who exercised absolute authority over all playhouses, both public and private, pretended that the Théâtre des Petits Appartements came within their jurisdiction, and that, consequently, the performances ought not to take place without their sanction. Hitherto they had contented themselves with sending a formal protest to the stage-manager, the Duc de la Vallière, which that nobleman appears to have ignored. But when, in January 1747, Richelieu entered upon his year of office, he at once decided that such an opportunity for annoying the favourite was too good to be lost, and issued an order prohibiting the musicians of the King's Chamber, who were under the control of the First Gentleman, and of whom the professional part of the orchestra was mainly composed, from accepting any engagements without his

[1] *Mémoires.*

permission; and on the Duc de la Vallière venturing to remonstrate, treated him with the greatest insolence, and "concluded by calling him a fool and snapping his fingers in his face."

The noble stage-manager naturally complained to Madame de Pompadour, who was furiously indignant, and hastened to bring the affair to the notice of the King. Louis, on this occasion, appears to have acted with that tact which he often displayed in matters of small importance. Instead of ordering the marshal to withdraw his prohibition to the musicians of the Chamber, or reprimanding him for his insolence to La Vallière, he at first declined to interfere, and then, one day on his return from the chase, when Richelieu, in his capacity as First Gentleman on duty, was removing his Majesty's riding-boots, a number of courtiers being in attendance as usual, suddenly observed: "By-the-bye, M. de Richelieu, how many times have you been in the Bastille?"

"Three times, Sire," answered the marshal, without changing countenance.

Nevertheless, he deemed it prudent to accept the hint so discreetly offered him, and, satisfied with the annoyance he had already caused the favourite, pretended that he had raised the difficulty about the musicians, not out of any ill-feeling towards the Duc de la Vallière, still less towards Madame de Pompadour, for whom he professed the most profound esteem, but solely in order to vindicate his own honour and that of his colleagues of the Chamber, as successive encroachments upon their privileges, if allowed to pass without protest, might easily lead to abuses, and that nothing had been farther from his thoughts than to cause inconvenience to any member of the company of the Petits Appartements.

Madame de Pompadour, on her side, was fain to accept the marshal's explanation, and a compromise was arrived at, whereby it was arranged that, in future, none of the musicians of the Chamber should play at the performances of the Petits Appartements without a written permission from the First Gentleman on duty, the latter undertaking never to withhold the same without good and sufficient reason.

With this trivial dispute, the antagonism between Richelieu and Madame de Pompadour came to an end. The former had the wisdom to perceive that he was playing a hazardous game; that "it was kicking against the pricks to rebel in any way against the mistress,"[1] and that, if he desired to retain the King's favour, it would be as well for him to accept the situation with as good a grace as he could command; while the favourite recognised that in Richelieu she had a dangerous and resourceful enemy, whom it was to her interest to conciliate without delay. A few weeks later, we find d'Argenson announcing that "a great and formal reconciliation had taken place between the marchioness and the marshal."

On February 21, 1749, Louis XV. received the felicitations of the superior courts, the University of Paris, and the Académie Française on the conclusion of the Peace of Aix-la-Chapelle. To Richelieu fell the task of delivering the harangue on behalf of the Academy. Luynes speaks of this discourse in high terms, and expresses his intention of inserting it in his *Mémoires*, if he can obtain a copy from the marshal; but, whatever might have been thought of the style and matter, its delivery would appear to have left a good deal to be desired, since d'Argenson tells us that at one point the orator came to a dead stop, and had to be prompted by a colleague, the Abbé d'Olivet.

Towards the end of April, came the disgrace of Maurepas, between whom and Madame de Pompadour the bitterest enmity had long existed. It was Maurepas who undoubtedly inspired, and, in some instances, it was shrewdly suspected, himself composed—for his talent in that direction was well known—the *Poissonades*, those virulent lampoons which held up the favourite to odium and ridicule. It was he who had stirred up the younger members of the Royal Family, with whom he was a great favourite, against her. It was he who had gone out of his way to protect her old enemy, Boyer, Bishop of Mirepoix, "whose destruction she had sworn as Herodias did that of John the Baptist,"[1] and had thwarted and derided her

[1] D'Argenson.

MADAME DE POMPADOUR

FROM THE PAINTING BY BOUCHER IN THE NATIONAL GALLERY AT EDINBURGH

pretensions whenever an opportunity presented itself. But, at length, he went too far.

One evening, at Marly, the marchioness discovered beneath her serviette a quatrain ridiculing her upon an infirmity very common in women of delicate constitution, but which she had been so careful to conceal that she was under the impression that no one was aware of it; and her fury and mortification may be imagined when she learned that copies of these atrocious verses had been distributed in Paris, and that her infirmity was now common property.

The police professed themselves unable to discover the writer, a highly suspicious circumstance, since Maurepas combined the office of Minister for Paris with that of Minister of Marine, and in the former capacity had authority over the police; and Madame de Pompadour, persuaded of that personage's culpability, declared open war against him, and from morning until night importuned the King to dismiss him, declaring her conviction that he intended to poison her, as he was reported to have poisoned her predecessor in his Majesty's affections,[1] and ostentatiously employing all kinds of precautions to protect herself.

These extravagances, as the astute lady had foreseen, soon exhausted the King's powers of resistance, and at one o'clock in the morning of April 25, d'Argenson, the Minister for War, was awakened from his slumbers by a royal messenger, bearing a *lettre de cachet*, dated from Madame de Pompadour's château of La Celle at eleven o'clock the previous evening, which he was directed to deliver to Maurepas at the earliest possible moment. This missive informed the Minister of Marine that his services were no longer required, and that he was exiled to Bourges, as his country-estate of Pontchartrain was too near Paris and Versailles.

The so-called *Mémoires* of Maurepas deny that the disgraced Minister was the author of the quatrain which so exasperated

[1] The only justification for this report was that Madame de Châteauroux had died somewhat suddenly, and that Maurepas had visited her a few days before her death, with the message from the King recalling her to Court.

Madame de Pompadour, and assert that it was Richelieu who wrote the verses, and caused them to be circulated in Paris, with the object of annoying the favourite, and, at the same time, of injuring Maurepas, upon whom he contrived that suspicion should fall.

There do not appear to be any grounds for attributing such Machiavellian conduct to the marshal, and, audacious though he was, he would scarcely have ventured to incur so grave a risk, the police not having the same reason for shielding him as they had in the case of Maurepas. If, however, Richelieu did not write the verses in question, it is not at all unlikely that he contrived to furnish Madame de Pompadour with what that lady considered to be convincing proofs of the guilt of their common enemy, and that he ably seconded her in her efforts to persuade the reluctant King to disgrace his favourite Minister, for, according to the Duc de Luynes, Maurepas's fall, which came as a great surprise to most people, was not unexpected by the marshal.

Maurepas received the *lettre de cachet* about eight o'clock on the morning of the 25th, at the house of Maupeou, First President of the Parlement of Paris, where he had passed the night, in order to attend the marriage of his host's daughter, Mlle. de Maupeou. "At that hour," writes Luynes, "M. de Richelieu was at the Parlement, to assist at the reception of the Maréchal de Belle-Isle. An intelligent man with whom I am well acquainted, and from whom I have what I am about to relate, met at the Parlement a friend of his, who said to him: 'Observe closely M. de Richelieu; he has the appearance of a man who is not himself. I should not be astonished if something which affects M. de Maurepas has not taken place.' The man who related to me this circumstance is a very truthful and unassuming person."

The fall of Maurepas brought about the resurrection of the ambitious hopes which Richelieu had buried in Madame de Châteauroux's grave, nor would they seem to have been entirely without justification, for that shrewd observer, the Marquis d'Argenson, writing at this time, gives it as his opinion that the marshal will become Prime Minister, and, notwithstanding his distrust of "this old butterfly, dabbling in politics," which he expresses earlier in his *Mémoires*, he appears to view such a prospect with complacency.

"In all the pressing circumstances," he writes, "pressing without, pressing within, pressing even in the domestic circle of the King, is it not to be expected that there must soon be a Prime Minister? The King will be compelled to appoint one. Two men alone at the Court can climb to that position by the tone which they have taken with the King: they are my brother and the Duc de Richelieu. If it be the first, we shall see in him a Jesuit, an old fox of a courtier on the throne; with an exterior of mildness, he will only do the show work of appearing without being; while beneath will be malignity and cruelty.[1] If it be the Maréchal Duc de Richelieu, we shall see boldness, good selections, some recklessness, rather too many views on a grand scale. He is, however, economical for himself; is it impossible that he may be the same for the State, when he sees with his own eyes all the horror of the means that it is now necessary to employ to procure money for great enterprises?

"Knowing the ground, one must believe that the Maréchal de Richelieu will be the man; my brother is only an adroit sycophant; the Richelieu, on the contrary, becomes, when the occasion requires, a *gouverneur* who astonishes and who pleases. He has the tone which the Cardinal de Richelieu must have adopted towards Louis XIII.: he who has not that tone with his master will never govern him, and will fall into a snare in trying to do good; that is what happened to me."

And he adds:

"It is singular that the said M. de Richelieu should have played with the King the *rôle* of missionary to make him quit his mistress and perform his Easter devotions, after having, six years ago, played a very different part in order to procure the domination of Madame de Châteauroux. But, at any rate, let

[1] There had been for some years past very little love lost between the brothers d'Argenson.

the evil cease, let the good come, from whatever quarter that it may, and it will be well."

Richelieu never had any opportunity of showing to what extent the hopes which the writer reposed in him were justified, for Madame de Pompadour distrusted him much too thoroughly to allow the reins of government to be placed in his hands, and, indeed, so far from becoming Prime Minister, he was not even admitted to the Council of State.

Madame de Pompadour's personal sentiments towards the marshal did not prevent her from considering his family a highly desirable one for hers to be connected with, and, about two years later, proposed to him an alliance between the Duc de Fronsac and her daughter, Alexandrine d'Étioles, so soon as that damsel, who was being educated in the Couvent de l'Assomption, should have reached a marriageable age. It is easy to conceive the feelings with which Richelieu must have listened to the proposal to mingle the blood of the great cardinal with that of a gentleman who had only escaped the wheel by the opportune discovery that the climate of his native land was unsuited to his health; but, since he was reluctant to give offence to the all-powerful favourite, he returned an evasive answer, to the effect that, while fully appreciating the honour Madame de Pompadour desired to confer upon his family and himself, he felt that he must first consult the wishes of the princes of the House of Lorraine, to whom his son was related on his mother's side.[1]

Madame de Pompadour, sensible of the *finesse* of this reply, allowed the matter to drop, and turned to another quarter of the Court in quest of a son-in-law. Negotiations were opened with the Duc and Duchesse de Chaulnes, who, being poor, were more inclined to complaisance, and it was arranged that, on attaining her thirteenth year, Alexandrine should espouse their eldest son, the Duc de Picquigny, in consideration of which alliance M. de Chaulnes was to receive the post of *gouverneur* to the eldest son of the Dauphin, and his wife that of *gouvernante* to the prince's daughter.

[1] *Vie privée de Louis XV.*

However, these plans were destined never to be realised, as, in the summer of 1754, the little girl upon whom so many hopes were centred died almost suddenly, to the inexpressible grief of her fond mother and the great disappointment of the impecunious Chaulnes.

# CHAPTER XIX

Comparatively uneventful period in Richelieu's life—He is appointed governor of Guienne—And is given the command of the troops stationed along the Mediterranean coast of France—Marriage of his daughter Septimanie to the Comte d'Egmont—Renewal of hostilities between England and France in America, followed by attacks of British privateers on French commerce—France prepares for war, and resolves upon an expedition against the island of Minorca—Imbecility of the British Government, who persist in the belief that a descent upon the English coast is meditated—The command of the expedition entrusted to Richelieu—He sails from Toulon—The British troops in Minorca resolve to confine their efforts to the defence of Fort St. Philip—Preparations of General Blakeney—Landing of the French at Ciudadella—Beginning of the siege of Fort St. Philip—Despatch of Admiral Byng to the Mediterranean—Voltaire's wager—Naval action off Port-Mahon, and retreat of Byng—Difficulties of the besiegers—Courage and energy of Richelieu—Night-assault on the outworks: heroism of both nations—Capitulation of the fortress—Indignation in England—Futile intervention of Voltaire and Richelieu on behalf of Byng, who is found guilty of neglect of duty and shot—Frantic rejoicings in Paris.

DURING the next few years—that is to say, until the spring of 1756—Richelieu's life appears to have been comparatively uneventful. He discharged his duties as First Gentleman of the Chamber, weighing gravely in the balance many vexed questions of etiquette and precedence; dominated the Academy, whose efforts to "immortalise" persons not regarded with favour in Court circles he sternly repressed; ruled with an iron hand the Comédie Française and the Opera;[1] engaged in a long lawsuit with the owners of a

[1] In April 1751, the *sociétaires* of the Comédie Française, without consulting the Gentlemen of the Chamber, constructed six new boxes. On learning of what had occurred, Richelieu immediately went down to the theatre, and, though the unfortunate players pleaded that the boxes had already been let, caused them to be demolished in his presence.

number of houses around the Palais-Royal, from which he expected to gain some 5,000,000 livres, but which ended in his being condemned to pay 150,000 in costs; quelled, not without cruelty, fresh religious disturbances in the Cevennes; bought the Château of Gennevilliers, and sold it again, after having had the misfortune to kill a peasant while shooting at a partridge, which gave him a disgust for the place; won and lost small fortunes at the card-table; formed "*un liaison du coin du feu*" with his old ally, Madame de Lauraguais, and made successful love to several younger ladies.[1]

At the end of September 1755, the government of Languedoc became vacant, owing to the death of the Prince de Dombes, and Richelieu, who, in addition to being one of the lieutenant-generals of that province, had since 1752 held the command of all the troops stationed there, expected to be given the appointment, the salary attached to which was 170,000 livres. But, to his great mortification, the Comte d'Eu, younger brother of the deceased prince, solicited permission to exchange his own government of Guienne for that of Languedoc, and Louis XV. felt obliged to accede to his request. Richelieu, therefore, had to be content with Guienne, which was only worth 120,000 livres.

The marshal, however, had no cause to complain of not receiving substantial proof of the royal favour and confidence, as, in the following January, he found himself selected for one of the most important military appointments in the kingdom, namely, the command of all the troops stationed in Provence and along the whole Mediterranean coast of France, the command of the Atlantic and Channel defences, from Bayonne to Dunkerque, being entrusted to Belle-Isle.

During this same winter, Richelieu married his daughter Septimanie, now fifteen years old, to the Comte d'Egmont. The manner in which the fate in store for her was announced

[1] He was still as resourceful as ever in his love-affairs, for in 1752 we hear of him gaining access to the chamber of an inamorata, who had the misfortune to be afflicted with a jealous husband, by means of a plank stretched across the street from the window of a friendly house on the opposite side of the way.

to the young lady is a singular illustration of the lengths to which paternal authority could be carried in those days. She was "in retreat" at the Abbey of Montmartre, when, one morning towards the end of January, Madame de Montmorency, the superior of the convent, sent for and informed her that her marriage had just been decided upon, and that she was to conduct her at once to the Hôtel d'Aiguillon. There, while the girl was being arrayed in costly lace and jewels, Madame d'Aiguillon told her of her father's decision, and she learned, for the first time, the name of her *fiancé*. He was formally presented to her the same day at the Hôtel d'Antin, where the relatives on both sides had assembled in full force, and, though highly indignant at the arbitrary way in which her hand had been disposed of, and far from prepossessed by the appearance of her future husband, she had, of course, no choice but to express in suitable terms her appreciation of the honour which he proposed to pay her.

The marriage-contract was signed on February 2, 1756, and on the 10th the nuptial ceremony was performed by M. de Guenet, Bishop of Saint-Pons-de-Tommière, in the presence of a brilliant company of relatives and friends. The wedding presents were magnificent, and in the *corbeille* of the bride figured the historic Egmont pearls, which were valued at more than 1,200,000 livres.[1]

Whatever we may think of Richelieu's conduct in entirely ignoring the feelings of his only daughter in so delicate a matter, it must be confessed that his choice of a husband for her was an excellent one from every point of view. The Comte d'Egmont was not only one of the greatest nobles in Europe,[2] and immensely wealthy, but he was a brave, honourable, chivalrous, and cultured gentleman, liked and esteemed by all who knew him. Although only twenty-nine, he was a widower;

[1] *Gazette de France*, February 14, 1756; the Comtesse d'Armaillé, *la Comtesse d'Egmont*.

[2] He was Marquis of Renti and Pignatelli, Duke of Bisaccia, Prince of Clèves, Duke of Gueldres and Agrigente, Count of Braisne, etc., a Knight of the Golden Fleece and a Grandee of Spain of the first class.

but, though this fact was scarcely calculated to commend him to a romantic maiden, in the eyes of her father it constituted a substantial guarantee for his daughter's happiness, since the count had already proved himself an excellent husband.

Richelieu had been very anxious to see his daughter established in life as early as possible, since great events were preparing, in which he would be called upon to play a prominent part.

At the time when the Peace of Aix-la-Chapelle was signed, no one in all Europe had believed in its permanence; and the history of the years which followed is the record of the political and other measures taken in preparation for the renewal of the conflict which was plainly inevitable. The animosity of Maria Theresa against Frederick the Great was, of course, the most disturbing element in the situation, but the rivalry between England and France, arising out of their conflicting colonial interests in both hemispheres, was an almost equally important factor.

In India, the open war between them, arrested for a brief space by the Peace, soon broke out again in a new form, the troops of the two nations appearing as "auxiliaries" on opposite sides in the struggle between Anwár-ud-din Khán and Chanda Sahib for the nawábship of the Karnátic. In North America, where the English settlers along the eastern coast of what is now the United States and the French in Canada and Louisiana were continually at variance, the outlook was still more threatening; and it was obvious that nothing but a complete understanding between the respective Governments could avert a conflict, which, once begun, would certainly not be confined to the New World.

Neither Government, however, showed any real desire for the maintenance of peace, the Whig oligarchy in England and the Ministry at Versailles being too occupied with their own quarrels to have any attention to spare for those so far away, and by the summer of 1754 the breach had widened beyond all hope of reconciliation.

Hostilities, indeed, had already broken out in America. In April, a party of 500 French descended the Alleghany, demolished the fort which the British were building at the forks of the Ohio, on a site selected by Washington,[1] and proceeded to erect a much larger one, which they called Fort Duquesne, in honour of the governor of Canada. Dinwiddie, governor of Virginia, and Washington decided to treat this incident as equivalent to a declaration of war; the latter at the head of a small force crossed the Alleghanies, and before May was out actual fighting was in progress.

The situation rapidly became more serious; regular troops were despatched from England to the assistance of the colonists; while British privateers fell upon the French shipping and inflicted considerable damage. The European war, though not declared, had begun.

In December 1755, the French Government addressed to England a demand for the liberation of the numerous vessels detained with their crews in our ports, and compensation for the loss inflicted on French commerce. The demand was refused, and France forthwith decided to commence operations in Europe.

Throughout the winter England was stirred by constantly recurring alarms of invasion, and as, thanks to the fatuity of Newcastle, the country was utterly unprepared for war, a state bordering on panic prevailed, and scarcely a French sail appeared in the Channel but it was expanded by popular rumour into a hostile fleet. "Our national confidence had dwindled under our pusillanimous rulers; a little longer, and we might all have sunk to the level of Newcastle."[2]

But, though the French boasted of their intended descent on England, and apparent preparations were in progress in all their ports from Brest to Dunkerque, they had secretly a very different object in view. This object was the conquest of the

[1] Washington, then a young man in his twenty-second year, was Adjutant-General of the Virginian Militia.

[2] Stanhope, "History of England from the Peace of Utrecht to the Peace of Versailles.'

island of Minorca, which had been seized by England in September 1708, and secured to her, five years later, by the Peace of Utrecht. Minorca, with its splendid harbour, Port-Mahon, would be an invaluable acquisition, which they might either offer to the Spaniards as the price of their alliance, or retain as a pledge to exchange against the conquests which the enemy might make in America.

The success of the undertaking depended, of course, on the secret being kept long enough to enable the French troops to reach Minorca before Great Britain could despatch to the Mediterranean a fleet to prevent their disembarkation; and, if the Government in London had not happened to be one of the most incapable with which this country has ever been burdened, it is scarcely possible to conceive how the project could have been executed. So convinced, however, were Newcastle and his colleagues that England herself was the French objective, that, though early in the year 1756 they received intelligence from several of our envoys and consuls both in Spain and Italy that troops were gathering along the Rhône, and that ships of the line and transports were being fitted out at Marseilles and Toulon, they did not attach any importance to these preparations, and insisted that they were but a feint to divert attention from our own shores. The whole of the British fleet was accordingly concentrated in the Channel, and the Mediterranean practically abandoned to the French.

The command of the expeditionary force was naturally entrusted to Richelieu, in virtue of his recent appointment as general-in-chief on the Mediterranean coast, nor could his fitness for an undertaking in which courage and energy would be the chief qualifications needed be questioned; that of the squadron which was to protect the transports and cover the siege of Port-Mahon was given to Admiral de la Gallissonnière, formerly governor of Canada, and one of the best sailors of his time.

Notwithstanding the paramount importance of the expedition sailing before the scales should fall from the eyes of the purblind

British Government, and the urgent representations of Richelieu, who, fearing, with good reason, that he might find himself forestalled, "spat fire and flame,"[1] Machault, who had succeeded Maurepas as Minister of Marine, could not be prevailed upon to hasten its departure, and much still remained to be done when, towards the end of March, the marshal, in despair, posted down to Toulon.

His presence and his authority had an excellent effect upon the progress of the preparations, and on April 10 the embarkation took place, and the squadron and the transports left the harbour of Toulon, though it was not until the 12th that they set sail for Minorca. "It is to the energy and the unwearying efforts of the Maréchal de Richelieu, the Comte de Maillebois, and the general officers that so prompt a departure, which is regarded as a phenomenon, is due," writes Portalis, the commissary of the army, to the Minister for War. "If matters had been left to the Marine, it would have remained here the entire month. That is the opinion of the most intelligent sailors."[2]

The expeditionary force was composed of twenty-five infantry battalions, a battalion of artillery, attached to a siege-train, and two companies of engineers, giving an effective total of about 15,000 men. Two lieutenant-generals, the Comtes de Maillebois and du Mesnil, and five *maréchaux de camp* served on Richelieu's staff. The transport fleet consisted of 173 vessels, and the squadron which escorted it of twelve ships of the line.

During the night of the 12th to 13th, a gale was encountered, which dispersed the transports, but little damage was done, and on the 18th the squadron dropped anchor off the port of Ciudadella, at the north-western end of Minorca. Two days earlier, a fast-sailing sloop had brought to General Blakeney, the governor, warning of the intended attack, and he had made such preparations as he could for the defence of Fort St. Philip,

[1] Cardinal de Bernis, *Mémoires et Lettres*.
[2] Portalis to the Comte d'Argenson, April 10, 1756, *Archives de la Guerre*, published by M. Waddington, *Louis XV. et le renversement des Alliances*.

which commanded the town and harbour of Mahon. As for defending the island, that was quite impossible, for Minorca has an area of 260 square miles, and is, though rocky, nearly all lowland; while the whole force which he had at his disposal consisted of four regiments, the Fourth, Twenty-third, Twenty-fourth, and Thirty-fourth of the Line, and a body of Marines, which Commodore Edgcombe, who was lying off Mahon with a squadron too weak to encounter that of La Gallissonnière, had sent to his assistance, before sailing away to Gibraltar. Of the officers belonging to these troops,[1] nearly forty were absent from duty, including the colonels of all four regiments; the chief engineer was confined to his quarters by gout; and Blakeney himself, who was over eighty and crippled by the same ailment, was quite unfit to sustain the incessant labours which a siege would entail. Nevertheless, from sheer dearth of senior officers, he was compelled to take upon himself the burden, and forthwith called in his advance-posts, including five companies which had been stationed at Ciudadella, demolished a number of houses and several windmills in the vicinity of the fort, in order to gain a clear range for his guns, and blocked the entrance to the harbour, by sinking a vessel there. He also caused a large herd of cattle to be driven into the fort, and engaged twenty-five Minorcan bakers to prepare biscuits and bread for the use of the garrison.[2]

The French troops disembarked on the 18th, on the beach at Ciudadella, without encountering any opposition from the British, who contented themselves with sending an officer to reconnoitre the enemy. Richelieu himself was one of the first to land, and lost no time in communicating his impressions to the Minister for War:

[1] The garrison, inclusive of the Marines, numbered some 2,000 men, according to Stanhope and Fortescue; but Richelieu, in his despatch of June 29, 1756, places the number which embarked for Gibraltar after the capitulation at 2,965 officers and soldiers and 120 Marines, while 171 men were in hospital, and about 100 had been killed or had died during the siege.

[2] Fortescue, "History of the British Army"; Stanhope, "History of England"; Grant, "British Battles."

"I have immediately despatched M. Dumesnil, with all the grenadiers and the Brigade de Royale, to encamp at Marcadale, and the day after to-morrow at Mahon. They [the British] have also abandoned the forts which defended the port of Fornella, which renders me absolute master of the whole island. It is impossible to display more demonstrations of the sincerest joy and more aversion for the English than the inhabitants of the island have shown. The situation in which I find myself is very advantageous, but for many days we shall be subjected to very great inconvenience, and the march from this town to Mahon, which is nine leagues distant, will be very trying for the officers, who have neither horses nor carriages, owing to the fearful heat of the sun, while the task of furnishing supplies will present many difficulties, from now until the moment when our magazines are established." [1]

On the 22nd, Richelieu received a letter from Blakeney, requesting to be informed of his reasons for invading the island while war was not yet declared between France and England, to which the marshal replied that "his intention was precisely similar to that of the fleets of his Britannic Majesty in regard to French vessels." [2]

On the 23rd, the French entered Mahon, when they soon discovered that the strength of Fort St. Philip had been greatly underrated. According to Bernis, the Ministry for War possessed no plan of the actual condition of the fortress, but only of the place in the days when the Spaniards held it. Since the British occupation it had been immensely strengthened, and was now one of the most formidable fortresses in Europe, surrounded by numerous redoubts, ravelins, and other outworks, and possessing a great number of subterranean mines and galleries, cut with incredible labour out of the solid rock, which afforded unusual protection to the defenders. "The place is very advantageously situated," wrote Richelieu to d'Argenson on the 27th, "and very strongly fortified and mined. There is a deafening artillery, and we are exposed to a murderous fire.

[1] Despatch of April 19, 1756, in Waddington.
[2] Cardinal de Bernis, *Mémoires et Lettres*.

We shall have to open trenches in the rock—a bad joke, which is likely to cost us a few people."

As there were no carts on the island and the mules were small and weak, it was found impossible to bring the siege-artillery and ammunition by road from Ciudadella ; and it was therefore re-shipped and conveyed by sea to the little bay of La Ravale, about a mile from Mahon. This naturally entailed much delay, and it was not until May 8 that the first cannon-shots were fired by the besiegers.

The opening of the siege was far from auspicious for the French. Richelieu had established several batteries on an eminence called St. Stephen's Hill, which overlooked the interior of the fort, but the distance rendered their fire ineffectual ; while those at La Ravale were soon silenced by the heavier guns of the defenders.

The French raised fresh batteries in every position whence they could annoy the besieged, and an incessant fire from mortars and cannon was maintained, day and night, on both sides ; but it was soon apparent that the reduction of the place would be the work of several weeks, during which Great Britain would certainly make an attempt to succour the garrison.

As a matter of fact, towards the end of March, the British Government had at last realised the true destination of the enemy's armaments, and on April 7 Admiral Byng [1] sailed from Spithead with ten ships of the line. He carried the Seventh Fusiliers on board, and had orders to touch at Gibraltar and embark another battalion, as a further reinforcement for the garrison of Fort St. Philip.

Although Byng was inferior in numbers to La Gallissonnière, and his ships were in poor condition and shamefully undermanned, no doubt as to his success appears to have been entertained in England, and heavy wagers at extravagant odds were laid that within four months Richelieu would be a prisoner in this country. "Take Port-Mahon, my hero," writes Voltaire to

[1] He was the second son of the admiral of that name, who had been created Viscount Torrington, and who, by a singular contrast, as it proved, had distinguished himself at the conquest of Minorca in 1708.

the marshal."[1] "I am personally interested. You know that a fool of an Englishman bets twenty to one that you will be brought prisoner to England before four months are over. I am sending instructions to London to deposit twenty guineas against this extravagant person, and I have good hopes of winning £200 sterling, with which I shall give a beautiful *feu de joie* the day I learn that you have made the garrison of St. Philip prisoners of war. I am not the only one who is betting on you. You will avenge France and you will enrich more than one Frenchman. I flatter myself that, notwithstanding the fatigues and the heat, glory is giving you health, both you and M. de Fronsac. You have with you all your family.[2] Permit me to hope that you are all drinking iced wine in this accursed fort, crowned with laurels, like the Romans triumphant over the Carthaginians."

On arriving at Gibraltar, Byng, in accordance with his instructions, demanded a battalion from the garrison, but General Fowke, who was in command at the Rock, refused to accede to his request, urging that the orders he himself had received on the subject left him full discretionary powers, and that he could not spare a battalion, having, indeed, barely sufficient men to furnish reliefs for the ordinary guards. Byng was therefore obliged to continue his voyage without the expected reinforcement, but he was joined by Commodore Edgecombe with one man-of-war and by Captain Harvey with another.[3] On May 19, he came in sight of Fort St. Philip, and the joy of the garrison may be imagined when they perceived the white sails of the British ships rising above the western

[1] He, at the same time, sent him an *épître*, beginning:

"Depuis plus de quarante années
Vous avez été mon héros.
J'ai présagé vos destinées."

and concluding with the prediction that

"Vous allez graver votre nom
Sur les débris de l'Angleterre."

[2] Richelieu's son-in-law, the Comte d'Egmont, had accompanied him, as well as Fronsac.

[3] Fortescue, "History of the British Army."

ADMIRAL BYNG

FROM AN ENGRAVING BY HOUSTON, AFTER THE PAINTING BY HUDSON

horizon. But their exultation was but short-lived, for, after fighting an indecisive action with La Gallissonnière's squadron, Byng, who, as the letters produced at his trial subsequently proved, had from the first despaired of success, held a council of war on board his flagship, the *Ramillies*, represented to the assembled officers that a new engagement, even if it resulted favourably, would not enable him to relieve St. Philip, while a reverse might compromise the safety of Gibraltar, and having obtained their consent to the abandonment of the enterprise, returned to Gibraltar, leaving Minorca to its fate (May 24).

The garrison, though bitterly disappointed at the departure of Byng, which was announced to them by the *feux de joie* fired from all the French lines, still cherished a hope that he would be reinforced and return to their relief, and continued their defence with unabated spirit.

The besiegers, on their side, in spite of the disappearance of the hostile squadron, were not free from grave anxiety. Hitherto they had made but little impression on the place, while they themselves had suffered severely from the well-directed fire of the fort; dysentery had broken out among the troops, due principally to their over-indulgence in the fruit in which the island abounds, and Richelieu had, in consequence, been obliged to order all the fruit trees in the neighbourhood to be destroyed; their ammunition was beginning to fail, and they were in daily apprehension of the reappearance of Byng in overwhelming force, in which event their communications with France would be cut off.[1]

Happily for the French, Richelieu, who, if he lacked experience in siege operations—the disposition of his batteries was somewhat severely criticised—showed plenty of courage, good sense, and energy, never for a moment lost heart. He was constantly in the trenches, encouraging the soldiers by his presence and by gifts of money, and his cheery optimism communicated itself to those under his command. He showed, too,

[1] La Gallissonnière informed Richelieu that, if the British admiral did return in superior force, he should have no alternative but to retreat, as his orders strictly forbade him to engage the enemy at a disadvantage.

a solicitude for the comfort of his men and a readiness to listen to their grievances very unusual in the French Army at this period, and enjoyed, in consequence, great popularity.

No further attempt was made by the British to relieve the fortress, and, the sea remaining open, fresh supplies of ammunition were brought from France. Reinforcements also arrived,[1] and by the end of the first week in June St. Philip's was invested by an army of 20,000 men, and bombarded day and night by over eighty guns and mortars, while an incessant fire of musketry was kept up from the roofs and windows of the town. The loss of the besieged was inconsiderable, since they were able to take shelter in the subterranean works, which were impervious to shot and shell; but before the middle of the month the donjon was a mere heap of stones, and more than one practicable breach had been made in the advance works, upon which the efforts of the besiegers were mainly concentrated.

The gallant fellows in St. Philip's, however, continued to receive and return the fire of the enemy with the utmost resolution, though "incessant duty and watching so exhausted the soldiers that they frequently fell asleep under a heavy cannonade."[2]

In proportion as the French brought their batteries nearer to the fort, their losses grew heavier, and in twelve days, June 2–14, seven officers and 207 men were killed or wounded. Their spirit, however, was admirable, and the wounded displayed the utmost *sang-froid.* "Our soldiers die with heroic firmness," writes the Chevalier de Couturelle to d'Argenson. "There was one, who, having had a foot carried off, remarked in jest that he did not intend to be the dupe of his captain, who that same day had ordered a pair of shoes to be given him, and that he should give him one of them back, since it was not fair that he should pay for two."[3]

On the 14th, a party of the garrison made a sally, and

[1] Four battalions of infantry and one of artillery.

[2] Records of the 34th Regiment, cited by Grant, "British Battles."

[3] Letter of June 21, 1756, in Waddington.

spiked several of the enemy's guns, but, pursuing their success too far, were surrounded and compelled to surrender.

This loss was a serious blow to the defenders ; nevertheless, Richelieu continued the bombardment until the 27th, by which time a fresh breach had been made in one of the ravelins and the other outworks so damaged, that he decided that the moment had come for a general assault. As wine was excellent and very cheap in Minorca, and there had been a great deal of drunkenness among the troops, which had caused the officers much trouble, the marshal, who well understood how to appeal to his countrymen's honour, issued an order of the day that any soldier found drunk should not be permitted to take part in the assault ; and the French became for the nonce an army of teetotalers.[1]

At ten o'clock that night, the French batteries having ceased fire, the signal for the attack was given by a single cannon-shot and four bombs fired from their signal-tower across the harbour,[2] and the besiegers, led by Richelieu in person, issued from their lines, and advanced rapidly across the open ground which lay between them and the fortifications.

They met, as might be expected, with a desperate resistance; even the sick and wounded officers and men who were in hospital coming forth to take part in the defence. The assailants, on their side, displayed the most splendid courage, Richelieu and the other general-officers setting them a worthy example; and the grenadiers of the Royal Italian Regiment, who had been selected to storm the Queen's Redoubt, finding their scaling-ladders too short to reach to the top of the ramparts—which were twenty-two feet high—drove their bayonets between the chinks of the stones, and mounted on their comrades' shoulders.

The French lost heavily from the withering fire of grape and musketry which was poured upon them from the ramparts, while several mines were sprung beneath their feet with deadly

[1] D'Argenson.

[2] Despatch of Richelieu to the King, June 28, 1756, in *Mémoires du duc de Luynes*.

effect.[1] But the assault was delivered simultaneously on so many different points, that the defenders, worn out with seventy days' incessant duty, were unable to repel them all; and when, at five o'clock on the following morning, a truce was agreed to, for the purpose of removing the wounded and burying the dead, three of the principal redoubts were in the possession of the French, while Lieutenant-Colonel Jefferies, the ablest officer of the garrison, was a prisoner in their hands,[2] and Major Cunningham, of the Engineers, whose skill and resource had been of inestimable value to the defence, had been severely wounded and rendered unfit for duty.

During this cessation of hostilities, Blakeney summoned a council of war, when, though several officers maintained that it was their duty to hold out to the last extremity, the majority, believing that they had done enough for honour, declared for a capitulation, if the enemy were disposed to offer honourable terms. "At two o'clock in the afternoon," writes Richelieu, "three deputies from the place arrived, who asked for twenty-four hours to propose articles of capitulation. I gave them until eight o'clock in the evening. At the hour named one of them returned, bringing me a draft of the articles, upon which I drew up a counter-draft, which I entrusted to the Comte de Redmond, who found the enemy so astounded by the prodigies performed by our infantry, and by the ardour of so great an assault, that they accepted the details of the conditions, which were not harsh." [3]

They were, in point of fact, the most honourable which it was in his power to accord, for the marshal was too overjoyed at having at last overcome the stubborn resistance of the heroic garrison, and too much in dread of the reappearance

[1] Several English writers speak of *three companies* of grenadiers having been destroyed by the explosion of a mine in the Queen's Redoubt, but, according to French authorities, only about fifty men were killed.

[2] Jefferies was taken prisoner in attempting to relieve the Queen's Redoubt. The Marquis de Monti, colonel of the Royal Italian Regiment, the officer who had defended the post of Voltri against the Austrians in 1748, seized him round the body, and held him fast until assistance arrived.

[3] Despatch of June 28, 1756, in Luynes

of the British squadron on the scene, to haggle over the terms on which the fortress was to be placed in his hands. The garrison, therefore, was permitted to march out with all the honours of war and shipped to Gibraltar. "The noble and strenuous defence which the British have made," wrote Richelieu, in reply to the second article proposed by Blakeney, "having merited all the marks of esteem and veneration that every soldier ought to show for such actions, and the Maréchal de Richelieu being very desirous to testify to General Blakeney the admiration due to the defence he has made, accords to the garrison all the honours of war that they can enjoy under the circumstances of their marching out for embarkation, namely, firelocks on their shoulders, drums beating, colours flying, twenty cartridges per man, and also lighted matches."[1]

On July 5, Richelieu and the bulk of the French sailed for Toulon, under the escort of La Gallissonnière's squadron, leaving eleven battalions to occupy Minorca. Two days later, the garrison of Fort St. Philip marched out and embarked for Gibraltar.

On their way, by the irony of Fate, they encountered seventeen British ships of the line under Admiral Hawke, who had replaced the discredited Byng in command of the Mediterranean squadron, and, unaware that the fortress had already capitulated, was hastening to its relief.

When, on July 14, the news of the loss of Minorca reached England, a very frenzy of indignation shook the country, which appalled even those who remembered the days of the Excise Bill and the South Sea Bubble. The Ministers were denounced for having neglected or delayed the necessary measures of defence; but it was upon Byng that the popular fury fastened itself, and the only doubt in men's minds seemed to be whether he was a traitor or a coward. In all the great towns the admiral was burned in effigy; his country-house in Hertfordshire was attacked by a raging mob, and with difficulty saved from total destruction; and from all parts of the kingdom addresses to

[1] Grant, "British Battles."

the King came crowding in praying for an inquiry into the loss of Minorca and for justice upon those responsible. The real delinquent, the Duke of Newcastle, only too willing that Byng should be sacrificed as a scapegoat for himself, did everything in his power to fan the popular resentment; and in December 1755 Byng was brought before a court-martial sitting at Portsmouth.

At the request of his old friend George Keith, Earl Marischal of Scotland, who had journeyed to Les Délices on purpose to plead the unfortunate admiral's cause, Voltaire, who had known Byng during his residence in England, wrote to Richelieu to beg him to vindicate the character of his fallen foe. Richelieu sent him an open letter, in which he expressed his conviction that Byng had done everything that could be expected from an able sailor and a brave man, and that, if he had continued the fight, the British fleet would have been totally destroyed. This letter Voltaire sent to Byng, and it was duly put in as evidence, but it was too obviously inspired by generous motives to produce much effect; and on January 27, 1757, the admiral, though acquitted on the charges of cowardice and treason, was found guilty of neglect of duty,[1] and condemned to death, in accordance with the 12th Article of War, the court having no power to inflict any lesser penalty. Courts-martial, it should be mentioned, had possessed discretionary power up to 1748; but, owing to its frequent abuse during the last war, it had been abolished by Act of Parliament. The sentence was accompanied by an earnest recommendation to mercy, but George II., contrary to the advice of Pitt, refused to entertain it, in which action modern authorities on naval questions seem to be of opinion that he was justified. According to Sir J. K. Laughton, it would have been imbecile, after passing the Act just referred to, to have shrunk from the first occasion of giving it effect.[2] The sentence was accordingly carried out, and the ill-fated admiral was shot on the quarter-deck of the *Monarque* in Portsmouth harbour (March 14, 1757), meeting his end with firmness and

[1] And not of "an error of judgment," as Macaulay says.

[2] See his article on Byng, in the "Dictionary of National Biography."

courage. He left grateful messages to Richelieu and Voltaire, and to the latter a copy of his defence.

While England was clamouring for the punishment of poor Byng, France—or, at any rate, Paris—was almost hysterical with joy.

At two o'clock in the morning of July 11, the Duc de Fronsac, "black as the devil and powdered like a courier," arrived at Compiègne, where the Court was then in residence, bearing his father's despatch of June 28; but, though he had passed through Paris, and it was generally believed that his arrival indicated that Fort St. Philip had fallen, nothing was known for certain until the afternoon of the 14th, while the official announcement was not made until the following day. Then the pent-up feelings of the Parisians found vent in a frantic outburst of delight. An enormous bonfire, to which Madame d'Egmont had been invited to apply the first torch, blazed to heaven from the middle of the Place de l'Hôtel de Ville; bells pealed forth from every steeple; cannon thundered until the glass fell out of all the neighbouring windows, and fountains ran wine. The name of Richelieu was in every mouth, and the fickle public, who had jeered at him after the Dunkerque fiasco, and was so soon to jeer at him again, now went about chanting his exploits:

> "Plein d'un noble audace,
> Richelieu presse, attaque la place," etc., etc.

# CHAPTER XX

First Treaty of Versailles between France and Austria—Disgrace of Machault and the Comte d'Argenson—Madame de Pompadour all-powerful—Second Treaty of Versailles—Intrigues for the command of the Grand Army: Conti, Richelieu, Soubise, and d'Estrées dispute the honour—Nomination of d'Estrées—The French cross the Rhine—Difficulties of d'Estrées: the forty-six generals—Pitiful strategy of the Duke of Cumberland—Battle of Hastenbeck—Intrigues against d'Estrées—He is superseded by Richelieu—Amusing *chanson* on the two marshals—Unfitness of Richelieu for the command of so large an army—He remains inactive at Oldendorf—He rejects Cumberland's proposal for an armistice, but seeks the intervention of Denmark—Despatch of Count Lynar to Stade—Conclusion of the Convention of Kloster-Zeven—Consternation of the French Government, who, however, decide to ratify the convention—Attitude of George II.

DURING Richelieu's absence in Minorca, France, at the bidding of Madame de Pompadour, had taken the first step on the road to ruin, and on May 1, 1756, Stahremberg, on behalf of Maria Theresa, and Bernis, on behalf of Louis XV., had signed the First Treaty of Versailles, by which the contracting parties bound themselves to guarantee and defend each other's possessions in Europe. At the end of August, Frederick, learning of the negotiations with the Czarina Elizabeth which the Cabinet of Vienna had been conducting simultaneously with those at Versailles, and that Augustus III. and Brühl, though they shrunk from committing themselves, were actively engaged in hounding Russia on, resolved to anticipate attack; and "threw open the theatre of war before the other actors were ready to appear upon the stage,"[1] by crossing the Saxon frontier. In the following year, came Damiens's attempt upon the Most Christian King's most

[1] Cardinal de Bernis, *Mémoires et Lettres.*

sacred person, and that new "Day of Dupes," which sent Machault and the Comte d'Argenson into exile.[1] Finally, on May 1, 1756—exactly a year after the Treaty of Versailles had been signed—Madame de Pompadour, whom the disgrace of the Ministers for War and the Marine, and the subsequent retirement of Saint-Séverin and Puisieux, had left almost as absolute for the moment as *le Grand Monarque*, succeeded in dragging the misguided Ministry into a second treaty with Austria, which had for its object the partition of Frederick's dominions.[2]

The favourite, not content with reconstructing Cabinets and negotiating treaties, now sought to control the French armies, or, at least, the generals who commanded them. By the Second Treaty of Versailles, France had undertaken to pay Austria a subsidy of 12,000,000 gulden a year, to take into her service 6,000 Würtembergers, and 4,000 Bavarians, and to bring into the field 105,000 troops of her own. The command of the Grand Army, 80,000 strong, which was to invade the Prussian dominions on the Lower Rhine, had been the subject of endless jealousy and intrigue at Versailles. The Prince de Conti, the Maréchal d'Estrées, Richelieu, and the Prince de Soubise all aspired to it, and all had powerful supporters. Maria Theresa had expressed a wish that the first-named should be appointed, and

[1] Both Ministers were dismissed on the same day (February 1, 1757). The Marquis de Paulmy, son of the Marquis d'Argenson, who had died a week earlier, succeeded his uncle at the War Office, in which he had been Assistant-Secretary of State for some years; while the Comte de Moras united the office of Minister of Marine with that of Comptroller-General of Finance. It would be difficult to say which of the new Ministers was the most incapable, and the disasters which overtook France during the Seven Years' War were largely the result of the imbecility with which their departments were administered.

[2] The advantage of this treaty, as is well known, was wholly on the side of Austria, who, in the event of the triumph of the coalition, would not only recover all the territory she had surrendered at Aix-la-Chapelle, and a great deal more besides, but would become absolutely supreme in Germany, as the only German power capable of thwarting her designs upon the independence of the minor states would be annihilated; while France, in return for the enormous sacrifices which she was called upon to make, would gain but a small portion of the Netherlands, which had become rather a burden than a source of strength to her new ally. It is, indeed, incomprehensible how any Government of rational men could have been brought to consent to so one-sided an arrangement.

the choice would have been a good one. Conti, besides being a brave soldier, was an intelligent and energetic officer, and had given proof of his ability in Italy during the War of the Austrian Succession. Louis XV. even went so far as to promise him the command ; but Madame de Pompadour detested the prince, who had not only refused to reveal to her the nature of the correspondence which he conducted on the King's behalf with his secret agents at the various European Courts,[1] but had endeavoured, some time before, to supplant her in the royal affections by a nominee of his own, one Madame de Coislin. She thereupon compelled the King to withdraw his promise, and refused to allow him to employ Conti in any military capacity whatever. The Commissary-General, Pâris-Duverney, who exercised a preponderating influence at the War Office, supported the claims of Richelieu, "having since the conquest of Minorca taken it into his head that the marshal was as great a warrior as he was a courtier and a man of intrigue."[2] But here again the prejudices of Madame de Pompadour proved an insurmountable obstacle. Since his return from Minorca, Richelieu, who was believed to disapprove of the alliance with the Court of Vienna, had been altogether out of favour with the marchioness, and she, moreover, suspected him, not, it would appear, without good reason, of having encouraged the *dévots* in their efforts to procure her dismissal during the King's illness. She herself desired to have the command given to her faithful friend, the Prince de Soubise, who had persuaded her that he only needed an opportunity to prove himself another Maurice de Saxe, and that the glory of her nominee would reflect upon herself. As, however, Soubise was only a lieutenant-general, and it was represented to her that his immediate appointment over the heads of all the marshals would create too great a scandal, she decided to exercise a little patience, and reluctantly acquiesced in the selection of the Maréchal d'Estrées, who was the candidate of Belle-Isle, whose failing

[1] On the secret diplomacy of Louis XV., see the late Duc de Broglie's interesting work, *le Secret du Roi.*

[2] Bernis.

health prevented him from taking the field in person, with the full determination that Soubise should supersede him on the first convenient opportunity.

At the beginning of April, the Grand Army crossed the Rhine near Wesel, which had been abandoned by the Prussians, though it was not until the end of the month, when d'Estrées arrived to assume the command, that the campaign actually began. Then the French advanced into Westphalia and marched slowly towards the Weser.

In numbers and equipment, it was as fine an army as France had ever put into the field ; in the matter of discipline, it was one of the worst. In the train of the generalissimo appeared three Princes of the Blood—the Duc d'Orléans, the Prince de Condé, and the Comte de la Marche—46 lieutenant-generals and 65 *maréchaux-de-camp*, drawn from the *élite* of the French nobility. The presence of the princes in the army was a serious trouble to d'Estrées, for not only did they bring with them numerous carriages and carts of all kinds, with hundreds of horses to transport them,[1] and an immense retinue of servants, but whole regiments had to be detached for the protection of their precious persons. Their example was followed by the senior officers, though, of course, on a more modest scale, notwithstanding that an ordinance of the previous March had strictly limited the number of horses and equipages which they were permitted to bring into the field. The result was that the difficulties of forage and transport were enormously aggravated, and the mobility of the whole army impeded.

Nor was this the only embarrassment. As the number of generals was out of all proportion to the size of the army, large though it was, and there were not enough brigades and divisions to go round, d'Estrées, in order to allay to some extent the jealousy which existed among them, adopted the expedient of utilising their services in turn. Thus one week a certain brigade would be commanded by the Duc de ——, the next by the Marquis de ——, and so on. The confusion which this

[1] According to Luynes, the Duc d'Orléans left Paris with 350 horses, the Prince de Condé with 225, and the Comte de la Marche with 100.

constant change of commanding officers occasioned may be easily conceived. Moreover, it was impossible with the best will in the world to provide even occasional employment for all, and those who were passed over, finding themselves without any other occupation than the ordinary routine of the march and the camp, spent their time in criticising the generalissimo and their more fortunate comrades and in revelry and gambling, and thus set a most deplorable example to the younger officers and the soldiers.

About the middle of April, the Duke of Cumberland had arrived from England, and taken command of a motley force of Hanoverians, Hessians, and other West German troops, together with a few hundred Prussians,[1] which was intended to oppose the advance of the French. His army[2] was much inferior to d'Estrées' in numbers—not more than 50,000 effectives—but the troops were brave and well trained, and under a skilful commander might have offered a successful resistance to the invaders. Cumberland's responsibility, however, seems to have been altogether too much for him. Frederick had strongly advised him to defend the Lower Rhine, but, instead of doing so, he fell back on the Weser—a river the passage of which was far more difficult to dispute than the Rhine—thus allowing the French to occupy nearly the whole of Westphalia without striking a blow.

The French, on their side, seemed in no hurry to take advantage of the enemy's retreat. They had the greatest difficulty in obtaining supplies, as the Prussian evacuation of Wesel had completely upset the calculations of Pâris-Duverney, the Commissary-General. That personage had calculated that a siege of two months would have been necessary to reduce the place, during which the bulk of the Grand Army would have remained on the Rhine to cover the siege, and have been able to draw their supplies from France. In consequence of

[1] The Prussian contingent, which had lately formed part of the garrison of Wesel, was soon recalled by Frederick, in disgust at the pitiful strategy of the duke.

[2] It was called the "Britannic Army of Observation," but, with the exception of Cumberland's personal staff, was "Britannic only in the money part."—Carlyle, „ Frederick the Great."

Duverney's want of foresight, and the bad condition of the roads, their advance was very slow, since, as d'Estrées observed, he "did not possess the talent to make an army advance by swimming or to make it live on air." [1]

As they advanced, Cumberland retreated before them,[2] and in the third week in June crossed the Weser, and placed that river between himself and the French.

After long delay—due partly to the causes we have mentioned and partly to his own irresolution—d'Estrées, spurred on by urgent despatches from Versailles, followed the duke, his passage of the Weser being practically undisputed, and at length came up with him at the village of Hastenbeck, near Hameln. Here, on July 26, a battle took place, which ended in a victory for the French, though no credit belonged to their commander, who had actually ordered a retrograde movement, under the impression that the day was lost, when he discovered that the main body of the enemy was in full retreat.

While d'Estrées was manœuvring in the Weser country, intrigues were going on against him at Versailles. The Comte de Maillebois, his chief of the staff, who had served under Richelieu in Minorca, and desired to see him occupying the place of d'Estrées, kept up a private correspondence with the Minister for War, whose sister he had married, in which he persistently exaggerated the shortcomings of his commanding officer, and represented him as absolutely incapable of maintaining discipline. Moreover, before leaving France, the marshal had quarrelled with Duverney, by refusing to discuss with him his plan of campaign, and had still further estranged that personage by the bitter complaints on the subject of the commissariat-service with which he seasoned his despatches. He had also committed the mistake of showing jealousy of the Court favourite, Soubise, who commanded the reserve, and who, among other acts of presumption, stamped the letters which he

[1] D'Estrées to Belle-Isle, May 27, 1757, in Waddington, *la Guerre de Sept Ans*.

[2] "I have never seen any one more out of his element in war than M. de Cumberland," writes Bésenval, in his *Mémoires*. "He seemed to be acting under our orders; as soon as we struck our tents to advance, he prepared to retreat."

sent to Versailles, "*Armée de Soubise.*" And, to crown all, his wife had mortally offended Madame de Pompadour, by conspiring against her with Mlle. Murphy ("*la petite Morfil*"), the reigning sultana of Louis XV.'s little seraglio, the Parc-aux-Cerfs.[1]

Early in June, Duverney, profiting by the anger of the favourite, the complaints of the Court of Vienna about the supineness of d'Estrées, and its demands for a more active co-operation in Germany, drew up a new plan of operations, which he prophesied would bring the war to an end in a single campaign. His proposal was that Richelieu should be sent to Western Germany, with a reinforcement of 25,000 men, and should supersede d'Estrées in command of the Grand Army, while Soubise, with an army of some 25,000 to 30,000, should operate in Saxony, in conjunction with the troops of the Circles,[2] keep Frederick there without risking a battle, and so give time to the Austrians to occupy Silesia. Paulmy, the Minister for War, was easily won over to the scheme by the arguments of his brother-in-law, Maillebois; while Madame de Pompadour, notwithstanding her dislike of Richelieu, could not but approve of an arrangement which got rid of d'Estrées, and gave to her "dear Soubise" an independent command.

Accordingly, after an interview between the favourite and Richelieu, "in which the marshal justified himself, and the marchioness simulated sentiments which were not in her heart,"[3] Duverney's proposals were accepted by the latter, and subsequently by Louis XV., though the marshal's appointment remained the secret of the conspirators until the second week in July.

After paying a brief visit to Bourbon-les-Bains, to bid

[1] For an account of Mlle. Murphy and the Parc-aux-Cerfs, see the author's *Madame de Pompadour* (London, Harper ; New York, Scribner, 1902).

[2] His original plan was that Soubise's corps should reinforce the Imperialists in Bohemia, but this was abandoned after he received intelligence of Frederick's defeat at Kolin (June 18) and his subsequent retreat into Saxony.

[3] Bernis. In his *Mémoires*, Bernis, who had lately succeeded Rouillé as Minister for Foreign Affairs, declares that he protested against Duverney's proposal, though this statement does not altogether accord with his correspondence on the matter with the Commissary-General.

farewell to Madame de Lauraguais, who was taking the waters there, Richelieu proceeded to Strasburg, to hasten on the mobilisation of the troops which were to reinforce his army. On August 3, he reached the French headquarters at Oldendorf, having purposely delayed his arrival in order not to precede the courier who was carrying to d'Estrées the order for his recall, and who had, for some reason unexplained, not left Versailles until July 24.

Great was his mortification to discover that, owing to his delay, the general whom he came to supersede had been permitted to gain a victory, the credit of which would otherwise have belonged to him; and that this success had been followed by the capitulation of Hameln and Münden, a letter from Schliestadt, Minister of the Duke of Brunswick, requesting a passport to permit him to treat with the French commander concerning the fate of his master's dominions, and a despatch announcing that a deputation from the town and the Council of Regency of Hanover was on its way to the French camp, with proposals for the neutrality of the electorate.

"If I had arrived ten days earlier," he writes to Duverney, "I should have been spared much irritation. But, in truth, the poor Maréchal d'Estrées has spoken to me so frankly and treated me so courteously, that I cannot be annoyed at what has happened."[1]

If d'Estrées contrived to conceal his wounded feelings in the presence of Richelieu, and subsequently abstained from any attack upon his successor, the *chansonniers* of Paris charged themselves with the duty of avenging him. Unaware of the good fortune that had gained him the battle of Hastenbeck, they saw in him only a victorious general sacrificed to a Court cabal, and chanted his praises, while they poured ridicule upon Richelieu:

"Nous avons deux généraux
Qui tous deux maréchaux,
Voilà la ressemblance.

[1] Letter of August 4, 1757, *Correspondance du Maréchal de Richelieu avec Pâris-Duverney* (London, 1789).

L'un de Mars est favori,
Et l'autre l'est de Louis,
Voilà la différence.

"Cumberland les craint tous deux
Et chercha à s'éloigner d'eux
Voilà la ressemblance.
De l'un il fuit le valeur
Et de l'autre l'odeur [1]
Voilà la différence.

"Dans un beau champ de lauriers
On aperçoit ces guerriers,
Voilà la ressemblance.
L'un a su les entasser,
L'autre vient les remasser,[2]
Voilà la différence." [3]

The friends of Richelieu at the Court, greatly embarrassed by the public indignation, exhorted him to justify his nomination by some brilliant success. "It is much hoped and desired here," wrote the Minister for War to the marshal, "that you will embark upon an energetic pursuit of the Duke of Cumberland's army and end by destroying it. You are, indeed, aware what is the best thing you can do to cover the successes which have preceded your arrival, and that, since it is of much more importance than these successes, it would prove them to be only imperfect." [4]

[1] Richelieu had a weakness for musk and other strong perfumes.

[2] A caricature of the day represents d'Estrées chastising the Duke of Cumberland with a branch of laurel, while Richelieu is engaged in gathering up the leaves that fall and making himself a crown.

[3] *Vie privée de Louis XV.*; *Journal de Barbier.* M. Waddington, in his *la Guerre de Sept Ans*, cites another version of this *chanson*, from which we select the following verses:

"Que pour eux dans les combats
La gloire a toujours d'appas!
L'un contre les ennemis,
L'autre contre les maris.
D'être utiles à notre roi
Tous deux se font la loi,
A Cythère l'un le sert,
Et l'autre sur le Weser."

[4] Despatch of July 1757, in Waddington, *la Guerre de Sept Ans.*

Richelieu needed no such exhortations to convince him of the urgency of justifying his selection, but, unfortunately for the accomplishment of his hopes, he found himself face to face with the material embarrassments which had hampered the movements of his predecessor. Moreover, the spirit of insubordination which had shown itself in complaints against the irresolution and supineness of d'Estrées, broke out in an aggravated form against the new commander-in-chief, who had not the prestige of recent victory to assist him in maintaining discipline. Although it was only the beginning of August, both officers and men, fatigued by long marches and miserable encampments, had come to the conclusion that they had had enough glory for one year, and sighed for the rest and comfort of winter-quarters ; and when they learned that it was Richelieu's intention to prosecute the campaign with vigour, they made no effort to conceal their disgust, and indulged in unpleasant jests at the expense of the Court favourite, whom they accused of seeking fresh laurels, out of jealousy of those which d'Estrées had culled. Maillebois, the chief of the staff, in consequence of his conduct at Hastenbeck, which, on his return to France, led to his being court-martialled and cashiered, had lost most of his authority; the Duc d'Orléans, who had been second in command to d'Estrées, indignant at Richelieu having been preferred to him, demanded his *congé* and returned to France; the generals of division were jealous of their commander and of each other, and the camp was divided into hostile factions.

At Genoa and again in Minorca, Richelieu had shown courage, energy, and resolution, but he did not possess the qualities indispensable for the command of an army such as the one to which he had been appointed. His splendid valour might inspire admiration on the field of battle, but, when not actually in the presence of the enemy, his frivolous character prevented him from commanding the confidence of his officers or the respect of his soldiers. Besides, if he were eager for glory, he was still more eager for money; and the immense contributions which he levied upon the conquered territory, and which he and his principal lieutenants diverted into their own pockets, encouraged marauding among the soldiers, to which Richelieu, seeing that he himself had set them the example, was naturally compelled to close his eyes.[1]

After his defeat at Hastenbeck, Cumberland, instead of falling back on Madgeburg, where he might have acted in conjunction with the Prussians, or making any attempt to defend the capital of his father's electorate, had retreated to Verden, the chief town of the duchy of that name, situated on the Aller, a little above the confluence of that river with the Weser, where he arrived on August 8.

For two weeks Richelieu made no attempt to pursue him, but remained in his camp at Oldendorf, levying contributions on the surrounding country and sending out detachments to secure the towns on the Weser. His explanation of his inaction was his belief that troops were on their way from England to reinforce Cumberland, and that that general was retreating towards the mouth of the Elbe in order to effect his junction with them,[2] and the unsatisfactory health of his army. "It would not be practical to resume the offensive," he writes to the Minister for War on August 12, "until after a period of repose, necessitated by the fatigue and sickly condition of the troops";[3] while he assures Duverney that "the army was exhausted by fatigue and dysentery caused by drinking bad water, and that it was necessary to reinstate it, by allowing it a little rest, and to drink wine and beer.[4]

As, when these despatches were written, the army had already been resting for more than a fortnight, it would appear that its indisposition to quit its comfortable quarters rather than the exigencies of its health was the real motive at work; and this seems to have been the opinion of the War Office, who informed Richelieu that his inaction was being severely criticised in Paris and that a rest of two or three days ought to be amply sufficient for the troops.

[1] Waddington, *la Guerre de Sept Ans.*

[2] Some 9,000 British troops had just embarked at Chatham. They were intended for a descent upon Rochefort, but the French could only conjecture their destination.

[3] Richelieu to Paulmy, August 12, 1757, cited by Waddington.

[4] *Correspondance du Maréchal de Richelieu avec Pâris-Duverney* (London, 1789).

WILLIAM AUGUSTUS, DUKE OF CUMBERLAND

FROM AN ENGRAVING BY L'EMPEREUR, AFTER THE PAINTING BY MORIER

At length, on August 19—after another week's repose—the Grand Army condescended to resume its march, and proceeded leisurely northwards in pursuit of Cumberland. On the 23rd, the French arrived at Mariensee, and on the same day the Hanoverians evacuated Verden and continued their retreat in the direction of Stade, where they hoped to be able to maintain themselves, at any rate for a time.

At Mariensee, Richelieu received a letter from Cumberland proposing a suspension of arms, "to permit the two Courts to arrange what I cannot call a peace, since I am not aware that war has been declared between France and the Electorate of Hanover." But the marshal replied that "the King his master had placed him at the head of his army to fight the enemies of his Allies, and not to negotiate."

"This answer," says Bernis, in his *Mémoires*, "was in conformity with the instructions which I had given him. In them he was formally ordered to send to Versailles all negotiations whatsoever which the enemy might endeavour to open with him, whether on the part of the King of England or on that of the King of Prussia and his allies. The Maréchal de Richelieu remembered this formal command on this occasion; he forgot it at Kloster-Zeven."[1]

Richelieu, indeed, soon abandoned his uncompromising attitude. Although very anxious for a success which should obliterate that of Hastenbeck, he considered it probable that Cumberland, instead of risking a battle against such vastly superior numbers, or surrendering at discretion, would throw himself into Stade;[2] and he doubted the expediency of beginning a siege so late in the year, and exposing his army to the diseases which a prolonged sojourn in a marshy region would inevitably invite. Besides, the farther he advanced northwards, the farther the distance between him and his real objectives, Halberstadt and Magdeburg, and the greater the danger of

[1] Cardinal de Bernis, *Mémoires et Lettres*.

[2] Cumberland was now in a kind of *cul-de-sac*, penned in between the Elbe, the sea, and the French. The Elbe, which is very broad at this point, was in the rear of the Hanoverian army, and there were no boats to transport it across the river into the duchy of Saxe-Lauenburg, in which it might otherwise have taken refuge.

Frederick breaking in upon his communications. For which reasons, he determined to seek the intervention of the neighbouring neutral State of Denmark, to bring about between the belligerents an arrangement which he was not authorised to conclude himself. Already the King of Denmark had proposed to the Court of France a convention relative to the Duchies of Bremen and Verden ; it would be easy to extend this convention to Hanover, Hesse, and Brunswick. The neutrality of Prussia's allies in North Germany secured, and, with it, his lines of communication, the Grand Army would be free to concentrate all its efforts against Frederick himself, and co-operate energetically with the Austrians.[1]

He accordingly communicated his views to Président Ogier, the French Ambassador at Copenhagen, and that diplomatist, who subsequently declared that the marshal gave him to understand that he was authorised to negotiate with Cumberland, lost no time in seeking the mediation of the Danish Court. Christian consented, all the more readily since he had lately received advances from George II., on behalf of himself and his allies in North Germany, in relation to the neutrality of his States and theirs; and Count Lynar, the Danish Viceroy of Oldenburgh, was forthwith despatched to Stade.

In the meanwhile, Richelieu had not been idle. Detachments of his army had occupied Verden, Bremen, and Harburg —a town on the lower arm of the Elbe, opposite Hamburg— while he himself, leaving the bulk of his forces at Weille, had established his headquarters at Kloster-Zeven, between Verden and Stade. Here, on September 5, he received a visit from Lynar, who brought a proposal from Cumberland for an armistice.

The marshal began by declining any arrangement which did not include the retirement of the Hanoverians beyond the Elbe and the surrender of Stade to a Danish garrison. To this Cumberland refused to consent, and Lynar's efforts to induce Richelieu to abate his terms proved ineffectual. Finally, however, on September 8, the Danish diplomatist, learning that

[1] Waddington, *la Guerre de Sept Ans*.

the French were preparing to advance, persuaded Cumberland to give him full powers to conclude the affair, and, two days later, that extraordinary document known as the Convention of Kloster-Zeven was signed. By its terms the Hessians, Brunswickers, and other auxiliaries were to be sent home and to observe the strictest neutrality until the end of the war; the Hanoverians were to pass the Elbe, and to be dispersed into different cantonments, leaving only a garrison in Stade; while the French remained in occupation of Hanover, Bremen, and Verden.

Richelieu was quite enchanted with his work. "I believe," he wrote to Paulmy, "that I could not have accomplished anything more glorious or more useful for the arms of the King";[1] and he hastened to inform all the Court and Paris of his triumph by private letters, "in which he spoke proudly of having forced a whole army to lay down its arms, and said that peace was made."[2]

The French Government was very far from sharing the marshal's jubilation. So soon as he was informed by Richelieu of Lynar's arrival at Kloster-Zeven, Bernis, who had no suspicion that it was the marshal himself who had suggested the mediation of Denmark, and that the negotiations were already far advanced, wrote to him that he had "no other negotiation to make with the Hanoverians than to force their camp at Stade and drive them into the Elbe." "After writing this and despatching the courier," he says, "I carried the Maréchal de Richelieu's letter to the King and informed him of the answer I had sent. He replied: 'You have answered properly; but you do not know the marshal; what he speaks of as a mere project may be half executed already. Send a second courier ordering M. de Richelieu to open no negotiations and to send at once to Fontainebleau (where the Court then was) all those that may have been begun.' I wrote under the eyes of the King, and almost at his dictation, and the second courier started instantly."[3]

[1] Richelieu to Paulmy, September 10, 1757, in Waddington.

[2] Bernis, *Mémoires et Lettres*.

[3] Bernis's second despatch, which is very emphatic, has been published by M. Waddington. It concludes as follows: "The King's intention is, Monsieur, that

It was then, however, September 12—two days after the convention had actually been signed—and, to the astonishment of Bernis, on the 15th the Duc de Duras arrived at Fontainebleau, bringing it with him.

The astonishment of the Minister was as nothing to the dismay with which he perused this unfortunate document, for it was not, as he fully expected to find it, a *capitulation*, that is to say, a military act complete in itself, but a *convention* [1]—a diplomatic act, which would be only binding if ratified by the respective Governments, in default of which it would become mere waste paper. Nor was this all, for Richelieu had, by some extraordinary oversight, omitted both to fix the date of the execution of the accepted articles and to prohibit Cumberland's troops from serving against the allies of France.

Since Richelieu had had no power whatever to conclude such a compact, Louis XV. might have repudiated it and brought its author before a court-martial. But, almost immediately after the signing of the convention, warned that Frederick was advancing towards the Saale, the marshal had marched with the bulk of his army on Halberstadt, leaving only six battalions and six squadrons to compel the Hanoverian army to execute the capitulation. Consequently, the King felt obliged to approve of his general's action, and to instruct him to inform Cumberland that France would ratify the convention so soon as Great Britain had done so.

Whatever might be the ultimate result of what the indignant

you confine yourself to listening to all the propositions which will be made to you, and that you only receive them to communicate them to his Majesty, who, after examining them, will deliberate upon them in his Council, as well as upon the reflexions with which you will accompany them, will decide as he thinks best, and inform you of his wishes. He desires that, in the meanwhile, you will not suspend the progress of your operations.

[1] It was, of course, to all intents and purposes, a capitulation, but Cumberland protested so strongly against the word being used, that Richelieu yielded the point, without taking into consideration the possible consequences of such a concession. The marshal has been accused of criminal carelessness in not insisting on the former compact, but it is probable that he considered the matter of very slight importance, as he anticipated that the convention would be merely a preliminary step to a treaty or the neutrality of Hanover, about which negotiations had been for some time in progress at Vienna.

Bernis stigmatises as "a masterpiece of clumsiness and imprudence," it was obvious that, for the time being, it placed North Germany completely prostrate at Richelieu's feet, and left him at liberty to proceed either against the Prussian territories of Halberstadt and Magdeburg, or to co-operate with Soubise in Saxony. In fact, "it would be difficult to decide," says Stanhope, "whether this convention excited most indignation at the English Court or in the Prussian camp." Frederick declared that Great Britain had undone him without mending her own situation; while George II. lost no time in recalling Cumberland to England, where, on the day following, the duke announced his resignation of the post of Captain-General and all his military employments, and withdrew into private life.[1]

Even before the return of the prince, George II. had determined not to ratify the convention. In this decision, in which he was supported by the British Ministers, he was no doubt technically in the right, but, at the same time, it is impossible to acquit him or the Government of the charges of bad faith brought against them by French writers. For, although the King wrote to the Hanoverian Council of Regency at Stade that it was his intention not to execute the treaty, he informed them that he should postpone the resumption of hostilities until the moment when "one can hope for a happy issue, and not to be exposed to still greater evils." And he added that "a victory gained by the King of Prussia would be a convenient occasion for falling unexpectedly upon the French who are quartered in our States, in such a manner that they may be surprised separately in their quarters or driven out of the country."[2]

[1] He could scarcely have acted otherwise after the "Here is my son, who has ruined me and disgraced himself," which the paternal Majesty let fall, at Kensington, the previous evening.

[2] Rescript to the Ministers of State at Stade, October 5, 1757, Newcastle Papers, British Museum.

# CHAPTER XXI

Richelieu marches on Halberstadt—He receives overtures for peace from Frederick—Letters of Voltaire and the King of Prussia to the marshal—The French Government refuse to entertain the King's proposals—Richelieu occupies Halberstadt—Instead of advancing on Magdeburg, he concludes an armistice until the spring of the following year—Refusal of the French Government to ratify the compact—Richelieu remains inactive at Halberstadt—Disputes with Versailles on the question of his army's winter-quarters—He sends reinforcements to Soubise—Crushing defeat of the latter at Rossbach entirely changes the situation of affairs—Richelieu falls back to the Aller, to hold the Hanoverians in check—Repudiation of the Convention of Kloster-Zeven—The marshal concentrates his forces at Zelle—Advance of Ferdinand of Brunswick—Richelieu, courageously refusing to listen to the pusillanimous counsels of his officers, passes the Aller and compels the Hanoverians to retreat—He is recalled to France, and succeeded by the Comte de Clermont—His conduct during the campaign of 1757 considered—His shameful rapacity the cause of the ruin of his army—The "Pavillon d'Hanovre."

IN the meanwhile, Richelieu was marching rapidly on Halberstadt—much too rapidly to suit his officers and men, who grumbled incessantly, the latter with some reason, since all the shoes which had been issued to them were worn out, and they had not been replaced.[1] At Brunswick, on September 20, he found one of Frederick's confidants named Eickstadt awaiting him, with a personal letter from the King containing overtures for peace. These overtures had been foreshadowed by a letter from Voltaire, who had conceived the idea of heaping coals of fire upon the head of his former protector, by acting as mediator between him and his victorious enemies It was as follows:

[1] According to the Comte de Gisors, 40,000 pairs of shoes were urgently needed. At the beginning of the campaign each man had received three pairs.

"MY HERO,

"You have seen and you have done extraordinary things. Here is one which is not less so, and which will occasion you no surprise. I confide it to your kindness for me, to your interest, to your wisdom, to your glory. He [Frederick] has taken it upon himself to write to me somewhat confidentially. He tells me that he is determined to kill himself, if he is without resources, and the Margravine,[1] his sister, writes to me that she will put an end to her life, if the King, her brother, puts an end to his. . . . It is not my province to meddle in politics ; but I ought to tell you that in my last letter to the Margravine, I could not prevent myself from allowing her to perceive how much I desire that you shall join the quality of arbiter to that of general. I am of opinion that if they wish to leave everything to the goodness and magnanimity of the King [of France], it would be better to address themselves to you than to any other."[2]

Frederick had lent himself very willingly to the suggestion of the patriarch of Ferney—for his situation at this moment was indeed a critical one—and he had been at pains to flatter his correspondent and persuade him to undertake the part which he desired him to play.

"I feel, M. le Duc," he writes, "that you have not been placed in the position you occupy for the purpose of negotiating. I am persuaded, however, that the nephew of the great Cardinal de Richelieu is made for signing treaties no less than for gaining battles. I address myself to you from an effect of the esteem with which you inspire even those who do not know you intimately.

"It is a mere trifle, Monsieur : only to make peace, if people are pleased to wish it ! I know not what your instructions are ; but, on the supposition that the King your master will have put it in your power to labour for the pacification of Germany, I send to you the Sieur Eickstadt, in whom you may place entire confidence.

[1] Wilhelmina, Margravine of Bayreuth.

[2] Letter of August 21, 1757, *Œuvres de Voltaire*, vol. lv.

"Although the events of the year offer me no hope that your Court is still favourably disposed towards my interests, I cannot persuade myself that a union which has lasted between us for sixteen years may not have left some trace in the mind. But, however that may be, I, in short, prefer to commit my interests to your master's hands rather than to any other's. If you have not, Monsieur, any instructions as to the proposal which is here made, I beg you to ask for them, and to acquaint me with their tenor.

"He who has merited statues at Genoa, he who has conquered the island of Minorca in the face of immense obstacles, he who is on the point of subjugating Lower Saxony—can do nothing more glorious than to labour to restore peace to Europe. Of all your laurels that will be the fairest."

Carlyle and several German historians assert that Eickstadt brought with him something more acceptable than flattery, to wit, a present of £15,000; but, if he did so, and Richelieu was not above taking it—which seems to us extremely improbable—it was a very unprofitable investment. For the marshal, having no instructions "to labour for the peace of Europe," wrote to the King to that effect and sent Frederick's epistle to Versailles. "The letter of the King of Prussia," writes Bernis, "was communicated to the Court of Vienna, which laughed, with good reason, at the trap laid for us to induce us to suspend the operations of the campaign, in order to give his Prussian Majesty time to recover from his losses at Kolin, and from various other checks he had received from time to time." [1]

Richelieu continued his advance on Halberstadt, which he occupied on September 29, the Prussian garrison having evacuated the town on his approach. This rapid march with an ill-provisioned and shoeless army was a movement which is generally acknowledged to reflect great credit on the marshal but, unfortunately for France, he neglected to profit by the advantage he had thereby gained.

The Marquis de Fraigne, formerly French Minister at Zerbst, who had been seized by Frederick and imprisoned at

[1] *Mémoires.*

Magdeburg, from which he had succeeded in making his escape, in female attire, subsequently declared that, while he was at large (love of the Dowager Princess of Zerbst having led him to return thither, he was recaptured by the Prussians and committed to a darksome dungeon), he notified Richelieu that Magdeburg was only garrisoned by 1,800 raw recruits, and blames him severely for not advancing at once upon the place and making himself master of it, together with its arsenal, treasure, and military stores, to say nothing of some 7,000 Austrian and Russian prisoners who were confined there.

Whether Richelieu would have found Magdeburg quite so easy a prey as the marquis imagined may be doubted. But the latter was certainly right in asserting that his advance would, at any rate, have compelled Frederick to abandon Saxony to Soubise, in order to hasten to its relief.[1] Anxious, however, to secure peaceful winter-quarters for his weary and discontented army, and very uneasy in regard to the Hanoverians and their allies in his rear, who had as yet shown no disposition to execute the articles of the Convention of Kloster-Zeven, the marshal proposed to Prince Ferdinand of Brunswick, who commanded in Magdeburg, an armistice up to the spring of 1758. Such an overture coincided only too well with Frederick's views for him not to authorise its immediate acceptance; and it was agreed, subject to the ratification of the French Government, that the Grand Army should evacuate the principality of Halberstadt and the adjoining districts, with the exception of Halberstadt itself, in which a garrison should be left, and winter around Brunswick and Wolfenbüttel, the Prussians to furnish them with the supplies needed, partly gratuitously and partly at a fixed price, and all hostilities in that region to be suspended until April 15, 1758.

All Richelieu's officers, "who were dying to get back to Paris for the winter,"[1] declared themselves in favour of this arrangement; but the Ministry at Versailles very properly declined to ratify a compact which would have left Frederick free to march at once upon Soubise, or to advance against the

[1] Bernis, *Mémoires et Lettres.*

Austrians in Silesia. Nevertheless, that astute monarch contrived to secure some advantage from the affair, as he caused the agreement to be printed, "adding articles which gave great umbrage to several of our allies, and causing it to be believed for a long time that we had signed them."[1]

During the whole of the month of October, Richelieu remained inactive at Halberstadt, conducting a somewhat acrimonious correspondence with Pâris-Duverney on the question of his army's winter-quarters. Duverney had decided that the army was to winter in and around Halberstadt, which, besides being an excellent base for the operations against Magdeburg, which were to begin in the spring, he fondly imagined to be a rich country, perfectly capable of supporting the troops. Richelieu maintained, and the correspondence of the Comte de Gisors and other officers[2] prove that he was perfectly right, that all the country for many miles round had been swept bare by the Prussians, and that the fortifications of Halberstadt were so weak that it would be the labour of months to render the place defensible, and urged that he should be allowed to evacuate it and fall back on the Ocker, where he would not only find suitable quarters for his army, but be in a position to keep a watchful eye on Cumberland's old troops.

Duverney, however, with the obstinacy of age—he was seventy-six—persisted in adhering to his original scheme, notwithstanding the representations of Richelieu, and it was not until the last days of October that the Government finally authorised the marshal to go into winter-quarters on the Ocker.

Meanwhile, the Grand Army had been very much weakened, since, early in October, Richelieu had despatched twenty battalions and eighteen squadrons to reinforce Soubise. Bernis in his *Mémoires*, blames the marshal for thus dividing his army, in view of the suspicious behaviour of the Hanoverians in his

[1] Bernis, *Mémoires*.

[2] See Camille Rousset, *le Comte de Gisors*. The Comte de Gisors was the only son of the Maréchal de Belle-Isle, and was colonel of the Régiment de Champagne. He was killed the following year at Crefeld.

rear; but he forgets, or more probably ignores, the fact that Richelieu was only acting according to the instructions he had received from Versailles, and the latter's despatches and the letters of the Comte de Gisors prove that he did so with extreme reluctance, and deeply resented the partiality of the Court for Soubise, which had imposed this obligation upon him.

On November 6, at the moment when the army was leaving Halberstadt, Richelieu received intelligence of the fatal battle of Rossbach and the total defeat of the aspiring Soubise. In a moment the situation of affairs had been entirely changed! Hard upon this came the news that the Hanoverians around Stade were moving, and that the French posts in the Electorate were threatened. The marshal found himself in a dilemma. The vanquished army summoned him on one side; the advancing Hanoverians demanded his attention on the other. On learning, however, that Soubise was neither pressed nor even pursued, he decided to march to the Aller and quarter his troops between Verden and Zelle, in the hope that this movement would compel the Hanoverians to remain within the limits assigned to them by the Convention of Kloster-Zeven.

On November 27, he reached Lüneburg, where the following day he received from Ferdinand of Brunswick, who, at the request of George II., had just been sent by Frederick to take command of the Hanoverian troops, a letter formally repudiating the armistice, and informing him of his intention to resume hostilities. After throwing reinforcements into Harburg, which was blockaded and bombarded by the enemy a few days later, Richelieu determined to concentrate his army at Zelle. His forces, already much reduced by sickness, were scattered over a considerable extent of country, and had Ferdinand at once advanced against him, his position would have been a perilous one. Even as matters stood, when, on December 13, the Hanoverian army appeared before Zelle, it was greatly superior in numbers to the French. The latter were by this time in a deplorable state—worn out by incessant marching, sickness, and want of food—and the general-officers, almost with one voice, implored Richelieu to abandon the line of the Aller and fall back towards the Rhine. But the marshal courageously refused to be influenced by the demoralisation of his staff, and announced his intention of passing the Aller and attacking the enemy.

This bold movement was executed on the night of December 23–24, and was completely successful, Ferdinand, on the advice of his lieutenants, abandoning his position and retreating on Lüneburg, without waiting to be attacked. Had he stood his ground and disputed the passage of the river, the result must have been extremely doubtful, for, though the French soldiers, unlike their officers, were eager for battle, sickness and starvation had rendered many of them quite unfit for the exertions that would have been required of them. "Give thanks to God," writes the Marquis de Crémille to Duverney, "that His divine goodness has preserved us from the misfortune of a battle. While crediting our soldiers with all the good-will which they, in fact, displayed on that day, I doubt if the strength of their debilitated bodies would have been able to respond to it, and, in truth, I believe that we are no longer in a position to take any risk at all."[1]

Richelieu appears to have entertained some thought of pursuing the enemy, but was dissuaded by the representation of his officers, of whose disinclination for any further exertions he complained bitterly to the Minister for War. "If I ought to judge the soldiers by what I have seen and what I know of them," he writes, "they are full of valour and will fight well; but I cannot say the same of the officers, from whom, indeed, we must fear the worst."[2]

Both armies now went into winter-quarters, and Richelieu demanded permission to return to Court, on the grounds that his health was affected, that it was most necessary for him to consult with the Ministers in regard to the campaign of the following spring, and that his own private affairs called urgently for his attention. The Government, who since the

[1] Camille Rousset, *le Comte de Gisors*.

[2] Richelieu to Paulmy, January 2, 1753, in Waddington.

rupture of the convention had regarded its author with a far from favourable eye, saw in this demand an excellent pretext for superseding him,[1] and on January 22, 1758, he received, at Hanover, a letter from Paulmy, informing him that, after considerable hesitation, due to his anxiety for the safety of his army, the King had decided to grant his request; but that, as his Majesty judged it very inadvisable to leave the army without a commander-in-chief, he was sending the Comte de Clermont—another friend of Madame de Pompadour, by the way—to replace him.[2]

This courteous intimation that his sovereign had decided to dispense with his services must have occasioned the marshal considerable mortification. Nevertheless, it is probable that he was not altogether sorry to be released from a position of which, notwithstanding his optimism and assurance, he can scarcely have failed to recognise the increasing difficulties. Any way, he carefully abstained from manifesting his annoyance, and, in acknowledging the War Minister's communication, merely expressed his sensibility of the King's kindness in acceding to his request to return to Court, and trusted that his Majesty was content with his services. At the same time, he asked permission to leave the army without waiting for the arrival of Clermont. This was granted, and early in February he set out for France.

As strategist and diplomat, Richelieu, as we have seen, had committed grave errors, though, in regard to the Convention of Kloster-Zeven, so high an authority as M. Waddington is of opinion that, while he is justly blamed for the careless manner in which it was drafted, he ought not to be held responsible for its rupture. This, he maintains, was mainly the fault of the French Government, and, in particular, of Bernis, as

[1] Bernis, writing to the Comte de Stainville (afterwards Duc de Choiseul), then French Ambassador at Vienna, on the last day of 1757, declared that "there was not a moment to lose in sending a general capable of imposing respect on the army and bringing order into everything."

[2] "The folly that he (Richelieu) showed in wishing to return in such critical circumstances decided his recall."—Bernis to Stainville, January 25, 1758, *Mémoires et Lettres du Cardinal de Bernis.*

Foreign Secretary, who ought to have concluded without delay arrangements with Brunswick and Hesse which would have prevented the troops of those States from rendering any further assistance to the Hanoverians, and thus have made it extremely hazardous for George II. to repudiate the convention. Much credit, too, is due to the marshal for the energy and resolution he displayed after the disaster of Rossbach; and his movement on Lüneburg, the strength of character he showed at Zelle in turning a deaf ear to the pusillanimous counsels of his staff, and the bold and skilful manœuvre by which he compelled a force superior in numbers to his own to retreat, prove him to have possessed a capacity which compares very favourably with most of the French generals of the Seven Years' War.

On the other hand, no condemnation can well be too severe for the general responsible for the efficiency and discipline of the army.

"Throughout the campaign of 1757," writes M. Waddington, "the want of discipline and marauding among the soldiers, the insubordination of the officers, their deplorable attitude towards their chiefs, the spirit of criticism and rivalry in the staff, were as many baneful influences which depreciated the value and profoundly affected the *morale* of the entire army. The bad example started from above; it was difficult to prevent the private soldier from imitating, in his often brutal way, the methods of spoliation, which, with more method and less grossness, it is true, were practised by the military authorities of every rank, beginning with the general-in-chief. How was it possible to expect restraint on the part of the subordinate when he could not be ignorant that his superiors had anticipated the requisitions or contributions levied on the conquered territories? In the correspondence of Richelieu, we find complaints concerning the excesses of the soldiers, the conduct and the language of the officers, the disobedience of the generals, and the embarrassments caused by their equipages; but he takes good care not to speak of the actions of the majority of his lieutenants, or to censure practices which were enriching the individual at the expense of the treasury of the army and the finances of the King."

The sacrifices demanded by the French intendants, both in kind and in money, from the conquered States, the distinguished historian goes on to point out, however heavy they may have seemed to the inhabitants, did not exceed those imposed by Frederick on Saxony. But, thanks to the vigilance of that prince and to the control which he exercised over his armies, the subsidies thus obtained were utilised for the sustenance of the troops and the conduct of the war, whereas, on the French side, where there was no such supervision, the intendants frequently found it impossible to obtain the expected contributions, owing to the people having been already bled white by the rapacious generals and commissaries. The intendant Lucé, writing to the Minister for War, from Wolfenbüttel, towards the end of September, declared that such immense sums had already been extorted from all the country round, that the inhabitants were quite unable to furnish the money he had demanded for the expenses of the troops' winter-quarters; and it was the same in many other districts. Thus, the soldiers were half-clothed and half-starved, while their leaders battened on their misery.

What was the amount which Richelieu obtained by this scandalous abuse of his position can only be conjectured; but, since an inquiry instituted by Clermont on his taking over the command of the army revealed the fact that he had actually received 150,000 livres in the Duchy of Brunswick, and 17,000 ducats in the Electorate of Hanover, merely from the sale of "safeguards,"—that is to say, exemptions from the duty of providing free quarters for the troops and of contributing to the general requisitions—he seems to have thoroughly earned the *sobriquet* of "*Père la Maraude*" which his soldiers bestowed upon him. "On Sunday, the 20th" (February), writes Barbier, "the Maréchal de Richelieu arrived in Paris. The rumour is general in Paris that he has greatly enriched himself by the excessive contributions which he has levied in the country of Hanover, and that he has discharged debts to the amount of

1,110,000 livres. If this be well founded, the King ought to punish him for setting the example to the generals."[1]

The King did nothing of the kind; on the contrary, he received the man whose neglect and rapacity had ruined that once splendid army[2] "with very marked graciousness."[3] Public opinion was less indulgent, and when, out of his ill-gotten gains, the marshal proceeded to purchase the garden of the Hôtel d'Antin and construct there an elegant mansion, the Parisians called it in derision "*le Pavillon d'Hanovre*."[4]

[1] Barbier, *Journal*.

[2] Clermont, writing on March 1, 1758, to his friend the Duc de Biron, draws a terrible picture of the condition in which he had found the army: "This poor army, however much one may complain of it, is in a miserable state, without clothing, without tents. There are companies in which there are not twelve men fit for duty. The hospitals are filthy and give forth a frightful stench; there are no hospital attendants, little linen, and little soup. In a word, we are in a condition of inconceivable demoralisation. Neither among the officers nor the men is there any discipline."

[3] "The Maréchal de Richelieu has arrived. He was present yesterday at the *coucher* of the king, who spoke to him for a moment in his cabinet, after which he appeared in public. The King treated him with very marked graciousness."—Luynes, February 21, 1758.

[4] "I have seen it; there is a chamber surrounded with looking-glasses, and hung with white lute-strings painted with roses. I wish you could see the antiquated Rinaldo who has built himself this romantic bower. Looking-glass never reflected so many wrinkles; you would think Rinaldo had lived till now."—Horace Walpole.

# CHAPTER XXII

Termination of Richelieu's military career—Outcry against him—Voltaire advises him to retire for a while into private life—He goes with his daughter to his government—Reaction in his favour consequent upon the incapacity of the Comte de Clermont—His pompous entry into Bordeaux—A squire of dames—Incident at a masked ball—Richelieu's scandalous conduct and tyranny end by alienating all classes of the Bordelais—He visits Voltaire at Ferney—The *beaux yeux* of Madame Cramer—Ruse of Voltaire to get rid temporarily of the lady's husband—A cruel rebuff—The advantages of an unsullied reputation in an actress in the eighteenth century, when combined with talent, exemplified by the case of Mlle. Raucourt—Extraordinary enthusiasm of the playgoing public—Voltaire, in a letter to Richelieu, destroys the illusion—Scene at the "Pavillon d'Hanovre"—Mlle. Raucourt discards virtue, and the public discards her—Marriage of the Duc de Fronsac to Mlle. d'Hautefort—Horace Walpole's impressions of Richelieu—And of the Comtesse d'Egmont.

WITH Richelieu's return from Germany, his long military career came to an end, as he was not employed again during the remainder of the war. It had extended over a period of forty-five years, and, apart from his conduct during the campaign of 1757, one must admit that it had been both a successful and an honourable one.

On the battlefield itself he was certainly splendid. "M. de Richelieu," wrote the Marquis d'Argenson, "despises death as a gambler despises ruin"—and it is therefore scarcely surprising that the historians of a nation in which mere personal courage has always been so highly esteemed should have shown themselves very indulgent towards his faults as a general, and that it should have been left to a thoroughly informed and impartial writer like M. Waddington to reveal how gross these faults were, and how disastrous the consequences they entailed.

Although Louis XV. seems to have been at pains to show

that, in spite of what had occurred in Germany, his old friend had not forfeited his favour, Richelieu's position was for some months a decidedly unpleasant one, since his enemies did not confine their accusations to rapacity and incompetence, but represented him as a traitor corrupted by the gold of France's enemies; and the Ministers in vain endeavoured to justify him. So fierce and so persistent, indeed, were these attacks that Voltaire, from his retreat at Ferney, wrote counselling him to retire to Richelieu, "to the bosom of his family," and remain there for a year or two at least: by which time the storm would no doubt have passed.

This suggestion did not commend itself to the marshal, to whom a prolonged absence from public life would have been intolerable, and who knew his countrymen too well to renounce the hope of seeing them at no very distant date revise their opinion concerning him. Nevertheless, he judged it expedient to withdraw for a time to his government of Guienne, of which he had not yet taken formal possession; and at the end of May he set out for Bordeaux, accompanied by his daughter, the Comtesse d'Egmont, whose husband had lately been summoned to Spain, on business connected with his estates there.

Soon after he quitted Paris, news arrived that his successor, the honest but absolutely incapable Clermont, who had already been forced by Ferdinand of Brunswick to evacuate Bremen and Verden and retreat in confusion across the Rhine, had permitted the enemy to pass that river without apparently offering the slightest opposition. Thereupon the fickle public promptly veered round, and declared that Richelieu ought never to have been superseded.

The friends of the marshal took advantage of this reaction in his favour [1] to prepare for him a magnificent reception at Bordeaux, into which he made his official entry "like a sovereign taking possession of his States." Vessels richly adorned with his coat-of-arms transported him, his daughter, and their suites from Blaye to Bordeaux. "When he appeared, all the ships

[1] The reaction was, of course, all the stronger after Clermont's disgraceful defeat at Crefeld, on June 23.

in the port, both French and foreign, fired salutes, to which the cannon of the Château-Trompette replied."

A military band preceded his vessel. On arriving at the Place-Royale, he found a triumphal arch, whither the Parlement came to receive and harangue him. There he mounted on horseback and passed through the town, followed by the nobility of the province, magnificently dressed and also on horseback, and proceeded to the cathedral, where he was received by the archbishop and the clergy. After the *Te Deum*, he returned in the same state to the governor's palace, which was to be his residence.

Splendid fêtes succeeded this pompous entry. "Never had there been a governor so magnificent; it seemed to be his intention to revive about him the imposing splendour which had greeted his youthful eyes at the Court of Louis XIV. Clothed with a portion of the authority of his successor, he deemed it incumbent upon him to act in a manner worthy of his master: he was King of Bordeaux."[1] Whenever he went out, he was preceded by a numerous guard, the captain of which was a cadet of the House of Rohan. On Sundays, covered with gold and embroidery, he attended Mass at the Cathedral, where musicians specially engaged for the occasion awaited his arrival to discourse the most heavenly music. His every action was accompanied by a pomp and ceremony which invested it with a theatrical splendour.

A few days after his arrival, he gave, in the garden of the governor's palace, a supper of four hundred covers. It had hitherto been the custom to confine such functions to the nobility and the magistracy; but Richelieu, in spite of his pretensions to conform to the traditions of the past in the way of magnificence, extended his hospitality to the *bourgeoisie*—or, at any rate, to their wives and daughters. This departure from established custom naturally occasioned a good deal of surprise, which was much increased when it was observed that only ladies—and those the prettiest present—had been invited to the governor's own table. Few men, even in that gallant age, would have

[1] *Mémoires du duc de Richelieu.*

felt equal to the task of entertaining such a bevy of beauties—there were twenty-nine of them—but the marshal worthily maintained his reputation as a squire of dames. "He was gallant towards them all," says the chronicler, "addressed to each a few agreeable words, and, if there was one whom he preferred, such was the skill with which he concealed his sentiments, that it was impossible for the others to take umbrage."[1]

The city returned the governor's hospitality by a grand masked ball. During the evening, Richelieu's curiosity was aroused by a domino, who several times approached and spoke to him, but who declined to reveal his or her identity. At length, however, the marshal insisting, the unknown exclaimed in a voice which could be heard by all standing round :

"Tu voudrais connaître mes traits
Et les sentiments de mon âme?
Si te crains, je suis Anglais,
Si t'aime, je suis Français,
Si te adore, je suis femme."

And straightway disappeared in the throng, and was seen no more.[2]

So long as Madame d'Egmont, "who had all her father's good qualities without any of his vices," remained at Bordeaux, Richelieu appears to have been immensely popular there, and nothing more serious than a love of ostentation could be alleged against him. But when, in the spring of 1759, the countess rejoined her husband in Paris, and the restraint imposed by her presence was removed, complaints about the new governor's behaviour soon began to be heard. The numerous gallantries in which he indulged with scarcely a pretence at concealment scandalised the more sober citizens, and his hôtel became "a place which modesty did not venture to approach without a blush."[3] The gambling orgies which took place almost nightly there, and at which several young men of good family were completely ruined, were also severely criticised, the more so that

[1] *Mémoires du duc de Richelieu.* [2] Rulhière, *Œuvres diverses.*
[3] *Mémoires du duc de Richelieu.*

the favourite medium of speculation was hazard, a game which had been repeatedly prohibited by the Parlement. Moreover, the evil example set by the King's representative had far-reaching consequences; gambling-houses sprang up on all sides like mushrooms; card-sharpers and courtesans from all the towns of South-western France flocked to Bordeaux, attracted thither by the laxity with which the laws against them were administered under the new *régime*, for a governor who himself "called the rattling main," and admitted ladies of notoriously easy virtue to his own table, was naturally inclined to leniency; and young people of the better classes vied with each other in the elegance of their dress and the irregularity of their lives. In short, in a year or two, if we are to believe Soulavie, Richelieu appears to have demoralised Bordeaux as completely as he had demoralised the Grand Army.[1]

Nor were these the only grievances which the Bordelais had against him. The Parlement complained bitterly of his arbitrary use of *lettres de cachet* and of his systematic encroachments upon their prerogatives, and an order which he issued prohibiting the carrying of arms, the espionage practised by his agents, and the imprisonment of several persons whose only offence seems to have been that they had openly expressed their disapproval of his conduct, were bitterly resented by the citizens. Finally, he succeeded in alienating all classes: the clergy, the magistracy, the *bourgeoisie*, and the people, and threatened to become almost as unpopular a governor as that Duc d'Épernon whom Voltaire once declared that he had taken for his model.

Richelieu and the philosopher had not met since November 1754, when the former, being on his way from Montpellier to Paris, had persuaded Voltaire, then living at Colmar, to spend a few days with him. However, in the early autumn of 1762, the marshal accepted his old friend's invitation to visit him at Ferney, where he arrived on October 1, accompanied by a suite of forty persons, and was lodged in the adjoining Château of

[1] It is possible that Soulavie has somewhat exaggerated his patron's delinquencies, though his account is perfectly in accord with what we know of the marshal's life from more trustworthy chroniclers.

Tournay, of which Voltaire had bought the life-lease from the Président de Brosses almost at the same time as he had purchased Ferney.

The arrival of so important a personage aroused quite a flutter of excitement at Geneva, and the French resident wrote to inform his government of the measures which the Council had decided to take to receive the celebrated marshal. His letter is interesting, as showing the importance attached to the minutiæ of etiquette in the eighteenth century, even in republican Geneva:

"MONSEIGNEUR,

"Although the Maréchal de Richelieu has not informed me of his arrival at M. de V——'s, I judged it proper that the Council should acquaint me with the honours which would be rendered to him.

"The old registers have been consulted, but they have not found any instance of a marshal of France having visited Geneva or the Republic. It was therefore necessary to deliberate upon the matter in the Council, and the following is what has been decided upon:

"That, in the event of the Maréchal de Richelieu coming to Ferney, district of Gex, to M. de V——'s, and notifying his arrival to the first syndic, the Council will send a former syndic and a councillor to compliment him.

"If the marshal comes to Geneva and pays a visit to the first syndic, a former syndic and two other members of the Council will be sent to his residence to compliment him.

"In case the Maréchal de Richelieu should give notice of his visit, the guard will be placed under arms, and the drummers will beat a salute, or if the marshal should not give notice, the guard will still be placed under arms, but the salute will not be beaten."[1]

After giving this weighty matter due consideration, the

[1] Archives of Geneva, published by Gaston Maugras and Lucien Perey, *la Vie intime de Voltaire aux Délices et à Ferney.*

Minister for Foreign Affairs replied that he approved what the Council had decided.

The Patriarch, arrayed in gala dress and followed by all his household—he had in his employ between sixty and seventy persons—came to welcome his distinguished guest, and overwhelmed him with attentions. He had invited to meet him the Duchesse d'Enville and her son, the Comte d'Harcourt, the Duc de Villars, Madame Ménage—a very pretty woman, who had come to Geneva to consult the celebrated Tronchin—and a number of friends from the neighbouring city, among them Gabriel Cramer, Voltaire's printer, and his charming and sprightly wife—"*une Parisienne égarée dans Calviniste Genève.*"

Richelieu's stay, which lasted about a week, was one round of fêtes, pleasure-parties, and plays, which were performed in the little gold-and-green theatre which the poet had constructed at Tourney. Voltaire himself was in the highest spirits, and exerted himself to the utmost to please his guest. "M. de Richelieu's visit," he writes, "has been rather gay. Geneva is sometimes in need of noblemen of jovial disposition."

The marshal's disposition, indeed, notwithstanding his sixty-six years, was still decidedly "jovial," and he was only too ready to make the most of his opportunities. He made love with ardour to the pretty women whom his friend had invited with an eye to his diversion, and Voltaire could not contain his delight on surprising him one day at the feet of Madame Ménage. She, however, it subsequently transpired, was not the lady upon whom his choice had fallen, for he confided to his host that the *beaux yeux* of Madame Cramer had completely subjugated him, and begged him to facilitate his suit, by getting her husband temporarily out of the way. The complaisant poet forthwith retired to his study and composed an *Épître au M. le Maréchal de Richelieu.* This effusion he handed to Cramer, with instructions to hurry to Geneva and arrange for several copies to be printed during the night, as he was most anxious that his celebrated guest should receive one as soon as he awoke the next morning. The unsuspecting printer set out at once, leaving the field free for Richelieu, who fondly imagined that he had only to throw the handkerchief for it to be picked up. But he had counted without Madame Cramer, who, when he asked for a rendezvous, had the impertinence to burst out laughing in his face. The only consolation he received for this cruel rebuff was the *épître*, which Cramer duly brought to his bedside next morning. For the first time in his life, he is said to have found Voltaire's flattering verses insipid.

After spending a day or two at Geneva, Richelieu returned to Paris, and he and Voltaire did not meet again until the Patriarch's last visit to the French capital in February 1778. They continued, however, to correspond, chiefly in regard to the affairs of the Academy and the Comédie-Française, and there can be no doubt that the marshal was influenced a good deal in his attitude towards both institutions by the letters he received from Ferney. One of these epistles, written in the spring of 1773, proved a veritable bombshell, so far as the theatrical world was concerned, and led to the deposition of one of the greatest idols which the playgoing public had ever set up.

At the end of the preceding year, there had appeared at the Comédie-Française, in the part of Dido, in Le Franc Pompignan's famous tragedy, a charming young actress of seventeen named Mlle. Raucourt, who had achieved an instantaneous and amazing success. Grimm predicted that she would be the "*gloire immortelle*" of the French stage; another critic declared that the annihilation of the British fleet alone could have aroused a deeper enthusiasm than her acting; while a third wrote: "It is impossible to describe the sensation she has created; nothing like it has ever been seen within the memory of living man."[1] The enthusiasm increased until it reached a veritable frenzy. On the days on which she was to appear, struggling crowds besieged the box-office of the theatre from an early hour in the morning, and those who had been intrepid enough to secure tickets were afterwards able to dispose of them at four and five times their face value. When the time for the performance drew near, the scene almost baffled description. All the streets leading to the Comédie-Française were

[1] *Mémoires secrets de la république des lettres.*

so blocked with people, that the actors themselves could with difficulty persuade their excited patrons to make way for them ; an enormous crowd surged round the theatre, forced the doors, and struggled and fought for the best places in the pit, and the victors were seen emerging from the *mêlée* with their clothes nearly torn from their backs, dishevelled hair ; and faces streaming with perspiration. "Do you think," inquired an old lady in Grimm's hearing one evening, "that if it had been a question of saving their country, these people would have exposed themselves like this?"[1]

The enthusiasm of the town spread to the Court, and the new actress was commanded to appear at Versailles, where she created a similar sensation. Louis XV. sent for and warmly complimented her, and made her a present of fifty louis, while Madame du Barry, the reigning favourite, gave her a magnificent *robe de théâtre*. In Paris, the *furore* she excited, so far from diminishing, seemed only to increase, and scarcely a day passed without some persons being more or less seriously injured in the struggle at the doors of the theatre.

The extraordinary popularity of Mlle. Raucourt with the playgoing public was materially enhanced by an unsullied reputation off the stage. "In vain was her heart besieged like the box-office of the theatre on the evenings on which she was to appear ; in vain her adorers prostrated themselves before her. She turned a deaf ear to the most brilliant propositions ; she repulsed with horror the most tempting offers."[2] Soon the lady's virtue became as celebrated as her talent ; it was the talk of the town ; the memoirs and correspondence of the times are full of it : "The virtue of the new actress still keeps up." "The virtue of the new actress resists the numerous assaults which are made upon it." "The new actress has begun to give *petits soupers*, which, it is hoped, may lead to what she has hitherto escaped" ; and so forth. Every evening the theatre resounded with acclamations, which were intended to be as much a tribute to her exemplary conduct—which, on the part

[1] Grimm, *Correspondance littéraire.*

[2] Emile Gaboriau, *les Comédiennes adorées.*

of an actress in those days, was as novel as it was laudable—as to her beauty and talent; devout ladies vied with one another in giving her good advice and in enriching her wardrobe; an old gentleman entered her dressing-room one day and deposited two rouleaux of one hundred louis each on her toilette-table, "as a proof of his esteem"; and when it was reported that she had rejected with scorn the "protection" of the Duc de Bourbon, a Prince of the Blood, together with an allowance of 24,000 livres, her idolaters could find no words in which to express their admiration.

But, alas! they were soon to be disillusioned. One day, it happened that Mlle. Raucourt was dining with Richelieu at the "Pavillon d'Hanovre," chaperoned by her father—a very dragon of vigilance, who, if we are to believe Grimm, invariably carried a loaded pistol in each pocket, "in order to blow out the brains of the first who should make an attempt on the virtue of his daughter."[1] D'Alembert, the Princesse de Beauvau, and the Marquis de Ximenès, a great patron of the stage, who, some years before, had half-ruined himself over Mlle. Clairon, were also present. While they were at table, a letter from Voltaire arrived for the host, who, as every one was anxious to know what the great man had to say, handed it, unopened, to Ximenès, with a request that he would read it to the company.

Now, the fame of Mlle. Raucourt's virtue had, of course, penetrated to Geneva, where it reached the ears of a gentleman of that city who had met the young lady in Spain—which she had visited with a travelling-company before coming to Paris—and claimed to have found her no more insensible to admiration than other daughters of Thespis. This gentleman, or one of his friends, informed Voltaire of the Spanish adventure, and presumably supported his statements with documentary evidence. Any way, the Patriarch, who, though circumstances sometimes obliged him to play the hypocrite himself, detested hypocrisy in others, and was filled with righteous indignation that a young *débutante* solely on account of an undeserved reputation for

[1] *Correspondance littéraire.*

virtue was being exalted above his beloved Adrienne Lecouvreur and his favourite interpreter, Mlle. Clairon, forthwith determined to unmask her, and had, in fact, done so in the very letter which Ximenès held in his hand.

The marquis, all unconscious of the bomb which the epistle contained, began to read, and proceeded until he had uttered the fatal sentence, when he stopped abruptly and began mumbling apologies. Terrible was the commotion which ensued. Mlle. Raucourt promptly swooned away; her father drew his sword, and brandishing it in the air, swore that he would proceed to Ferney and run the Patriarch through the body; the Princesse de Beauvau called the maladroit Ximenès a fool; while old Richelieu, it is safe to presume, looked on choking with suppressed merriment.

Next day, thanks no doubt to the malevolent activity of Richelieu, the story was all over Paris. The first feeling was one of incredulity; and Court and town were so indignant at the aspersions that had been cast upon their idol, that Voltaire, warned by d'Alembert of the feeling against him, and perhaps alarmed for the future reception of his tragedies, hastened to pour the balm of his flattery upon the wound he had inflicted, and sent the actress some of his most flattering verses. But all the flattery in the world could not repair the mischief that had been done. Gradually people began to think that there might be more truth in the story about the Genevese lover than they had at first supposed; Mlle. Raucourt's *soupirants* redoubled their attentions, and refused any longer to believe her indignant protestations. Nothing is more disheartening than to make sacrifices in which the world does not believe, and, whether Voltaire's accusation was true or not, the lady speedily came to the conclusion that she had made enough of them, and, one fine day, the town "learned with stupefaction" that the virtue of its idol had at length succumbed.

Once embarked upon the downward course, Mlle. Raucourt, as if determined to make up for lost time, showed herself utterly indifferent to public opinion, and plunged into a course of dissipation which "scandalised even those who were least susceptible to scandal." [1] With her reputation for virtue, her renown as a *tragédienne* disappeared also, for the public, having come to the conclusion that it had been the dupe of an unscrupulous hypocrite, was positively burning with righteous indignation. Those who had been loudest in chanting her praises were foremost in ridicule and abuse, and such was the general odium which she had contrived to arouse, that she counted herself fortunate if her appearance on the stage was received in silence. "Never," wrote Grimm, "was idol worshipped with more infatuation; never was idol broken with more contempt."

In 1776, Mlle. Raucourt had to fly from France, in order to escape the too-pressing attentions of her creditors, and remained in exile three years. Then she returned, and was reinstated as a *sociétaire* of the Comédie-Française by the Gentlemen of the Chamber, in spite of the indignant protests of the players, who represented that her misconduct had injured the company in the estimation of its patrons. Her reinstatement was bitterly resented by the public, and on her first appearance she was greeted with a perfect tempest of hisses, groans, and cat-calls. Gradually, however, by the exercise of patience and tact, she contrived to conciliate the opposition, and in a few years had regained much of her former popularity.[2]

In March 1764, Richelieu married his son, the Duc de Fronsac, to Mlle. d'Hautefort, with the greatest *éclat*. The wedding ceremony was followed by a dinner, to which the *Nouvelles à la main* report that one hundred ladies were invited, while in the evening there was a sumptuous supper, a ball, and performances by the players of the Comédie Française and the Comédie-Italienne. It was certainly time that the young gentleman settled down, since his taste for feminine society was as marked as his father's had been at his age, with this difference, that, whereas the one preferred to make love, the other was content to buy it ready-made. However, M. de

[1] Grimm, *Correspondance littéraire.*

[2] For a full account of Mlle. Raucourt's romantic career, see the author's "Later Queens of the French Stage" (London, Harper; New York, Scribner, 1905).

Fronsac's marriage does not appear to have cured him of his penchant for the coarser forms of gallantry.[1]

In the autumn of 1765, Horace Walpole visited Paris. In a letter to the Earl of Hertford, written some months before, he had declared that Richelieu was one of the persons whom he was most anxious to see, and his correspondence during his stay in France contains frequent references to the marshal, which, however, are far from complimentary:

"I saw the Duc de Richelieu in waiting, who is pale, except his nose, which is red, much wrinkled, and exactly a remnant of that age which produced General Churchill,[2] Robert Wilks,[3] the Duke of Argyll, etc."[4]

And again:

"The Duc de Richelieu is a lean old resemblance of old General Churchill, and, like him, affects still to have his Boothbies! Alas, poor Boothbies!" And, in a third epistle, written after a supper at the marshal's hôtel, he describes his host as "an old piece of tawdry, worn out, but endeavouring to brush itself up"; adding that he put him in mind of Lord Chesterfield, "for they laugh before they know what he has said—and are in the right, for I think they would not laugh afterwards."[5]

On the other hand, Madame d'Egmont seems to have made a highly favourable impression upon him.

"There is a young Comtesse d'Egmont, daughter of Marshal Richelieu," he writes to Lady Suffolk, "so pretty and pleasing that, if I thought that it would break anybody's heart in England, I would be in love with her. Nay, Madam, I might

[1] But, in justice to M. de Fronsac, it should be said that his bringing-up seems to have left a good deal to be desired. Horace Walpole tells us that, at the age of ten, being reproached for his ignorance of Latin, he replied that his father never knew the language, notwithstanding which he had enjoyed the favours of the prettiest women in France.

[2] General Charles Churchill, sometime Member of Parliament for Castle Rising, celebrated for his wit and his amours.

[3] The Drury Lane actor.

[4] Walpole to Chute, October 3, 1765.

[5] Walpole to Hon. Seymour Conway, December 5, 1765.

be so within all the rules here; I am twenty years on the right side of red heels, which her father wears still, and he has still a wrinkle to come before he leaves them off."[1]

And to Lady Harvey he describes her "as delightful, pretty, and civil, and gay, and conversable."[2]

[1] Letter of December 5, 1765.

[2] Letter of January 2, 1766.

# CHAPTER XXIII

Madame du Barry—Richelieu, although not responsibe for her elevation to the "sunlit heights," one of her staunchest adherents—In his capacity as First Gentleman of the Chamber, he overcomes the difficulties in the way of the new favourite's presentation—Singular alliance between the Du Barry faction and the religious party against Choiseul—Fall of Choiseul—Louis XV. refuses to gratify the marshal's political ambitions, and he is compelled to content himself with the post of Mentor *in petto* to the new Ministry—The *coup d'État* Maupeou—Richelieu expels the members of the Cour des Aides and the Châtelet, and the recalcitrant magistrates of the Parlement of Bordeaux—Death of the Comtesse d'Egmont—Richelieu high in favour with the King—A *bon mot* of the marshal—Last illness of Louis XV.—The battle of the Sacraments begins—Richelieu and the Archbishop of Paris—Diplomatic conduct of the Grand Almoner—Provisional dismissal of Madame du Barry—Fronsac and the curé of Versailles—Administration of the Sacraments—Death of the King.

THE name of Richelieu, inseparable from the advent or the disgrace of all the mistresses of Louis XV., figures prominently in the history of the favourite who was to fill up the measure of the royal degradation. Some contemporary writers even assert that that feather-brained but generous-hearted little courtesan who, under the name of the Comtesse du Barry, the scandalised Court saw installed at Versailles in the closing weeks of 1768, was indebted for her elevation to the "sunlight heights of harlotry and rascaldom"[1] largely to his machinations. This, however, does not appear to have been the case. It is true that Richelieu was well acquainted with Jean du Barry—the "*Roué*"—the astute personage who first introduced the daughter of the Vaucouleurs sempstress to the gay world,[2] and whose younger brother, the

[1] Carlyle, "French Revolution."

[2] What Walpole says, in his letter of December 2, 1768 to Sir Horace Mann, in regard to the services rendered by the "*Roué*" to Richelieu is confirmed by the reports of the police.

complaisant "Comte" Guillaume, subsequently lent her the ægis of his name and supposititious title. But, as we have pointed out in another work,[1] the weight of evidence goes to show that the future Madame du Barry first attracted the attention of her sovereign on the occasion of certain visits which she paid to the Prime Minister, the Duc de Choiseul, at Versailles, to solicit the continuance in her and her mother's favour of an army-contract which had been surrendered to them by the "*Roué*," and that the only intermediary was the King's confidential *valet de chambre*, Lebel, whom his Majesty commissioned to "arrange matters" with the lady herself.

However, if Richelieu had no part in determining the choice of the King, the new favourite was to find in him one of her staunchest adherents. Bitterly jealous of Choiseul's ascendency over Louis XV., and incensed by the Minister's refusal to allow him scope for that meddlesome activity which he mistook for genius, he had viewed with unalloyed satisfaction the advent of a rival influence. At first, having no great confidence in the permanence of the monarch's latest passion, he hesitated to commit himself too deeply, but, once convinced that the affair was something more than a caprice, he resolved to lend his support to Madame du Barry, hoping thereby to ensure the undoing of his enemy and the realisation of those political ambitions which Madame de Châteauroux's death and Madame de Pompadour's hostility had frustrated.

And the support which Richelieu was able to give Madame du Barry was a very material factor in securing the official recognition of her position, that is to say, her formal presentation to the King. For until that important ceremony had taken place, it was impossible for her to ride in the royal carriages, to be admitted to his Majesty's *petits soupers*, to pay her court to the Dauphin or the King's daughters (*Mesdames*), to be present at Court functions, to enjoy, in a word, any of those privileges "without which the mistress was nothing but a mistress, with which the mistress was the favourite."[2]

[1] See the author's "Madame du Barry" (London, Harper : New York, Scribner, 1904).

[2] E. and J. de Goncourt, *la Du Barry*.

On January 1, 1769, Richelieu had entered upon his term of office as First Gentleman of the Chamber, in which capacity he had charge of the presentations for the ensuing year. His duties also gave him many opportunities for private conversations with his royal master, and there can be very little doubt that he took advantage of them to overcome any lingering scruples which the King might have entertained concerning the acknowledgment of his new mistress. Nor did his services to Madame du Barry end there, for when one great lady after another who was requested to undertake the duty of *marraine* to the new postulant had indignantly refused or taken refuge in specious excuses, so that it almost seemed as if the presentation would have to be abandoned, it was Richelieu who persuaded the impecunious old Comtesse de Béarn, in consideration of the payment of her debts, to step into the breach.

French history affords few more singular spectacles than the alliance between the Du Barry faction, and the bigoted old Duc de la Vauguyon and the religious party at the Court, who had never forgiven Choiseul his expulsion of the Jesuits, for the overthrow of their common enemy. But, thanks to the support of Choiseul's ambitious colleagues, Maupeou and Terray, and to the King's well-founded belief that his Minister was endeavouring to drag Spain, and France with her, into war with England over the question of the Falkland Islands, the coalition triumphed, and on January 24, 1770, the man who since the death of Madame de Pompadour had been the virtual master of France was dismissed from office and exiled to his estates.

To the victors went the spoils, but Richelieu's share fell very much below his expectations, for, though the amorous old monarch could refuse little to his mistress, he did refuse her the marshal's admission to the Council of State. Perhaps Louis considered that his old friend knew too many secrets for his presence there to be altogether desirable; perhaps he was of opinion that, having rather against his will taken the Duc d'Aiguillon for Prime Minister, he had done enough for the family. Any way, Richelieu had to content himself with the position of Mentor *in petto* to the new Ministry and a pension of 30,000 livres on the Treasury for the Duc de Fronsac, which considerably relieved the paternal exchequer.

During the contest between the King and the Parlements, which ended in Maupeou's famous *coup d'État* of January 19, 1771, Richelieu, in whom respect for the royal authority was combined with a personal animosity towards the magistracy, owing to their recent prosecution of his nephew d'Aiguillon,[1] was one of the most strenuous advocates of violent measures. In April, parodying Cromwell, he entered the Cour des Aides and the chambers of the Châtelet, at the head of the Swiss Guards, turned the judges out into the street and locked the doors against them; and in September he accepted with alacrity the still more congenial mission of expelling the recalcitrant members of the Parlement of Bordeaux. "I hear," writes Horace Walpole, "that the Parlement of Bordeaux have made as much stand as they could, and enough to frighten the old Richelieu out of the remains of his old senses. They said they knew not what he meant by *lettres de cachet;* they acknowledged no such power. He retreated to his seat at Fronsac on the Dordogne, and has despatched a courier to Versailles for a squadron of powers. I suppose it will end in his plundering the city, and building a new Pavillon in his garden."[2]

Walpole, it should be remembered, was an intimate friend of Madame du Deffand, one of the most zealous of Choiseul's partisans, and therefore not unnaturally prejudiced against Richelieu; and the idea of the man who had led the charge of the Household cavalry at Fontenoy and the night-assault on the outworks of Fort St. Philip being "frightened out of his senses" by a few angry lawyers may well provoke a smile. However, when the "squadron of powers" arrived, the marshal returned to Bordeaux, and made very short work of the gentlemen of the long robe.

In 1773, Richelieu lost his daughter, the Comtesse d'Egmont,

[1] For a full account of these proceedings, see the author's "Madame du Barry."

[2] Letter of September 26, 1771.

who died on October 14 of that year, at the early age of thirty-three, from consumption. Since the beginning of 1771, her relations with her father had been very strained, in consequence of her refusal to pay her court to Madame du Barry; and for some time the despotic old man, furious at his wishes being disregarded, had treated his daughter with much harshness and even forbidden her to approach him. He does not appear to have been greatly affected by her death, for three days afterwards he was selecting the plays to be performed before the Court at Fontainebleau, and the following month he assisted at the marriage-fêtes of the Comte d'Artois (afterwards Charles X.).

Although Louis XV. had refused to gratify Richelieu's political ambitions, the marshal seems to have been in as high favour as he had ever been during the last years of the King's life, for he and Madame du Barry were perhaps the only two persons who were capable of arousing the old monarch from those fits of ennui from which he had suffered all his life, and which, with the decline of his physical powers, were becoming more frequent and more prolonged. The familiar terms on which he stood with his sovereign are well illustrated by the following anecdote.

When, in Holy Week 1773, the Abbé de Beauvais preached that unpleasantly outspoken sermon before the Court on the evil example set by dissipated old men of exalted position,[1] the King, as they left the chapel, turned to Richelieu with the remark: "It seems to me that the abbé was throwing stones into your garden." "True, Sire," answered the marshal, laughing, "but some of them were thrown so hard that they rebounded into the park of Versailles."

[1] In this sermon, the following passage is said to have occurred: "Solomon, satiated with voluptuousness, tired of having extinguished, in the endeavour to revive his withered senses, every sort of pleasure that surrounded the throne, ended by seeking one of a new kind in *the vile dregs of public corruption.*" M. Vatel, who discusses this question at some length in his *Histoire de Madame du Barry*, with the view, apparently, of vindicating the character of the Jewish monarch, is of opinion that the Abbé de Beauvais never used the words imputed to him, as they are not to be found in his collected sermons. Perhaps, however, as an English biographer of the lady, Mr. R. B. Douglas, suggests, they were omitted by a timid editor.

A little more than a year later (Tuesday, April 27, 1774), Louis XV. was taken ill at the Petit-Trianon; on the following afternoon, he was removed to Versailles; on the 29th, the doctors—there were eleven present, besides three apothecaries! —diagnosed small-pox, and by the Sunday, the King was so exhausted that it was the general impression that he could not survive more than a couple of days, and the same contest over the question of the Sacraments which had marked his illnesses in 1744 and 1757 forthwith began. On this occasion, however, the previous order of things was reversed: it was the patrons of the philosophers—that is to say, the Choiseul party—who cried out against the scandal of allowing the King to remain any longer in a state of sin; while the *dévots* supported Richelieu and the other intimates of the favourite in their contention that confession and absolution would effectually destroy any chance of recovery his Majesty might have, as everything depended on concealing his true condition from him.

In the midst of this unseemly wrangle, news arrived that Christophe de Beaumont, the Archbishop of Paris, had announced his intention of visiting the King on the following day. No one doubted that the object of the prelate's visit was to exhort his Majesty to repentance and confession, and the Du Barry party, in great alarm, held a council of war, which was attended by the favourite, d'Aiguillon, Richelieu, and Fronsac.

After some discussion, it was decided that, as it was impossible to keep the archbishop away from the King, the best course to pursue was to ensure that the Duc d'Orléans, first Prince of the Blood, should be in the room all the time, that the visit should be one of courtesy only, and that no mention should be made of the Sacraments. Madame Adélaïde, Louis XV.'s eldest daughter, whom the doctors of the favourite's faction had assured that the question of Eternity was premature and that it would be her father's death-blow, joined the conspiracy.

To Richelieu was entrusted the task of reconciling the metropolitan to the neglect of his very obvious duty, and when, at eleven o'clock the next morning, M. de Beaumont—

LOUIS FRANÇOIS ARMAND DU PLESSIS, MARÉCHAL DUC DE RICHELIEU

FROM AN ENGRAVING AFTER A COPY OF THE PAINTING BY GAULT DE SAINT-GERMAIN

an imposing figure in his violet robes—presented himself at the door of the King's ante-chamber, he was met by the marshal, who led him into the Cabinet du Conseil, made him sit down by his side, and spoke to him "with great vehemence and animated gestures."

Now, the archbishop was an honest and pious, if narrow-minded, man, who had endured exile and persecution for the truth's sake, or rather for that of the Bull *Unigenitus.* He deplored the irregularities of the King, but he fully appreciated the services which Madame du Barry had rendered to the party of which he was the ecclesiastical head by the overthrow of Choiseul, the elevation of d'Aiguillon, and the destruction of the Jansenist Parlement. He had come to insist on the dismissal of the favourite, as an indispensable preliminary to confession and the Sacraments, to the saving of the King's soul; but when Richelieu, with brutal frankness, pointed out to him that the saving of the King's soul meant the return of Choiseul and the Parlement, the triumph, in fact, of the enemies of the Church, he began to wonder whether his Majesty's salvation was indeed worth so great a sacrifice.

While he thus "hesitated between his zeal and his conscience," the Duc d'Aumont came to announce that the King awaited him. The prelate rose and entered the sick-room, where he found the Duc d'Orléans, who had been charged by Madame Adélaïde to take care that M. de Beaumont did not say anything which might alarm her father. The prince's representations calmed the archbishop's last scruples, and, after remaining a few minutes, and condoling with his Majesty on the unfortunate event which had temporarily deprived his loving subjects of the joy of seeing him amongst them, he went back to Paris, without saying a word about confession; while the King, inferring from the prelate's avoidance of this unpleasant subject that the doctors could not consider him in any danger, sent at once for Madame du Barry, "wept with joy, and covered her hands with kisses."

The "Anti-Barriens," furious at the weakness of the archbishop, now fell back upon the Grand Almoner, the Cardinal de la Roche-Aymon. Incited by them, the Bishop of Carcassonne, an honest man who sincerely desired his sovereign's salvation, brandishing his pectoral cross before the cardinal's eyes, summoned him, in the name of that cross, to do his duty and propose the Sacraments to the King.

The cardinal found himself in very much the same predicament as had Père Pérusseau, at Metz, thirty years before; but, being an exceedingly supple and cautious ecclesiastic, he was determined not to commit himself. He therefore replied that, as the doctors were opposed to anything which might tend to alarm the King, he could not propose to administer the Sacraments openly, but that he would avail himself of the first opportunity of putting his Majesty in the right way. He then went to visit the King, but conversed with him in so low a tone that no one else could hear what was said. In this way, his Eminence was able to give his own version of what passed between Louis and himself.

That day a slight improvement was observed in the royal patient's condition, and the hopes of the Du Barry party rose high, while the spirits of the rival faction were correspondingly depressed. But during the night the disease took an alarming turn, and the following morning Louis questioned his first surgeon La Martinière, who felt obliged to tell him that he was suffering from small-pox.

In an agony of terror, the conscience-stricken monarch at once resolved to purchase absolution by the dismissal, or rather the apparent dismissal, of his mistress. Accordingly, that evening when Madame du Barry was brought to the sick-room, he called her to his bedside, and desired her to go to the Duc d'Aiguillon's château at Rueil, where she was "to await his orders."

At four o'clock the following afternoon (May 5), the favourite left Versailles, the joy of the "Anti-Barriens" at her departure being considerably discounted by the reflection that Rueil was but two leagues from Versailles, and that such a very modified form of exile probably implied a speedy recall in the event of the King's recovery. Louis's mind, indeed, was far more occupied by his mistress than by his confessor, and the inquiries he addressed to his *valet de chambre* La Borde and d'Aiguillon concerning her, showed but too plainly that the lady's departure was merely a precautionary measure.

In the course of the evening, a disgraceful scene took place in the ante-chamber. The curé of Versailles announced his intention of entering the sick-room to exhort the King to place himself in a state of grace without further delay; upon which the Duc de Fronsac, acting presumably on his father's instructions, threatened to throw him out of the window, if he dared even to mention the word "confession" in his Majesty's hearing. "If I am not killed, I shall return by the door," replied the priest, "for it is my duty." However, the attitude of the duke was so threatening that the curé eventually decided to remain silent.

The following day passed without any perceptible change in the King's condition, but during the night of the 6th to 7th he had a relapse, and calling the Duc de Duras, the First Gentleman of the Chamber on duty that year, bade him summon his confessor, the Abbé Maudoux. The duke, a bitter enemy of d'Aiguillon, obeyed the order with alacrity, and the abbé, who was an honest man, told his Majesty very plainly that it was impossible for him to give him absolution so long as his stone of stumbling was anywhere in the neighbourhood. Louis thereupon sent for d'Aiguillon, and having confided to him what the abbé had said, desired him to inform Madame du Barry that she must retire to Richelieu's château at Chinon, in Touraine. The Minister, who, on the principle that while there is life there is hope, was determined not to abandon the struggle, assured the King that he must have misunderstood his *directeur*, and, instead of sending Madame du Barry to Chinon, hurried off to the Cardinal de la Roche-Aymon and the Abbé Maudoux, to endeavour to persuade them to administer the Sacraments unconditionally. He met, as might be expected, with considerable opposition from the abbé; but the cardinal was complaisant enough, and, in the end, the matter was settled to d'Aiguillon's satisfaction.

At six o'clock the next morning, preceded by the clergy of the parish and the chapel, surrounded by bishops, and followed by the Dauphin and his brothers, the Princes and Princesses of the Blood, the grand officers of the Crown, the Ministers and Secretaries of State, and nearly the whole of the Court, all with lighted tapers in their hands, the Host was brought in solemn state to the apartments of the dying King. The clergy, *Mesdames*, and the princes entered the royal bedchamber, where the Cardinal de la Roche-Aymon, after delivering a brief and perfectly inaudible exhortation to his Majesty, administered the Holy Sacrament.

But the ceremony was not yet over, for, as the cardinal turned away, the Abbé Maudoux, "with anxious, acidulated face," plucked him by the sleeve and whispered in his ear, whereupon La Roche-Aymon advanced to the door, and there repeated the formula of repentance drawn up by the Archbishop of Paris, the bishops, and the confessor:

"Messieurs, the King charges me to inform you that he asks pardon of God for having offended Him, and for the scandal he has given his people; that if God restores him to health, he will occupy himself with the maintenance of religion and the welfare of his people."

Two voices broke the silence which ensued. One was that of the King, who murmured: "I should have wished for sufficient strength to say it myself"; the other was that of old Richelieu, who had listened "with mastiff-face growing blacker" to the declaration of penitence, and, on its conclusion, growled out some uncomplimentary reference to the Grand Almoner, which Bésenval, who records the incident, is too modest to repeat. "Old Richelieu, conqueror of Minorca, companion of Flying-Table orgies, perforator of bedroom walls, is thy day also done?" [1]

Not yet. Louis XV. died at a quarter-past three on May 9, but Richelieu survived till the very eve of the Revolution, and expiated, to some extent at least, his gallant adventures and the scandals of his long life.

[1] Carlyle, "French Revolution."

# CHAPTER XXIV

*L'affaire* Saint-Vincent—Madame de Saint-Vincent confined by her relatives in the Couvent des Benedictines, at Millau—Her correspondence with Richelieu—Her first forgeries of the marshal's name—She obtains money on the strength of a letter purporting to be written by him—She is removed to the Ursuline convent, at Tarbes, and thence to the Couvent de Catherinettes, at Poitiers—Her intrigue with Védel, major in the Régiment Dauphin—Conspiracy against Richelieu's coffers—She is visited by the marshal at Poitiers—A septuagenarian escapade—Madame de Saint-Vincent obtains her removal to Paris—Ruse by which she succeeds in compromising Richelieu—Inauspicious opening of the campaign—New plan of operations decided upon—An ecclesiastical dupe—The Jew Ruby—A hard bargain—The plot discovered after four forged bills have been discounted—Letter of Richelieu to Madame de Saint-Vincent—Impudent reply of the latter—Arrest of Madame de Saint-Vincent, her accomplices, and dupes—Her reply to the Lieutenant Criminel—A *cause célèbre* in the eighteenth century—Ingenuity of the accused—Serious position of Richelieu: prejudice of the judges against him—Evidence of Mlle. Maury de Saint-Victor for the prosecution—An amazing verdict.

WRITING under date September 16, 1775, to George Selwyn, Horace Walpole says: "A great-grand-daughter of Madame de Sévigné pretends, for it is not certain, that she has been debauched by ancient Richelieu, and half the world thinks that she is more guilty of forgery. The memoirs of the two parties are half as voluminous as M. de Guines,[1] and more are to appear."

The matter to which Horace Walpole refers was the famous *l'affaire* Saint-Vincent, one of the most extraordinary of the *causes célèbres* of the eighteenth century, in which for three years the old marshal was compelled to struggle against a gang of clever and audacious swindlers to save his fortune and his honour.

[1] The Duc de Guines, at this time French Ambassador in England. The writer is referring to his lawsuit with Tort de la Sonde.

To discover the genesis of this singular affair we must go back to the year 1766. At that time, there was residing as a *pensionnaire* in the Couvent des Benedictines, at Millau, a certain Marquise de Saint-Vincent, wife of a president of the Parlement of Aix. Madame de Saint-Vincent was not a voluntary inmate of this cloistral retreat, where she had lived since February 1753, as she had been conducted there in virtue of a *lettre de cachet*, issued on the joint application of her husband and her father, "*pour cause de libertinage et conduite scandaleuse.*" Divorce being at this period unknown to the French law, confinement in a convent was the approved method of dealing with ladies whose marriage vows sat lightly upon them, though, as the motive in most cases seems to have been rather a precautionary than a vindictive one, the delinquent's lot was by no means so unpleasant as might be supposed. Thus, unless orders had been sent to the contrary, or the superior happened to be unusually austere, she was permitted to furnish her apartments according to her own taste, to wear and to order what she pleased, and to visit and receive any friends she might have in the neighbourhood, at stated hours. Madame de Saint-Vincent enjoyed all these privileges, and, being a lady of considerable personal attractions and great charm of manner, was regarded as a decided acquisition to the society of Millau.

Now, Madame de Saint-Vincent was rather given to boasting of the great people whom she had known in the days before her unfortunate sensibility to admiration had rendered it undesirable for her to remain any longer under the conjugal roof; and on one occasion she happened to mention the celebrated Maréchal de Richelieu, adding that he was a distant relative of her own. The lady's acquaintance with the marshal was, as a matter of fact, of the slightest, being confined to a single meeting at Aix, when Richelieu, passing through that city on his way to the coast to embark for Genoa, had paid a visit of courtesy to her father, M. de Vence; for, though the relationship of which Madame de Saint-Vincent spoke was so very distant as to be quite beyond the range of normal vision, the great man had condescended to acknowledge it.

One of the nuns of the convent, who was present when Richelieu's name was mentioned, begged Madame de Saint Vincent to endeavour to enlist the good offices of her distinguished "cousin" on behalf of her brother, a M. des Angles, for whom she was anxious to obtain some military post. Prompted by vanity and the desire of appearing to maintain her intercourse with the great world, the lady, though very dubious as to the reception which her letter was likely to meet with, consented; and, to her surprise and gratification, received a favourable answer. Although so many years had passed since their meeting, the gallant marshal wrote that he still remembered it, and that it would give him great pleasure to accord her the favour she solicited.

From that moment, one knows not by what caprice of the old man, he wrote to her almost every week, and a regular correspondence was soon established between them, of which Madame de Saint-Vincent did not fail to take advantage. An extravagant and open-handed woman, she had greatly exceeded the limits of the pension which her husband allowed her, and was heavily in debt; and it now occurred to her to procure a respite from her creditors by putting to practical use a dangerous talent which she had acquired during the long and idle hours in the convent—that of imitating handwriting. She accordingly set herself to counterfeit the writing of the marshal, and succeeded so well that soon it was impossible to distinguish the true from the false. Then she proceeded to compose imaginary letters, couched in a much more intimate tone than her correspondent usually employed, and holding out hopes of financial assistance in the near future. These letters, with much apparent reluctance and many blushes, she showed to her creditors, who were so impressed thereby that they forthwith ceased to persecute her.

However, as the months went by without the marshal showing any intention of coming to the rescue of his distressed relative, their patience became exhausted, and in the summer of 1768, Madame de Saint-Vincent was obliged to confide her impoverished condition to Richelieu. Contrary to his habit, for he was far from generous with women, the latter sent her an order on his Bordeaux bankers for 3,000 livres. It was to prove the most costly present he ever made in his life.

Three thousand livres represented but a small part of Madame de Saint-Vincent's liabilities, but, encouraged by the success of her first stratagem, she determined to take a second, and much more serious, step on the downward path. She carefully copied the document, added a cipher, and found herself the possessor of an order for 30,000 livres. She did not, however, go so far as to present it for payment or get it discounted, but adopted a much more astute line of action. Sending for one of her friends, a certain Baron de la Capelle Montauriol, she gave him the document and begged him to show it to her creditors, in order to pacify them. The baron complied, and the long-suffering tradesmen readily agreed to accord the lady a further period of grace, and, in several cases, an extension of credit.

Most happily for Richelieu, as it eventually proved, the forgery had a witness, in the person of a young lady, named Mlle. Maury de Saint-Victor, also a *pensionnaire* in the convent, who had surprised Madame de Saint-Vincent in the very act. On the latter's assurance that it was merely a ruse to persuade a particularly pressing creditor to wait her convenience, she had decided to say nothing about it; but from that moment she avoided Madame de Saint-Vincent as much as possible.

In the spring of 1769, it suddenly occurred to Madame de Saint-Vincent that it would be a sinful squandering of opportunities were she not to exploit the gratitude of M. des Angles, the gentleman whom Richelieu had befriended at her request. Accordingly, she invited him to visit her, and handed him a letter purporting to have been written to him by the marshal, under cover to herself, in which he begged M. des Angles to endeavour to put his cousin's affairs in order, and informed him that he held in trust for her the sum of 10,000 livres, representing a legacy which had been left her by her mother, and would be paid in the following November. On the strength of this forged letter, Des Angles advanced the lady between 5,000 and 6,000 livres, and, though he subsequently learned, from a friend of Madame de Saint-Vincent, that the legacy had never existed save in the latter's imagination, the sight of the order for 30,000 reassured him; and not only did he pardon the trick of which he had been the victim, but actually lent her a further sum. He must have been a gentleman of a singularly unsuspicious nature.

Some months later, Madame de Saint-Vincent made the discovery that the climate of Millau was unsuited to her health, and accordingly petitioned to be allowed to change her residence. After some delay, her request was granted, and on August 10, 1774, an exempt of police escorted her to the Ursuline convent at Tarbes.

The pretty Pyrenean town was altogether a much more congenial spot for a lady who was fond of society than Millau, and one might have supposed that Madame de Saint-Vincent would have been content to remain there, at least for a while. The contrary was the case. Scarcely had she arrived, than she gave way to the bitterest lamentations. "They had buried her alive," she declared; "her apartment, the roof of which she could touch with her head, was nothing but a horrible sepulchre, looking out on to the cemetery of the nuns. She saw nothing from this lugubrious hole but cypress-trees and tombs." The Archbishop of Tarbes—a very gallant old gentleman—to whom she hastened to appeal, sanctioned her removal to a comfortable private house, commanding a charming view, which he himself had selected for her. But, so far from being grateful for this concession, she speedily found new grounds for complaint, and addressed to Richelieu the most heartrending letters. The marshal wrote to the archbishop; the archbishop wrote to the lady's husband; and at the beginning of April 1771, the Duc de la Vrillière, *Commandeur des Ordres* to the King, sent a new order, in virtue of which Madame de Saint-Vincent was transferred to the Couvent des Catherinettes, at Poitiers, where, through the thoughtfulness of Richelieu, two luxurious apartments had been prepared for her reception.

Now, as the reader will have doubtless surmised, there was something behind the extreme anxiety of Madame de Saint-Vincent to leave Tarbes. This something was a lover, one

M. Védel du Montel, a major in the Régiment Dauphin, then in garrison at Poitiers. The major was long past his *première jeunesse*—nearer fifty than forty—but he was none the less a remarkably handsome man, with regular features, bright dark eyes, perfect teeth, and a smile that was worth a dowry of 100,000 livres at a conservative estimate. That he had not yet secured the hand of an heiress was due to the unfortunate circumstance that his moral qualities altogether discounted his personal attractions. He was, in fact, though an excellent soldier, who had obtained the cross of Saint-Louis, an unmitigated rogue, debauched, cunning, avaricious, and unscrupulous. Madame de Saint-Vincent had made his acquaintance at Millau, when he came there to visit Mlle. Maury de Saint-Victor, to whom he was betrothed. No sooner did she set eyes on the fascinating major than she loved him to distraction, and determined to put a stop to the proposed marriage. She accordingly informed Mlle. de Saint-Victor of a discreditable episode in M. Védel's past which had come to her knowledge. Mlle. de Saint-Victor, in turn, informed her parents, who, finding that the charge—that of having played Lovelace to the Clarissa of a damsel of good family at Nîmes—was true, broke off the match.

M. de Védel was naturally much chagrined at the loss of his *fiancée*, or rather of his money, but found consolation, both sentimental and pecuniary, in a liaison with Madame de Saint-Vincent. From this liaison resulted several things: First a very passionate correspondence—at any rate, on the lady's side—which afterwards greatly edified the Paris courts. Secondly, a son, the paternity of which the lady subsequently endeavoured to foist upon Richelieu. Thirdly, a most audacious conspiracy, of which Védel was the head, Madame de Saint-Vincent the hand, Paris the theatre, and the old marshal the victim.

The first move of this precious pair was to compromise Richelieu. This was easily effected, for Poitiers was on the road from Paris to Bordeaux, and the old gentleman was naturally anxious to behold his fair correspondent; and in the early hours of a fine May morning in 1772, the inmates of the Couvent des Catherinettes were awakened from their slumbers by the arrival of a courier, with a letter for Madame de Saint-Vincent announcing that the marshal would reach Poitiers in the course of the day.

Richelieu alighted at the episcopal palace, where he dined, and afterwards, accompanied by the Bishop of Poitiers, paid a visit of ceremony to the convent. What he saw of Madame de Saint-Vincent pleased him so much that, when the shades of night had fallen, he returned, this time, needless to say, without the bishop, who must have been greatly shocked when he learned next morning of the escapade of his septuagenarian guest. Thanks to the activity of Védel, it was all over the town.

The marshal paid four other visits to the convent on his journeys to and from Bordeaux; but, as the bishop had presumably given the superior a piece of his mind, there were no more private interviews. However, the one of which we have spoken had served the conspirators' purpose.

The next move in the game was for Madame de Saint-Vincent to get herself transferred to Paris, and, thanks to the influence of her intended victim, the end of March 1773 found her an inmate of the Couvent des Filles de la Miséricorde, in the Rue Vieux-Colombier.

The lady subsequently declared that she had come at the marshal's instigation, "in order to precipitate herself into his arms." But the marshal confined his attentions to returning the visit which Madame de Saint-Vincent hastened to pay to the Hôtel de Richelieu, and the cunning Provençale, fearing that her rather mature charms might not be sufficient to bring him back, modestly effaced herself, and pushed forward one of her friends, a charming young English "*miladi.*"

The old *roué* fell into the trap prepared for him, and almost every day his well-known liveries were seen at the convent gate. "Here I am back from Versailles, my dear cousin," he writes. "I saw the Chancellor [Maupeou], who spoke to me about your husband. I will tell you of this after dinner, for I shall not be able to dine, but I hope to find you after dinner still with the amiable companion with whom you were so kind as to invite me to dine." And again: "Here, my dear cousin, are the letters which you confided to me and which I return to you. Those little words of *miladi* have suspended my affliction, but, in order to dissipate it altogether, I must *hear* her say them herself. Farewell, *dear* cousin, I love you very tenderly."

Having now succeeded in compromising the marshal in Paris, as well as at Poitiers, Madame de Saint-Vincent judged that the moment for executing the plans which she had been so carefully maturing had arrived. She and Védel, who had preceded her to Paris, had already found an efficient confederate, in the person of a Gascon adventurer, named Bénaven, and three useful tools, in a certain Comtesse de Saint-Jean, a friend of Madame de Saint-Vincent, the Abbé Froment, chaplain of the Couvent de la Miséricorde, and the Abbé de Villeneuve-Flayosc, a son of Madame de Saint-Vincent's elder sister.

On June 27, 1773, Madame de Saint-Vincent called upon the Comtesse de Saint-Jean, at the latter's house in the Rue de la Chaise, and, having confided to her friend the passion with which she had inspired the Maréchal de Richelieu and the brilliant lot which awaited her, showed her an order for 100,000 écus (300,000 livres) accepted by his Bordeaux banker, Peschot. It was as follows: "The Maréchal de Richelieu requests the sieur Peschot to pay to Madame de Saint-Vincent the three hundred thousand livres which belong to her and of which he will hold him discharged." Some days later, she sent her *femme de chambre* to the countess to ask if she could get it discounted for her, and an admirer of Madame de Saint-Jean, named Dumas, a brigadier in the Army, took the document to his banker, M. Julien of the Rue Simon-le-Franc. Julien, who had had many dealings with Peschot, no sooner glanced at his signature than he declared it to be a forgery, which so astounded the poor brigadier that, as he subsequently declared, he came within measurable distance of an apoplectic fit.[1]

[1] *Déposition de Barbe-Thérèse d'Oraison, comtesse de Saint-Jean et de M. Dumas, Archives du Parlement de Paris*, published by Mary-Lafon, *les Dernières Armes de Richelieu : le Maréchal de Richelieu et Madame de Saint-Vincent.*

This fiasco naturally threw the conspirators into great consternation; but, as neither Julien nor their dupes seemed inclined to talk about the matter, they regained their courage, and, having taken the advice of a legal friend as to the best method of drawing bills, without, of course, allowing him to suspect their criminal intentions, they resolved to operate by means of bills for less sensational amounts, made payable to bearer.

To the Church fell the honour of opening the campaign. At Madame de Saint-Vincent's request, the unsuspecting Abbé Froment, chaplain of her convent, took a bill for 60,000 livres, and, provided with an introduction from a notary of his acquaintance, had no difficulty in persuading M. Bouché de Préville, a high Government official, to discount it.

Seeing the confidence which the clergy seemed to inspire, Madame de Saint-Vincent entrusted her nephew, the Abbé de Villeneuve-Flayosc, with a similar commission. But his attempt to place two bills, one for 25,000 livres and the other for 20,000, with a bill-discounter of the Quartier Montmartre failed, as the abbé's refusal to disclose the name of the holder aroused suspicion.

Then Védel and Bénaven entered the field, and called upon a broker of the Halles, named Ruby, a gentleman of Jewish origin, who combined with his ordinary business a good deal of secret usury, and offered two bills bearing Richelieu's signature, one for 35,000, dated April 4, 1773, and payable in three years, the other for 20,000, payable in thirty-three months. Ruby began by refusing to entertain the transaction, assuring them that he nowadays confined his attentions entirely to his trade, and it was not until Védel and Bénaven intimated that the holder of the bills would be prepared to accept part of their value in furniture that he asked to see the documents. With the shrewdness of his race, he had already decided that there was something distinctly suspicious about the affair, but he was prepared to undertake the risk, in view of the immense profit which it offered him. At the same time, he took every precaution to excuse his error and to prove that he was acting in good faith. First, he insisted on being given the name of the holder of the bills, and made his clients sign a paper certifying that the sums they represented were "legitimately due from the seigneur Duc de Richelieu to Madame la Marquise de Saint-Vincent." Then, since the marshal's signature was unknown to him, he declared that he must have it verified before concluding the business. So perfect, however, was the forgery, that Védel and Bénaven had no fear upon that score, and, at their suggestion, they all three repaired to the office of Richelieu's notary, Dumoulin, in the Rue Saint-Antoine. Carefully folding one of the bills so that the signature alone was visible, Védel placed it before the man of law and asked if he recognised the writing of his noble client. "Yes, gentlemen," answered Dumoulin, "it is the marshal's signature; it is, however, a little thin; still, I believe that it is his." He then took some documents from his desk, and having found one which bore Richelieu's signature, compared it with that upon the bill, and observed: "The writing on this is thicker than the one you have, but the letters are formed in the same way. I presume that the marshal has signed this hurriedly, with a pen which was not his own. I believe, however, that it is the marshal's signature, but, if you wish to be certain, you can see his intendant."

Ruby, however, being of opinion that the notary's testimony would be sufficient to exonerate him, professed himself satisfied, and he with the conspirators returned to the Halles, where he proceeded to drive a bargain worthy of Shylock himself. For the two bills, representing 55,000 livres, he persuaded them to accept 6,000 livres in cash, and a quantity of second-hand furniture, *objets d'art*, porcelain, and jewellery, for the most part quite worthless; for when it all came to be sold some time afterwards, it only realised 713 livres!

The campaign continued, but with results which fell very far short of the conspirators' expectations. With the exception of Ruby, who consented to discount a further bill for 35,000 livres on the same terms as the others, the financial world was very shy indeed, and no one seemed at all anxious to possess the marshal's signature, though they hawked it industriously all over the town. This was extremely mortifying, but worse was to follow; for at the end of July 1774, they were invited to exchange their castle in Spain for his Majesty's château of the Bastille.

It was Ruby who had given the game away. That astute gentleman, ascertaining that he was only one among many to whom M. de Richelieu's "paper" had been offered, perceived that his suspicions had been but too well founded, and determined to get on the safe side of the fence with the least possible delay. He accordingly sent his notary to interview Marion, the marshal's intendant—Richelieu himself was at Bordeaux—to inform that functionary that he had a client who held certain bills signed by his master, which, however, he would be prepared to exchange for some other form of security, if the marshal desired.

Marion, after looking at the bills and pronouncing the signatures genuine—which was another point in Ruby's favour—denied all knowledge of them, but promised to communicate with his master. He did so, and Richelieu, in a great rage, replied that the bills were forgeries, and ordered him to have the notary and his client arrested. Both were taken to For l'Évêque, where Ruby at once named the persons from whom he had received the bills. Marion informed the marshal, who sent a courier to Madame de Saint-Vincent, with the following letter:

"I learn with the greatest astonishment, my dear cousin, that bills for 200,000 livres signed by me are in circulation, and what astounds me, is that it is said that you are concerned in it, which I cannot believe. I beg you to listen patiently to the sieur Marion and to assist him to unravel the thread of this villainy. You are as much interested as myself in not allowing it to go unpunished. I shall not speak of anything else in this letter."

It is evident from this epistle that the marshal believed Madame de Saint-Vincent to be innocent, and that the forger had been making use of her name. But he was speedily undeceived when his courier returned, and handed him the following masterpiece of impudence:

"MY DEAR COUSIN,

"I am at a loss to understand the fuss which Marion is making here. He *dares* to assert that I have fabricated these bills under your signature, which was *false*. It is clear that he has not spoken by your directions, and I believe it so little, that I hope you will make him repent this step; and if you do not, then I and all my family will undertake it. Necessity has compelled me to transfer the bills which you gave me. But I took, at the same time, measures to prevent your ever learning it, and that it should not upset you. Through an indiscretion, my secret had been divulged; but, since it has happened, and since the sieur Marion forces me to speak plainly, in order to prove that I am incapable of forgery, I shall tell the whole truth. Further, I shall prove the truth of everything I say, and until my last breath I shall defend my own honour and that of my family. It is already informed of all this, and I shall perish with my friends and my relatives sooner than fail to sustain my impeached honour. That is my determination, and I shall adhere to it, as well as to my sentiments of gratitude for all the benefits which I have received from you, my dear cousin.

"VENCE DE SAINT-VINCENT"[1]

Madame de Saint-Vincent was as good as her word. Learning from Marion that it was his intention to invoke the assistance of the police to discover the criminals, she determined to anticipate him; and on July 19, accompanied by Védel, in full uniform and with the cross of Saint-Louis on his breast, Bénaven, and a *maître des requêtes* of her acquaintance, she called boldly upon Sartine, the Lieutenant of Police, and showed him a number of bills bearing Richelieu's signature and several letters purporting to refer to them, and which were, of course,

[1] Published by Mary-Lafon.

also skilful forgeries. Sartine received the party very courteously, but, five days later, he caused the lady and both her accomplices to be arrested and conveyed to the Bastille. Through the influence of her relatives, who, though caring nothing for the lady herself, were greatly concerned about their family honour, she was soon allowed to leave the Bastille, and returned to her convent, an exempt of police being instructed to keep a vigilant eye upon her; while Védel was transferred to his house and closely guarded likewise. The Abbé de Villeneuve-Flayosc and several other persons who had been employed to negotiate the forged bills were imprisoned in the Conciergerie or For l'Évêque.

When examined by the Lieutenant Criminel on August 17, Madame de Saint-Vincent displayed the utmost *sang-froid.* She declared that she had received in all from Richelieu bills and orders to the value of 1,020,000 livres, viz. an order for 100,000 écus on Peschot—the one offered the banker Julien—which, recognising the difficulty of discounting, she had subsequently exchanged for a number of bills payable to bearer; two bills for a similar sum, and two of 60,000 livres each. Asked what was the consideration which Richelieu had received for so much money, she laughed disdainfully, and replied: "A consideration with which M. le Marèchal was satisfied.".

On March 7, 1775, a decree of the Tournelle (the Court of criminal jurisdiction) directed that the case should be referred to the Parlement, to be tried by the assembled Chambers,[1] the peers sitting with them.

Paris adores sensational trials, and the serious character of the charge, the celebrity of the prosecutor, the rank and beauty of the principal accused, and the romantic nature of the relations which had existed between them—all combined to provide one after its own heart. It was a duel, too, not only between Richelieu and Madame de Saint-Vincent, but between the ermine and the *cordon bleu*, between the Parlement and the

[1] That is to say, by the Grande Chambre, the Cour des Requêtes, and Cour des Enquêtes.

Court, for the accused was the wife of a judge, and the prosecutor one of the most implacable enemies of the magistracy. Keen and bitter was the struggle. Money was poured out on both sides like water, for all the prisoner's relatives—the Saint-Vincents, the Vences, the Castellanes—all the noblesse of Provence, rallied to the side of the persecuted lady; the best champions of the Bar entered the arena on one side or the other; the ablest experts in handwriting wrinkled their brows over the bills and letters; the most scurrilous gutter-poets were employed to compose *chansons;* and the most bitter pens in France, among which that of Voltaire was easily recognisable,[1] dashed off pamphlet after pamphlet, memoir after memoir.

The point of supreme importance for the accused was to furnish a satisfactory explanation of Richelieu's supposed generosity—a generosity which was little short of extraordinary on the part of a man who was notoriously parsimonious in his treatment of his mistresses. What was the motive which had induced him to give this middle-aged inamorata bills to the value of over a million livres?

It had been Madame de Saint-Vincent's original intention to maintain that the marshal was the father of her little son born at Poitiers, and that the money he had given her was intended to repair the wrong he had committed and to make provision for the child; and, with this idea, she had forged a letter, in which Richelieu gave her certain directions concerning the education of the boy. When, however, she reflected that the evidence as to the nature of her relations with Védel—their correspondence had fallen into the hands of the police—was such as to render this line of defence untenable, she promptly abandoned it, and declared that, although the marshal was not the father of her child, "she had persuaded him to believe that he was, in order to extract money from him."

[1] Beaumarchais also supported Richelieu, and Madame de Saint-Vincent wrote him a reproachful letter. "In what Jordan," she asks, "will you purify that pen which you have sullied with the blood of an innocent person?"

This adroit move, while it cost her the sympathy of many of her supporters, immensely strengthened her case, since it gave to the forged letter an appearance of authenticity. It was obvious to every one—and Richelieu's leading counsel frankly admitted it—that if the marshal had really entertained this illusion, that alone was quite sufficient to account for his munificence towards the accused.

Matters now began to look very serious indeed for Richelieu, for it must be remembered that the majority of the Parlement were, for political reasons, violently prejudiced against him, and would have cheerfully given a good round sum to find a plausible pretext for an adverse verdict.[1] In spite of the evidence of Des Angles in regard to the pretended letter of the marshal, on the strength of which he had advanced money to Madame de Saint-Vincent, the sympathies of the court seemed entirely with the accused, and nothing can be more certain than that the marshal would have found himself a disgraced and ruined man, had it not been for the intervention of Mlle. Maury de Saint-Victor, the young lady who had been a fellow-*pensionnaire* of Madame de Saint-Vincent at the Couvent des Benedictines, at Millau, and who had witnessed the forgery of the order for 30,000 livres which the marchioness had used to deceive her creditors.

Mlle. de Saint-Victor, who was now residing with her parents at Montauban, had been interrogated by the *lieutenant criminel* of the district, but, unwilling to be mixed up in so unsavoury an affair, had firmly refused to answer his questions. Warned, however, by Des Angles, that she might be able to give most important evidence, Richelieu wrote a very courteous letter to her father, pointing out the desperate position he was in, and the vital importance of persuading the girl to reveal everything she knew. His letter was not without effect, and, about the middle of September 1776, M. de Saint-Victor and his daughter arrived in Paris.

[1] One of the judges openly declared in the course of the trial that he intended to vote against the marshal, "because a man who had carried fire and sword into the sanctuary of the laws deserved no consideration."

Mlle. de Saint-Victor's evidence and her subsequent confrontation with the accused created a most profound impression, and, though the defence made desperate efforts to discount the importance of her testimony, by casting the most scandalous aspersions on the moral character of the poor girl, and charging her with having been suborned by the prosecution, they were unsuccessful.

Despite the hatred with which they regarded Richelieu, the Parlement was unable to close its eyes to such evidence. Nevertheless, it continued to prolong the trial for several months longer; and it was not until May 6, 1777, that it finally delivered what is surely one of the most astonishing verdicts to be found in history! Shorn of legal phraseology, it was as follows:

The court found that all the bills and orders supposed to have been signed by Richelieu were forgeries, and that the letters purporting to have accompanied them were also forgeries. But it found that there was *insufficient evidence* to connect Madame de Saint-Vincent with the crime, and therefore discharged both her and her accomplices, condemning the marchioness to pay to Bouchet de Préville and Ruby the amount of the bills discounted by them—which, needless to say, she never did—and cautioning Védel and Bénaven to be "more circumspect in the future." It further condemned Richelieu to pay 30,000 livres damages to the Abbé de Villeneuve-Flayosc, and various smaller sums, amounting in all to another 35,200 livres, to nine other persons whom he had caused to be arrested for having attempted to negotiate the bills.

What the affair cost the marshal from beginning to end, it is impossible to say; but, having regard to the length of the trial, the eminent counsel engaged, the cost of commissioning, printing, and circulating the pamphlets and memoirs issued on his behalf, and the expense entailed in bringing witnesses from distant provinces to Paris and maintaining them there for long periods, it must have been something enormous. However, when we remember what his past life had been, it is difficult to feel much sympathy for him.[1]

[1] But this was not the opinion of Madame de Gaze, an old flame of Richelieu in the far-off days when he frequented the Duchesse du Maine's little Court at Sceaux. On her death, in the previous March, she left him her whole fortune, amounting to some 150,000 livres, at the same time declaring that it was her desire that "no advocate or attorney should put his nose into her affairs, or his foot into her house." "*Parbleu!*" the marshal is reported to have said on hearing of the legacy, "if all the women who have been in love with me had been so thoughtful, I should be richer than the King."

## CHAPTER XXV

The return of Voltaire—His note to Richelieu—Death of the Patriarch—The marshal's opiate—Opinion of d'Alembert—Portrait of Richelieu in 1780 by the Duc de Lévis—Serious illness of the marshal—Conduct of Fronsac—Richelieu marries for the third time, at the age of eighty-four !—A happy marriage—Episode of Louis XVI.'s dressing-gown—Richelieu is reconciled to Maurepas—He persecutes the mayor of Bordeaux—And engages in a lawsuit with Arthur, the paper-manufacturer—His last years—His death, on August 8, 1788, at the age of ninety-two.

ON February 10, 1778, Voltaire arrived in Paris, to enjoy that amazing ovation which was intended to atone for his twenty-eight years of exile—and to die. Scarcely had he arrived, than he wrote to Richelieu, to say that he was expecting him "with all the uneasiness of an old man who has not a moment to lose, and the impatience of a young girl eager to embrace her lover." The marshal lost no time in responding to so pressing an invitation, and assisted the author of *Irène* in the delicate task of assigning the parts. He was, of course, present at Voltaire's reception by the Academy on March 30, and at the extraordinary scene at the Comédie-Française a little later in the day. "*Ah! Dieu!* You will kill me with glory!" exclaimed the Patriarch, as Brizard, on behalf of the *sociétaires*, placed the crown of laurel on his head.

The words were, unhappily, prophetic. The excitement, the perpetual ovations, the work which he insisted on undertaking in connection with his great scheme for the Academy Dictionary, proved too much for the old man's slender reserve of strength. On May 12, he was compelled to take to his bed; at a quarter-past eleven on the night of the 30th, he was dead.

In connection with Voltaire's last days, a curious story was current. Here is the version which is given by the *Mémoires secrets*, under date May 24—that is to say six days before the patriarch died:

"M. de Voltaire, enchanted at the good health enjoyed by the Maréchal Duc de Richelieu, asked him what he did to induce sleep. The marshal told him of an excellent narcotic which he possessed, promised to share it with him ["like a brother," says another account], and sent him a certain quantity. The old philosopher, who is very anxious to live, took so strong a dose of it, that it made him very ill. It appears that there was too much opium in the elixir, and since that time he calls the marshal 'his brother Cain.'"

Now, it is not disputed that Richelieu did send his old friend the opiate in question—one which he was accustomed to take during his attacks of gout—probably on the night of the 20th, when Voltaire, being in great pain, sent to ask him for it. But it is not certain that he took it; and still less certain that, even if he did, it had the injurious effect ascribed to it; while the "brother Cain" part of the story seems to be a pure invention.

But let us listen to what d'Alembert, always a trustworthy witness, and who was with Voltaire constantly in his last illness, has to say on the matter:

"I do not believe that he [Voltaire] said to M. de Richelieu the jesting words that are attributed to him: '*Ah! frère Caïn, tu m'as tué!*' I saw him constantly during his illness, and I met the marshal there several times. I never heard the words; his family and all his friends never heard them. It is true that the remark is a jesting one, and very similar to those he often made, but it would appear to have been invented by some one who believed it; and it is not true that the patriarch was poisoned by the laudanum which the marshal gave him. He did certainly give him some, but the bottle was broken, through the fault of the servants, before he had taken a drop.

"It is very certain that, some days before his illness, he took a great deal of coffee, to enable him to work better at different things which he wished to do. He overheated his blood, was unable to sleep, and suffered much from strangury; and, to obtain relief, drank laudanum, which he sent to an apothecary for, and which probably ended by killing him."[1]

Richelieu survived the friend to whose purse and pen he was so much indebted ten years. He was now in his eighty-third year, but, except for his "mastiff-face," might well have been mistaken for a man of sixty-five. The Duc de Lévis, who seems to have entertained for the marshal an unbounded admiration, has left us the following interesting portrait of him at this period of his life:

"It is only at rare intervals that one meets with beings privileged by Nature to combine talents with personal attractions, and the gifts of the mind with the charms of wit. Fascinating in youth, brilliant in mature age, superior in society as in affairs, their company was at all periods of their lives as agreeable as it was sought after. Such were Alcibiades, among the Greeks, and among the French, the Maréchal de Richelieu.

"When I knew him, he was more than eighty years old. It was impossible to recognise in his person the hero of so many gallant adventures, for he had not those noble features which time withers without effacing. Deep wrinkles furrowed his face in every direction; and he strove in vain to conceal the shrinking of his figure, which in youth was only of medium height, by wearing excessively high heels. His mind had not experienced the same decay. He had doubtless no longer the animation and sprightliness of youth, but his memory was excellent; he was interested in the affairs of the day, and used to relate with as much simplicity as grace those of the past. He judged with admirable discernment both men and things, and his jests were piquant without being spiteful."[2]

[1] Letter of d'Alembert to Frederick the Great, August 18, 1788, in Desnoiresterres, *Voltaire et la Société française au XVIII^e siècle*, vol. viii.

[2] *Souvenirs*.

We may add that his activity was positively astonishing. The *Mémoires secrets*, under date May 24, 1778, inform us that he mounted his horse "like a young soldier performing his exercise," and, a few months later, we hear of him dancing a minuet at a State ball at Versailles with all the zest of a youth of twenty.

Towards the end of the following year, however, he fell so seriously ill "of an indigestion," that the doctors declared that the end was only a question of hours. A servant on horseback was despatched to Fronsac, who was hunting in the plain of Gennevilliers, to bid him return in all haste, if he wished to see his father alive. The duke, whose grief, if we are to trust Soulavie, was a good deal tempered by material considerations, galloped *ventre-à-terre* to Paris to find the old gentleman unconscious and displaying scarcely any sign of life. Being unable to endure so pathetic a sight, he withdrew to the house of his brother-in-law, the Comte d'Egmont, bidding the servants inform him when the fatal moment arrived. After waiting some hours, however, a messenger presented himself with the news that Heaven had had compassion upon his despair, and that his father was much better. He returned to the Hôtel de Richelieu and ascended to the sick-room, where a voice from under the bed-clothes muttered: "I am not dead yet; you are not going to inherit this time!" The marshal, on regaining consciousness, had been informed of the arrival and speedy departure of his heir, and had resolved to read him a lesson.

In a day or two he had completely recovered, but, being of opinion that he had now arrived at an age when he required some one to take care of him, he began to look about for a third wife. At first, he appears to have entertained some thought of espousing a certain Madame Portail; next, a German princess; but eventually, in the spring of 1780, he offered his hand and heart, his title, and his eighty-four years to Madame de Rooth, the pretty and penniless widow of an officer in the service of the French East India Company, who accepted them with becoming gratitude.

Fronsac was greatly alarmed on learning of the paternal intentions, fearing that, if a son were born, the marshal would bequeath the child everything that he was able to leave away from the title. But he was somewhat reassured when his father informed him that, in the event of his having a son, it was his intention to make him a cardinal, that he might follow in the footsteps of the illustrious founder of the family fortunes. However, the prospective cardinal never arrived, as the only issue of the marriage was a stillborn child.

In other respects, Richelieu's third experiment in matrimony was as fortunate as the one which had preceded it, for the new duchess was not only a very pretty, but an extremely amiable, woman, and was sincerely attached to her venerable consort,[1] who, despite his advanced age, still appears to have retained some remnants of the adoration with which the opposite sex had once regarded him. Aware of this, and fearing lest another Madame de Saint-Vincent should appear upon the scene, the duchess took the most elaborate precautions to keep her husband's feet in the straight path. But, notwithstanding all her vigilance, they occasionally strayed from it; and there were tales about a Mlle. Colombe, a pretty actress of the Comédie-Italienne, in whom the marshal was reported to take something more than a paternal interest.

Very unfavourably regarded by Louis XVI. and Marie Antoinette—the former had, soon after his accession, given orders that he was not to reside in his government, except when the commandant of the province, the Marquis de Mouchy, was in residence at Bordeaux—Richelieu continued to discharge his duties as First Gentleman of the Chamber for some years. At length, annoyed at the thoughtlessness of Louis XVI., who, one evening at his *coucher*, happening to be deep in a discussion about hunting, allowed the old man to follow him round the room for several minutes, holding his Majesty's dressing-gown with outstretched arms, he resigned his office in favour of

[1] So much so, that we are assured that she used to watch over him while he was taking his afternoon siesta, in order to brush away the flies which might interrupt the ducal slumbers.

Fronsac, who had been granted the reversion after the conquest of Minorca.

His chief friend at Versailles under the new reign seems to have been his once deadly enemy Maurepas, who had been recalled by Louis XVI., after twenty-seven years in exile, and made Prime Minister. Finding themselves the only representatives of the Court of *le Grand Monarque*, the two old men decided to forget their differences, and spent many an hour together recalling the glories of the past and bewailing the degenerate tendencies of the present age.

Although, after his marriage, yielding to the wishes of the duchess, who considered that it was inadvisable for him to undertake long journeys, he ceased to visit Bordeaux, he continued to occupy himself with the details of his government; and he fell into a terrible passion on learning that one evening the mayor, M. de Noé, had had the unparalleled audacity to occupy the governor's box at the theatre, notwithstanding the remonstrances of the door-keeper. As the mayor refused to appear before the tribunal of the Marshals of France to answer for his conduct, the infuriated old man obtained an order for his arrest, which directed that he was to be brought bound hand and foot to Paris. Noé, however, preferred to expatriate himself, and did not return to France until the death of his persecutor.

Not long after this, undeterred by his sad experience in the Saint-Vincent case, the marshal embarked upon another interminable lawsuit, with a rich paper-manufacturer named Arthur, who had built a warehouse on the Boulevard des Italiens, facing the "Pavillon d'Hanovre," which M. de Richelieu alleged interfered with his enjoyment of the view on that side. After nearly two years of litigation, however, the parties arrived at a settlement.

During his last years the marshal became very deaf, and his memory frequently failed him. He continued, however, a marvel of activity, and one day greatly astonished the Archbishop of Paris, who had invited him to dine at his country seat at Conflans, by arriving on horseback and departing at a gallop.

At last, just when people were beginning to fancy him immortal, he caught a chill which he was unable to shake off; and in the evening of August 8, 1788, he died, in his ninety-third year, eleven months before the beginning of the cataclysm which was to destroy that brilliant and corrupt society whose most typical representative he undoubtedly was.

Fronsac, who now became fourth Duc de Richelieu, did not long survive his father, as he died on February 4, 1791, at the age of fifty-four. In spite of his debauched life, he had not lived altogether in vain, as, besides two daughters, who married respectively the Marquis de Montcalm and the Marquis de Jumilhac, and were well-known figures in Paris society under the Restoration, he left a son, Armand Emmanuel Sophie Septimanie du Plessis, fifth Duc de Richelieu, who worthily upheld the honour of the name. At the end of the year 1789, he went to Vienna, fought with his friend the Prince de Ligne against the Turks, and was present at the taking of Ismailia. He then took service with Russia, and, after a brief visit to France, became, in 1803, governor of Odessa, which city owes a deep debt of gratitude to his admirable administration. Returning to France at the Restoration, he accompanied Louis XVIII. to Ghent, and, after the Hundred Days, was offered a place in the Ministry, which, owing to his dislike of Fouché, he declined. After the dismissal of that personage, however, he became Prime Minister, with the portfolio of Foreign Affairs (September 27, 1815), and held office until December 20, 1818. He was Prime Minister for the second time from February 21, 1820, until December 14, 1821. Five months later (May 17, 1822), he died, after a short illness, in his fifty-sixth year. He had no children, but by royal ordinance his title and peerage passed to his nephew, the Marquis de Jumilhac.

# INDEX

PRINTED BY
WILLIAM CLOWES AND SONS, LIMITED,
LONDON AND BECCLES.

# A CATALOGUE OF BOOKS PUBLISHED BY METHUEN AND COMPANY: LONDON 36 ESSEX STREET W.C.

CONTENTS



OCTOBER 1909

A CATALOGUE OF

# MESSRS. METHUEN'S PUBLICATIONS

In this Catalogue the order is according to authors. An asterisk denotes that the book is in the press.

Colonial Editions are published of all Messrs. METHUEN'S Novels issued at a price above 2s. 6d., and similar editions are published of some works of General Literature. Colonial editions are only for circulation in the British Colonies and India.

All books marked net are not subject to discount, and cannot be bought at less than the published price. Books not marked net are subject to the discount which the bookseller allows.

Messrs. METHUEN'S books are kept in stock by all good booksellers. If there is any difficulty in seeing copies, Messrs. Methuen will be very glad to have early information, and specimen copies of any books will be sent on receipt of the published price *plus* postage for net books, and of the published price for ordinary books.

I.P.L. represents Illustrated Pocket Library.

## PART I.—GENERAL LITERATURE

**Abraham (George D.).** THE COMPLETE MOUNTAINEER. With 75 Illustrations. *Second Edition. Demy 8vo.* 15s. *net.*

**Acatos (M. J.).** See Junior School Books.

**Addleshaw (Percy).** SIR PHILIP SIDNEY. With 12 Illustrations. *Demy 8vo.* 10s. 6d. *net.*

**Adeney (W. F.),** M.A. See Bennett (W. H.)

**Ady (Cecilia M.).** A HISTORY OF MILAN UNDER THE SFORZA. With 20 Illustratious and a Map. *Demy 8vo.* 10s. 6d. *net.*

**Aeschylus.** See Classical Translations.

**Ainsworth (W. Harrison).** See I.P.L.

**Aldis (Janet).** THE QUEEN OF LETTER WRITERS, MARQUISE DE SÉVIGNÉ, DAME DE BOURBILLY, 1626-96. With 18 Illustrations. *Second Edition. Demy 8vo.* 12s. 6d. *net.*

**Alexander (William),** D.D., Archbishop of Armagh. THOUGHTS AND COUNSELS OF MANY YEARS. *Demy 16mo.* 2s. 6d.

**Alken (Henry).** See I.P.L.

**Allen (Charles C.).** See Textbooks of Technology.

**Allen (L. Jessie).** See Little Books on Art.

**Allen (J. Romilly),** F.S.A. See Antiquary's Books.

**Almack (E.),** F.S.A. See Little Books on Art.

**Amherst (Lady).** A SKETCH OF EGYPTIAN HISTORY FROM THE EARLIEST TIMES TO THE PRESENT DAY. With many Illustrations and Maps. *A New and Cheaper Issue Demy 8vo.* 7s. 6d. *net.*

**Anderson (F. M.).** THE STORY OF THE BRITISH EMPIRE FOR CHILDREN. With 42 Illustrations. *Cr. 8vo.* 2s.

**Anderson (J. G.),** B.A., NOUVELLE GRAMMAIRE FRANÇAISE, À L'USAGE DES ÉCOLES ANGLAISES. *Crown 8vo.* 2s.

EXERCICES DE GRAMMAIRE FRANÇAISE. *Cr. 8vo.* 1s. 6d.

**Andrewes (Bishop).** PRECES PRIVATAE. Translated and edited, with Notes, by F. E. BRIGHTMAN. M.A., of Pusey House, Oxford. *Cr. 8vo.* 6s.

See also Library of Devotion.

**'Anglo-Australian.'** AFTER-GLOW MEMORIES. *Cr. 8vo.* 6s.

**Anon.** THE BUDGET, THE LAND AND THE PEOPLE. *Second Edition. Crown 8vo.* 6d. *net.*

HEALTH, WEALTH, AND WISDOM. *Crown 8vo.* 1s. *net.*

THE WESTMINSTER PROBLEMS BOOK. Prose and Verse. Compiled from *The Saturday Westminster Gazette* Competitions, 1904-1907. *Cr. 8vo.* 3s. 6d. *net.*

VENICE AND HER TREASURES. With many Illustrations. *Round corners. Fcap. 8vo.* 5s. *net.*

**Aristotle.** THE ETHICS OF. Edited, with an Introduction and Notes by JOHN BURNET, M.A., *Cheaper issue. Demy 8vo.* 10s. 6d. *net.*

**Asman (H. N.),** M.A., B.D. AN INTRODUCTION TO THE HISTORY OF ROME. With Maps and Illustrations. *Cr. 8vo.* 2s. 6d. See also Junior School Books.

**Atkins (H. G.).** See Oxford Biographies.

**Atkinson (C. M.).** JEREMY BENTHAM. *Demy 8vo.* 5s. *net.*

**Atkinson (C. T.),** M.A., Fellow of Exeter College, Oxford, sometime Demy of Magdalen College. A HISTORY OF GERMANY, from 1713 to 1815. With 35 Maps and Plans *Demy 8vo.* 15s. *net.*

**Atkinson (T. D.).** ENGLISH ARCHITECTURE. With 196 Illustrations. *Fcap. 8vo.* 3*s.* 6*d. net.*

A GLOSSARY OF TERMS USED IN ENGLISH ARCHITECTURE. With 265 Illustrations. *Second Edition. Fcap. 8vo.* 3*s.* 6*d. net.*

**Atteridge (A. H.).** NAPOLEON'S BROTHERS. With 24 Illustrations. *Demy 8vo.* 18*s. net.*

**Auden (T.),** M.A., F.S.A. See Ancient Cities.

**Aurelius (Marcus).** WORDS OF THE ANCIENT WISE. Thoughts from Epictetus and Marcus Aurelius. Edited by W. H. D. ROUSE, M.A., Litt. D. *Fcap. 8vo.* 3*s.* 6*d. net.*
See also Standard Library.

**Austen (Jane).** See Standard Library, Little Library and Mitton (G. E.).

**Aves (Ernest).** CO-OPERATIVE INDUSTRY. *Crown 8vo.* 5*s. net.*

**Bacon (Francis).** See Standard Library and Little Library.

**Bagot (Richard).** THE LAKES OF NORTHERN ITALY. With 37 Illustrations and a Map. *Fcap. 8vo.* 5*s. net.*

**Bailey (J. C.),** M.A. See Cowper (W.).

**Bain (R. Nisbet).** THE LAST KING OF POLAND AND HIS CONTEMPORARIES. With 16 Illustrations. *Demy 8vo.* 10*s.* 6*d. net.*

**Baker (W. G.),** M.A. See Junior Examination Series.

**Baker (Julian L.),** F.I.C., F.C.S. See Books on Business.

**Balfour (Graham).** THE LIFE OF ROBERT LOUIS STEVENSON. With a Portrait. *Fourth Edition in one Volume. Cr. 8vo. Buckram,* 6*s.*

**Ballard (A.),** B.A., LL.D. See Antiquary's Books.

**Bally (S. E.).** See Commercial Series.

**Barham (R. H.).** See Little Library.

**Baring (The Hon. Maurice).** WITH THE RUSSIANS IN MANCHURIA. *Third Edition. Demy 8vo.* 7*s.* 6*d. net.*

A YEAR IN RUSSIA. *Second Edition. Demy 8vo.* 10*s.* 6*d. net.*

RUSSIAN ESSAYS AND STORIES. *Second Edition. Cr. 8vo.* 5*s. net.*
Also published in a Colonial Edition.

**Baring-Gould (S.).** THE LIFE OF NAPOLEON BONAPARTE. With nearly 200 Illustrations, including a Photogravure Frontispiece. *Second Edition. Wide Royal 8vo.* 10*s.* 6*d. net.*

THE TRAGEDY OF THE CÆSARS: A STUDY OF THE CHARACTERS OF THE CÆSARS OF THE JULIAN AND CLAUDIAN HOUSES. With numerous Illustrations from Busts, Gems, Cameos, etc. *Sixth Edition. Royal 8vo.* 10*s.* 6*d. net.*

A BOOK OF FAIRY TALES. With numerous Illustrations by A. J. GASKIN. *Second Edition. Cr. 8vo. Buckram.* 6*s.*, also *Medium 8vo.* 6*d.*

OLD ENGLISH FAIRY TALES. With numerous Illustrations by F. D. BEDFORD. *Third Edition. Cr. 8vo. Buckram.* 6*s.*

THE VICAR OF MORWENSTOW. Revised Edition. With a Portrait. *Third Edition. Cr. 8vo.* 3*s.* 6*d.*

OLD COUNTRY LIFE. With 69 Illustrations. *Fifth Edition. Large Crown 8vo.* 6*s.*

A GARLAND OF COUNTRY SONG: English Folk Songs with their Traditional Melodies. Collected and arranged by S. BARING-GOULD and H. F. SHEPPARD. *Demy 4to.* 6*s.*

SONGS OF THE WEST: Folk Songs of Devon and Cornwall. Collected from the Mouths of the People. By S. BARING-GOULD, M.A., and H. FLEETWOOD SHEPPARD, M.A. New and Revised Edition, under the musical editorship of CECIL J. SHARP. *Large Imperial 8vo.* 5*s. net.*

A BOOK OF NURSERY SONGS AND RHYMES. Edited by S. BARING-GOULD. Illustrated. *Second and Cheaper Edition. Large Cr. 8vo.* 2*s.* 6*d. net.*

STRANGE SURVIVALS: SOME CHAPTERS IN THE HISTORY OF MAN. Illustrated. *Third Edition. Cr. 8vo.* 2*s.* 6*d. net.*

YORKSHIRE ODDITIES: INCIDENTS AND STRANGE EVENTS. *Fifth Edition. Cr. 8vo.* 2*s.* 6*d. net.*

THE BARING-GOULD SELECTION READER. Arranged by G. H. ROSE. Illustrated. *Crown 8vo.* 1*s.* 6*d.*

THE BARING-GOULD CONTINUOUS READER. Arranged by G. H. ROSE. Illustrated. *Crown 8vo.* 1*s.* 6*d.*

A BOOK OF CORNWALL. With 33 Illustrations. *Second Edition. Cr. 8vo.* 6*s.*

A BOOK OF DARTMOOR. With 60 Illustrations. *Second Edition. Cr. 8vo.* 6*s.*

A BOOK OF DEVON. With 35 Illustrations. *Third Edition. Cr. 8vo.* 6*s.*

A BOOK OF NORTH WALES. With 49 Illustrations. *Cr. 8vo.* 6*s.*

A BOOK OF SOUTH WALES. With 57 Illustrations. *Cr. 8vo.* 6*s.*

A BOOK OF BRITTANY. With 69 Illustrations. *Second Edition Cr. 8vo.* 6*s.*

A BOOK OF THE RHINE: From Cleve to Mainz. With 8 Illustrations in Colour by TREVOR HADDEN, and 48 other Illustrations. *Second Edition. Cr. 8vo.* 6*s.*

A BOOK OF THE RIVIERA. With 40 Illustrations. *Cr. 8vo.* 6*s.*

A BOOK OF THE PYRENEES. With 25 Illustrations. *Cr. 8vo.* 6*s.*
See also Little Guides.

**Barker (Aldred F.).** See Textbooks of Technology.

**Barker (E.),** M.A. (Late) Fellow of Merton College, Oxford. THE POLITICAL THOUGHT OF PLATO AND ARISTOTLE. *Demy 8vo.* 10*s.* 6*d. net.*

**Barnes (W. E.),** D.D. See Churchman's Bible.

**Barnett (Mrs. P. A.).** See Little Library.

**Baron (R. R. N.), M.A.** FRENCH PROSE COMPOSITION. *Fourth Edition. Cr. 8vo.* 2s. 6d. *Key*, 3s. *net.*
See also Junior School Books.

**Barron (H. M.), M.A.**, Wadham College, Oxford. TEXTS FOR SERMONS. With a Preface by Canon SCOTT HOLLAND. *Cr. 8vo.* 3s. 6d.

**Bartholomew (J. G.)**, F.R.S.E. See Robertson (C. G.).

**Bastable (C. F.), LL.D.** THE COMMERCE OF NATIONS. *Fourth Ed. Cr. 8vo.* 2s. 6d.

**Bastian (H. Charlton)**, M.A., M.D., F.R.S. THE EVOLUTION OF LIFE. With Diagrams and many Photomicrographs. *Demy 8vo.* 7s. 6d. *net.*

**Batson (Mrs. Stephen).** A CONCISE HANDBOOK OF GARDEN FLOWERS. *Fcap. 8vo.* 3s. 6d.

THE SUMMER GARDEN OF PLEASURE. With 36 Illustrations in Colour by OSMUND PITTMAN. *Wide Demy 8vo.* 15s. *net.*

**Bayley (R. Child).** THE COMPLETE PHOTOGRAPHER. With over 100 Illustrations. With Note on Direct Colour Process. *Third Edition. Demy 8vo.* 10s. 6d. *net.*

**Beard (W. S.).** EASY EXERCISES IN ALGEBRA FOR BEGINNERS. *Cr. 8vo.* 1s. 6d. With Answers. 1s. 9d.
See also Junior Examination Series and Beginner's Books.

**Beckett (Arthur).** THE SPIRIT OF THE DOWNS: Impressions and Reminiscences of the Sussex Downs, and Downland People and Places. With 20 Illustrations in Colour by STANLEY INCHBOLD. *Second Edition. Demy 8vo.* 10s. 6d. *net.*

**Beckford (Peter).** THOUGHTS ON HUNTING. Edited by J. OTHO PAGET, and Illustrated by G. H. JALLAND. *Second Edition. Demy 8vo.* 6s.

**Beckford (William).** See Little Library.

**Beeching (H. C.), M.A.**, Canon of Westminster. See Library of Devotion.

**Beerbohm (Max).** A BOOK OF CARICATURES. *Imperial 4to.* 21s. *net.*

**Begbie (Harold).** MASTER WORKERS. Illustrated. *Demy 8vo.* 7s. 6d. *net.*

**Behmen (Jacob).** DIALOGUES ON THE SUPERSENSUAL LIFE. Edited by BERNARD HOLLAND. *Fcap. 8vo.* 3s. 6d.

**Bell (Mrs. Arthur G.).** THE SKIRTS OF THE GREAT CITY. With 16 Illustrations in Colour by ARTHUR G. BELL, 17 other Illustrations, and a Map. *Second Edition. Cr. 8vo.* 6s.

**Belloc (H.)** PARIS. With 7 Maps and a Frontispiece in Photogravure. *Second Edition, Revised. Cr. 8vo.* 6s.

HILLS AND THE SEA. *Second Edition. Crown 8vo.* 6s.

ON NOTHING AND KINDRED SUBJECTS. *Second Edition. Fcap. 8vo.* 5s.

ON EVERYTHING. *Fcap. 8vo.* 5s.

MARIE ANTOINETTE. With 35 Portraits and Illustrations. *Demy 8vo.* 15s. *net.*

THE PYRENEES. With 46 Sketches by the Author, and 22 Maps. *Second Edition. Demy 8vo.* 7s. 6d. *net.*

**Bellot (H. H. L.), M.A.** See Jones (L. A. A.).

**Bennett (Joseph).** FORTY YEARS OF MUSIC, 1865-1905. With 24 Illustrations. *Demy 8vo.* 16s. *net.*

**Bennett (W. H.), M.A.** A PRIMER OF THE BIBLE. *Fifth Edition. Cr. 8vo.* 2s. 6d.

**Bennett (W. H.)** and **Adeney (W. F.).** A BIBLICAL INTRODUCTION. With a concise Bibliography. *Fifth Edition. Cr. 8vo.* 7s. 6d.

**Benson (Archbishop)** GOD'S BOARD. Communion Addresses. *Second Edition. Fcap. 8vo.* 3s. 6d. *net.*

**Benson (A. C.), M.A.** See Oxford Biographies.

**Benson (R. M.).** THE WAY OF HOLINESS. An Exposition of Psalm cxix. Analytical and Devotional. *Cr. 8vo.* 5s.

**Bernard (E. R.), M.A.**, Canon of Salisbury THE ENGLISH SUNDAY: ITS ORIGINS AND ITS CLAIMS. *Fcap. 8vo.* 1s. 6d.

**Berry (W. Grinton), M.A.** FRANCE SINCE WATERLOO. With 16 Illustrations and Maps. *Cr. 8vo.* 6s.

**Beruete (A. de).** See Classics of Art.

**Betham-Edwards (Miss).** HOME LIFE IN FRANCE. With 20 Illustrations. *Fifth Edition. Crown 8vo.* 6s.

**Bethune-Baker (J. F.), M.A.** See Handbooks of Theology.

**Bindley (T. Herbert), B.D.** THE OECUMENICAL DOCUMENTS OF THE FAITH. With Introductions and Notes. *Second Edition. Cr. 8vo.* 6s. *net.*

**Binns (H. B.).** THE LIFE OF WALT WHITMAN. Illustrated. *Demy 8vo.* 10s. 6d. *net.*

**Binyon (Mrs. Laurence).** NINETEENTH CENTURY PROSE. Selected and arranged by. *Crown 8vo.* 6s.

**Binyon (Laurence).** THE DEATH OF ADAM AND OTHER POEMS. *Cr. 8vo.* 3s. 6d. *net.*
See also Blake (William).

**Birch (Walter de Gray), LL.D., F.S.A.** See Connoisseur's Library.

**Birnstingl (Ethel).** See Little Books on Art.

**Blackmantle (Bernard).** See I.P.L.

**Blair (Robert).** See I.P.L.

**Blake (William).** THE LETTERS OF WILLIAM BLAKE, TOGETHER WITH A LIFE BY FREDERICK TATHAM. Edited from the Original Manuscripts, with an Introduction and Notes, by ARCHIBALD G. B. RUSSELL. With 12 Illustrations. *Demy 8vo.* 7s. 6d. *net.*

ILLUSTRATIONS OF THE BOOK OF JOB. With General Introduction by LAURENCE BINYON. *Quarto.* 21s. *net.*
See also I.P.L., and Little Library.

**Bloom (J. Harvey)**, M.A. See Antiquary's Books.

**Blouet (Henri).** See Beginner's Books.

**Boardman (T. H.)**, M.A. See French (W.).

**Bode (Wilhelm)**, Ph.D. See Classics of Art.

**Bodley (J. E. C.)** THE CORONATION OF EDWARD VII. *Demy 8vo.* 21*s. net.* By Command of the King.

**Body (George)**, D.D. THE SOUL'S PILGRIMAGE: Devotional Readings from the Published and Unpublished writings of George Body, D.D. Selected and arranged by J. H. BURN, B.D., F.R.S.E. *Demy 16mo.* 2*s.* 6*d.*

**Bona (Cardinal).** See Library of Devotion.

**Bonnor (Mary L.).** See Little Books on Art.

**Boon (F. C.).**, B.A. See Commercial Series.

**Borrow (George).** See Little Library.

**Bos (J. Ritzema).** AGRICULTURAL ZOOLOGY. Translated by J. R. AINSWORTH DAVIS, M.A. With 155 Illustrations. *Second Edition. Cr. 8vo.* 3*s.* 6*d.*

**Botting (C. G.)**, B.A. EASY GREEK EXERCISES. *Cr. 8vo.* 2*s.* See also Junior Examination Series.

**Boulting (W.)** TASSO AND HIS TIMES. With 24 Illustrations. *Demy 8vo.* 10*s.* 6*d. net.*

**Boulton (E. S.)**, M.A. GEOMETRY ON MODERN LINES. *Cr. 8vo.* 2*s.*

**Boulton (William B.).** SIR JOSHUA REYNOLDS, P.R.A. With 49 Illustrations. *Second Edition. Demy 8vo.* 7*s.* 6*d. net.*

**Bovill (W. B. Forster).** HUNGARY AND THE HUNGARIANS. With 16 Illustrations in Colour by WILLIAM PASCOE, 12 other Illustrations and a Map. *Demy 8vo.* 7*s.* 6*d. net.*

**Bowden (E. M.).** THE IMITATION OF BUDDHA: Being Quotations from Buddhist Literature for each Day in the Year. *Fifth Edition. Cr. 16mo.* 2*s.* 6*d.*

**Bower (E.)**, B.A. See New Historical Series.

**Boyle (W.).** CHRISTMAS AT THE ZOO. With Verses by W. BOYLE and 24 Coloured Pictures by H. B. NEILSON. *Super Royal 16mo.* 2*s.*

**Brabant (F. G.)**, M.A. RAMBLES IN SUSSEX. With 30 Illustrations. *Crown 8vo.* 6*s.* See also Little Guides.

**Bradley (A. G.).** ROUND ABOUT WILTSHIRE. With 14 Illustrations, in Colour by T. C. GOTCH, 16 other Illustrations, and a Map. *Second Edition. Cr. 8vo.* 6*s.*

THE ROMANCE OF NORTHUMBERLAND. With 16 Illustrations in Colour by FRANK SOUTHGATE, R.B.A., and 12 from Photographs. *Second Edition. Demy 8vo.* 7*s.* 6*d net.*

**Bradley (John W.).** See Little Books on Art.

**Braid (James)**, Open Champion, 1901, 1905 and 1906. ADVANCED GOLF. With 88 Photographs and Diagrams. *Fifth Edition. Demy 8vo.* 10*s.* 6*d. net.*

**Braid (James) and Others.** GREAT GOLFERS IN THE MAKING. Edited by HENRY LEACH. With 24 Illustrations. *Second Edition. Demy 8vo.* 7*s.* 6*d. net.*

**Brailsford (H. N.).** MACEDONIA: ITS RACES AND THEIR FUTURE. With 32 Illustrations and 2 Maps. *Demy 8vo.* 12*s.* 6*d. net.*

**Brentano (C.).** See Simplified German Texts.

**Brightman (F. E.)**, M.A. See Andrewes (Lancelot).

**Brodrick (Mary) and Morton (A. Anderson).** A CONCISE DICTIONARY OF EGYPTIAN ARCHÆOLOGY. A Hand-Book for Students and Travellers. With 80 Illustrations and many Cartouches. *Cr. 8vo.* 3*s.* 6*d.*

**Brooks (E. E.)**, B.Sc. (Lond.), Leicester Municipal Technical School, and **James (W. H. N.)**, A.M.I.E.E., A.R.C.Sc., Municipal School of Technology, Manchester. See Textbooks of Technology.

**Brown (S. E.)**, M.A., B.Sc., Senior Science Master at Uppingham. A PRACTICAL CHEMISTRY NOTE-BOOK FOR MATRICULATION AND ARMY CANDIDATES. Easy Experiments on the Commoner Substances. *Cr. 4to.* 1*s.* 6*d. net.*

**Brown (J. Wood)**, M.A. THE BUILDERS OF FLORENCE. With 74 Illustrations by HERBERT RAILTON. *Demy 4to.* 18*s. net.*

**Browne (Sir Thomas).** See Standard Library.

**Brownell (C. L.).** THE HEART OF JAPAN. Illustrated. *Third Edition. Cr. 8vo.* 6*s.* Also *Medium 8vo.* 6*d.*

**Browning (Robert).** BROWNING AND PARACELSUS. The Text of Browning's Poem, edited with Introduction, Footnotes, and Bibliography, by MARGARET L. LEE, Lecturer in English Literature to the Women's Department, King's College, and KATHRINE B. LOCOCK. *Fcap. 8vo.* 3*s.* 6*d. net.* See also Little Library.

**Bryant (Walter W.)**, B.A., F.R.A.S., F.R. Met. Soc., of the Royal Observatory, Greenwich. A HISTORY OF ASTRONOMY. With 47 Illustrations. *Demy 8vo.* 7*s.* 6*d. net.*

**Buckland (Francis T.).** CURIOSITIES OF NATURAL HISTORY. Illustrated by H. B. NEILSON. *Cr. 8vo.* 3*s.* 6*d.*

**Buckton (A. M.)** THE BURDEN OF ENGELA. *Second Edition. Cr. 8vo.* 3*s.* 6*d. net.*

EAGER HEART: A Mystery Play. *Seventh Edition. Cr. 8vo.* 1*s. net.*

KINGS IN BABYLON: A Drama. *Cr. 8vo.* 1*s. net.*

SONGS OF JOY. *Cr. 8vo.* 1*s. net.*

**Budge (E. A. Wallis).** THE GODS OF THE EGYPTIANS. With over 100 Coloured Plates and many Illustrations. *Two Volumes. Royal 8vo.* £3, 3*s. net.*

***Bulst (H. Massac).** THE COMPLETE AERONAUT. With many Illustrations. *Demy 8vo.* 12*s.* 6*d. net.*

**Bull (Paul)**, Army Chaplain. GOD AND OUR SOLDIERS. *Second Edition. Cr. 8vo.* 6*s.*

**Bulley (Miss).** See Dilke (Lady).

**Bunyan (John).** THE PILGRIM'S PROGRESS. Edited, with an Introduction by C. H. FIRTH, M.A. With 39 Illustrations by R. ANNING BELL. *Crown 8vo.* 6*s.* See also Standard Library and Library of Devotion.

**Burch (G. J.),** M.A., F.R.S. A MANUAL OF ELECTRICAL SCIENCE. Illustrated. *Cr. 8vo.* 3*s.*

**Burgess (Gelett).** GOOPS AND HOW TO BE THEM. Illustrated. *Small 4to.* 6*s.*

**Burke (Edmund).** See Standard Library.

**Burn (A. E.),** D.D., Rector of Handsworth and Prebendary of Lichfield. See Handbooks of Theology.

**Burn (J. H.),** B. D., F. R. S. E. THE CHURCHMAN'S TREASURY OF SONG: Gathered from the Christian poetry of all ages. Edited by. *Fcap. 8vo.* 3*s.* 6*d. net.* See also Library of Devotion.

**Burnet (John),** M.A. See Aristotle.

**Burns (Robert),** THE POEMS. Edited by ANDREW LANG and W. A. CRAIGIE. With Portrait. *Third Edition. Wide Demy 8vo, gilt top.* 6*s.*
See also Standard Library.

**Burnside (W. F.),** M.A. OLD TESTAMENT HISTORY FOR USE IN SCHOOLS. *Third Edition. Cr. 8vo.* 3*s.* 6*d.*

**Burton (Alfred).** See I.P.L.

**Bury (J. B.),** M.A., Litt. D. See Gibbon (Edward).

**Bussell (F. W.),** D.D. CHRISTIAN THEOLOGY AND SOCIAL PROGRESS (The Bampton Lectures of 1905). *Demy 8vo.* 10*s.* 6*d. net.*

**Butler (Joseph),** D.D. See Standard Library.

**Butlin (F. M.).** AMONG THE DANES. With 12 Illustrations in Colour by ELLEN WILKINSON, and 15 from Photographs. *Demy 8vo.* 7*s.* 6*d. net.*

**Cain (Georges),** Curator of the Carnavalet Museum, Paris. WALKS IN PARIS. Translated by A. R. ALLINSON, M.A. With a Frontispiece in Colour by MAXWELL ARMFIELD, and 118 other Illustrations. *Demy 8vo.* 7*s.* 6*d. net.*

**Caldecott (Alfred),** D.D. See Handbooks of Theology.

**Calderwood (D. S.),** Headmaster of the Normal School, Edinburgh. TEST CARDS IN EUCLID AND ALGEBRA. In three packets of 40, with Answers. 1*s.* each. Or in three Books, price 2*d.*, 2*d.*, and 3*d.*

**Cameron (Mary Lovett).** OLD ETRURIA AND MODERN TUSCANY. With 32 Illustrations. *Crown 8vo.* 6*s. net.*

**Cannan (Edwin),** M.A. See Smith (Adam).

**Canning (George).** See Little Library.

**Capey (E. F. H.).** See Oxford Biographies.

**Carden (Robert W.).** THE CITY OF GENOA. With 12 Illustrations in Colour by WILLIAM PARKINSON, and 20 other Illustrations. *Demy 8vo.* 10*s.* 6*d. net.*

**Careless (John).** See I.P.L.

**Carlyle (Thomas).** THE FRENCH REVOLUTION. Edited by C. R. L. FLETCHER, Fellow of Magdalen College, Oxford. *Three Volumes. Cr. 8vo.* 18*s.*

THE LETTERS AND SPEECHES OF OLIVER CROMWELL. With an Introduction by C. H. FIRTH, M.A., and Notes and Appendices by Mrs. S. C. LOMAS. *Three Volumes. Demy 8vo.* 18*s. net.*

**Carlyle (R. M. and A. J.),** M.A. See Leaders of Religion.

**Carmichael (Philip).** ALL ABOUT PHILIPPINE. With 8 Illustrations. *Cr. 8vo.* 2*s.* 6*d.*

**Carpenter (Margaret Boyd).** THE CHILD IN ART. With 50 Illustrations. *Second Edition. Large Cr. 8vo.* 6*s.*

**Carter (George),** M.A. THE STORY OF MILTON'S 'PARADISE LOST.' *Crown 8vo.* 1*s.* 6*d.*

**Cavanagh (Francis),** M.D. (Edin.). See New Library of Medicine.

**Celano (Brother Thomas of).** THE LIVES OF FRANCIS OF ASSISI. Translated by A. G. FERRERS HOWELL. With a Frontispiece. *Cr. 8vo.* 5*s. net.*

**Chambers (A. M.).** A CONSTITUTIONAL HISTORY OF ENGLAND. *Crown 8vo.* 6*s.*

**Chamisso (A. von).** See Simplified German Texts.

**Chandler (Arthur),** Bishop of Bloemfontein. ARA CŒLI: AN ESSAY IN MYSTICAL THEOLOGY. *Third Edition. Crown 8vo.* 3*s.* 6*d. net.*

**Channer (C. C.) and Roberts (M. E.).** LACEMAKING IN THE MIDLANDS, PAST AND PRESENT. With 17 full-page Illustrations. *Cr. 8vo.* 2*s.* 6*d.*

**Chapman (S. J.).** See Books on Business.

**Chatterton (Thomas).** See Standard Library.

**Chesterfield (Lord),** THE LETTERS OF THE EARL OF CHESTERFIELD TO HIS SON. Edited, with an Introduction by C. STRACHEY, with Notes by A. CALTHROP. *Two Volumes. Cr. 8vo.* 12*s.*

**Chesterton (G.K.).** CHARLES DICKENS. With two Portraits in Photogravure. *Fifth Edition. Cr. 8vo.* 6*s.*

ALL THINGS CONSIDERED. *Fifth Edition. Fcap. 8vo.* 5*s.*

TREMENDOUS TRIFLES. *Second Edition. Fcap. 8vo.* 5*s.*

**Childe (Charles P.),** B.A., F.R.C.S. See New Library of Medicine.

**Cicero.** See Classical Translations.

**Clapham (J. H.),** Professor of Economics in the University of Leeds. THE WOOLLEN AND WORSTED INDUSTRIES. With 21 Illustrations and Diagrams. *Cr. 8vo.* 6*s.*

**Clarke (F. A.),** M.A. See Leaders of Religion.

**Clausen (George),** A.R.A., R.W.S. SIX LECTURES ON PAINTING. With 16

Illustrations. *Third Edition. Large Post 8vo.* 3s. 6d. *net.*
AIMS AND IDEALS IN ART. Eight Lectures delivered to the Students of the Royal Academy of Arts. With 32 Illustrations. *Second Edition. Large Post 8vo.* 5s. *net.*

**Clay (Rotha Mary).** See Antiquary's Books.

**Cleather (A. L.).** See Wagner (R).

**Clinch (G.),** F.G.S. See Antiquary's Books and Little Guides.

**Clough (W. T.)** and **Dunstan (A. E.).** See Junior School Books and Textbooks of Science.

**Clouston (T. S.),** M.D., C.C.D., F.R.S.E. See New Library of Medicine.

***Clutton - Brock.** SHELLEY: THE MAN AND THE POET. With 8 Illustrations. *Demy 8vo.* 7s. 6d. *net.*

**Coast (W. G.),** B.A. EXAMINATION PAPERS IN VERGIL. *Cr. 8vo.* 2s.

**Cobb (W. F.),** M.A. THE BOOK OF PSALMS: with an Introduction and Notes. *Demy 8vo.* 10s. 6d. *net.*

**Cockshott (Winnifred),** St. Hilda's Hall, Oxford. THE PILGRIM FATHERS, THEIR CHURCH AND COLONY. With 12 Illustrations. *Demy 8vo.* 7s. 6d. *net.*

**Collingwood (W. G.),** M.A. THE LIFE OF JOHN RUSKIN. With Portrait. *Sixth Edition. Cr. 8vo.* 2s. 6d. *net.*

**Collins (W. E.),** M.A. See Churchman's Library.

**Colvill (Helen H.).** ST. TERESA OF SPAIN. With 20 Illustrations. *Demy 8vo.* 7s. 6d. *net.*

**Combe (William).** See I.P.L.

**Conrad (Joseph).** THE MIRROR OF THE SEA: Memories and Impressions. *Third Edition. Cr. 8vo.* 6s.

**Cook (A. M.),** M.A., and **Marchant (E. C.),** M.A. PASSAGES FOR UNSEEN TRANSLATION. Selected from Latin and Greek Literature. *Fourth Ed. Cr. 8vo.* 3s. 6d.
LATIN PASSAGES FOR UNSEEN TRANSLATION. *Cr. 8vo.* 1s. 6d.

**Cooke-Taylor (R. W.).** THE FACTORY SYSTEM. *Cr. 8vo.* 2s. 6d.

**Coolidge (W. A. B.),** M.A. THE ALPS. With many Illustrations. *Demy 8vo.* 7s. 6d. *net.*

**Cooper (C. S.),** F.R.H.S. See Westell (W. P.)

**Corkran (Alice).** See Little Books on Art.

**Cotes (Rosemary).** DANTE'S GARDEN. With a Frontispiece. *Second Edition. Fcap. 8vo.* 2s. 6d.; *leather,* 3s. 6d. *net.*
BIBLE FLOWERS. With a Frontispiece and Plan. *Fcap. 8vo.* 2s. 6d. *net.*

**Cotton (Charles).** See I.P.L. and Little Library.

**Coulton (G. G.).** CHAUCER AND HIS ENGLAND. With 32 Illustrations. *Second Edition. Demy 8vo.* 10s. 6d. *net.*

**Cowley (Abraham).** See Little Library.

**Cowper (William).** THE POEMS. Edited with an Introduction and Notes by J. C. BAILEY, M.A. Illustrated, including two unpublished designs by WILLIAM BLAKE. *Demy 8vo.* 10s. 6d. *net.*

**Cox (J. Charles).** See Ancient Cities, Antiquary's Books, and Little Guides.

**Cox (Harold),** B.A., M.P. LAND NATIONALIZATION AND LAND TAXATION. *Second Edition revised. Cr. 8vo.* 3s. 6d. *net.*

**Crabbe (George).** See Little Library.

**Craik (Mrs.).** See Little Library.

**Crane (C. P.),** D.S.O. See Little Guides.

**Crane (Walter),** R.W.S. AN ARTIST'S REMINISCENCES. With 123 Illustrations by the Author and others from Photographs. *Second Edition. Demy 8vo.* 18s. *net.*
INDIA IMPRESSIONS. With 84 Illustrations from Sketches by the Author. *Second Edition. Demy 8vo.* 7s. 6d. *net.*

**Crashaw (Richard).** See Little Library.

**Crispe (T. E.),** K.C. REMINISCENCES OF A K.C. With 2 Portraits. *Demy 8vo.* 10s. 6d. *net.*

**Cross (J. A.),** M.A. THE FAITH OF THE BIBLE. *Fcap. 8vo.* 2s. 6d. *net.*

**Crowley (Ralph H.).** THE HYGIENE OF SCHOOL LIFE. *Cr. 8vo.* 3s. 6d. *net.*

**Cruikshank (G.).** THE LOVING BALLAD OF LORD BATEMAN. With 11 Plates. *Cr. 16mo.* 1s. 6d. *net.*

**Crump (B.).** See Wagner (R.).

**Cruttwell (C. T.),** M.A., Canon of Peterborough. See Handbooks of English Church History.

**Cunynghame (H. H.),** C.B. See Connoisseur's Library.

**Cutts (E. L.),** D.D. See Leaders of Religion.

**Daniell (G. W.),** M.A. See Leaders of Religion.

**Dante (Alighieri).** LA COMMEDIA DI DANTE. The Italian Text edited by PAGET TOYNBEE, M.A., D.Litt. *Cr. 8vo.* 6s.
THE DIVINE COMEDY. Translated by H. F. CARY. Edited with a Life of Dante and Introductory Notes by PAGET TOYNBEE, M.A., D.Litt. *Demy 8vo.* 6d.
THE PURGATORIO OF DANTE. Translated into Spenserian Prose by C. GORDON WRIGHT. With the Italian text. *Fcap. 8vo.* 2s. 6d. *net.*
See also Little Library, Toynbee (Paget), and Vernon (Hon. W. Warren).

**Darley (George).** See Little Library.

**D'Arcy (R. F.),** M.A. A NEW TRIGONOMETRY FOR BEGINNERS. With numerous diagrams. *Cr. 8vo.* 2s. 6d.

**Daudet (Alphonse).** See Simplified French Texts.

**Davenport (Cyril).** See Connoisseur's Library and Little Books on Art.

**Davenport (James).** THE WASHBOURNE FAMILY. With 15 Illustrations and a Map. *Royal 8vo.* 21s. *net.*

**Davey (Richard.)** THE PAGEANT OF LONDON. With 40 Illustrations in Colour by JOHN FULLEYLOVE, R.I. *In Two Volumes. Demy 8vo.* 15s. *net.*
See also Romantic History.

**Davies (Gerald S.).** See Classics of Art.

**Davies (W. O. P.).** See Junior Examination Series.

**Davis (H. W. C.),** M.A., Fellow and Tutor of Balliol College. ENGLAND UNDER THE NORMANS AND ANGEVINS: 1066-1272. With Maps and Illustrations. *Second Edition. Demy 8vo.* 10s. 6d. *net.*

**Dawson (Nelson).** See Connoisseur's Library.

**Dawson (Mrs. Nelson).** See Little Books on Art.

**Deane (A. C.).** See Little Library.

**Deans (Storry R.).** THE TRIALS OF FIVE QUEENS: KATHARINE OF ARAGON, ANNE BOLEYN, MARY QUEEN OF SCOTS, MARIE ANTOINETTE and CAROLINE OF BRUNSWICK. With 12 Illustrations. *Demy 8vo.* 10s. 6d. *net.*

**Dearmer (Mabel).** A CHILD'S LIFE OF CHRIST. With 8 Illustrations in Colour by E. FORTESCUE-BRICKDALE. *Large Cr. 8vo.* 6s.

**D'Este (Margaret).** IN THE CANARIES WITH A CAMERA. With 50 Illustrations, of which one is in Colour, from Photographs by Mrs. R. M. KING, and a Map. *Cr. 8vo* 7s. 6d. *net.*

**Delbos (Leon).** THE METRIC SYSTEM. *Cr. 8vo.* 2s.

**Demosthenes.** AGAINST CONON AND CALLICLES. Edited by F. DARWIN SWIFT, M.A. *Second Edition. Fcap. 8vo.* 2s.

**Dickens (Charles).** See Little Library, I.P.L., and Chesterton (G. K.).

**Dickinson (Emily).** POEMS. *Cr. 8vo.* 4s. 6d. *net.*

**Dickinson (G. L.),** M.A., Fellow of King's College, Cambridge. THE GREEK VIEW OF LIFE. *Sixth Edition. Cr. 8vo.* 2s. 6d.

**Dilke (Lady), Bulley (Miss),** and **Whitley (Miss).** WOMEN'S WORK. *Cr. 8vo.* 2s. 6d.

**Dillon (Edward),** M.A. See Connoisseur's Library, Little Books on Art, and Classics of Art.

**Ditchfield (P. H.),** M.A., F.S.A. THE STORY OF OUR ENGLISH TOWNS. With an Introduction by AUGUSTUS JESSOPP, D.D. *Second Edition. Cr. 8vo.* 6s.

OLD ENGLISH CUSTOMS: Extant at the Present Time. *Cr. 8vo.* 6s.

ENGLISH VILLAGES. With 100 Illustrations. *Second Edition. Cr. 8vo.* 2s. 6d. *net.*

THE PARISH CLERK. With 31 Illustrations. *Third Edition. Demy 8vo.* 7s. 6d. *net.*

THE OLD-TIME PARSON. With 17 Illustrations. *Second Edition. Demy 8vo.* 7s. 6d. *net.*

**Dixon (W. M.),** M.A. A PRIMER OF TENNYSON. *Third Edition. Cr. 8vo.* 2s. 6d.

ENGLISH POETRY FROM BLAKE TO BROWNING. *Second Edition. Cr. 8vo.* 2s. 6d.

**Dobbs (W. J.),** M.A. See Textbooks of Science.

**Doney (May).** SONGS OF THE REAL. *Cr. 8vo.* 3s. 6d. *net.*

**Douglas (Hugh A.).** VENICE ON FOOT. With the Itinerary of the Grand Canal. With 75 Illustrations and 11 Maps. *Fcap. 8vo.* 5s. *net.*

**Douglas (James).** THE MAN IN THE PULPIT. *Cr. 8vo.* 2s. 6d. *net.*

**Dowden (J.),** D.D., Lord Bishop of Edinburgh. FURTHER STUDIES IN THE PRAYER BOOK. *Cr. 8vo.* 6s.

See also Churchman's Library.

**Drage (G.).** See Books on Business.

**Driver (S. R.),** D.D., D.C.L., Regius Professor of Hebrew in the University of Oxford. SERMONS ON SUBJECTS CONNECTED WITH THE OLD TESTAMENT. *Cr. 8vo.* 6s.

See also Westminster Commentaries.

**Dry (Wakeling).** See Little Guides.

**Dryhurst (A. R.).** See Little Books on Art.

**Duff (Nora).** MATILDA OF TUSCANY. With many Illustrations. *Demy 8vo.* 10s. 6d. *net.*

**Duguid (Charles).** See Books on Business.

**Dumas (Alexandre).** THE CRIMES OF THE BORGIAS AND OTHERS. With an Introduction by R. S. GARNETT. With 9 Illustrations. *Cr. 8vo.* 6s

THE CRIMES OF URBAIN GRANDIER AND OTHERS. With 8 Illustrations. *Cr. 8vo.* 6s.

THE CRIMES OF THE MARQUISE DE BRINVILLIERS AND OTHERS. With 8 Illustrations. *Cr. 8vo.* 6s.

THE CRIMES OF ALI PACHA AND OTHERS. With 8 Illustrations. *Cr. 8vo.* 6s.

MY MEMOIRS. Translated by E. M. WALLER. With an Introduction by ANDREW LANG. With Frontispieces in Photogravure. In six Volumes. *Cr. 8vo.* 6s. *each volume.*
VOL. I. 1802-1821. VOL. IV. 1830-1831.
VOL. II. 1822-1825. VOL. V. 1831-1832.
VOL. III. 1826-1830. VOL. VI. 1832-1833.

MY PETS. Newly translated by A. R. ALLINSON, M.A. With 16 Illustrations by V. LECOMTE. *Cr. 8vo.* 6s.

See also Simplified French Texts.

**Duncan (David),** D Sc., LL.D. THE LIFE AND LETTERS OF HERBERT SPENCER. With 17 Illustrations. *Demy 8vo.* 15s.

**Dunn (J. T.),** D.Sc., **and Mundella (V. A.).** GENERAL ELEMENTARY SCIENCE. With 114 Illustrations. *Second Edition. Cr. 8vo.* 3s. 6d.

**Dunn-Pattison (R. P.).** NAPOLEON'S MARSHALS. With 20 Illustrations. *Demy 8vo. Second Edition.* 12s. 6d. *net.*

**Dunstan (A. E.),** B.Sc. (Lond.). See Textbooks of Science, and Junior School Books.

**Durham (The Earl of).** A REPORT ON CANADA. With an Introductory Note. *Demy 8vo.* 4s. 6d. *net.*

**Dutt (W. A.).** THE NORFOLK BROADS. With coloured Illustrations by FRANK SOUTHGATE, R.B.A. *Second Edition. Cr. 8vo.* 6s.

WILD LIFE IN EAST ANGLIA. With 16 Illustrations in colour by FRANK SOUTHGATE, R.B.A. *Second Edition. Demy 8vo.* 7*s.* 6*d.* *net.*

SOME LITERARY ASSOCIATIONS OF EAST ANGLIA. With 16 Illustrations in Colour by W. DEXTER, R.B.A., and 16 other Illustrations. *Demy 8vo.* 10*s.* 6*d.* *net.* See also Little Guides.

**Earle (John)**, Bishop of Salisbury. MICROCOSMOGRAPHIE, OR A PIECE OF THE WORLD DISCOVERED. *Post 16mo.* 2*s.* *net.*

**Edmonds (Major J. E.)**, R.E.; D.A.Q.-M.G. See Wood (W. Birkbeck).

**Edwardes (Tickner).** THE LORE OF THE HONEY BEE. With 24 Illustrations. *Cr. 8vo.* 6*s.*

**Edwards (Clement)**, M.P. RAILWAY NATIONALIZATION. *Second Edition, Revised. Crown 8vo.* 2*s.* 6*d.* *net.*

**Edwards (W. Douglas).** See Commercial Series.

**Egan (Pierce).** See I.P.L.

**Egerton (H. E.)**, M.A. A HISTORY OF BRITISH COLONIAL POLICY. *Second Ed., Revised. Demy 8vo.* 7*s.* 6*d.* *net.*

**Ellaby (C. G.).** See Little Guides.

**Ellerton (F. G.).** See Stone (S. J.).

**Epictetus.** See Aurelius (Marcus).

**Erasmus.** A Book called in Latin ENCHIRIDION MILITIS CHRISTIANI, and in English the Manual of the Christian Knight. *Fcap. 8vo.* 3*s.* 6*d.* *net.*

**Erckmann-Chatrian.** See Simplified French Texts.

**Evagrius.** See Byzantine Texts.

**Everett-Green (Mary Anne).** ELIZABETH; ELECTRESS PALATINE AND QUEEN OF BOHEMIA. Revised by her Niece S. C. LOMAS. With a Prefatory Note by A. W. WARD, Litt.D. *Demy 8vo.* 10*s.* 6*d.* *net.*

**Ewald (Carl).** TWO LEGS, AND OTHER STORIES. Translated from the Danish by ALEXANDER TEIXEIRA DE MATTOS. Illustrated by AUGUSTA GUEST. *Large Cr. 8vo.* 6*s.*

**Ezekiel.** See Westminster Commentaries.

**Facon (H. T.)**, B.A. See Junior Examination Series.

**Fairbrother (W. H.)**, M.A. THE PHILOSOPHY OF T. H. GREEN. *Second Edition. Cr. 8vo.* 3*s.* 6*d.*

**Fea (Allan).** THE FLIGHT OF THE KING. With over 70 Sketches and Photographs by the Author. *New and revised Edition. Demy 8vo.* 7*s.* 6*d.* *net.*

SECRET CHAMBERS AND HIDING-PLACES. With 80 Illustrations. *New and revised Edition. Demy 8vo.* 7*s.* 6*d.* *net.*

JAMES II. AND HIS WIVES. With 40 Illustrations. *Demy 8vo.* 10*s.* 6*d.* *net.*

**Fell (E. F. B.).** THE FOUNDATIONS OF LIBERTY. *Cr. 8vo.* 5*s.* *net.*

**Ferrier (Susan).** See Little Library.

**Fidler (T. Claxton)**, M.Inst. C.E. See Books on Business.

**Fielding (Henry).** See Standard Library.

**Finn (S. W.)**, M.A. See Junior Examination Series.

**Firth (J. B.).** See Little Guides.

**Firth (C. H.)**, M.A., Regius Professor of Modern History at Oxford. CROMWELL'S ARMY: A History of the English Soldier during the Civil Wars, the Commonwealth, and the Protectorate. *Cr. 8vo.* 6*s.*

**Firth (Edith E.).** See Beginner's Books and Junior School Books.

**FitzGerald (Edward).** THE RUBÁIYÁT OF OMAR KHAYYÁM. Printed from the Fifth and last Edition. With a Commentary by Mrs. STEPHEN BATSON, and a Biography of Omar by E. D. ROSS. *Cr. 8vo.* 6*s.* See also Miniature Library.

**FitzGerald (H. P.).** A CONCISE HANDBOOK OF CLIMBERS, TWINERS, AND WALL SHRUBS. Illustrated. *Fcap. 8vo.* 3*s.* 6*d.* *net.*

**Fitzpatrick (S. A. O.).** See Ancient Cities.

**Flecker (W. H.)**, M.A., D.C.L., Headmaster of the Dean Close School, Cheltenham. THE STUDENT'S PRAYER BOOK. THE TEXT OF MORNING AND EVENING PRAYER AND LITANY. With an Introduction and Notes. *Cr. 8vo.* 2*s.* 6*d.*

**Fletcher (C. R. L.)**, M.A. *See* Carlyle (Thomas).

**Fletcher (J. S.).** A BOOK OF YORKSHIRE. With 16 Illustrations in Colour by WAL PAGET and FRANK SOUTHGATE, R.B.A., 16 other Illustrations and a Map. *Demy 8vo.* 7*s.* 6*d.* *net.*

**Flux (A. W.)**, M.A., William Dow Professor of Political Economy in M'Gill University, Montreal. ECONOMIC PRINCIPLES. *Demy 8vo.* 7*s.* 6*d.* *net.*

**Foat (F. W. G.)**, D.Litt., M.A. A LONDON READER FOR YOUNG CITIZENS. With Plans and Illustrations. *Cr. 8vo.* 1*s.* 6*d.*

**Ford (H. G.)**, M.A., Assistant Master at Bristol Grammar School. See Junior School Books.

**Forel (A.).** THE SENSES OF INSECTS. Translated by MACLEOD YEARSLEY. With 2 Illustrations. *Demy 8vo.* 10*s.* 6*d.* *net.*

**Fortescue (Mrs. G.).** See Little Books on Art.

**Fouqué (La Motte).** SINTRAM AND HIS COMPANIONS. Translated by A. C. FARQUHARSON. With 20 Illustrations by EDMUND J. SULLIVAN, and a Frontispiece in Photogravure from an engraving by ALBRECHT DÜRER. *Demy 8vo.* 7*s.* 6*d.* *net. Half White Vellum,* 10*s.* 6*d.* *net.* See also Simplified German Texts.

**Fraser (J. F.).** ROUND THE WORLD ON A WHEEL. With 100 Illustrations. *Fifth Edition Cr. 8vo.* 6*s.*

**French (W.)**, M.A. See Textbooks of Science.

**Freudenreich (Ed. von).** DAIRY BACTERIOLOGY. A Short Manual for Students. Translated by J. R. AINSWORTH DAVIS, M.A. *Second Edition. Revised. Cr. 8vo.* 2*s.* 6*d.*

**Fursdon (F. R. M).** FRENCH AND ENGLISH PARALLELS. *Fcap. 8vo.* 3*s*. 6*d*. *net*.

**Fyvie (John).** TRAGEDY QUEENS OF THE GEORGIAN ERA. With 16 Illustrations. *Second Ed. Demy 8vo.* 12*s*. 6*d*. *net*.

**Gallaher (D.) and Stead (W. J.).** THE COMPLETE RUGBY FOOTBALLER, ON THE NEW ZEALAND SYSTEM. With 35 Illustrations. *Second Ed. Demy 8vo.* 10*s*. 6*d*. *net*.

**Gallichan (W. M.).** See Little Guides.

**Galton (Sir Francis),** F.R.S.; D.C.L., Oxf.; Hon. Sc.D., Camb.; Hon. Fellow Trinity College, Cambridge. MEMORIES OF MY LIFE. With 8 Illustrations. *Third Edition. Demy 8vo.* 10*s*. 6*d*. *net*.

**Gambado (Geoffrey, Esq.).** See I.P.L.

**Garnett (Lucy M. J.).** THE TURKISH PEOPLE: THEIR SOCIAL LIFE, RELIGIOUS BELIEFS AND INSTITUTIONS, AND DOMESTIC LIFE. With 21 Illustrations. *Demy 8vo.* 10*s*. 6*d*. *net*.

**Gaskell (Mrs.).** See Little Library, Standard Library and Sixpenny Novels.

**Gasquet,** the Right Rev. Abbot. O.S.B. See Antiquary's Books.

**Gee (Henry),** D.D., F.S.A. See Handbooks of English Church History.

**George (H. B.),** M.A., Fellow of New College, Oxford. BATTLES OF ENGLISH HISTORY. With numerous Plans. *Fourth Edition Revised. Cr. 8vo.* 3*s*. 6*d*.

A HISTORICAL GEOGRAPHY OF THE BRITISH EMPIRE. *Fourth Edition. Cr. 8vo.* 3*s*. 6*d*.

**Gibbins (H. de B.),** Litt.D., M.A. INDUSTRY IN ENGLAND: HISTORICAL OUTLINES. With 5 Maps. *Sixth Edition. Demy 8vo.* 10*s*. 6*d*.

THE INDUSTRIAL HISTORY OF ENGLAND. With Maps and Plans. *Fifteenth Edition, Revised. Cr. 8vo.* 3*s*.

ENGLISH SOCIAL REFORMERS. *Second Edition. Cr. 8vo.* 2*s*. 6*d*.

See also Hadfield (R. A.), and Commercial Series.

**Gibbon (Edward).** MEMOIRS OF MY LIFE AND WRITINGS. Edited by G. BIRKBECK HILL, LL.D *Cr. 8vo.* 6*s*.

*THE DECLINE AND FALL OF THE ROMAN EMPIRE. Edited, with Notes, Appendices, and Maps, by J. B. BURY. M.A., Litt.D., Regius Professor of Modern History at Cambridge. In Seven Volumes. With many Illustrations and Maps. *Demy 8vo. Gilt top. Each* 10*s*. 6*d*. *net*.

**Gibbs (Philip).** THE ROMANCE OF GEORGE VILLIERS: FIRST DUKE OF BUCKINGHAM, AND SOME MEN AND WOMEN OF THE STUART COURT. With 20 Illustrations. *Second Edition. Demy 8vo.* 15*s*. *net*.

**Gibson (E. C. S.),** D.D., Lord Bishop of Gloucester. See Westminster Commentaries. Handbooks of Theology, and Oxford Biographies.

**Gilbert (A. R.).** See Little Books on Art.

**Gloag (M. R.)** and **Wyatt (Kate M.).** A BOOK OF ENGLISH GARDENS. With 24 Illustrations in Colour. *Demy 8vo.* 10*s*. 6*d*. *net*.

**Glover (T. R.),** M.A., Fellow and Classical Lecturer of St. John's College, Cambridge. THE CONFLICT OF RELIGIONS IN THE EARLY ROMAN EMPIRE. *Third Edition. Demy 8vo.* 7*s*. 6*d*. *net*.

**Godfrey (Elizabeth).** A BOOK OF REMEMBRANCE. Being Lyrical Selections for every day in the Year. Arranged by. *Second Edition. Fcap. 8vo.* 2*s*. 6*d*. *net*.

ENGLISH CHILDREN IN THE OLDEN TIME. With 32 Illustrations. *Second Edition. Demy 8vo.* 7*s*. 6*d*. *net*.

**Godley (A. D.),** M.A., Fellow of Magdalen College, Oxford. OXFORD IN THE EIGHTEENTH CENTURY. With 16 Illustrations. *Second Edition. Demy 8vo.* 7*s*. 6*d*. *net*.

Also published in a Colonial Edition.

LYRA FRIVOLA. *Fourth Edition. Fcap. 8vo.* 2*s*. 6*d*.

VERSES TO ORDER. *Second Edition. Fcap. 8vo.* 2*s*. 6*d*.

SECOND STRINGS. *Fcap. 8vo.* 2*s*. 6d.

**Goldsmith (Oliver).** See I.P.L. and Standard Library.

**Goll (August).** CRIMINAL TYPES IN SHAKESPEARE. Authorised Translation from the Danish by Mrs. CHARLES WEEKES. *Cr. 8vo.* 5*s*. *net*.

**Gomme (G. L.).** See Antiquary's Books.

**Gordon (Lina Duff)** (Mrs. Aubrey Waterfield). HOME LIFE IN ITALY: LETTERS FROM THE APENNINES. With 13 Illustrations by AUBREY WATERFIELD and 15 Illustrations from Photographs. *Second Edition. Demy 8vo.* 10*s*. 6*d*. *net*.

**Gorst (Rt. Hon. Sir John).** See New Library of Medicine.

**Gostling (Frances M.).** THE BRETONS AT HOME. With 12 Illustrations in Colour by GASTON FANTY LESCURE, and 32 from Photographs. *Demy 8vo.* 10*s*. 6*d*. *net*.

**Goudge (H. L.),** M.A., Principal of Wells Theological College. See Westminster Commentaries.

**Graham (Harry).** A GROUP OF SCOTTISH WOMEN. With 16 Illustrations. *Second Edition. Demy 8vo.* 10*s*. 6*d*. *net*.

**Graham (P. Anderson).** THE RURAL EXODUS. The Problem of the Village and the Town. *Cr. 8vo.* 2*s*. 6*d*.

**Grahame (Kenneth).** THE WIND IN THE WILLOWS. With a Frontispiece by GRAHAM ROBERTSON. *Fourth Edition. Cr. 8vo.* 6*s*.

**Granger (F. S.),** M.A., Litt.D. PSYCHOLOGY. *Fourth Edition. Cr. 8vo.* 2*s*. 6*d*.

THE SOUL OF A CHRISTIAN. *Cr. 8vo.* 6*s*.

**Gray (E. M'Queen).** GERMAN PASSAGES FOR UNSEEN TRANSLATION. *Cr. 8vo.* 2s. 6d.

**Gray (P. L.),** B.Sc. THE PRINCIPLES OF MAGNETISM AND ELECTRICITY. With 181 Diagrams. *Cr. 8vo.* 3s. 6d.

**Green (G. Buckland),** M.A., late Fellow of St. John's College, Oxon. NOTES ON GREEK AND LATIN SYNTAX. *Second Ed. revised. Crown 8vo.* 3s. 6d.

**Greenidge (A. H. J.),** M.A., D.Litt. A HISTORY OF ROME: From the Tribunate of Tiberius Gracchus to the end of the Jugurthine War, B.C. 133-104. *Demy 8vo.* 10s. 6d. *net.*

**Gregory (Miss E. C.).** See Library of Devotion.

**Grubb (H. C.).** See Textbooks of Technology.

**Gwynn (Stephen),** M.P. A HOLIDAY IN CONNEMARA. With 16 Illustrations. *Demy 8vo.* 10s. 6d. *net.*

**Hadfield (R. A.)** and **Gibbins (H. de B.).** A SHORTER WORKING DAY. *Cr. 8vo.* 2s. 6d.

**Hall (Cyril).** THE YOUNG CARPENTER. With many Diagrams, and 15 Photographic Illustrations. *Cr. 8vo.* 5s.

**Hall (Hammond).** THE YOUNG ENGINEER: OR MODERN ENGINES AND THEIR MODELS. With 85 Illustrations. *Second Edition. Cr. 8vo.* 5s.

**Hall (Mary).** A WOMAN'S TREK FROM THE CAPE TO CAIRO. With 64 Illustrations and 2 Maps. *Second Edition. Demy 8vo.* 16s. *net.*

**Hamel (Frank).** FAMOUS FRENCH SALONS. With 20 Illustrations. *Third Edition. Demy 8vo.* 12s. 6d. *net.*

**Hannay (D.).** A SHORT HISTORY OF THE ROYAL NAVY. Vol. I., 1217-1688. Vol. II., 1689-1815. *Demy 8vo. Each* 7s. 6d. *net.*

**Hannay (James O.),** M.A. THE SPIRIT AND ORIGIN OF CHRISTIAN MONASTICISM. *Cr. 8vo.* 6s.

THE WISDOM OF THE DESERT. *Fcap. 8vo.* 3s. 6d. *net.*

**Hardie (Martin).** See Connoisseur's Library.

**Hare (A. T.),** M.A. THE CONSTRUCTION OF LARGE INDUCTION COILS. With 35 Illustrations. *Demy 8vo.* 6s.

**Harker (Alfred),** M.A., F.R.S., Fellow of St. John's College, and Lecturer in Petrology in the University of Cambridge. THE NATURAL HISTORY OF IGNEOUS ROCKS. With 112 Diagrams and 2 Plates. *Demy 8vo.* 12s. 6d. *net.*

**Harper (Charles G.).** 'THE AUTOCAR' ROAD-BOOK. In four Volumes. *Crown 8vo. Each* 7s. 6d. *net.*

Vol. I.—SOUTH OF THE THAMES.

**Harvey (Alfred),** M.B. See Ancient Cities and Antiquary's Books.

**Hawthorne (Nathaniel).** See Little Library.

**Headley (F. W.).** DARWINISM AND MODERN SOCIALISM. *Cr. 8vo.* 5s. *net.*

**Heath (Frank R.).** See Little Guides.

**Heath (Dudley).** See Connoisseur's Library.

**Henderson (B. W.),** Fellow of Exeter College, Oxford. THE LIFE AND PRINCIPATE OF THE EMPEROR NERO. Illustrated. *New and cheaper issue. Demy 8vo.* 7s. 6d. *net.*

AT INTERVALS. *Fcap 8vo.* 2s. 6d. *net.*

**Henderson (M. Sturge).** GEORGE MEREDITH: NOVELIST, POET, REFORMER. With a Portrait in Photogravure. *Second Edition. Crown 8vo.* 6s.

**Henderson (T. F.).** See Little Library and Oxford Biographies.

**Henderson (T. F.), and Watt (Francis).** SCOTLAND OF TO-DAY. With 20 Illustrations in colour and 24 other Illustrations. *Second Edition. Cr. 8vo.* 6s.

**Henley (W. E.).** ENGLISH LYRICS. CHAUCER TO POE, 1340-1849. *Second Edition. Cr. 8vo.* 2s. 6d. *net.*

**Henley (W. E.)** and **Whibley (C.)** A BOOK OF ENGLISH PROSE, CHARACTER, AND INCIDENT, 1387-1649. *Cr. 8vo.* 2s. 6d. *net.*

**Herbert (George).** See Library of Devotion.

**Herbert of Cherbury (Lord).** See Miniature Library.

**Hett (Walter S.),** B.A. A SHORT HISTORY OF GREECE TO THE DEATH OF ALEXANDER THE GREAT. With 3 Maps and 4 Plans. *Cr. 8vo.* 3s. 6d.

**Hewins (W. A. S.),** B.A. ENGLISH TRADE AND FINANCE IN THE SEVENTEENTH CENTURY. *Cr. 8vo.* 2s. 6d.

**Hewitt (Ethel M.)** A GOLDEN DIAL. A Day Book of Prose and Verse. *Fcap. 8vo.* 2s. 6d. *net.*

**Hey (H.),** Inspector, Surrey Education Committee, and **Rose (G. H.),** City and Guilds Woodwork Teacher. A WOODWORK CLASS-BOOK. Pt. I. Illustrated. *4to.* 2s.

**Heywood (W.).** See St. Francis of Assisi.

**Hill (Clare).** See Textbooks of Technology.

**Hill (George Francis).** ONE HUNDRED MASTERPIECES OF SCULPTURE. with 101 Illustrations. *Demy 8vo.* 10s. 6d. *net.*

**Hill (Henry),** B.A., Headmaster of the Boy's High School, Worcester, Cape Colony. A SOUTH AFRICAN ARITHMETIC. *Cr. 8vo.* 3s. 6d.

**Hind (C. Lewis).** DAYS IN CORNWALL. With 16 Illustrations in Colour by WILLIAM PASCOE, and 20 other Illustrations and a Map. *Second Edition. Cr. 8vo.* 6s.

**Hirst (F. W.)** See Books on Business.

**Hobhouse (L. T.),** late Fellow of C.C.C., Oxford. THE THEORY OF KNOWLEDGE. *Demy 8vo.* 10s. 6d. *net.*

**Hobson (J. A.),** M.A. INTERNATIONAL TRADE: A Study of Economic Principles. *Cr. 8vo.* 2s. 6d. *net.*

PROBLEMS OF POVERTY. An Inquiry

into the Industrial Condition of the Poor. *Seventh Edition. Cr. 8vo.* 2s. 6d.
THE PROBLEM OF THE UNEMPLOYED. *Fourth Edition. Cr. 8vo.* 2s. 6d.
**Hodgetts (E. A. Brayley).** THE COURT OF RUSSIA IN THE NINETEENTH CENTURY. With 20 Illustrations. *Two Volumes. Demy 8vo.* 24s. *net.*
**Hodgkin (T.),** D.C.L. See Leaders of Religion.
**Hodgson (Mrs. W.)** HOW TO IDENTIFY OLD CHINESE PORCELAIN. With 40 Illustrations. *Second Edition. Post 8vo.* 6s.
**Holden-Stone (G. de).** See Books on Business.
**Holdich (Sir T. H.),** K.C.I.E., C.B., F.S.A. THE INDIAN BORDERLAND, 1880-1900. With 22 Illustrations and a Map. *Second Edition. Demy 8vo.* 10s. 6d. *net.*
**Holdsworth (W. S.),** D.C.L. A HISTORY OF ENGLISH LAW. *In Four Volumes. Vols. I., II., III. Demy 8vo. Each* 10s. 6d. *net.*
**Holland (Clive).** TYROL AND ITS PEOPLE. With 16 Illustrations in Colour by ADRIAN STOKES, 31 other Illustrations and a Map. *Demy 8vo.* 10s. 6d. *net.*
**Holland (H. Scott),** Canon of St. Paul's. See Newman (J. H.).
**Hollings (M. A.),** M.A. See Six Ages of European History.
**Hollway-Calthrop (H. C.),** late of Balliol College, Oxford; Bursar of Eton College. PETRARCH: HIS LIFE, WORK, AND TIMES. With 24 Illustrations. *Demy 8vo.* 12s. 6d. *net.*
**Holmes (T. Scott).** See Ancient Cities.
**Holyoake (G. J.).** THE CO-OPERATIVE MOVEMENT OF TO-DAY. *Fourth Ed. Cr. 8vo.* 2s. 6d.
**Hone (Nathaniel J.).** See Antiquary's Books.
**Hook (A.)** HUMANITY AND ITS PROBLEMS. *Cr. 8vo.* 5s. *net.*
**Hoppner.** See Little Galleries.
**Horace.** See Classical Translations.
**Horsburgh (E. L. S.),** M.A. LORENZO THE MAGNIFICENT: AND FLORENCE IN HER GOLDEN AGE. With 24 Illustrations and 2 Maps. *Second Edition. Demy 8vo.* 15s. *net.*
WATERLOO: With Plans. *Second Edition. Cr. 8vo.* 5s.
See also Oxford Biographies.
**Horth (A. C.).** See Textbooks of Technology.
**Horton (R. F.),** D.D. See Leaders of Religion.
**Hosie (Alexander).** MANCHURIA. With 30 Illustrations and a Map. *Second Edition Demy 8vo.* 7s. 6d. *net.*
**How (F. D.).** SIX GREAT SCHOOLMASTERS. With 13 Illustrations. *Second Edition. Demy 8vo.* 7s. 6d.
**Howell (A. G. Ferrers).** FRANCISCAN DAYS. Being Selections for every day in the year from ancient Franciscan writings. *Cr. 8vo.* 3s. 6d. *net.*
**Howell (G.).** TRADE UNIONISM—NEW AND OLD. *Fourth Edition. Cr. 8vo.* 2s. 6d.
**Huggins (Sir William),** K.C.B., O.M., D.C.L., F.R.S. THE ROYAL SOCIETY; OR, SCIENCE IN THE STATE AND IN THE SCHOOLS. With 25 Illustrations. *Wide Royal 8vo.* 4s. 6d. *net.*
**Hughes (C. E.).** THE PRAISE OF SHAKESPEARE. An English Anthology. With a Preface by SIDNEY LEE. *Demy 8vo.* 3s. 6d. *net.*
**Hugo (Victor).** See Simplified French Texts.
**Hulton (Samuel F.).** THE CLERK OF OXFORD IN FICTION. With 12 Illustrations. *Demy 8vo.* 10s. 6d. *net.*
**Hume (Martin),** M.A. See Romantic History.
**Hutchinson (Horace G.)** THE NEW FOREST. Illustrated in colour with 50 Pictures by WALTER TYNDALE and 4 by LUCY KEMP-WELCH. *Fourth Edition. Cr. 8vo.* 6s.
**Hutton (A. W.),** M.A. See Leaders of Religion and Library of Devotion.
**Hutton (Edward).** THE CITIES OF UMBRIA. With 20 Illustrations in Colour by A. PISA, and 12 other Illustrations. *Third Edition. Cr. 8vo.* 6s.
THE CITIES OF SPAIN. With 24 Illustrations in Colour, by A. W. RIMINGTON, 20 other Illustrations and a Map. *Third Edition. Cr. 8vo.* 6s.
FLORENCE AND THE CITIES OF NORTHERN TUSCANY, WITH GENOA. With 16 Illustrations in Colour by WILLIAM PARKINSON, and 16 other Illustrations. *Second Edition. Cr. 8vo.* 6s.
ENGLISH LOVE POEMS. Edited with an Introduction. *Fcap. 8vo.* 3s. 6d. *net.*
COUNTRY WALKS ABOUT FLORENCE. With 32 Drawings by ADELAIDE MARCHI and 20 other Illustrations. *Fcap. 8vo.* 5s. *net.*
IN UNKNOWN TUSCANY. With an Appendix by WILLIAM HEYWOOD. With 8 Illustrations in Colour and 20 others. *Second Edition. Demy 8vo.* 7s. 6d. *net.*
ROME. With 16 Illustrations in Colour by MAXWELL ARMFIELD, and 12 other Illustrations. *Cr. 8vo.* 6s.
**Hutton (R. H.).** See Leaders of Religion.
**Hutton (W. H.),** M.A. THE LIFE OF SIR THOMAS MORE. With Portraits after Drawings by HOLBEIN. *Second Edition. Cr. 8vo.* 5s.
See also Leaders of Religion.
**Hyde (A. G.)** GEORGE HERBERT AND HIS TIMES. With 32 Illustrations. *Demy 8vo.* 10s. 6d. *net.*
**Hyett (F. A.).** FLORENCE: HER HISTORY AND ART TO THE FALL OF THE REPUBLIC. *Demy 8vo.* 7s. 6d. *net.*
**Ibsen (Henrik).** BRAND. A Drama. Translated by WILLIAM WILSON. *Third Edition. Cr. 8vo.* 3s. 6d.
**Inge (W. R.),** M.A., Fellow and Tutor of Hertford College, Oxford. CHRISTIAN MYSTICISM. (The Bampton Lectures of 1899.) *Demy 8vo.* 12s. 6d. *net.*
See also Library of Devotion.

**Innes (A. D.)**, M.A. A HISTORY OF THE BRITISH IN INDIA. With Maps and Plans. *Cr. 8vo.* 6*s.*

ENGLAND UNDER THE TUDORS. With Maps. *Second Edition. Demy 8vo.* 10*s.* 6*d. net.*

**Innes (Mary).** SCHOOLS OF PAINTING. With 76 Illustrations. *Cr. 8vo.* 5*s. net.*

**Isaiah.** See Churchman's Bible.

**Jackson (C. E.)**, B.A. See Textbooks of Science.

**Jackson (S.)**, M.A. See Commercial Series.

**Jackson (F. Hamilton).** See Little Guides.

**Jacob (F.)**, M.A. See Junior Examination Series.

**Jeans (J. Stephen).** TRUSTS, POOLS, AND CORNERS AS AFFECTING COMMERCE AND INDUSTRY. *Cr. 8vo.* 2*s.* 6*d.*

See also Books on Business.

**Jebb (Camilla).** A STAR OF THE SALONS: JULIE DE LESPINASSE. With 20 Illustrations. *Demy 8vo.* 10*s.* 6*d. net.*

**Jeffery (Reginald W.)**, M.A. THE HISTORY OF THE THIRTEEN COLONIES OF NORTH AMERICA 1497-1763. With 8 Illustrations and a Map. *Demy 8vo.* 7*s.* 6*d. net.*

**Jeffreys (D. Gwyn).** DOLLY'S THEATRICALS. *Super Royal 16mo.* 2*s.* 6*d.*

**Jenks (E.)**, M.A., B.C.L. AN OUTLINE OF ENGLISH LOCAL GOVERNMENT. *Second Ed.* Revised by R. C. K. ENSOR, M.A. *Cr. 8vo.* 2*s.* 6*d.*

**Jenner (Mrs. H.).** See Little Books on Art.

**Jennings (A. C.)**, M.A. See Handbooks of English Church History.

**Jennings (Oscar)**, M.D. EARLY WOODCUT INITIALS. *Demy 4to.* 21*s. net.*

**Jerningham (Charles Edward).** THE MAXIMS OF MARMADUKE. *Fcap. 8vo.* 5*s.*

**Jessopp (Augustus)**, D.D. See Leaders of Religion.

**Jevons (F. B.)**, M.A., Litt.D., Principal of Hatfield Hall, Durham. RELIGION IN EVOLUTION. *Cr. 8vo.* 3*s.* 6*d. net.*

See also Churchman's Library and Handbooks of Theology.

**Johnson (A. H.)**, M.A. See Six Ages of European History.

**Johnston (Sir H. H.)**, K.C.B. BRITISH CENTRAL AFRICA. With nearly 200 Illustrations and Six Maps. *Third Edition. Cr. 4to.* 18*s. net.*

**Jones (H.).** See Commercial Series.

**Jones (H. F.).** See Textbooks of Science.

**Jones (L. A. Atherley)**, K.C., M.P., and **Bellot (Hugh H. L.)**, M.A., D.C.L. THE MINER'S GUIDE TO THE COAL MINES REGULATION ACTS AND THE LAW OF EMPLOYERS AND WORKMEN. *Cr. 8vo.* 2*s.* 6*d. net.*

COMMERCE IN WAR. *Royal 8vo.* 21*s. net.*

**Jones (R. Compton)**, M.A. POEMS OF THE INNER LIFE. Selected by. *Thirteenth Edition. Fcap. 8vo.* 2*s.* 6*d. net.*

**Jonson (Ben).** See Standard Library.

**Julian (Lady) of Norwich.** REVELATIONS OF DIVINE LOVE. Ed. by GRACE WARRACK. *Third Ed. Cr. 8vo.* 3*s.* 6*d.*

**Juvenal.** See Classical Translations.

**'Kappa.'** LET YOUTH BUT KNOW: A Plea for Reason in Education. *Second Edition. Cr. 8vo.* 3*s.* 6*d. net.*

**Kaufmann (M.)**, M.A. SOCIALISM AND MODERN THOUGHT. *Second Edition Revised and Enlarged. Cr. 8vo.* 2*s.* 6*d. net*

**Keats (John).** THE POEMS. Edited with Introduction and Notes by E. de SÉLINCOURT, M.A. With a Frontispiece in Photogravure. *Second Edition Revised. Demy 8vo.* 7*s.* 6*d. net.*

REALMS OF GOLD. Selections from the Works of. *Fcap. 8vo.* 3*s.* 6*d. net.*

See also Little Library and Standard Library.

**Keble (John).** THE CHRISTIAN YEAR. With an Introduction and Notes by W. LOCK, D.D., Warden of Keble College. Illustrated by R. ANNING BELL. *Third Edition Fcap. 8vo.* 3*s.* 6*d.*; *padded morocco*, 5*s*

See also Library of Devotion.

**Kelynack (T. N.)**, M.D., M.R.C.P. See New Library of Medicine.

**Kempis (Thomas à).** THE IMITATION OF CHRIST. With an Introduction by DEAN FARRAR. Illustrated by C. M. GERE. *Third Edition. Fcap. 8vo.* 3*s.* 6*d.*; *padded morocco.* 5*s.*

Also Translated by C. BIGG, D.D. *Cr. 8vo.* 3*s.* 6*d.*

See also Montmorency (J. E. G. de)., Library of Devotion, and Standard Library.

**Kennedy (James Houghton)**, D.D., Assistant Lecturer in Divinity in the University of Dublin. See St. Paul.

**Kerr (S. Parnell).** GEORGE SELWYN AND THE WITS. With 16 Illustrations. *Demy 8vo.* 12*s.* 6*d. net.*

**Kimmins (C. W.)**, M.A. THE CHEMISTRY OF LIFE AND HEALTH. Illustrated. *Cr. 8vo.* 2*s.* 6*d.*

**Kinglake (A. W.).** See Little Library.

**Kipling (Rudyard).** BARRACK-ROOM BALLADS. *91th Thousand. Twenty-sixth Edition. Cr. 8vo.* 6*s.* Also *Fcap. 8vo, Leather.* 5*s.*

THE SEVEN SEAS. *79th Thousand. Fifteenth Edition. Cr. 8vo.* 6*s.* Also *Fcap. 8vo, Leather.* 5*s.*

THE FIVE NATIONS. *68th Thousand. Sixth Edition. Cr. 8vo.* 6*s.* Also *Fcap. 8vo, Leather.* 5*s.*

DEPARTMENTAL DITTIES. *Eighteenth Edition. Cr. 8vo.* 6*s.* Also *Fcap. 8vo, Leather.* 5*s.*

**Knight (Albert E.).** THE COMPLETE CRICKETER. With 50 Illustrations. *Demy 8vo.* 7*s.* 6*d. net.*

**Knowling (R. J.)**, M.A., Professor of New Testament Exegesis at King's College, London. See Westminster Commentaries.

**Knox (Winifred F.).** THE COURT OF A SAINT. With 16 Illustrations. *Demy 8vo.* 10s. 6d. *net.*

**Kropotkin (Prince).** THE TERROR IN RUSSIA. An Appeal to the Nation. *Seventh Edition. Cr. 8vo.* 2d. *net.*

**Laboulaye (Edouard).** See Simplified French Texts.

**Lamb (Charles and Mary),** THE WORKS. Edited by E. V. LUCAS. Illustrated. *In Seven Volumes. Demy 8vo.* 7s. 6d. *each.*
See also Little Library and Lucas (E. V.)

**Lambert (F. A. H.).** See Little Guides.

**Lambros (Professor S. P.).** See Byzantine Texts.

**Lane-Poole (Stanley).** A HISTORY OF EGYPT IN THE MIDDLE AGES. With 101 Illustrations and a Map. *Cr. 8vo.* 6s.

**Langbridge (F.),** M.A. BALLADS OF THE BRAVE: Poems of Chivalry, Enterprise, Courage, and Constancy. *Fourth Edition. Cr. 8vo.* 2s. 6d.

**Lankester (Sir E. Ray),** K.C.B., F.R.S. SCIENCE FROM AN EASY CHAIR. With many Illustrations, of which 2 are in Colour. *Cr. 8vo.* 6s.

**Law (William).** See Library of Devotion and Standard Library.

**Leach (Henry).** THE SPIRIT OF THE LINKS. *Cr. 8vo.* 6s.
See also Braid (James).

**Le Braz (Anatole).** THE LAND OF PARDONS. Translated by FRANCES M. GOSTLING. With 12 Illustrations in Colour by T. C. GOTCH, and 40 other Illustrations. *Third Edition. Crown 8vo.* 6s.

**Lee (Margaret L.).** See Browning (Robert).

**Lees (Beatrice).** See Six Ages of European History.

**Lees (Frederick).** A SUMMER IN TOURAINE. With 12 Illustrations in Colour by MAXWELL ARMFIELD, and 87 from Photographs. Also a Map. *Second Edition. Demy 8vo.* 10s. 6d. *net.*

**Lehmann (R. C.),** M.P. THE COMPLETE OARSMAN. With 59 Illustrations. *Demy 8vo.* 10s. 6d. *net.*

**Lewes (V. B.),** M.A. AIR AND WATER. Illustrated. *Cr. 8vo.* 2s. 6d.

**Lewis (B. M. Gwyn).** A CONCISE HANDBOOK OF GARDEN SHRUBS. With 20 Illustrations. *Fcap. 8vo.* 3s. 6d. *net.*

**Lindsay (Lady Mabel).** ANNI DOMINI: A GOSPEL STUDY. *In Two Volumes. Super Royal 8vo.* 10s. *net.*

**Lindsay (W. M.),** Fellow of Jesus College, Oxford. See Plautus.

**Lisle (Fortunée de).** See Little Books on Art.

**Littlehales (H.).** See Antiquary's Books.

**Llewellyn (Owen) and Raven-Hill (L.).** THE SOUTH-BOUND CAR. With 85 Illustrations. *Crown 8vo.* 6s.

**Lock (Walter),** D.D., Warden of Keble College. ST. PAUL, THE MASTER-BUILDER. *Second Ed. Cr. 8vo.* 3s. 6d.

THE BIBLE AND CHRISTIAN LIFE. *Cr. 8vo.* 6s.
See also Keble (J.) and Leaders of Religion.

**Locker (F.).** See Little Library.

**Locock (Katherine B.).** See Browning (Rt.).

**Lodge (Sir Oliver),** F.R.S. THE SUBSTANCE OF FAITH, ALLIED WITH SCIENCE: A Catechism for Parents and Teachers. *Ninth Ed. Cr. 8vo.* 2s *net.*

MAN AND THE UNIVERSE: A STUDY OF THE INFLUENCE OF THE ADVANCE IN SCIENTIFIC KNOWLEDGE UPON OUR UNDERSTANDING OF CHRISTIANITY. *Seventh Edition. Demy 8vo.* 7s. 6d. *net.*

THE SURVIVAL OF MAN: A STUDY OF UNRECOGNISED HUMAN FACULTY. *Demy 8vo.* 7s. 6d. *net.*

**Lodge (Eleanor C.).** See Six Ages of European History.

**Lofthouse (W. F.),** M.A. ETHICS AND ATONEMENT. With a Frontispiece. *Demy 8vo.* 5s. *net.*

**Longfellow (H. W.).** See Little Library.

**Lorimer (George Horace).** LETTERS FROM A SELF-MADE MERCHANT TO HIS SON. *Seventeenth Edition. Cr. 8vo.* 3s. 6d.

OLD GORGON GRAHAM. *Second Edition. Cr. 8vo.* 6s.

***Lorimer (Norma).** BY THE WATERS OF EGYPT. With 16 Illustrations in Colour by BENTON FLETCHER, and 32 other Illustrations. *Demy 8vo.* 16s. *net.*

**Lover (Samuel).** See I.P.L.

**Lucas (E. V.).** THE LIFE OF CHARLES LAMB. With 28 Illustrations. *Fourth and Revised Edition in One Volume. Demy 8vo.* 7s. 6d. *net.*

A WANDERER IN HOLLAND. With 20 Illustrations in Colour by HERBERT MARSHALL, 34 Illustrations after old Dutch Masters, and a Map. *Ninth Edition. Cr. 8vo.* 6s.

A WANDERER IN LONDON. With 16 Illustrations in Colour by NELSON DAWSON, 36 other Illustrations and a Map. *Seventh Edition. Cr. 8vo.* 6s.

A WANDERER IN PARIS. With 16 Illustrations in Colour by WALTER DEXTER, and 32 from Photographs after Old Masters. *Third Edition. Cr. 8vo.* 6s.

THE OPEN ROAD: a Little Book for Wayfarers. *Fifteenth Edition. Fcap. 8vo.* 5s.; *India Paper,* 7s. 6d.

THE FRIENDLY TOWN: a Little Book for the Urbane. *Fourth Edition. Fcap. 8vo.* 5s.; *India Paper,* 7s. 6d.

FIRESIDE AND SUNSHINE. *Fifth Edition. Fcap. 8vo.* 5s.

CHARACTER AND COMEDY. *Fifth Edition. Fcap. 8vo.* 5s.

THE GENTLEST ART. A Choice of Letters by Entertaining Hands. *Fifth Edition. Fcap. 8vo.* 5s.

A SWAN AND HER FRIENDS. With 24 Illustrations. *Demy 8vo.* 12s. 6d. *net.*

HER INFINITE VARIETY: A FEMININE PORTRAIT GALLERY *Fourth Edition. Fcap. 8vo.* 5s.

LISTENER'S LURE: AN OBLIQUE NARRATION. *Sixth Edition. Fcap. 8vo.* 5s.

GOOD COMPANY: A RALLY OF MEN. *Fcap.* 8*vo.* 5*s.*
ONE DAY AND ANOTHER: A VOLUME OF ESSAYS. *Second Ed. Fcap.* 8*vo.* 5*s.*
OVER BEMERTON'S: AN EASY-GOING CHRONICLE. *Sixth Edition. Fcap.* 8*vo.* 5*s.*
See also Lamb (Charles).
**Lucian.** See Classical Translations.
**Lyde (L. W.),** M.A. See Commercial Series.
**Lydon (Noel S.).** A PRELIMINARY GEOMETRY. With numerous Diagrams. *Cr.* 8*vo.* 1*s.*
See also Junior School Books.
**Lyttelton (Hon. Mrs. A.).** WOMEN AND THEIR WORK. *Cr.* 8*vo.* 2*s.* 6*d.*
**M. (R.).** THE THOUGHTS OF LUCIA HALIDAY. With some of her Letters. Edited by R. M. *Fcap.* 8*vo.* 2*s.* 6*d. net.*
**Macaulay (Lord).** CRITICAL AND HISTORICAL ESSAYS. Edited by F. C. MONTAGUE, M.A. *Three Volumes. Cr.* 8*vo.* 18*s.*
**M'Allen (J. E. B.),** M.A. See Commercial Series.
**McCabe (Joseph)** (formerly Very Rev. F. ANTONY, O.S.F.). THE DECAY OF THE CHURCH OF ROME. *Second Edition. Demy* 8*vo.* 7*s.* 6*d. net.*
**MacCunn (Florence A.).** MARY STUART. With 44 Illustrations, in cluding a Frontispiece in Photogravure. *New and Cheaper Edition. Large Cr.* 8*vo.* 6*s.*
See also Leaders of Religion.
**McDermott (E. R.).** See Books on Business.
**McDougall (William),** M.A. (Oxon., M.B. (Cantab.). AN INTRODUCTION TO SOCIAL PSYCHOLOGY. *Second Ed. Cr.* 8*vo.* 5*s. net.*
**M'Dowall (A. S.).** See Oxford Biographies.
**MacFie (Ronald C.),** M.A., M.B. See New Library of Medicine.
**Mackay (A. M.),** B.A. See Churchman's Library.
**Mackenzie (W. Leslie),** M.A., M.D., D.P.H., etc. THE HEALTH OF THE SCHOOL CHILD. *Cr.* 8*vo.* 2*s.* 6*d.*
**Macklin (Herbert W.),** M.A. See Antiquary's Books.
**M'Neile (A. H.),** B.D. See Westminster Commentaries.
**'Mdlle Mori' (Author of).** ST. CATHERINE OF SIENA AND HER TIMES. With 28 Illustrations. *Second Edition. Demy* 8*vo.* 7*s.* 6*d. net.*
**Maeterlinck (Maurice).** THE BLUE BIRD: A FAIRY PLAY IN FIVE ACTS. Translated by ALEXANDER TEIXERA DE MATTOS. *Second Edition. Fcap.* 8*vo. Deckle Edges.* 3*s.* 6*d. net.*
**Magnus (Laurie),** M.A. A PRIMER OF WORDSWORTH. *Cr.* 8*vo.* 2*s.* 6*d.*
**Mahaffy (J. P.),** Litt.D. A HISTORY OF THE EGYPT OF THE PTOLEMIES. With 79 Illustrations. *Cr.* 8*vo.* 6*s.*
**Maitland (F. W.),** M.A., LL.D. ROMAN CANON LAW IN THE CHURCH OF ENGLAND. *Royal* 8*vo.* 7*s.* 6*d.*
**Major (H.),** B.A., B.Sc. A HEALTH AND TEMPERANCE READER. *Cr.* 8*vo.* 1*s.*
**Malden (H. E.),** M.A. ENGLISH RECORDS. A Companion to the History of England. *Cr.* 8*vo.* 3*s.* 6*d.*
THE RIGHTS AND DUTIES OF A CITIZEN. *Seventh Edition. Cr.* 8*vo.* 1*s.* 6*d.*
See also School Histories.
**Marchant (E. C.),** M.A., Fellow of Peterhouse, Cambridge. A GREEK ANTHOLOGY *Second Edition. Cr.* 8*vo.* 3*s.* 6*d.*
See also Cook (A. M.).
**Marett (R. R.),** M.A., Fellow and Tutor of Exeter College, Oxford. THE THRESHOLD OF RELIGION. *Cr.* 8*vo.* 3*s.* 6*d net.*
**Marks (Jeannette),** M.A. ENGLISH PASTORAL DRAMA from the Restoration to the date of the publication of the 'Lyrical Ballads' (1660-1798). *Cr.* 8*vo.* 5*s. net.*
**Marr (J. E.),** F.R.S. Fellow of St John's College, Cambridge. THE SCIENTIFIC STUDY OF SCENERY. *Third Edition.* Revised. Illustrated. *Cr.* 8*vo.* 6*s.*
AGRICULTURAL GEOLOGY. Illustrated. *Cr.* 8*vo.* 6*s.*
**Marriott (Charles).** A SPANISH HOLIDAY. With 8 Illustrations by A. M. FOWERAKER, R.B.A., and 22 other Illustrations. *Demy* 8*vo.* 7*s.* 6*d. net.*
**Marriott (J. A. R.),** M.A. THE LIFE AND TIMES OF LORD FALKLAND. With 23 Illustrations. *Second Edition. Demy* 8*vo.* 7*s.* 6*d. net.*
See also Six Ages of European History.
**Marvell (Andrew).** See Little Library.
**Masefield (John).** SEA LIFE IN NELSON'S TIME. With 16 Illustrations. *Cr.* 8*vo.* 3*s.* 6*d. net.*
ON THE SPANISH MAIN: or, SOME ENGLISH FORAYS IN THE ISTHMUS OF DARIEN. With 22 Illustrations and a Map. *Demy* 8*vo.* 10*s.* 6*d. net.*
A SAILOR'S GARLAND. Selected and Edited by. *Second Ed. Cr.* 8*vo.* 3*s.* 6*d. net.*
AN ENGLISH PROSE MISCELLANY. Selected and Edited by. *Cr.* 8*vo.* 6*s.*
**Maskell (A.).** See Connoisseur's Library.
**Mason (A. J.),** D.D. See Leaders of Religion.
**Masterman (C. F. G.),** M.A., M.P. TENNYSON AS A RELIGIOUS TEACHER. *Cr.* 8*vo.* 6*s.*
THE CONDITION OF ENGLAND. *Third Edition. Cr.* 8*vo.* 6*s.*
**Masterman (J. H. B.),** M.A. See Six Ages of European History.
**Matheson (E. F.).** COUNSELS OF LIFE. *Fcap.* 8*vo.* 2*s.* 6*d. net.*
**Maude (J. H.),** M.A. See Handbooks of English Church History.
**May (Phil).** THE PHIL MAY ALBUM. *Second Edition.* 4*to.* 1*s. net.*
**Mayne (Ethel Colburn).** ENCHANTERS OF MEN. With 24 Illustrations. *Demy* 8*vo.* 10*s.* 6*d. net.*

**Meakin (Annette M. B.)**, Fellow of the Anthropological Institute. WOMAN IN TRANSITION. *Cr. 8vo.* 6*s.*
GALICIA: THE SWITZERLAND OF SPAIN. With 105 Illustrations and a Map. *Demy 8vo.* 12*s.* 6*d. net.*
***Medley (D. J.)**, M.A., Professor of History in the University of Glasgow. ORIGINAL ILLUSTRATIONS OF ENGLISH CONSTITUTIONAL HISTORY, COMPRISING A SELECTED NUMBER OF THE CHIEF CHARTERS AND STATUTES. *Cr. 8vo.* 7*s.* 6*d. net.*
**Mellows (Emma S.)**. A SHORT STORY OF ENGLISH LITERATURE. *Cr. 8vo.* 3*s.* 6*d.*
**Mérimee (P.)**. See Simplified French Texts.
**Methuen (A. M. S.)**, M.A. THE TRAGEDY OF SOUTH AFRICA. *Cr. 8vo.* 2*s. net.* *Also Cr. 8vo.* 3*d. net.*
ENGLAND'S RUIN: DISCUSSED IN FOURTEEN LETTERS TO A PROTECTIONIST. *Ninth Edition. Cr. 8vo.* 3*d. net.*
**Meynell (Everard)**. COROT AND HIS FRIENDS. With 28 Illustrations. *Demy 8vo* 10*s.* 6*d. net.*
**Miles (Eustace)**, M.A. LIFE AFTER LIFE: OR, THE THEORY OF REINCARNATION. *Cr. 8vo.* 2*s.* 6*d. net.*
THE POWER OF CONCENTRATION: HOW TO ACQUIRE IT. *Third Edition. Cr. 8vo.* 3*s.* 6*d. net.*
**Millais (J. G.)**. THE LIFE AND LETTERS OF SIR JOHN EVERETT MILLAIS, President of the Royal Academy. With many Illustrations, of which 2 are in Photogravure. *New Edition. Demy 8vo.* 7*s.* 6*d. net.*
See also Little Galleries.
**Millin (G. F.)**. PICTORIAL GARDENING. With 21 Illustrations. *Crown 8vo.* 3*s.* 6*d. net.*
**Millis (C. T.)**, M.I.M.E. See Textbooks of Technology.
**Milne (J. G.)**, M.A. A HISTORY OF EGYPT UNDER ROMAN RULE. With 143 Illustrations. *Cr. 8vo.* 6*s.*
**Milton (John)**. A DAY BOOK OF MILTON. Edited by R. F. TOWNDROW. *Fcap. 8vo.* 2*s.* 6*d. net.*
See also Little Library and Standard Library.
**Minchin (H. C.)**, M.A. See Peel (R.).
**Mitchell (P. Chalmers)**, M.A. OUTLINES OF BIOLOGY. With 74 Illustrations. *Second Edition. Cr. 8vo.* 6*s.*
**Mitton (G. E.)**. JANE AUSTEN AND HER TIMES. With 21 Illustrations. *Second and Cheaper Edition. Large Cr. 8vo.* 6*s.*
**Moffat (Mary M.)**. QUEEN LOUISA OF PRUSSIA. With 20 Illustrations. *Fourth Edition. Crown 8vo.* 6*s.*
**Moil (A.)**. See Books on Business.
**Moir (D. M.)**. See Little Library.
**Molinos (Dr. Michael de)**. See Library of Devotion.
**Money (L. G. Chiozza)**, M.P. RICHES AND POVERTY. *Eighth Edition Demy 8vo.* 5*s. net.* Also *Cr. 8vo.* 1*s. net.*
**Montagu (Henry)**, Earl of Manchester. See Library of Devotion.
**Montaigne.** A DAY BOOK OF. Edited by C. F. POND. *Fcap. 8vo.* 2*s.* 6*d. net.*
**Montgomery (H. B.)** THE EMPIRE OF THE EAST. With a Frontispiece in Colour and 18 other Illustrations. *Second Edition. Demy 8vo.* 7*s.* 6*d. net.*
**Montmorency (J. E. G. de)**, B.A., LL.B. THOMAS A KEMPIS, HIS AGE AND BOOK. With 22 Illustrations. *Second Edition. Demy 8vo.* 7*s.* 6*d. net.*
**Moore (H. E.)**. BACK TO THE LAND. *Cr. 8vo.* 2*s.* 6*d.*
**Moore (T. Sturge)**. ART AND LIFE. With 88 Illustrations. *Cr. 8vo.* 5*s. net.*
**Moorhouse (E. Hallam)**. NELSON'S LADY HAMILTON. With 51 Portraits. *Second Edition. Demy 8vo.* 7*s.* 6*d. net.*
**Moran (Clarence G.)**. See Books on Business.
**More (Sir Thomas)**. See Standard Library.
**Morfill (W. R.)**, Oriel College, Oxford. A HISTORY OF RUSSIA FROM PETER THE GREAT TO ALEXANDER II. With 12 Maps and Plans. *Cr. 8vo.* 3*s.* 6*d.*
**Morich (R. J.)**. See School Examination Series.
**Morley (Margaret W.)**, Founded on. THE BEE PEOPLE. With 74 Illustrations. *Sq. Crown 8vo.* 2*s.* 6*d.*
LITTLE MITCHELL: THE STORY OF A MOUNTAIN SQUIRREL TOLD BY HIMSELF. With 26 Illustrations. *Sq. Cr. 8vo.* 2*s.* 6*d.*
**Morris (J.)**. THE MAKERS OF JAPAN. With 24 Illustrations. *Demy 8vo.* 12*s.* 6*d. net.*
**Morris (Joseph E.)**. See Little Guides.
**Morton (A. Anderson)**. See Brodrick (M.).
**Moule (H. C. G.)**, D.D., Lord Bishop of Durham. See Leaders of Religion.
**Muir (M. M. Pattison)**, M.A. THE CHEMISTRY OF FIRE. Illustrated. *Cr. 8vo.* 2*s.* 6*d.*
**Mundella (V. A.)**, M.A. See Dunn (J. T.).
**Munro (R.)**, M.A., LL.D. See Antiquary's Books.
**Musset (Alfred de)**. See Simplified French Text.
**Myers (A. Wallis)**, THE COMPLETE LAWN TENNIS PLAYER. With 90 Illustrations. *Second Edition. Demy 8vo.* 10*s.* 6*d. net.*
**Naval Officer (A)**. See I. P. L.
**Newman (Ernest)**. See New Library of Music.
**Newman (George)**, M.D., D.P.H., F.R.S.E. See New Library of Medicine.
**Newman (J. H.) and others.** See Library of Devotion.
**Newsholme (Arthur)**, M.D., F.R.C.P. See New Library of Medicine.
**Nichols (Bowyer)**. See Little Library.
**Nicklin (T.)**, M.A. EXAMINATION PAPERS IN THUCYDIDES. *Cr. 8vo.* 2*s.*
**Nimrod.** See I. P. L.
**Norgate (G. Le Grys)**. THE LIFE OF

SIR WALTER SCOTT. With 53 Illustrations by JENNY WYLIE. *Demy 8vo. 7s. 6d. net.*

**Norway (A. H.).** NAPLES. PAST AND PRESENT. With 25 Coloured Illustrations by MAURICE GREIFFENHAGEN. *Third Edition. Cr. 8vo. 6s.*

**Novalis.** THE DISCIPLES AT SAÏS AND OTHER FRAGMENTS. Edited by Miss UNA BIRCH. *Fcap. 8vo. 3s. 6d. net.*

**Officer (An).** See I. P. L.

**Oldfield (W. J.),** M.A., Prebendary of Lincoln. A PRIMER OF RELIGION. BASED ON THE CATECHISM OF THE CHURCH OF ENGLAND. *Crown 8vo. 2s. 6d.*

**Oldham (F. M.),** B.A. See Textbooks of Science.

**Oliphant (Mrs.).** See Leaders of Religion.

**Oliver, Thomas,** M.D. See New Library of Medicine.

**Oman (C. W. C.),** M.A., Fellow of All Souls', Oxford. A HISTORY OF THE ART OF WAR IN THE MIDDLE AGES. Illustrated. *Demy 8vo. 10s. 6d. net.*

ENGLAND BEFORE THE CONQUEST. With Maps. *Demy 8vo. 10s. 6d. net.*

**Oppé (A. P.).** See Classics of Art.

**Ottley (R. L.),** D.D. See Handbooks of Theology and Leaders of Religion.

**Overton (J. H.).** See Leaders of Religion.

**Owen (Douglas).** See Books on Business.

**Oxford (M. N.),** of Guy's Hospital. A HANDBOOK OF NURSING. *Fifth Edition. Cr. 8vo. 3s. 6d.*

**Pakes (W. C. C.).** THE SCIENCE OF HYGIENE. Illustrated. *Demy 8vo. 15s.*

**Parker (Eric).** A BOOK OF THE ZOO; BY DAY AND NIGHT. With 24 Illustrations from Photographs by HENRY IRVING. *Cr. 8vo. 6s.*

**Parker (Gilbert),** M.P. A LOVER'S DIARY. *Fcap. 8vo. 5s.*

**Parkes (A. K.).** SMALL LESSONS ON GREAT TRUTHS. *Fcap. 8vo. 1s. 6d.*

**Parkinson (John).** PARADISI IN SOLE PARADISUS TERRESTRIS, OR A GARDEN OF ALL SORTS OF PLEASANT FLOWERS. *Folio. £3, 3s. net.*

**Parsons (Mrs. C.).** GARRICK AND HIS CIRCLE. With 36 Illustrations. *Second Edition. Demy 8vo. 12s. 6d. net.*

THE INCOMPARABLE SIDDONS. With 20 Illustrations. *Demy 8vo. 12s. 6d. net.*

**Pascal.** See Library of Devotion.

**Paston (George).** SOCIAL CARICATURE IN THE EIGHTEENTH CENTURY. With 214 Illustrations. *Imperial Quarto. £2, 12s. 6d. net.*

LADY MARY WORTLEY MONTAGU AND HER TIMES With 24 Illustrations. *Second Edition. Demy 8vo. 15s. net.*

See also Little Books on Art and I.P.L.

**Patmore (K. A.).** THE COURT OF LOUIS XIII. With 16 Illustrations. *Second Edition. Demy 8vo. 10s. 6d. net.*

**Patterson (A. H.).** NOTES OF AN EAST COAST NATURALIST. Illustrated in Colour by F. SOUTHGATE, R.B.A. *Second Edition. Cr. 8vo. 6s.*

NATURE IN EASTERN NORFOLK. With 12 Illustrations in Colour by FRANK SOUTHGATE, R.B.A. *Second Edition. Cr. 8vo. 6s.*

WILD LIFE ON A NORFOLK ESTUARY. With 40 Illustrations by the Author, and a Prefatory Note by Her Grace the DUCHESS OF BEDFORD. *Demy 8vo. 10s. 6d. net.*

MAN AND NATURE ON TIDAL WATERS. With Illustrations by the Author. *Cr. 8vo. 6s.*

**Peacock (Netta).** See Little Books on Art.

**Peake (C. M. A.),** F.R.H.S. A CONCISE HANDBOOK OF GARDEN ANNUAL AND BIENNIAL PLANTS. With 24 Illustrations. *Fcap. 8vo. 3s. 6d. net.*

**Peel (Robert),** and **Minchin (H. C.),** M.A. OXFORD. With 100 Illustrations in Colour. *Cr. 8vo. 6s.*

**Peel (Sidney),** late Fellow of Trinity College, Oxford, and Secretary to the Royal Commission on the Licensing Laws. PRACTICAL LICENSING REFORM. *Second Edition. Cr. 8vo. 1s. 6d.*

**Pentin (Herbert),** M.A. See Library of Devotion.

**Petrie (W. M. Flinders),** D.C.L., LL.D., Professor of Egyptology at University College. A HISTORY OF EGYPT. Fully Illustrated. *In six volumes. Cr. 8vo. 6s. each.*

VOL. I. FROM THE EARLIEST KINGS TO XVITH DYNASTY. *Sixth Edition.*

VOL. II. THE XVIITH AND XVIIITH DYNASTIES. *Fourth Edition.*

VOL. III. XIXTH TO XXXTH DYNASTIES.

VOL. IV. EGYPT UNDER THE PTOLEMAIC DYNASTY. J. P. MAHAFFY, Litt.D.

VOL. V. EGYPT UNDER ROMAN RULE. J. G. MILNE, M.A.

VOL. VI. EGYPT IN THE MIDDLE AGES. STANLEY LANE-POOLE, M.A.

RELIGION AND CONSCIENCE IN ANCIENT EGYPT. Lectures delivered at University College, London. Illustrated. *Cr. 8vo. 2s. 6d.*

SYRIA AND EGYPT, FROM THE TELL EL AMARNA LETTERS. *Cr. 8vo. 2s. 6d.*

EGYPTIAN TALES. Translated from the Papyri. First Series, IVth to XIIth Dynasty. Edited by W. M. FLINDERS PETRIE. Illustrated by TRISTRAM ELLIS. *Second Edition. Cr. 8vo. 3s. 6d.*

EGYPTIAN TALES. Translated from the Papyri. Second Series. XVIIIth to XIXth Dynasty. Illustrated by TRISTRAM ELLIS. *Crown 8vo. 3s. 6d.*

EGYPTIAN DECORATIVE ART. A Course of Lectures delivered at the Royal Institution. Illustrated. *Cr. 8vo. 3s. 6d.*

**Phillips (W. A.).** See Oxford Biographies.

**Phillpotts (Eden).** MY DEVON YEAR. With 38 Illustrations by J. LEY PETHYBRIDGE. *Second and Cheaper Edition. Large Cr. 8vo. 6s.*

UP-ALONG AND DOWN-ALONG Illustrated by CLAUDE SHEPPERSON. *Cr. 4to. 5s. net.*

**Phythian (J. Ernest).** TREES IN NATURE, MYTH, AND ART. With 24 Illustrations. *Crown 8vo.* 6s.
**Plarr (Victor G.).** M.A. See School Histories.
**Plato.** See Standard Library.
**Plautus.** THE CAPTIVI. Edited, with an Introduction, Textual Notes, and a Commentary, by W. M. LINDSAY, Fellow of Jesus College, Oxford. *Demy 8vo.* 10s. 6d. *net.*
**Plowden-Wardlaw (J. T.),** B.A. See School Examination Series.
**Podmore (Frank).** MODERN SPIRITUALISM. *Two Volumes. Demy 8vo.* 21s. *net.*
MESMERISM AND CHRISTIAN SCIENCE: A Short History of Mental Healing. *Demy 8vo.* 10s. 6d. *net.*
**Pollard (Alice).** See Little Books on Art.
**Pollard (Alfred W.).** THE SHAKESPEARE FOLIOS AND QUARTOS. With numerous Facsimiles. *Folio. One Guinea net.*
**Pollard (Eliza F.).** See Little Books on Art.
**Pollock (David),** M.I.N.A. See Books on Business.
**Potter (M. C.),** M.A., F.L.S. AN ELEMENTARY TEXT-BOOK OF AGRICULTURAL BOTANY. Illustrated. *Third Edition. Cr. 8vo.* 4s. 6d.
**Powell (A. E.).** LIEUTENANT ROYAL ENGINEERS. *Crown 8vo.* 3s. 6d. *net.*
**Power (J. O'Connor).** THE MAKING OF AN ORATOR. *Cr. 8vo.* 6s.
**Price (Eleanor C.).** A PRINCESS OF THE OLD WORLD. With 21 Illustrations. *Demy 8vo.* 12s. 6d. *net.*
**Price (L. L.),** M.A., Fellow of Oriel College, Oxon. A HISTORY OF ENGLISH POLITICAL ECONOMY FROM ADAM SMITH TO ARNOLD TOYNBEE. *Fifth Edition. Cr. 8vo.* 2s. 6d.
**Protheroe (Ernest).** THE DOMINION OF MAN. GEOGRAPHY IN ITS HUMAN ASPECT. With 32 full-page Illustrations. *Second Edition. Cr. 8vo.* 2s.
**Psellus.** See Byzantine Texts.
**Pullen-Burry (B.).** IN A GERMAN COLONY; or, FOUR WEEKS IN NEW BRITAIN. With 8 Illustrations and 2 Maps. *Cr. 8vo.* 5s. *net.*
**Pycraft (W. P.).** BIRD LIFE. With 2 Illustrations in Colour by G. E. LODGE, and many from Drawings and Photographs. *Demy 8vo.* 10s. 6d. *net.*
**'Q' (A. T. Quiller Couch).** THE GOLDEN POMP. A PROCESSION OF ENGLISH LYRICS FROM SURREY TO SHIRLEY. *Second and Cheaper Edition. Cr. 8vo.* 2s. 6d. *net.*
**G. R. and E. S.** MR. WOODHOUSE'S CORRESPONDENCE. *Cr. 8vo.* 6s.
Also published in a Colonial Edition.
**Rackham (R. B.),** M.A. See Westminster Commentaries.
**Ragg (Laura M.).** THE WOMEN ARTISTS OF BOLOGNA. With 20 Illustrations. *Demy 8vo.* 7s. 6d. *net.*
**Ragg (Lonsdale).** B.D., Oxon. DANTE AND HIS ITALY. With 32 Illustrations. *Demy 8vo.* 12s. 6d. *net.*
**Rahtz (F. J.),** M.A., B.Sc. HIGHER ENGLISH. *Fourth Edition. Cr. 8vo.* 3s. 6d.
JUNIOR ENGLISH. *Fourth Edition. Cr. 8vo.* 1s. 6d.
**Randolph (B. W.),** D.D. See Library of Devotion.
**Rannie (D. W.),** M.A. A STUDENT'S HISTORY OF SCOTLAND. *Cr. 8vo.* 3s. 6d.
WORDSWORTH AND HIS CIRCLE. With 20 Illustrations. *Demy 8vo.* 12s. 6d *net.*
**Rashdall (Hastings),** M.A., Fellow and Tutor of New College, Oxford. DOCTRINE AND DEVELOPMENT. *Cr. 8vo.* 6s.
**Raven (J. J.),** D.D., F.S.A. See Antiquary's Books.
**Raven-Hill (L.).** See Llewellyn (Owen).
**Rawlings (Gertrude Burford).** COINS AND HOW TO KNOW THEM. With 206 Illustrations. *Second Edition. Cr. 8vo.* 6s.
**Rawstorne (Lawrence, Esq.).** See I.P.L.
**Raymond (Walter).** See School Histories.
**Rea (Lilian).** THE LIFE AND TIMES OF MARIE MADELEINE COUNTESS OF LA FAYETTE. With 20 Illustrations. *Demy 8vo.* 10s. 6d. *net.*
**Read (C. Stanford),** M.B. (Lond.), M.R.C.S., L.R.C.P. FADS AND FEEDING. *Cr. 8vo.* 2s. 6d.
**Real Paddy (A).** See I.P.L.
**Reason (W.),** M.A. UNIVERSITY AND SOCIAL SETTLEMENTS. Edited by *Cr. 8vo.* 2s. 6d.
**Redpath (H. A.),** M.A., D.Litt. See Westminster Commentaries.
**Rees (J. D.),** C.I.E., M.P. THE REAL INDIA. *Second Edition. Demy 8vo.* 10s. 6d. *net.*
**Reich (Emil),** Doctor Juris. WOMAN THROUGH THE AGES. With 36 Illustrations. *Two Volumes. Demy 8vo.* 21s. *net.*
**Reynolds (Sir Joshua).** See Little Galleries
**Rhodes (W. E.).** See School Histories.
**Ricketts (Charles).** See Classics of Art.
**Richardson (Charles).** THE COMPLETE FOXHUNTER. With 46 Illustrations, of which 4 are in Colour. *Second Edition. Demy 8vo.* 12s. 6d. *net.*
**Richmond (Wilfrid),** Chaplain of Lincoln's Inn. THE CREED IN THE EPISTLES. *Cr. 8vo.* 2s. 6d. *net.*
**Riehl (W. H.).** See Simplified German Texts.
**Roberts (M. E.).** See Channer (C. C.).
**Robertson (A.),** D.D., Lord Bishop of Exeter. REGNUM DEI. (The Bampton Lectures of 1901). *A New and Cheaper Edition. Demy 8vo.* 7s. 6d. *net.*
**Robertson (C. Grant).** M.A., Fellow of All Souls' College, Oxford. SELECT STATUTES, CASES, AND CONSTITUTIONAL DOCUMENTS, 1660-1832. *Demy 8vo.* 10s. 6d. *net.*

**Robertson (C. Grant)** and **Bartholomew (J. G.)**, F.R.S.E., F.R.G.S. A HISTORICAL AND MODERN ATLAS OF THE BRITISH EMPIRE. *Demy Quarto.* 4s. 6d. *net.*

**Robertson (Sir G. S.)**, K.C.S.I. CHITRAL: THE STORY OF A MINOR SIEGE. With 8 Illustrations. *Third Edition. Demy 8vo.* 10s. 6d. *net.*

**Robinson (Cecilia).** THE MINISTRY OF DEACONESSES. With an Introduction by the late Archbishop of Canterbury. *Cr. 8vo.* 3s. 6d.

**Robinson (F. S.).** See Connoisseur's Library.

**Rochefoucauld (La).** See Little Library.

**Rodwell (G.)**, B.A. NEW TESTAMENT GREEK. A Course for Beginners. With a Preface by WALTER LOCK, D.D., Warden of Keble College. *Fcap. 8vo.* 3s. 6d.

**Roe (Fred).** OLD OAK FURNITURE. With many Illustrations by the Author, including a frontispiece in colour. *Second Edition. Demy 8vo.* 10s. 6d. *net.*

**Rogers (A. G. L.)**, M.A. See Books on Business.

**Roland.** See Simplified French Texts.

**Romney (George).** See Little Galleries.

**Roscoe (E. S.).** See Little Guides.

**Rose (Edward).** THE ROSE READER. Illustrated. *Cr. 8vo.* 2s. 6d. *Also in 4 Parts. Parts I. and II.* 6d. *each; Part III.* 8d.; *Part IV.* 10d.

**Rose (G. H.).** See **Hey (H.)** and **Baring-Gould (S).**

**Rowntree (Joshua).** THE IMPERIAL DRUG TRADE. A RE-STATEMENT OF THE OPIUM QUESTION. *Third Edition Revised. Cr. 8vo.* 2s. *net.*

**Royde-Smith (N. G.).** THE PILLOW BOOK: A GARNER OF MANY MOODS. Collected by. *Second Edition. Cr. 8vo.* 4s. 6d. *net.*

POETS OF OUR DAY. Selected, with an Introduction, by. *Fcap. 8vo.* 5s.

**Rubie (A. E.)**, D.D. See Junior School Books.

**Rumbold (The Right Hon. Sir Horace).** Bart., G. C. B., G. C. M. G. THE AUSTRIAN COURT IN THE NINETEENTH CENTURY. With 16 Illustrations. *Second Ed. Demy 8vo.* 18s. *net.*

**Russell (Archibald G. B.).** See Blake (William.)

**Russell (W. Clark).** THE LIFE OF ADMIRAL LORD COLLINGWOOD. With 12 Illustrations by F. BRANGWYN. *Fourth Edition. Cr. 8vo.* 6s.

**Ryley (M. Beresford).** QUEENS OF THE RENAISSANCE. With 24 Illustrations. *Demy 8vo.* 10s. 6d. *net.*

**Sainsbury (Harrington)**, M.D., F.R.C.P. PRINCIPIA THERAPEUTICA. *Demy 8vo.* 7s. 6d. *net.*
See also New Library of Medicine.

**St. Anselm.** See Library of Devotion.

**St. Augustine.** See Library of Devotion.

**St. Bernard.** See Library of Devotion.

**St. Cyres (Viscount).** See Oxford Biographies.

**St. Francis of Assisi.** THE LITTLE FLOWERS OF THE GLORIOUS MESSER, AND OF HIS FRIARS. Done into English, with Notes by WILLIAM HEYWOOD. With 40 Illustrations from Italian Painters. *Demy 8vo.* 5s. *net.*
See also Library of Devotion and Standard Library.

**St. Francis de Sales.** See Library of Devotion.

**St. James.** See Churchman's Bible and Westminster Commentaries.

**St. Luke.** See Junior School Books.

**St. Mark.** See Junior School Books and Churchman's Bible.

**St. Matthew.** See Junior School Books.

**St. Paul.** SECOND AND THIRD EPISTLES OF PAUL THE APOSTLE TO THE CORINTHIANS. Edited by JAMES HOUGHTON KENNEDY, D.D., Assistant Lecturer in Divinity in the University of Dublin. With Introduction, Dissertations, and Notes by J. SCHMITT. *Cr. 8vo.* 6s. See also Churchman's Bible and Westminster Commentaries.

**'Saki' (H. Munro).** REGINALD. *Second Edition. Fcap. 8vo.* 2s. 6d. *net.*

**Salmon (A. L.).** See Little Guides.

**Sanders (Lloyd).** THE HOLLAND HOUSE CIRCLE. With 24 Illustrations. *Second Edition. Demy 8vo.* 12s. 6d. *net.*

**Sathas (C.).** See Byzantine Texts.

**Schmitt (John).** See Byzantine Texts.

**Schofield (A. T.)**, M.D., Hon. Phys. Freidenham Hospital. See New Library of Medicine.

**Scudamore (Cyril).** See Little Guides.

**Scupoli (Dom. L.).** See Library of Devotion.

**Ségur (Madame de).** See Simplified French Texts.

**Sélincourt (E. de.)** See Keats (John).

**Sélincourt (Hugh de).** GREAT RALEGH. With 16 Illustrations. *Demy 8vo.* 10s. 6d. *net.*

**Sells (V. P.)**, M.A. THE MECHANICS OF DAILY LIFE. Illustrated. *Cr. 8vo.* 2s. 6d.

**Selous (Edmund).** TOMMY SMITH'S ANIMALS. Illustrated by G. W. ORD. *Eleventh Edition. Fcap. 8vo.* 2s. 6d.
*School Edition,* 1s. 6d.

TOMMY SMITH'S OTHER ANIMALS. Illustrated by AUGUSTA GUEST. *Fifth Edition. Fcap. 8vo.* 2s 6d.
*School Edition,* 1s. 6d.

**Senter (George)**, B.Sc. (Lond.), Ph.D. See Textbooks of Science.

**Shakespeare (William).**

THE FOUR FOLIOS, 1623; 1632; 1664; 1685. Each £4, 4s. *net,* or a complete set, £12, 12s. *net.*
Folios 2, 3 and 4 are ready.

THE POEMS OF WILLIAM SHAKESPEARE. With an Introduction and Notes

by GEORGE WYNDHAM. *Demy* 8*vo. Buckram, gilt top,* 10*s.* 6*d.*
See also Arden Shakespeare, Standard Library and Little Quarto Shakespeare.
**Sharp (A.).** VICTORIAN POETS. *Cr.* 8*vo.* 2*s.* 6*d.*
**Sharp (Cecil).** See Baring-Gould (S.).
**Sharp (Elizabeth).** See Little Books on Art.
**Shedlock (J. S.)** THE PIANOFORTE SONATA. *Cr.* 8*vo.* 5*s.*
**Shelley (Percy B.).** See Standard Library.
**Sheppard (H. F.),** M.A. See Baring-Gould (S.).
**Sherwell (Arthur),** M.A. LIFE IN WEST LONDON. *Third Edition. Cr.* 8*vo.* 2*s.* 6*d.*
**Shipley (Mary E.).** AN ENGLISH CHURCH HISTORY FOR CHILDREN. With a Preface by the Bishop of Gibraltar. With Maps and Illustrations. *Cr.* 8*vo. Each part* 2*s.* 6*d. net.*
PART I.—To the Norman Conquest.
PART II.—To the Reformation.
**Sichel (Walter).** See Oxford Biographies.
**Sidgwick (Mrs. Alfred).** HOME LIFE IN GERMANY. With 16 Illustrations. *Second Edition. Demy* 8*vo.* 10*s.* 6*d. net.*
**Sime (John).** See Little Books on Art.
**Simonson (G. A.).** FRANCESCO GUARDI. With 41 Plates. *Imperial* 4*to.* £2, 2*s. net.*
**Sketchley (R. E. D.).** See Little Books on Art.
**Skipton (H. P. K.).** See Little Books on Art.
**Sladen (Douglas).** SICILY: The New Winter Resort. With over 200 Illustrations. *Second Edition. Cr.* 8*vo.* 5*s. net.*
**Smallwood (M. G.).** See Little Books on Art.
**Smedley (F. E.).** See I.P.L.
**Smith (Adam).** THE WEALTH OF NATIONS. Edited with an Introduction and numerous Notes by EDWIN CANNAN, M.A. *Two volumes. Demy* 8*vo.* 21*s. net.*
**Smith (H. Bompas),** M.A. A NEW JUNIOR ARITHMETIC. *Crown* 8*vo.* Without Answers, 2*s.* With Answers, 2*s.* 6*d.*
**Smith (H. Clifford).** See Connoisseur's Library.
**Smith (Horace and James).** See Little Library.
**Smith (R. Mudie).** THOUGHTS FOR THE DAY. Edited by. *Fcap.* 8*vo.* 3*s.* 6*d. net.*
**Smith (Nowell C.).** See Wordsworth (W).
**Smith (John Thomas).** A BOOK FOR A RAINY DAY: Or, Recollections of the Events of the Years 1766-1833. Edited by WILFRED WHITTEN. Illustrated. *Wide Demy* 8*vo.* 12*s.* 6*d. net.*
**Snell (F. J.).** A BOOK OF EXMOOR. Illustrated. *Cr.* 8*vo.* 6*s.*
**Snowden (C. E.).** A HANDY DIGEST OF BRITISH HISTORY. *Demy* 8*vo.* 4*s.* 6*d.*
**Sophocles.** See Classical Translations.
**Sornet (L. A.),** and **Acatos (M. J.)** See Junior School Books.
**Southey (R.).** ENGLISH SEAMEN Edited by DAVID HANNAY.
Vol. I. (Howard, Clifford, Hawkins, Drake, Cavendish). *Second Edition. Cr.* 8*vo.* 6*s.*
Vol. II. (Richard Hawkins, Grenville, Essex, and Raleigh). *Cr.* 8*vo.* 6*s.*
See also Standard Library.
**Souvestre (E.).** See Simplified French Texts.
**Spence (C. H.),** M.A. See School Examination Series.
**Spicer (A. Dykes),** M.A. THE PAPER TRADE. A Descriptive and Historical Survey. With Diagrams and Plans. *Demy* 8*vo.* 12*s.* 6*d. net.*
**Spooner (W. A.),** M.A. See Leaders of Religion.
**Spragge (W. Horton),** M.A. See Junior School Books.
**Staley (Edgcumbe).** THE GUILDS OF FLORENCE Illustrated. *Second Edition. Royal* 8*vo.* 16*s. net.*
**Stanbridge (J. W.),** B.D. See Library of Devotion.
**'Stancliffe.'** GOLF DO'S AND DONT'S. *Second Edition. Fcap.* 8*vo.* 1*s.*
**Stead (D. W.).** See Gallaher (D.).
**Stedman (A. M. M.),** M.A.
INITIA LATINA: Easy Lessons on Elementary Accidence. *Eleventh Edition. Fcap.* 8*vo.* 1*s.*
FIRST LATIN LESSONS. *Eleventh Edition. Cr.* 8*vo.* 2*s.*
FIRST LATIN READER. With Notes adapted to the Shorter Latin Primer and Vocabulary. *Seventh Edition.* 18*mo.* 1*s.* 6*d.*
EASY SELECTIONS FROM CÆSAR. The Helvetian War. *Fourth Edition.* 18*mo.* 1*s.*
EASY SELECTIONS FROM LIVY. The Kings of Rome. *Second Edition.* 18*mo.* 1*s.* 6*d.*
EASY LATIN PASSAGES FOR UNSEEN TRANSLATION. *Thirteenth Ed. Fcap.* 8*vo.* 1*s.* 6*d.*
EXEMPLA LATINA. First Exercises in Latin Accidence. With Vocabulary. *Fourth Edition. Cr.* 8*vo.* 1*s.*
EASY LATIN EXERCISES ON THE SYNTAX OF THE SHORTER AND REVISED LATIN PRIMER. With Vocabulary. *Thirteenth Ed. Cr.* 8*vo.* 1*s.* 6*d.* KEY, 3*s. net.*
THE LATIN COMPOUND SENTENCE: Rules and Exercises. *Second Edition. Cr.* 8*vo.* 1*s.* 6*d.* With Vocabulary. 2*s.*
NOTANDA QUAEDAM: Miscellaneous Latin Exercises on Common Rules and Idioms. *Fifth Edition. Fcap.* 8*vo.* 1*s.* 6*d.* With Vocabulary. 2*s.* KEY, 2*s. net.*
LATIN VOCABULARIES FOR REPETITION: Arranged according to Subjects. *Sixteenth Edition. Fcap.* 8*vo.* 1*s.* 6*d.*
A VOCABULARY OF LATIN IDIOMS. 18*mo. Fourth Edition.* 1*s.*

STEPS TO GREEK. *Fourth Edition.* 18*mo.* 1*s.*

A SHORTER GREEK PRIMER. *Third Edition. Cr.* 8*vo.* 1*s.* 6*d.*

EASY GREEK PASSAGES FOR UNSEEN TRANSLATION. *Fourth Edition, revised. Fcap.* 8*vo.* 1*s.* 6*d.*

GREEK VOCABULARIES FOR REPETITION. Arranged according to Subjects. *Fourth Edition. Fcap.* 8*vo.* 1*s* 6*d.*

GREEK TESTAMENT SELECTIONS. For the use of Schools. With Introduction, Notes, and Vocabulary. *Fourth Edition. Fcap.* 8*vo.* 2*s.* 6*d.*

STEPS TO FRENCH. *Ninth Edition.* 18*mo.* 8*d.*

FIRST FRENCH LESSONS. *Ninth Edition. Cr.* 8*vo.* 1*s.*

EASY FRENCH PASSAGES FOR UNSEEN TRANSLATION. *Sixth Edition. Fcap.* 8*vo.* 1*s.* 6*d.*

EASY FRENCH EXERCISES ON ELEMENTARY SYNTAX. With Vocabulary. *Fourth Edition. Cr.* 8*vo.* 2*s.* 6*d.* KEY. 3*s. net.*

FRENCH VOCABULARIES FOR REPETITION: Arranged according to Subjects. *Fourteenth Edition. Fcap.* 8*vo.* 1*s.*

See also School Examination Series.

**Steel (R. Elliott),** M.A., F.C.S. THE WORLD OF SCIENCE. With 147 Illustrations. *Second Edition. Cr.* 8*vo.* 2*s.* 6*d.*

See also School Examination Series.

**Stephenson (C.),** of the Technical College, Bradford, and **Suddards (F.)** of the Yorkshire College, Leeds. A TEXTBOOK DEALING WITH ORNAMENTAL DESIGN FOR WOVEN FABRICS. With 66 full-page Plates and numerous Diagrams in the Text. *Third Edition. Demy* 8*vo.* 7*s.* 6*d.*

**Sterne (Laurence).** See Little Library.

**Steuart (Katherine).** BY ALLAN WATER. *Second Edition. Cr.* 8*vo.* 6*s.*

RICHARD KENNOWAY AND HIS FRIENDS. A Sequel to 'By Allan Water.' *Demy* 8*vo.* 7*s.* 6*d. net.*

**Stevenson (R. L.)** THE LETTERS OF ROBERT LOUIS STEVENSON TO HIS FAMILY AND FRIENDS. Selected and Edited by SIDNEY COLVIN. *Eighth Edition.* 2 *vols. Cr.* 8*vo.* 12*s.*

VAILIMA LETTERS. With an Etched Portrait by WILLIAM STRANG. *Seventh Edition. Cr.* 8*vo. Buckram.* 6*s.*

THE LIFE OF R. L. STEVENSON. See Balfour (G.).

**Stevenson (M. I.).** FROM SARANAC TO THE MARQUESAS. Being Letters written by Mrs. M. I. STEVENSON during 1887-88. *Cr.* 8*vo.* 6*s. net.*

LETTERS FROM SAMOA, 1891-95. Edited and arranged by M. C. BALFOUR With many Illustrations. *Second Edition Cr.* 8*vo.* 6*s. net.*

**Stoddart (Anna M.).** See Oxford Biographies.

**Stokes (F. G.),** B.A. HOURS WITH RABELAIS. From the translation of SIR T. URQUHART and P. A. MOTTEUX. With a Portrait in Photogravure. *Cr.* 8*vo.* 3*s.* 6*d. net.*

**Stone (S. J.).** POEMS AND HYMNS. With a Memoir by F. G. ELLERTON, M.A. With Portrait. *Cr.* 8*vo.* 6*s.*

**Storr (Vernon F.),** M.A., Canon of Winchester. DEVELOPMENT AND DIVINE PURPOSE *Cr.* 8*vo.* 5*s. net.*

**Story (Alfred T.).** AMERICAN SHRINES IN ENGLAND. With 4 Illustrations in Colour, and 19 other Illustrations. *Crown* 8*vo.* 6*s.*

See also Little Guides.

**Straker (F.).** See Books on Business.

**Streane (A. W.),** D.D. See Churchman's Bible.

**Streatfeild (R. A.).** MODERN MUSIC AND MUSICIANS. With 24 Illustrations. *Second Ed. Demy* 8*vo.* 7*s.* 6*d. net.*

See also New Library of Music.

**Stroud (Henry),** D.Sc., M.A. ELEMENTARY PRACTICAL PHYSICS. With 115 Diagrams. *Second Edit., revised. Cr.* 8*vo.* 4*s.* 6*d.*

**Sturch (F.),** Staff Instructor to the Surrey County Council. MANUAL TRAINING DRAWING (WOODWORK). With Solutions to Examination Questions, Orthographic, Isometric and Oblique Projection. With 50 Plates and 140 Figures. *Foolscap.* 5*s. net.*

**Suddards (F.).** See Stephenson (C.).

**Surtees (R. S.).** See I.P.L.

**Sutherland (William).** OLD AGE PENSIONS IN THEORY AND PRACTICE, WITH SOME FOREIGN EXAMPLES. *Cr.* 8*vo.* 3*s.* 6*d. net.*

**Swanton (E. W.),** Member of the British Mycological Society. FUNGI AND HOW TO KNOW THEM. With 16 Coloured Plates by M. K. SPITTAL, and 32 Monotone Plates. *Cr.* 8*vo.* 5*s. net.*

**Symes (J. E.),** M.A. THE FRENCH REVOLUTION. *Second Edition. Cr.* 8*vo.* 2*s.* 6*d.*

**Sympson (E. Mansel),** M.A., M.D. See Ancient Cities.

**Tabor (Margaret E.).** THE SAINTS IN ART. With 20 Illustrations. *Fcap.* 8*vo.* 3*s.* 6*d. net.*

**Tacitus.** AGRICOLA. Edited by R. F. DAVIS, M.A. *Cr.* 8*vo.* 2*s.*

GERMANIA. By the same Editor. *Cr.* 8*vo.* 2*s.*

See also Classical Translations.

**Tallack (W.).** HOWARD LETTERS AND MEMORIES. *Demy* 8*vo.* 10*s.* 6*d. net.*

**Tatham (Frederick).** See Blake (William).

**Tauler (J.).** See Library of Devotion.

**Taylor (A. E.).** THE ELEMENTS OF METAPHYSICS. *Second Edition. Demy* 8*vo.* 10*s.* 6*d. net.*

**Taylor (F. G.),** M.A. See Commercial Series.

**Taylor (I. A.).** See Oxford Biographies.

**Taylor (John W.).** THE COMING OF THE SAINTS. With 26 Illustrations. *Demy* 8*vo.* 7*s.* 6*d. net.*

**Taylor (T. M.)**, M.A., Fellow of Gonville and Caius College, Cambridge. A CONSTITUTIONAL AND POLITICAL HISTORY OF ROME. To the Reign of Domitian. *Cr. 8vo.* 7*s.* 6*d.*

**Teasdale-Buckell (G. T.).** THE COMPLETE SHOT. With 53 Illustrations. *Third Edition. Demy 8vo.* 12*s.* 6*d. net.*

**Tennyson (Alfred, Lord).** EARLY POEMS. Edited, with Notes and an Introduction, by J. CHURTON COLLINS, M.A. *Cr. 8vo.* 6*s.*

IN MEMORIAM, MAUD, AND THE PRINCESS. Edited by J. CHURTON COLLINS, M.A. *Cr. 8vo.* 6*s.*

See also Little Library.

**Terry (C. S.).** See Oxford Biographies.

**Terry (F. J.)**, B.A. ELEMENTARY LATIN. *Cr. 8vo.* 2*s.*

TEACHER'S HANDBOOK TO ELEMENTARY LATIN. Containing the necessary supplementary matter to Pupil's edition. *Cr. 8vo.* 3*s.* 6*d. net.*

**Thackeray (W. M.).** See Little Library.

**Theobald (F. V.)**, M.A. INSECT LIFE. Illustrated. *Second Edition Revised. Cr. 8vo.* 2*s.* 6*d.*

**Thibaudeau (A. C.).** BONAPARTE AND THE CONSULATE. Translated and Edited by G. K. FORTESQUE, LL.D. With 12 Illustrations. *Demy 8vo.* 10*s.* 6*d. net.*

**Thompson (A. H.).** See Little Guides.

**Thompson (Francis).** SELECTED POEMS OF FRANCIS THOMPSON. With a Biographical Note by WILFRID MEYNELL. With a Portrait in Photogravure. *Second Ed. Fcap. 8vo.* 5*s. net.*

**Thompson (A. P.).** See Textbooks of Technology.

**Thompson (J. M.)**, Fellow and Dean of Divinity of Magdalen College, Oxford. JESUS ACCORDING TO ST. MARK. *Cr. 8vo.* 5*s. net.*

**Tileston (Mary W.).** DAILY STRENGTH FOR DAILY NEEDS. *Sixteenth Edition. Medium 16mo.* 2*s.* 6*d. net.* Also an edition in superior binding, 6*s.*

**Tompkins (H. W.)**, F.R.H.S. See Little Books on Art and Little Guides.

**Toynbee (Paget)**, M.A., D.Litt. IN THE FOOTPRINTS OF DANTE. A Treasury of Verse and Prose from the works of Dante. *Small Cr. 8vo.* 4*s.* 6*d. net.*

DANTE IN ENGLISH LITERATURE: FROM CHAUCER TO CARY. *Two vols. Demy 8vo.* 21*s. net.*

See also Oxford Biographies and Dante.

**Tozer (Basil).** THE HORSE IN HISTORY. With 25 Illustrations. *Cr. 8vo.* 6*s.*

**Tremayne (Eleanor E.).** See Romantic History.

**Trench (Herbert).** DEIRDRE WEDDED, AND OTHER POEMS. *Second and Revised Edition. Large Post 8vo.* 6*s.*

NEW POEMS. *Second Edition. Large Post 8vo.* 6*s.*

APOLLO AND THE SEAMAN. *Large Post 8vo. Paper,* 1*s.* 6*d. net; cloth,* 2*s.* 6*d. net.*

**Trevelyan (G. M.)**, Fellow of Trinity College, Cambridge. ENGLAND UNDER THE STUARTS. With Maps and Plans. *Third Edition. Demy 8vo.* 10*s.* 6*d. net.*

ENGLISH LIFE THREE HUNDRED YEARS AGO: Being the first two chapters of *England under the Stuarts.* Edited by J. TURRAL, B.A. *Cr. 8vo.* 1*s.*

**Triggs (H. Inigo)**, A.R.I.B.A. TOWN PLANNING: PAST, PRESENT, AND POSSIBLE. With 173 Illustrations. *Wide Royal 8vo.* 15*s. net.*

**Troutbeck (G. E.).** See Little Guides.

**Tyler (E. A.)**, B.A., F.C.S. See Junior School Books.

**Tyrrell-Gill (Frances).** See Little Books on Art.

**Unwin (George).** See Antiquary's Books.

**Vardon (Harry).** THE COMPLETE GOLFER. With 63 Illustrations. *Tenth Edition. Demy 8vo.* 10*s.* 6*d. net.*

**Vaughan (Henry).** See Little Library.

**Vaughan (Herbert M.)**, B.A. (Oxon.). THE LAST OF THE ROYAL STUARTS, HENRY STUART, CARDINAL, DUKE OF YORK. With 20 Illustrations. *Second Edition. Demy 8vo.* 10*s.* 6*d. net.*

THE MEDICI POPES (LEO X. AND CLEMENT VII. With 20 Illustrations. *Demy 8vo.* 15*s. net.*

THE NAPLES RIVIERA. With 25 Illustrations in Colour by MAURICE GREIFFENHAGEN. *Second Edition. Cr. 8vo.* 6*s.*

**Vernon (Hon. W. Warren)**, M.A. READINGS ON THE INFERNO OF DANTE. With an Introduction by the Rev. Dr. MOORE. *In Two Volumes. Second Edition. Cr. 8vo.* 15*s. net.*

READINGS ON THE PURGATORIO OF DANTE. With an Introduction by the late DEAN CHURCH. *In Two Volumes. Third Edition. Cr. 8vo.* 15*s. net.*

READINGS ON THE PARADISO OF DANTE. With an Introduction by the BISHOP OF RIPON. *In Two Volumes. Second Edition. Cr. 8vo.* 15*s. net.*

**Vincent (J. E.).** THROUGH EAST ANGLIA IN A MOTOR CAR. With 16 Illustrations in Colour by FRANK SOUTHGATE, R.B.A., and a Map. *Cr. 8vo.* 6*s.*

**Voegelin (A.)**, M.A. See Junior Examination Series.

**Waddell (Col. L. A.)**, LL.D., C.B. LHASA AND ITS MYSTERIES. With a Record of the Expedition of 1903–1904. With 155 Illustrations and Maps. *Third and Cheaper Edition. Medium 8vo.* 7*s.* 6*d. net.*

**Wade (G. W.)**, D.D. OLD TESTAMENT HISTORY. With Maps. *Sixth Edition. Cr. 8vo.* 6*s.*

**Wade (G. W.)**, D.D., and **Wade (J. H.)**, M.A. See Little Guides.

**Wagner (Richard).** RICHARD WAGNER'S MUSIC DRAMAS: Interpretations, embodying Wagner's own explanations. By ALICE LEIGHTON CLEATHER and BASIL CRUMP. *In Three Volumes. Fcap 8vo.* 2*s.* 6*d. each.*

VOL. I.—THE RING OF THE NIBELUNG. *Third Edition.*
VOL. II.—PARSIFAL, LOHENGRIN and THE HOLY GRAIL.
VOL. III.—TRISTAN AND ISOLDE.

**Waineman (Paul).** A SUMMER TOUR IN FINLAND. With 16 Illustrations in Colour by ALEXANDER FEDERLEY, 16 other Illustrations and a Map. *Demy 8vo.* 10s. 6d. *net.*

**Walkley (A. B.).** DRAMA AND LIFE. *Cr. 8vo.* 6s.

**Wall (J. C.).** See Antiquary's Books.

**Wallace-Hadrill (F.),** Second Master at Herne Bay College. REVISION NOTES ON ENGLISH HISTORY. *Cr. 8vo.* 1s.

**Walters (H. B.).** See Little Books on Art and Classics of Art.

**Walton (F. W.),** M.A. See School Histories.

**Walton (Izaak) and Cotton (Charles).** See I.P.L. and Little Library.

**Waterhouse (Elizabeth).** WITH THE SIMPLE-HEARTED: Little Homilies to Women in Country Places. *Second Edition. Small Pott 8vo.* 2s. *net.*

COMPANIONS OF THE WAY. Being Selections for Morning and Evening Reading. Chosen and arranged by ELIZABETH WATERHOUSE. *Large Cr. 8vo.* 5s. *net.*

THOUGHTS OF A TERTIARY. *Pott 8vo.* 1s. *net.*

See also Little Library.

**Watt (Francis).** See Henderson (T. F.).

**Weatherhead (T. C.),** M.A. EXAMINATION PAPERS IN HORACE. *Cr. 8vo.* 2s.

See also Junior Examination Series.

**Webb (George W.),** B.A. A SYSTEMATIC GEOGRAPHY OF THE BRITISH ISLES. With Maps and Diagrams. *Cr. 8vo.* 1s.

**Webber (F. C.).** See Textbooks of Technology.

***Weigall (Arthur E. P.).** A GUIDE TO THE ANTIQUITIES OF UPPER EGYPT: From Abydos to the Sudan Frontier. With 67 Maps, and Plans. *Cr. 8vo.* 7s. 6d. *net.*

**Weir (Archibald),** M.A. AN INTRODUCTION TO THE HISTORY OF MODERN EUROPE. *Cr. 8vo.* 6s.

**Welch (Catharine).** THE LITTLE DAUPHIN. With 16 Illustrations. *Cr. 8vo.* 6s.

**Wells (Sidney H.)** See Textbooks of Science.

**Wells (J.),** M.A., Fellow and Tutor of Wadham College. OXFORD AND OXFORD LIFE. *Third Edition. Cr. 8vo.* 3s. 6d.

A SHORT HISTORY OF ROME. *Ninth Edition.* With 3 Maps. *Cr. 8vo.* 3s. 6d.

See also Little Guides.

**Wesley (John).** See Library of Devotion.

**Westell (W. Percival).** THE YOUNG NATURALIST. A GUIDE TO BRITISH ANIMAL LIFE With 8 Coloured Plates by C. F. NEWALL, and 240 specially selected Photographs from the collections of well-known amateur photographers. *Cr. 8vo.* 6s.

**Westell (W. Percival),** F.L.S., M.B.O.U., and **Cooper (C. S.),** F.R.H.S. THE YOUNG BOTANIST. With 8 Coloured and 63 Black and White Plates drawn from Nature, by C. F. NEWALL. *Cr. 8vo.* 3s. 6d. *net.*

**Whibley (C.).** See Henley (W. E.).

**Whibley (L.),** M.A., Fellow of Pembroke College, Cambridge. GREEK OLIGARCHIES: THEIR ORGANISATION AND CHARACTER. *Cr. 8vo.* 6s.

**White (Eustace E.).** THE COMPLETE HOCKEY PLAYER. With 32 Illustrations. *Second Edition. Demy 8vo.* 5s. *net.*

**White (George F.),** Lieut.-Col. A CENTURY OF SPAIN AND PORTUGAL. *Demy 8vo.* 12s. 6d. *net.*

**White (Gilbert).** See Standard Library.

**Whitfield (E. E.),** M.A. See Commercial Series.

**Whitehead (A. W.).** GASPARD DE COLIGNY, ADMIRAL OF FRANCE. With 26 Illustrations and 10 Maps and Plans. *Demy 8vo.* 12s. 6d. *net.*

**Whiteley (R. Lloyd),** F.I.C., Principal of the Municipal Science School, West Bromwich. AN ELEMENTARY TEXT-BOOK OF INORGANIC CHEMISTRY. *Cr. 8vo.* 2s. 6d.

**Whitley (Miss).** See Dilke (Lady).

**Whitling (Miss L.),** late Staff Teacher of the National Training School of Cookery. THE COMPLETE COOK. With 42 Illustrations. *Demy 8vo.* 7s. 6d. *net.*

**Whitten (W.).** See Smith (John Thomas).

**Whyte (A. G.),** B.Sc. See Books on Business.

**Wilberforce (Wilfrid).** See Little Books on Art.

**Wilde (Oscar).** DE PROFUNDIS. *Twelfth Edition. Cr. 8vo.* 5s. *net.*

THE WORKS OF OSCAR WILDE. In 12 Volumes. *Fcap. 8vo. Gilt top. Deckle edge.* 5s. *net each volume.*

I. LORD ARTHUR SAVILE'S CRIME and the PORTRAIT OF MR. W. H. II. THE DUCHESS OF PADUA. III. POEMS (including 'The Sphinx,' 'The Ballad of Reading Gaol,' and 'Uncollected Pieces') IV. LADY WINDERMERE'S FAN. V. A WOMAN OF NO IMPORTANCE. VI. AN IDEAL HUSBAND. VII. THE IMPORTANCE OF BEING EARNEST. VIII. A HOUSE OF POMEGRANATES. IX. INTENTIONS. X. DE PROFUNDIS and PRISON LETTERS. XI. ESSAYS ('Historical Criticism,' 'English Renaissance,' 'London Models,' 'Poems in Prose'). XII. SALOMÉ, A FLORENTINE TRAGEDY, LA SAINTE COURTISANE.

**Wilkins (W. H.),** B.A. THE ALIEN INVASION. *Cr. 8vo.* 2s. 6d.

**Williams (H. Noel).** THE WOMEN BONAPARTES. The Mother and three Sisters of Napoleon. With 36 Illustrations. *In Two Volumes Demy 8vo.* 24s *net.*

A ROSE OF SAVOY: MARIE ADELÉIDE OF SAVOY, DUCHESSE DE BOURGOGNE, MOTHEF OF LOUIS XV. With a Frontispiece in Photogtavure and 16 other Illustrations. *Second Edition. Demy 8vo.* 15s. *net*

**Williams (A.).** PETROL PETER: or Pretty Stories and Funny Pictures. Illustrated in Colour by A. W. MILLS. *Demy 4to.* 3*s.* 6*d.* *net.*

**Williamson (M. G.)**, M.A. See Ancient Cities.

**Williamson (W.)**, B.A. See Junior Examination Series, Junior School Books, and Beginner's Books.

**Wilmot-Buxton (E. M.)**, F. R. Hist. S. MAKERS OF EUROPE. Outlines of European History for the Middle Forms of Schools. With 12 Maps. *Tenth Edition. Cr. 8vo.* 3*s.* 6*d.*

THE ANCIENT WORLD. With Maps and Illustrations. *Cr. 8vo.* 3*s.* 6*d.*

A BOOK OF NOBLE WOMEN. With 16 Illustrations. *Cr. 8vo.* 3*s.* 6*d.*

A HISTORY OF GREAT BRITAIN: FROM THE COMING OF THE ANGLES TO THE YEAR 1870. With 20 Maps. *Second Edition. Cr. 8vo.* 3*s.* 6*d.*

BY ROAD AND RIVER. A Descriptive Geography of the British Isles. With 12 Illustrations and 12 Maps. *Cr. 8vo.* 2*s.*

See also Beginner's Books and New Historical Series.

**Wilson (Bishop.).** See Library of Devotion.

**Wilson (A. J.).** See Books on Business.

**Wilson (H. A.).** See Books on Business.

**Wilton (Richard)**, M.A. LYRA PASTORALIS: Songs of Nature, Church, and Home. *Pott 8vo.* 2*s.* 6*d.*

**Winbolt (S. E.)**, M.A. EXERCISES IN LATIN ACCIDENCE. *Cr. 8vo.* 1*s.* 6*d.*

LATIN HEXAMETER VERSE: An Aid to Composition. *Cr. 8vo.* 3*s.* 6*d.* KEY, 5*s.* *net.*

**Windle (B. C. A.)**, D.Sc., F.R.S., F.S.A. See Antiquary's Books, Little Guides, Ancient Cities, and School Histories.

**Wood (Sir Evelyn)**, F. M., V.C., G.C.B., G.C.M.G. FROM MIDSHIPMAN TO FIELD-MARSHAL. With Illustrations, and 29 Maps. *Fifth and Cheaper Edition. Demy 8vo.* 7*s.* 6*d.* *net.*

THE REVOLT IN HINDUSTAN. 1857-59. With 8 Illustrations and 5 Maps. *Second Edition. Cr. 8vo.* 6*s.*

**Wood (J. A. E.).** See Textbooks of Technology.

**Wood (J. Hickory).** DAN LENO. Illustrated. *Third Edition. Cr. 8vo.* 6*s.*

**Wood (W. Birkbeck)**, M.A., late Scholar of Worcester College, Oxford, and **Edmonds (Major J. E.)**, R.E., D.A.Q.-M.G. A HISTORY OF THE CIVIL WAR IN THE UNITED STATES. With an Introduction by H. SPENSER WILKINSON. With 24 Maps and Plans. *Second Edition. Demy 8vo.* 12*s.* 6*d.* *net.*

**Wordsworth (Christopher)**, M.A. See Antiquary's Books.

**Wordsworth (W.).** THE POEMS OF. With an Introduction and Notes by NOWELL C. SMITH, late Fellow of New College, Oxford. *In Three Volumes. Demy 8vo.* 15*s.* *net.*

POEMS BY WILLIAM WORDSWORTH. Selected with an Introduction by STOPFORD A. BROOKE. With 40 Illustrations by E. H. NEW, including a Frontispiece in Photogravure. *Cr. 8vo.* 7*s.* 6*d.* *net.*

See also Little Library.

**Wordsworth (W.)** and **Coleridge (S. T.).** See Little Library.

**Wright (Arthur)**, D.D., Fellow of Queen's College, Cambridge. See Churchman's Library.

**Wright (C. Gordon).** See Dante.

**Wright (J. C.).** TO-DAY. Thoughts on Life for every day. *Demy 16mo.* 1*s.* 6*d.* *net.*

**Wright (Sophie).** GERMAN VOCABULARIES FOR REPETITION. *Fcap. 8vo.* 1*s.* 6*d.*

**Wyatt (Kate M.).** See Gloag (M. R.).

**Wylde (A. B.).** MODERN ABYSSINIA. With a Map and a Portrait. *Demy 8vo.* 15*s.* *net.*

**Wyllie (M. A.).** NORWAY AND ITS FJORDS. With 16 Illustrations, in Colour by W. L. WYLLIE, R.A., and 17 other Illustrations. *Crown 8vo.* 6*s.*

**Wyndham (Geo.).** See Shakespeare (Wm.).

**Yeats (W. B.).** A BOOK OF IRISH VERSE. *Revised and Enlarged Edition. Cr. 8vo.* 3*s.* 6*d.*

**Young (Filson).** THE COMPLETE MOTORIST. With 138 Illustrations. *New Edition (Seventh), with many additions. Demy. 8vo.* 12*s.* 6*d.* *net.*

THE JOY OF THE ROAD: An Appreciation of the Motor Car. With a Frontispiece in Photogravure. *Sm. Demy 8vo.* 5*s.* *net.*

**Zachariah of Mitylene.** See Byzantine Texts.

**Zimmern (Antonia).** WHAT DO WE KNOW CONCERNING ELECTRICITY? *Fcap. 8vo.* 1*s.* 6*d.* *net.*

## Ancient Cities

General Editor, B. C. A. WINDLE, D.Sc., F.R.S.

*Cr. 8vo.* 4*s.* 6*d.* *net.*

BRISTOL. By Alfred Harvey, M.B. Illustrated by E. H. New.

CANTERBURY. By J. C. Cox, LL.D., F.S.A. Illustrated by B. C. Boulter.

CHESTER. By B. C. A. Windle, D.Sc. F.R.S. Illustrated by E. H. New.

DUBLIN. By S. A. O. Fitzpatrick. Illustrated by W. C. Green.

EDINBURGH. By M. G. Williamson, M.A. Illustrated by Herbert Railton.

LINCOLN. By E. Mansel Sympson, M.A., M.D. Illustrated by E. H. New.

SHREWSBURY. By T. Auden, M.A., F.S.A. Illustrated by Katharine M. Roberts.

WELLS and GLASTONBURY. By T. S. Holmes. Illustrated by E. H. New.

## The Antiquary's Books

General Editor, J. CHARLES COX, LL.D., F.S.A.

*Demy 8vo. 7s. 6d. net.*

ARCHÆOLOGY AND FALSE ANTIQUITIES. By R. Munro, LL.D. With 81 Illustrations.

BELLS OF ENGLAND, THE. By Canon J. J. Raven, D.D., F.S.A. With 60 Illustrations. *Second Edition.*

BRASSES OF ENGLAND, THE. By Herbert W. Macklin, M.A. With 85 Illustrations. *Second Edition.*

CELTIC ART IN PAGAN AND CHRISTIAN TIMES. By J. Romilly Allen, F.S.A. With 44 Plates and numerous Illustrations.

DOMESDAY INQUEST, THE. By Adolphus Ballard, B.A., LL.B. With 27 Illustrations.

ENGLISH CHURCH FURNITURE. By J. C. Cox, LL.D., F.S.A., and A. Harvey, M.B. With 121 Illustrations. *Second Edition.*

ENGLISH COSTUME. From Prehistoric Times to the End of the Eighteenth Century. By George Clinch, F.G.S. With 131 Illustrations.

ENGLISH MONASTIC LIFE. By the Right Rev. Abbot Gasquet, O.S.B. With 50 Illustrations, Maps and Plans. *Fourth Edition.*

ENGLISH SEALS. By J. Harvey Bloom. With 93 Illustrations.

FOLK-LORE AS AN HISTORICAL SCIENCE. By G. L. Gomme. With 28 Illustrations.

GILDS AND COMPANIES OF LONDON, THE. By George Unwin. With 37 Illustrations.

MANOR AND MANORIAL RECORDS, THE. By Nathaniel J. Hone. With 54 Illustrations.

MEDIÆVAL HOSPITALS OF ENGLAND, THE. By Rotha Mary Clay. With many Illustrations.

OLD SERVICE BOOKS OF THE ENGLISH CHURCH. By Christopher Wordsworth, M.A., and Henry Littlehales. With 38 Coloured and other Illustrations.

PARISH LIFE IN MEDIÆVAL ENGLAND. By the Right Rev. Abbott Gasquet, O.S.B. With 39 Illustrations. *Second Edition.*

REMAINS OF THE PREHISTORIC AGE IN ENGLAND. By B. C. A. Windle, D.Sc., F.R.S. With 94 Illustrations. *Second Edition.*

ROYAL FORESTS OF ENGLAND, THE. By J. C. Cox, LL.D., F.S.A. With 25 Plates and 23 other Illustrations.

SHRINES OF BRITISH SAINTS. By J. C. Wall. With 28 Plates and 50 other Illustrations.

## The Arden Shakespeare

*Demy 8vo. 2s. 6d. net each volume.*

An edition of Shakespeare in single Plays. Edited with a full Introduction, Textual Notes, and a Commentary at the foot of the page.

ALL'S WELL THAT ENDS WELL. Edited by W. O. Brigstocke.

ANTONY AND CLEOPATRA. Edited by R. H. Case.

CYMBELINE. Edited by E. Dowden.

COMEDY OF ERRORS, THE. Edited by Henry Cuningham.

HAMLET. Edited by E. Dowden. *Second Edition.*

JULIUS CAESAR. Edited by M. Macmillan.

KING HENRY V. Edited by H. A. Evans.

KING HENRY VI. PT. I. Edited by H. C. Hart.

KING HENRY VI. PT. II. Edited by H. C. Hart and C. K. Pooler.

KING LEAR. Edited by W. J. Craig.

KING RICHARD III. Edited by A. H. Thompson.

LIFE AND DEATH OF KING JOHN, THE. Edited by Ivor B. John.

LOVE'S LABOUR'S LOST. Edited by H. C. Hart.

*MACBETH. Edited by H. Cuningham.

MEASURE FOR MEASURE. Edited by H. C. Hart.

MERCHANT OF VENICE, THE. Edited by C. K. Pooler.

MERRY WIVES OF WINDSOR, THE. Edited by H. C. Hart.

A MIDSUMMER NIGHT'S DREAM. Edited by H. Cuningham.

OTHELLO. Edited by H. C. Hart.

PERICLES. Edited by K. Deighton.

ROMEO AND JULIET. Edited by Edward Dowden.

TAMING OF THE SHREW, THE. Edited by R. Warwick Bond.

TEMPEST, THE. Edited by M. Luce.

TIMON OF ATHENS. Edited by K. Deighton.

TITUS ANDRONICUS. Edited by H. B. Baildon.

TROILUS AND CRESSIDA. Edited by K. Deighton.

TWO GENTLEMEN OF VERONA, THE. Edited by R. W. Bond.

TWELFTH NIGHT. Edited by M. Luce.

## The Beginner's Books

Edited by W. WILLIAMSON, B.A.

EASY DICTATION AND SPELLING. By W. Williamson, B.A. *Seventh Ed. Fcap. 8vo.* 1s.

EASY EXERCISES IN ARITHMETIC. Arranged by W. S. Beard. *Third Edition. Fcap. 8vo.* Without Answers, 1s. With Answers. 1s. 3d.

EASY FRENCH RHYMES. By Henri Blouet. *Second Edition.* Illustrated. *Fcap. 8vo.* 1s.

AN EASY POETRY BOOK. Selected and arranged by W. Williamson, B.A. *Second Edition. Cr. 8vo.* 1s.

EASY STORIES FROM ENGLISH HISTORY. By E. M. Wilmot-Buxton, F.R.Hist.S. *Fifth Edition. Cr. 8vo.* 1s.

A FIRST HISTORY OF GREECE. By E. E. Firth. With 7 Maps. *Cr. 8vo.* 1s. 6d.

STORIES FROM ROMAN HISTORY. By E. M. Wilmot-Buxton. *Second Edition. Cr. 8vo.* 1s. 6d.

STORIES FROM THE OLD TESTAMENT. By E. M. Wilmot-Buxton. *Cr. 8vo.* 1s. 6d.

## Books on Business

*Cr. 8vo.* 2s. 6d. *net.*

AUTOMOBILE INDUSTRY, THE. G. Holden-Stone.

BREWING INDUSTRY, THE. J. L. Baker, F.I.C., F.C.S. With 28 Illustrations.

BUSINESS OF ADVERTISING, THE. C. G. Moran, With 11 Illustrations.

BUSINESS SIDE OF AGRICULTURE, THE. A. G. L. Rogers.

BUSINESS OF INSURANCE, THE. A. J. Wilson.

CIVIL ENGINEERING. C. T. Fidler. With 15 Illustrations.

COTTON INDUSTRY AND TRADE, THE. S. J. Chapman. With 8 Illustrations.

THE ELECTRICAL INDUSTRY: LIGHTING, TRACTION, AND POWER. A. G. Whyte,

IRON TRADE OF GREAT BRITAIN, THE. J. S. Jeans. With 12 Illustrations.

LAW IN BUSINESS. H. A. Wilson.

MINING AND MINING INVESTMENTS. A. Moil.

MONEY MARKET, THE. F. Straker.

MONOPOLIES, TRUSTS, AND KARTELLS. F. W. Hirst.

PORTS AND DOCKS. Douglas Owen.

RAILWAYS. E. R. McDermott.

SHIPBUILDING INDUSTRY THE: Its History, Practice, Science, and Finance. David Pollock, M.I.N.A.

STOCK EXCHANGE, THE. C. Duguid. *Second Edition.*

TRADE UNIONS. G. Drage.

## Byzantine Texts

Edited by J. B. BURY, M.A., Litt.D.

THE SYRIAC CHRONICLE KNOWN AS THAT OF ZACHARIAH OF MITYLENE. Translated by F. J. Hamilton, D.D., and E. W. Brooks. *Demy 8vo.* 12s. 6d. *net.*

EVAGRIUS. Edited by L. Bidez and Léon Parmentier. *Demy 8vo.* 10s. 6d. *net.*

THE HISTORY OF PSELLUS. Edited by C. Sathas. *Demy 8vo.* 15s. *net.*

ECTHESIS CHRONICA AND CHRONICON ATHENARUM. Edited by Professor S. P. Lambros. *Demy 8vo.* 7s. 6d. *net.*

THE CHRONICLE OF MOREA. Edited by John Schmitt. *Demy 8vo.* 15s. *net.*

## The Churchman's Bible

General Editor, J. H. BURN, B.D., F.R.S.E.

*Fcap. 8vo.* 1s. 6d. *net each.*

THE EPISTLE OF ST. PAUL THE APOSTLE TO THE GALATIANS. Explained by A. W. Robinson, M.A. *Second Edition.*

ECCLESIASTES. Explained by A. W. Streane, D.D.

THE EPISTLE OF ST. PAUL THE APOSTLE TO THE PHILIPPIANS. Explained by C. R. D. Biggs, D.D. *Second Edition.*

THE EPISTLE OF ST. JAMES. Explained by H. W. Fulford M.A.

ISAIAH. Explained by W. E. Barnes, D.D. *Two Volumes.* With Map. 2s. *net each.*

THE EPISTLE OF ST. PAUL THE APOSTLE TO THE EPHESIANS. Explained by G. H. Whitaker, M.A.

THE GOSPEL ACCORDING TO ST. MARK. Explained by J. C. Du Buisson, M.A. 2s. 6d. *net.*

THE EPISTLE OF PAUL THE APOSTLE TO THE COLOSSIANS AND PHILEMON. Explained by H. J. C. Knight. 2s. *net.*

## The Churchman's Library

General Editor, J. H. BURN, B.D., F.R.S.E.

*Crown 8vo. 3s. 6d. each.*

THE BEGINNINGS OF ENGLISH CHRISTIANITY. By W. E. Collins, M.A. With Map.

THE CHURCHMAN'S INTRODUCTION TO THE OLD TESTAMENT. By A. M. Mackay, B.A. *Second Edition.*

EVOLUTION. By F. B. Jevons, M.A., Litt.D.

SOME NEW TESTAMENT PROBLEMS. By Arthur Wright, D.D. 6s.

THE WORKMANSHIP OF THE PRAYER BOOK: Its Literary and Liturgical Aspects. By J. Dowden, D.D. *Second Edition, Revised and Enlarged.*

## Classical Translations

*Crown 8vo.*

AESCHYLUS—The Oresteian Trilogy (Agamemnon, Choëphoroe, Eumenides). Translated by Lewis Campbell, LL.D. 5s.

CICERO—De Oratore I. Translated by E. N. P. Moor, M.A. *Second Edition.* 3s. 6d.

CICERO—The Speeches against Cataline and Antony and for Murena and Milo. Translated by H. E. D. Blakiston, M.A. 5s.

CICERO—De Natura Deorum. Translated by F. Brooks, M.A. 3s. 6d.

CICERO—De Officiis. Translated by G. B. Gardiner, M.A. 2s. 6d.

HORACE—The Odes and Epodes. Translated by A. D. Godley, M.A. 2s.

LUCIAN—Six Dialogues Translated by S. T. Irwin, M.A. 3s. 6d.

SOPHOCLES—Ajax and Electra. Translated by E. D. Morshead, M.A. 2s. 6d.

TACITUS—Agricola and Germania. Translated by R. B. Townshend. 2s. 6d.

JUVENAL—Thirteen Satires. Translated by S. G. Owen, M.A. 2s. 6d.

## Classics of Art

Edited by DR. J. H. W. LAING.

*Wide Royal 8vo. Gilt top.*

THE ART OF THE GREEKS. By H. B. Walters. With 112 Plates and 18 Illustrations in the Text. *12s. 6d. net.*

FLORENTINE SCULPTORS OF THE RENNAISANCE. By Wilhelm Bode, Ph.D. Translated by Jessie Haynes. With 94 Plates. *12s. 6d. net.*

GHIRLANDAIO. By Gerald S. Davies, Master of the Charterhouse. With 50 Plates. *Second Edition.* 10s. 6d.

MICHELANGELO. By Gerald S. Davies, Master of the Charterhouse. With 126 Plates. *12s. 6d. net.*

RUBENS. By Edward Dillon, M.A. With a Frontispiece in Photogravure and 483 Plates. *25s. net.*

RAPHAEL. By A. P. Oppé. With a Frontispiece in Photogravure and 200 Illustrations. *12s. 6d. net.*

*TITIAN. By Charles Ricketts. With about 200 Illustrations. *12s. 6d. net.*

VELAZQUEZ. By A. de Beruete. With 94 Plates. *10s. 6d. net.*

## Commercial Series

*Crown 8vo.*

BRITISH COMMERCE AND COLONIES FROM ELIZABETH TO VICTORIA. By H. de B. Gibbins, Litt.D., M.A. *Fourth Edition.* 2s.

COMMERCIAL EXAMINATION PAPERS. By H. de B. Gibbins, Litt.D., M.A. 1s. 6d.

THE ECONOMICS OF COMMERCE, By H. de B. Gibbins, Litt.D., M.A. *Second Edition.* 1s. 6d.

A GERMAN COMMERCIAL READER. By S. E. Bally. With Vocabulary. 2s.

A COMMERCIAL GEOGRAPHY OF THE BRITISH EMPIRE. By L. W. Lyde, M.A. *Seventh Edition.* 2s.

A COMMERCIAL GEOGRAPHY OF FOREIGN NATIONS. By F. C. Boon, B.A. 2s.

A PRIMER OF BUSINESS. By S. Jackson, M.A. *Fourth Edition.* 1s. 6d.

A SHORT COMMERCIAL ARITHMETIC. By F. G. Taylor, M.A. *Fourth Edition.* 1s. 6d.

FRENCH COMMERCIAL CORRESPONDENCE. By S. E. Bally. With Vocabulary. *Fourth Edition.* 2s.

GERMAN COMMERCIAL CORRESPONDENCE. By S. E. Bally. With Vocabulary. *Second Edition.* 2s. 6d.

A FRENCH COMMERCIAL READER. By S. E. Bally. With Vocabulary. *Second Edition.* 2s.

PRECIS WRITING AND OFFICE CORRESPONDENCE. By E. E. Whitfield, M.A. *Second Edition.* 2s.

AN ENTRANCE GUIDE TO PROFESSIONS AND BUSINESS. By H. Jones. 1s. 6d.

THE PRINCIPLES OF BOOK-KEEPING BY DOUBLE ENTRY. By J. E. B. M'Allen, M.A. 2s.

COMMERCIAL LAW. By W. Douglas Edwards. *Second Edition.* 2s.

## The Connoisseur's Library

*Wide Royal 8vo. 25s. net.*

MEZZOTINTS. By Cyril Davenport. With 40 Plates in Photogravure.

PORCELAIN. By Edward Dillon. With 19 Plates in Colour, 20 in Collotype, and 5 in Photogravure.

MINIATURES. By Dudley Heath. With 9 Plates in Colour, 15 in Collotype, and 15 in Photogravure.

IVORIES. By A. Maskell. With 80 Plates in Collotype and Photogravure.

ENGLISH FURNITURE. By F. S. Robinson. With 160 Plates in Collotype and one in Photogravure. *Second Edition.*

ENGLISH COLOURED BOOKS. By Martin Hardie. With 28 Illustrations in Colour and Collotype.

EUROPEAN ENAMELS. By Henry H. Cunynghame, C.B. With 54 Plates in Collotype and Half-tone and 4 Plates in Colour.

GOLDSMITHS' AND SILVERSMITHS' WORK. By Nelson Dawson. With 51 Plates in Collotype and a Frontispiece in Photogravure. *Second Edition.*

GLASS. By Edward Dillon. With 37 Illustrations in Collotype and 12 in Colour.

SEALS. By Walter de Gray Birch. With 52 Illustrations in Collotype and a Frontispiece in Photogravure.

JEWELLERY. By H. Clifford Smith. With 50 Illustrations in Collotype, and 4 in Colour. *Second Edition.*

## Handbooks of English Church History

Edited by J. H. BURN, B.D. *Crown 8vo. 2s. 6d. net.*

THE FOUNDATIONS OF THE ENGLISH CHURCH. J. H. Maude.

THE SAXON CHURCH AND THE NORMAN CONQUEST. C. T. CRUTTWELL.

THE MEDIÆVAL CHURCH AND THE PAPACY A. C. Jennings.

THE REFORMATION PERIOD. By Henry Gee.

## The Illustrated Pocket Library of Plain and Coloured Books

*Fcap 8vo. 3s. 6d. net each volume.*

### COLOURED BOOKS

OLD COLOURED BOOKS. By George Paston. With 16 Coloured Plates. *Fcap. 8vo. 2s. net.*

THE LIFE AND DEATH OF JOHN MYTTON, ESQ. By Nimrod. With 18 Coloured Plates by Henry Alken and T. J. Rawlins. *Fourth Edition.*

THE LIFE OF A SPORTSMAN. By Nimrod. With 35 Coloured Plates by Henry Alken.

HANDLEY CROSS. By R. S. Surtees. With 17 Coloured Plates and 100 Woodcuts in the Text by John Leech. *Second Edition.*

MR. SPONGE'S SPORTING TOUR. By R. S. Surtees. With 13 Coloured Plates and 90 Woodcuts in the Text by John Leech.

JORROCKS' JAUNTS AND JOLLITIES. By R. S. Surtees. With 15 Coloured Plates by H. Alken. *Second Edition.*

ASK MAMMA. By R. S. Surtees. With 13 Coloured Plates and 70 Woodcuts in the Text by John Leech.

THE ANALYSIS OF THE HUNTING FIELD. By R. S. Surtees. With 7 Coloured Plates by Henry Alken, and 43 Illustrations on Wood.

THE TOUR OF DR. SYNTAX IN SEARCH OF THE PICTURESQUE. By William Combe. With 30 Coloured Plates by T. Rowlandson.

THE TOUR OF DOCTOR SYNTAX IN SEARCH OF CONSOLATION. By William Combe. With 24 Coloured Plates by T. Rowlandson.

THE THIRD TOUR OF DOCTOR SYNTAX IN SEARCH OF A WIFE. By William Combe. With 24 Coloured Plates by T. Rowlandson.

THE HISTORY OF JOHNNY QUAE GENUS: the Little Foundling of the late Dr. Syntax. By the Author of 'The Three Tours.' With 24 Coloured Plates by Rowlandson.

THE ENGLISH DANCE OF DEATH, from the Designs of T. Rowlandson, with Metrical Illustrations by the Author of 'Doctor Syntax.' *Two Volumes.*

This book contains 76 Coloured Plates.

THE DANCE OF LIFE: A Poem. By the Author of 'Doctor Syntax.' Illustrated with 26 Coloured Engravings by T. Rowlandson.

LIFE IN LONDON: or, the Day and Night Scenes of Jerry Hawthorn, Esq., and his Elegant Friend, Corinthian Tom. By Pierce Egan. With 36 Coloured Plates by I. R. and G. Cruikshank. With numerous Designs on Wood.

REAL LIFE IN LONDON: or, the Rambles and Adventures of Bob Tallyho, Esq., and his Cousin, The Hon. Tom Dashall. By an Amateur (Pierce Egan). With 31 Coloured Plates by Alken and Rowlandson, etc. *Two Volumes.*

THE LIFE OF AN ACTOR. By Pierce Egan. With 27 Coloured Plates by Theodore Lane, and several Designs on Wood.

THE VICAR OF WAKEFIELD. By Oliver Goldsmith. With 24 Coloured Plates by T. Rowlandson.

THE MILITARY ADVENTURES OF JOHNNY NEWCOME. By an Officer. With 15 Coloured Plates by T. Rowlandson.

ILLUSTRATED POCKET LIBRARY OF PLAIN AND COLOURED BOOKS—*continued.*

THE NATIONAL SPORTS OF GREAT BRITAIN. With Descriptions and 50 Coloured Plates by Henry Alken.

THE ADVENTURES OF A POST CAPTAIN. By A Naval Officer. With 24 Coloured Plates by Mr. Williams.

GAMONIA: or, the Art of Preserving Game; and an Improved Method of making Plantations and Covers, explained and illustrated by Lawrence Rawstorne, Esq. With 15 Coloured Plates by T. Rawlins.

AN ACADEMY FOR GROWN HORSEMEN: Containing the completest Instructions for Walking, Trotting, Cantering, Galloping, Stumbling, and Tumbling. Illustrated with 27 Coloured Plates, and adorned with a Portrait of the Author. By Geoffrey Gambado, Esq.

REAL LIFE IN IRELAND, or, the Day and Night Scenes of Brian Boru, Esq., and his Elegant Friend, Sir Shawn O'Dogherty. By a Real Paddy. With 19 Coloured Plates by Heath, Marks, etc.

THE ADVENTURES OF JOHNNY NEWCOME IN THE NAVY. By Alfred Burton. With 16 Coloured Plates by T. Rowlandson.

THE OLD ENGLISH SQUIRE: A Poem. By John Careless, Esq. With 20 Coloured Plates after the style of T. Rowlandson

THE ENGLISH SPY. By Bernard Blackmantle. An original Work, Characteristic, Satirical, Humorous, comprising scenes and sketches in every Rank of Society, being Portraits of the Illustrious, Eminent, Eccentric, and Notorious. With 72 Coloured Plates by R. CRUIKSHANK, and many Illustrations on wood. *Two Volumes.* 7*s. net.*

PLAIN BOOKS

THE GRAVE: A Poem. By Robert Blair. Illustrated by 12 Etchings executed by Louis Schiavonetti from the original Inventions of William Blake. With an Engraved Title Page and a Portrait of Blake by T. Phillips, R.A.

The illustrations are reproduced in photogravure.

ILLUSTRATIONS OF THE BOOK OF JOB. Invented and engraved by William Blake.

These famous Illustrations—21 in number—are reproduced in photogravure.

WINDSOR CASTLE By W. Harrison Ainsworth. With 22 Plates and 87 Woodcuts in the Text by George Cruikshank.

THE TOWER OF LONDON. By W. Harrison Ainsworth. With 40 Plates and 58 Woodcuts in the Text by George Cruikshank.

FRANK FAIRLEGH. By F. E. Smedley. With 30 Plates by George Cruikshank.

HANDY ANDY. By Samuel Lover. With 24 Illustrations by the Author.

THE COMPLEAT ANGLER. By Izaak Walton and Charles Cotton. With 14 Plates and 77 Woodcuts in the Text.

THE PICKWICK PAPERS. By Charles Dickens. With the 43 Illustrations by Seymour and Phiz, the two Buss Plates, and the 32 Contemporary Onwhyn Plates.

## Junior Examination Series

Edited by A. M. M. STEDMAN, M.A. *Fcap. 8vo.* 1*s.*

JUNIOR ALGEBRA EXAMINATION PAPERS. By S. W. Finn, M.A.

JUNIOR ARITHMETIC EXAMINATION PAPERS. By W. S. Beard. *Fifth Edition.*

JUNIOR ENGLISH EXAMINATION PAPERS. By W. Williamson, B.A. *Second Edition.*

JUNIOR FRENCH EXAMINATION PAPERS. By F. Jacob, M.A. *Second Edition.*

JUNIOR GENERAL INFORMATION EXAMINATION PAPERS. By W. S. Beard. KEY, 3*s.* 6*d. net.*

JUNIOR GEOGRAPHY EXAMINATION PAPERS. By W. G. Baker, M.A.

JUNIOR GERMAN EXAMINATION PAPERS. By A. Voegelin, M.A.

JUNIOR GREEK EXAMINATION PAPERS. By T. C. Weatherhead, M.A. KEY, 3*s.* 6*d. net.*

JUNIOR LATIN EXAMINATION PAPERS. By C. G. Botting, B.A. *Sixth Edition.* KEY, 3*s.* 6*d. net.*

JUNIOR HISTORY EXAMINATION PAPERS. By W. O. P. Davies.

## Methuen's Junior School-Books

Edited by O. D. INSKIP, LL.D., and W. WILLIAMSON, B.A.

A CLASS-BOOK OF DICTATION PASSAGES. By W. Williamson, B.A. *Fifteenth Edition. Cr. 8vo.* 1*s.* 6*d.*

THE GOSPEL ACCORDING TO ST. MATTHEW. Edited by E. Wilton South, M.A. With Three Maps. *Cr. 8vo.* 1*s.* 6*d.*

THE GOSPEL ACCORDING TO ST. MARK. Edited by A. E. Rubie, D.D. With Three Maps. *Cr. 8vo.* 1*s.* 6*d.*

A JUNIOR ENGLISH GRAMMAR. By W. Williamson, B.A. With numerous passages for parsing and analysis, and a chapter on Essay Writing. *Fourth Edition. Cr. 8vo.* 2*s.*

A JUNIOR CHEMISTRY. By E. A. Tyler, B.A., F.C.S. With 78 Illustrations. *Fifth Edition. Cr. 8vo.* 2*s.* 6*d.*

THE ACTS OF THE APOSTLES. Edited by A. E. Rubie, D.D. *Cr. 8vo.* 2*s.*

METHUEN'S JUNIOR SCHOOL BOOKS—*continued.*

A JUNIOR FRENCH GRAMMAR. By L. A. Sornet and M. J. Acatos. *Third Edition. Cr. 8vo.* 2s.

ELEMENTARY EXPERIMENTAL SCIENCE. PHYSICS by W. T. Clough, A.R.C.Sc. (Lond.), F.C.S. CHEMISTRY by A. E. Dunstan, B.Sc. (Lond.), F.C.S. With 2 Plates and 154 Diagrams. *Eighth Edition. Cr. 8vo.* 2s. 6d.

A JUNIOR GEOMETRY. By Noel S. Lydon. With 276 Diagrams. *Seventh Edition. Cr. 8vo.* 2s.

ELEMENTARY EXPERIMENTAL CHEMISTRY. By A. E. Dunstan, B.Sc. (Lond.), F.C.S. With 4 Plates and 109 Diagrams. *Third Edition. Cr. 8vo.* 2s.

A JUNIOR FRENCH PROSE. By R. R. N. Baron, M.A. *Fourth Edition. Cr. 8vo.* 2s.

THE GOSPEL ACCORDING TO ST. LUKE. With an Introduction and Notes by William Williamson, B.A. With Three Maps. *Cr. 8vo.* 2s.

THE FIRST BOOK OF KINGS. Edited by A. E. RUBIE, D.D. With 4 Maps. *Cr. 8vo.* 2s.

A JUNIOR GREEK HISTORY. By W. H. Spragge, M.A. With 4 Illustrations and 5 Maps. *Cr. 8vo.* 2s. 6d.

A SCHOOL LATIN GRAMMAR. By H. G. Ford, M.A. *Cr. 8vo.* 2s. 6d.

A JUNIOR LATIN PROSE. By H. N. Asman, M.A., B.D. *Cr. 8vo.* 2s. 6d.

*ELEMENTARY EXPERIMENTAL ELECTRICITY AND MAGNETISM. By W. T. Clough, A.R.C.Sc. (Lond.), F.C.S. With 200 Illustrations and Diagrams. *Cr. 8vo.* 2s. 6d.

ENGLISE LITERATURE FOR SCHOOLS. By Edith E. Firth. With 4 Maps. *Cr. 8vo.* 2s. 6d.

## Leaders of Religion

Edited by H. C. BEECHING, M.A., Canon of Westminster. *With Portraits. Cr. 8vo.* 2s. *net.*

CARDINAL NEWMAN. By R. H. Hutton.

JOHN WESLEY. By J. H. Overton, M.A.

BISHOP WILBERFORCE. By G. W. Daniell, M.A.

CARDINAL MANNING. By A. W. Hutton, M.A.

CHARLES SIMEON. By H. C. G. Moule, D.D.

JOHN KNOX. By F. MacCunn. *Second Edition.*

JOHN HOWE. By R. F. Horton, D.D.

THOMAS KEN. By F. A. Clarke, M.A.

GEORGE FOX, THE QUAKER. By T. Hodgkin, D.C.L. *Third Edition.*

JOHN KEBLE. By Walter Lock, D.D.

THOMAS CHALMERS. By Mrs. Oliphant.

LANCELOT ANDREWES. By R. L. Ottley, D.D. *Second Edition.*

AUGUSTINE OF CANTERBURY. By E. L. Cutts, D.D.

WILLIAM LAUD. By W. H. Hutton, M.A. *Third Edition.*

JOHN DONNE. By Augustus Jessopp, D.D.

THOMAS CRANMER. By A. J. Mason, D.D.

BISHOP LATIMER. By R. M. Carlyle and A. J. Carlyle, M.A.

BISHOP BUTLER. By W. A. Spooner, M.A.

## The Library of Devotion

With Introductions and (where necessary) Notes.

*Small Pott 8vo, cloth,* 2s. ; *leather,* 2s. 6d. *net.*

THE CONFESSIONS OF ST. AUGUSTINE. Edited by C. Bigg, D.D. *Seventh Edition.*

THE IMITATION OF CHRIST : called also the Ecclesiastical Music. Edited by C. Bigg, D.D. *Fifth Edition.*

THE CHRISTIAN YEAR. Edited by Walter Lock, D.D. *Fourth Edition.*

LYRA INNOCENTIUM. Edited by Walter Lock, D.D. *Second Edition.*

THE TEMPLE. Edited by E. C. S. Gibson, D.D. *Second Edition.*

A BOOK OF DEVOTIONS. Edited by J. W. Stanbridge. B.D. *Second Edition.*

A SERIOUS CALL TO A DEVOUT AND HOLY LIFE. Edited by C. Bigg, D.D. *Fourth Ed.*

A GUIDE TO ETERNITY. Edited by J. W. Stanbridge, B.D.

THE INNER WAY. By J. Tauler. Edited by A. W. Hutton, M.A. *Second Edition.*

ON THE LOVE OF GOD. By St. Francis de Sales. Edited by W. J. Knox-Little, M.A.

THE PSALMS OF DAVID. Edited by B. W. Randolph, D.D.

LYRA APOSTOLICA. By Cardinal Newman and others. Edited by Canon Scott Holland, M.A., and Canon H. C. Beeching, M.A.

THE SONG OF SONGS. Edited by B. Blaxland, M.A.

THE THOUGHTS OF PASCAL. Edited by C. S. Jerram, M.A.

A MANUAL OF CONSOLATION FROM THE SAINTS AND FATHERS. Edited by J. H. Burn, B.D.

DEVOTIONS FROM THE APOCRYPHA. Edited, with an Introduction, by Herbert Pentin, M.A.

THE LIBRARY OF DEVOTION—*continued.*

THE SPIRITUAL COMBAT. By Dom Lorenzo Scupoli. Newly translated, with an Introduction and Notes, by Thomas Barns, M.A.

THE DEVOTIONS OF ST. ANSELM. Edited by C. C. J. Webb, M.A.

GRACE ABOUNDING TO THE CHIEF OF SINNERS. By John Bunyan. Edited by S. C. Freer, M.A.

BISHOP WILSON'S SACRA PRIVATA. Edited by A. E. Burn, B.D.

LYRA SACRA: A Book of Sacred Verse. Edited by Canon H. C. Beeching, M.A. *Second Edition, revised.*

A DAY BOOK FROM THE SAINTS AND FATHERS. Edited by J. H. Burn, B.D.

A LITTLE BOOK OF HEAVENLY WISDOM. A Selection from the English Mystics. Edited by E. C. Gregory.

LIGHT, LIFE, and LOVE. A Selection from the German Mystics. Edited by W. R. Inge, M.A.

AN INTRODUCTION TO THE DEVOUT LIFE. By St. Francis de Sales. Translated and Edited by T. Barns, M.A.

THE LITTLE FLOWERS OF THE GLORIOUS MESSER ST. FRANCIS AND OF HIS FRIARS. Done into English by W. Heywood. With an Introduction by A. G. Ferrers Howell.

MANCHESTER AL MONDO: a Contemplation of Death and Immortality. By Henry Montagu Earl of Manchester. With an Introduction by Elizabeth Waterhouse, Editor of 'A Little Book of Life and Death.'

THE SPIRITUAL GUIDE, which Disentangles the Soul and brings it by the Inward Way to the Fruition of Perfect Contemplation, and the Rich Treasure of Internal Peace. Written by Dr. Michael de Molinos, Priest. Translated from the Italian copy, printed at Venice, 1685. Edited with an Introduction by Kathleen Lyttelton. And a Note by Canon Scott Holland.

DEVOTIONS FOR EVERY DAY OF THE WEEK AND THE GREAT FESTIVALS. By John Wesley. Edited, with an Introduction by Canon C. Bodington.

PRECES PRIVATAE. By Lancelot Andrewes, Bishop of Winchester. Selections from the Translation by Canon F. E. Brightman. Edited, with an Introduction, by A. E. Burn, D.D.

HORAE MYSTICAE: A Day Book from the Writings of Mystics of Many Nations. Edited by E. C. Gregory.

## Little Books on Art

*With many Illustrations. Demy 16mo. 2s. 6d. net.*

Each volume consists of about 200 pages, and contains from 30 to 40 Illustrations, including a Frontispiece in Photogravure.

ALBRECHT DÜRER. J. Allen.
ARTS OF JAPAN, THE. E. Dillon.
BOOKPLATES. E. Almack.
BOTTICELLI. Mary L. Bonnor.
BURNE-JONES. F. de Lisle.
CHRIST IN ART. Mrs. H. Jenner.
CLAUDE. E. Dillon.
CONSTABLE. H. W. Tompkins.
COROT. A. Pollard and E. Birnstingl.
ENAMELS. Mrs. N. Dawson.
FREDERIC LEIGHTON. A. Corkran.
GEORGE ROMNEY. G. Paston.
GREEK ART. H. B. Walters.
GREUZE AND BOUCHER. E. F. Pollard.
HOLBEIN. Mrs. G. Fortescue.
ILLUMINATED MANUSCRIPTS. J. W. Bradley.
JEWELLERY. C. Davenport.
JOHN HOPPNER. H. P. K. Skipton.
SIR JOSHUA REYNOLDS. J. Sime.
MILLET. N. Peacock.
MINIATURES. C. Davenport.
OUR LADY IN ART. Mrs. H. Jenner.
RAPHAEL. A. R. Dryhurst. *Second Edition.*
REMBRANDT. Mrs. E. A. Sharp.
TURNER. F. Tyrrell-Gill.
VANDYCK. M. G. Smallwood.
VELASQUEZ. W. Wilberforce and A. R. Gilbert.
WATTS. R. E. D. Sketchley.

## The Little Galleries

*Demy 16mo. 2s. 6d. net.*

Each volume contains 20 plates in Photogravure, together with a short outline of the life and work of the master to whom the book is devoted.

A LITTLE GALLERY OF REYNOLDS.
A LITTLE GALLERY OF ROMNEY.
A LITTLE GALLERY OF HOPPNER.
A LITTLE GALLERY OF MILLAIS.
A LITTLE GALLERY OF ENGLISH POETS.

## The Little Guides

With many Illustrations by E. H. NEW and other artists, and from photographs.

*Small Pott 8vo, cloth, 2s. 6d. net.; leather, 3s. 6d. net.*

The main features of these Guides are (1) a handy and charming form; (2) illustrations from photographs and by well-known artists; (3) good plans and maps; (4) an adequate but compact presentation of everything that is interesting in the natural features, history, archæology, and architecture of the town or district treated.

CAMBRIDGE AND ITS COLLEGES. A. H. Thompson. *Second Edition.*
ENGLISH LAKES, THE. F. G. Brabant.
ISLE OF WIGHT. THE. G. Clinch.
MALVERN COUNTRY, THE B. C. A. Windle.
NORTH WALES. A. T. Story.
OXFORD AND ITS COLLEGES. J. Wells. *Eighth Edition.*
SHAKESPEARE'S COUNTRY. B. C. A. Windle. *Third Edition.*
ST. PAUL'S CATHEDRAL. G. Clinch.
WESTMINSTER ABBEY. G. E. Troutbeck. *Second Edition.*

BUCKINGHAMSHIRE. E. S. Roscoe.
CHESHIRE. W. M. Gallichan.
CORNWALL. A. L. Salmon.
DERBYSHIRE. J. C. Cox.
DEVON. S. Baring-Gould.
DORSET. F. R. Heath. *Second Edition.*
ESSEX. J. C. Cox.
HAMPSHIRE. J. C. Cox.
HERTFORDSHIRE. H. W. Tompkins.
KENT. G. Clinch.
KERRY. C. P. Crane.
MIDDLESEX. J. B. Firth.
MONMOUTHSHIRE. G. W. Wade and J. H. Wade.
NORFOLK. W. A. Dutt.
NORTHAMPTONSHIRE. W. Dry.
OXFORDSHIRE. F. G. Brabant.
SOMERSET. G. W. and J. H. Wade.
SUFFOLK. W. A. Dutt.
SURREY. F. A. H. Lambert.
SUSSEX. F. G. Brabant. *Second Edition.*
YORKSHIRE, THE EAST RIDING. J. E. Morris.
YORKSHIRE, THE NORTH RIDING. J. E. Morris.

BRITTANY. S. Baring-Gould.
NORMANDY. C. Scudamore.
ROME. C. G. Ellaby.
SICILY. F. H. Jackson.

## The Little Library

With Introductions, Notes, and Photogravure Frontispieces.

*Small Pott 8vo. Each Volume, cloth, 1s. 6d. net; leather, 2s. 6d. net.*

**Anon.** A LITTLE BOOK OF ENGLISH LYRICS. *Second Edition.*

**Austen (Jane).** PRIDE AND PREJUDICE. Edited by E. V. LUCAS. *Two Vols.*
NORTHANGER ABBEY. Edited by E. V. LUCAS.

**Bacon (Francis).** THE ESSAYS OF LORD BACON. Edited by EDWARD WRIGHT.

**Barham (R. H.).** THE INGOLDSBY LEGENDS. Edited by J. B. ATLAY. *Two Volumes.*

**Barnett (Mrs. P. A.).** A LITTLE BOOK OF ENGLISH PROSE. *Second Edition.*

**Beckford (William).** THE HISTORY OF THE CALIPH VATHEK. Edited by E. DENISON ROSS.

**Blake (William).** SELECTIONS FROM WILLIAM BLAKE. Edited by M. PERUGINI.

**Borrow (George).** LAVENGRO. Edited by F. HINDES GROOME. *Two Volumes.*
THE ROMANY RYE. Edited by JOHN SAMPSON.

**Browning (Robert).** SELECTIONS FROM THE EARLY POEMS OF ROBERT BROWNING. Edited by W. HALL GRIFFIN, M.A.

**Canning (George).** SELECTIONS FROM THE ANTI-JACOBIN: with GEORGE CANNING'S additional Poems. Edited by LLOYD SANDERS.

**Cowley (Abraham).** THE ESSAYS OF ABRAHAM COWLEY. Edited by H. C. MINCHIN.

**Crabbe (George).** SELECTIONS FROM GEORGE CRABBE. Edited by A. C. DEANE.

**Craik (Mrs.).** JOHN HALIFAX, GENTLEMAN. Edited by ANNIE MATHESON. *Two Volumes.*

**Crashaw (Richard).** THE ENGLISH POEMS OF RICHARD CRASHAW. Edited by EDWARD HUTTON.

**Dante (Alighieri).** THE INFERNO OF DANTE. Translated by H. F. CARY. Edited by PAGET TOYNBEE, M.A., D.Litt.
THE PURGATORIO OF DANTE. Translated by H. F. CARY. Edited by PAGET TOYNBEE, M.A., D.Litt.
THE PARADISO OF DANTE. Translated by H. F. CARY. Edited by PAGET TOYNBEE, M.A., D.Litt.

**Darley (George).** SELECTIONS FROM THE POEMS OF GEORGE DARLEY. Edited by R. A. STREATFEILD.

THE LITTLE LIBRARY—*continued.*

**Deane (A. C.).** A LITTLE BOOK OF LIGHT VERSE.

**Dickens (Charles).** CHRISTMAS BOOKS. *Two Volumes.*

**Ferrier (Susan).** MARRIAGE. Edited by A. GOODRICH-FREER and LORD IDDESLEIGH. *Two Volumes.*

THE INHERITANCE. *Two Volumes.*

**Gaskell (Mrs.).** CRANFORD. Edited by E. V. LUCAS. *Second Edition.*

**Hawthorne (Nathaniel).** THE SCARLET LETTER. Edited by PERCY DEARMER.

**Henderson (T. F.).** A LITTLE BOOK OF SCOTTISH VERSE.

**Keats (John).** POEMS. With an Introduction by L. BINYON, and Notes by J. MASEFIELD.

**Kinglake (A. W.).** EOTHEN. With an Introduction and Notes. *Second Edition.*

**Lamb (Charles).** ELIA, AND THE LAST ESSAYS OF ELIA. Edited by E. V. LUCAS.

**Locker (F.).** LONDON LYRICS. Edited by A. D. GODLEY, M.A. A reprint of the First Edition.

**Longfellow (H. W.).** SELECTIONS FROM LONGFELLOW. Edited by L. M. FAITHFULL.

**Marvell (Andrew).** THE POEMS OF ANDREW MARVELL. Edited by E. WRIGHT.

**Milton (John).** THE MINOR POEMS OF JOHN MILTON. Edited by H. C. BEECHING, M.A.

**Moir (D. M.).** MANSIE WAUCH. Edited by T. F. HENDERSON.

**Nichols (J. B. B.).** A LITTLE BOOK OF ENGLISH SONNETS.

**Rochefoucauld (La).** THE MAXIMS OF LA ROCHEFOUCAULD. Translated by Dean STANHOPE. Edited by G. H. POWELL.

**Smith (Horace and James).** REJECTED ADDRESSES. Edited by A. D. GODLEY, M.A.

**Sterne (Laurence).** A SENTIMENTAL JOURNEY. Edited by H. W. PAUL.

**Tennyson (Alfred, Lord).** THE EARLY POEMS OF ALFRED, LORD TENNYSON. Edited by J. CHURTON COLLINS, M.A.

IN MEMORIAM. Edited by H. C. BEECHING, M.A.

THE PRINCESS. Edited by ELIZABETH WORDSWORTH.

MAUD. Edited by ELIZABETH WORDSWORTH.

**Thackeray (W. M.).** VANITY FAIR. Edited by S. GWYNN. *Three Volumes.*

PENDENNIS. Edited by S. GWYNN. *Three Volumes.*

ESMOND. Edited by S. GWYNN.

CHRISTMAS BOOKS. Edited by S. GWYNN.

**Vaughan (Henry).** THE POEMS OF HENRY VAUGHAN. Edited by EDWARD HUTTON.

**Walton (Izaak).** THE COMPLEAT ANGLER. Edited by J. BUCHAN.

**Waterhouse (Elizabeth).** A LITTLE BOOK OF LIFE AND DEATH. Edited by. *Twelfth Edition.*

**Wordsworth (W.).** SELECTIONS FROM WORDSWORTH. Edited by NOWELL C. SMITH.

**Wordsworth (W.)** and **Coleridge (S. T.).** LYRICAL BALLADS. Edited by GEORGE SAMPSON.

## The Little Quarto Shakespeare

Edited by W. J. CRAIG. With Introductions and Notes.

*Pott 16mo. In 40 Volumes. Leather, price* 1*s. net each volume.*

*Mahogany Revolving Book Case.* 10*s. net.*

## Miniature Library

Reprints in miniature of a few interesting books which have qualities of humanity, devotion, or literary genius.

EUPHRANOR: A Dialogue on Youth. By Edward FitzGerald. From the edition published by W. Pickering in 1851. *Demy 32mo. Leather,* 2*s. net.*

THE LIFE OF EDWARD, LORD HERBERT OF CHERBURY. Written by himself. From the edition printed at Strawberry Hill in the year 1764. *Demy 32mo. Leather,* 2*s. net.*

POLONIUS: or Wise Saws and Modern Instances. By Edward FitzGerald. From the edition published by W. Pickering in 1852. *Demy 32mo. Leather,* 2*s. net.*

THE RUBÁIYÁT OF OMAR KHAYYÁM. By Edward FitzGerald. From the 1st edition of 1859, *Fourth Edition. Leather,* 1*s. net.*

## A New Historical Series

Edited by the Rev. H. N. ASMAN, M.A., B.D.

*STORIES FROM ANCIENT HISTORY. By E. Bower, B.A. *Cr. 8vo.* 1s. 6d.

STORIES FROM MODERN HISTORY. By E. M. Wilmot-Buxton, F.R.Hist.S. *Cr. 8vo.* 1s. 6d.

## The New Library of Medicine

Edited by C. W. SALEEBY, M.D., F.R.S.Edin. *Demy 8vo.*

CARE OF THE BODY, THE. F. Cavanagh. *Second Edition.* 7s. 6d. *net.*
CHILDREN OF THE NATION, THE. Right Hon. Sir John Gorst. 7s. 6d. *net.*
CONTROL OF A SCOURGE, THE: or, How Cancer is Curable. Chas. P. Childe. 7s. 6d. *net.*
DISEASES OF OCCUPATION. Sir Thomas Oliver. 10s. 6d. *net.*
DRINK PROBLEM, THE, in its Medico-Sociological Aspects. Edited by T. N. Kelynack. 7s. 6d. *net.*
DRUGS AND THE DRUG HABIT. H. Sainsbury.
FUNCTIONAL NERVE DISEASES. A. T. Schofield. 7s. 6d. *net.*
HYGIENE OF MIND, THE. T. S. Clouston. *Fifth Edition.* 7s. 6d. *net.*
INFANT MORTALITY. George Newman. 7s. 6d. *net.*
PREVENTION OF TUBERCULOSIS (CONSUMPTION), THE. Arthur Newsholme. 10s. 6d. *net.*
AIR AND HEALTH. Ronald C. Macfie, M.A., M.B. 7s. 6d. *net.*

## The New Library of Music

Edited by ERNEST NEWMAN. *Demy 8vo.* 7s. 6d. *net.*

HUGO WOLF. By Ernest Newman. With 13 Illustrations.

HANDEL. By R. A. Streatfeild. With 12 Illustrations.

## Oxford Biographies

*Fcap. 8vo. Each volume, cloth,* 2s. 6d. *net; leather,* 3s. 6d. *net.*

DANTE ALIGHIERI. By Paget Toynbee, M.A., D.Litt. With 12 Illustrations. *Third Edition.*
GIROLAMO SAVONAROLA. By E. L. S. Horsburgh, M.A. With 12 Illustrations. *Second Edition.*
JOHN HOWARD. By E. C. S. Gibson, D.D., Bishop of Gloucester. With 12 Illustrations.
ALFRED TENNYSON. By A. C. BENSON, M.A. With 9 Illustrations. *Second Edition.*
SIR WALTER RALEIGH. By I. A. Taylor. With 12 Illustrations.
ERASMUS. By E. F. H. Capey. With 12 Illustrations.
THE YOUNG PRETENDER. By C. S. Terry. With 12 Illustrations.
ROBERT BURNS. By T. F. Henderson. With 12 Illustrations.
CHATHAM. By A. S. M'Dowall. With 12 Illustrations.
FRANCIS OF ASSISI. By Anna M. Stoddart. With 16 Illustrations.
CANNING. By W. Alison Phillips. With 12 Illustrations.
BEACONSFIELD. By Walter Sichel. With 12 Illustrations.
JOHANN WOLFGANG GOETHE. By H. G. Atkins. With 16 Illustrations.
FRANÇOIS FENELON. By Viscount St Cyres. With 12 Illustrations.

## Romantic History

Edited by MARTIN HUME, M.A. *With Illustrations. Demy 8vo.*

A series of attractive volumes in which the periods and personalities selected are such as afford romantic human interest, in addition to their historical importance.

THE FIRST GOVERNESS OF THE NETHERLANDS, MARGARET OF AUSTRIA. By Eleanor E. Tremayne. 10s. 6d. *net.*
TWO ENGLISH QUEENS AND PHILIP. By Martin Hume, M.A. 15s. *net.*
THE NINE DAYS' QUEEN. By Richard Davey. With a Preface by Martin Hume, M.A. With 12 Illustrations. 10s. 6d. *net.*

## School Examination Series

Edited by A. M. M. STEDMAN, M.A. *Crown 8vo.* *2s. 6d.*

EXAMINATION PAPERS IN ENGLISH HISTORY. By J. Tait Plowden-Wardlaw, B.A.

FRENCH EXAMINATION PAPERS. By A. M. M. Stedman, M.A. *Fifteenth Edition.*
KEY. *Sixth Edition.* *6s. net.*

GENERAL KNOWLEDGE EXAMINATION PAPERS. By A. M. M. Stedman, M.A. *Sixth Edition.*
KEY. *Fourth Edition.* *7s. net.*

GERMAN EXAMINATION PAPERS. By R. J. Morich. *Seventh Edition.*
KEY. *Third Edition.* *6s. net.*

GREEK EXAMINATION PAPERS. By A. M. M. Stedman, M.A. *Ninth Edition.*
KEY. *Fourth Edition.* *6s. net.*

HISTORY AND GEOGRAPHY EXAMINATION PAPERS. By C. H. Spence, M.A. *Third Edition.*

LATIN EXAMINATION PAPERS. By A. M. M. Stedman, M.A. *Fourteenth Edition.*
KEY. *Seventh Edition.* *6s. net.*

PHYSICS EXAMINATION PAPERS. By R. E. Steel, M.A., F.C.S.

## School Histories

*Illustrated.* *Crown 8vo.* *1s. 6d.*

A SCHOOL HISTORY OF WARWICKSHIRE. By B. C. A. Windle, D.Sc., F.R.S.

A SCHOOL HISTORY OF SOMERSET. By Walter Raymond. *Second Edition.*

A SCHOOL HISTORY OF LANCASHIRE. By W. E. Rhodes, M.A.

A SCHOOL HISTORY OF SURREY. By H. E. Malden, M.A.

A SCHOOL HISTORY OF MIDDLESEX. By V. G. Plarr, M.A., and F. W. Walton, M.A.

## Simplified French Texts

Edited by T. R. N. CROFTS, M.A.

*Fcap 8vo.* *1s.*

ABDALLAH. By Edouard Laboulaye. Adapted by J. A. Wilson.

DEUX CONTES. By P. Mérimée. Adapted by J. F. Rhoades.

EDMOND DANTÈS. By A. Dumas. Adapted by M. Ceppi.

JEAN VALJEAN. By Victor Hugo. Adapted by F. W. M. Draper, M.A.

LA BATAILLE DE WATERLOO. By Erckmann-Chatrian. Adapted by G. H. Evans.

LA BOUILLIE AU MIEL. By A. Dumas. Adapted by P. B. Ingham, M.A.

LA CHANSON DE ROLAND. Adapted by H. Rieu, M.A. *Second Edition.*

LE CONSCRIT DE 1813. By Erckmann-Chatrian. Adapted by H. Rieu.

LE DOCTEUR MATHÉUS. By Erckmann-Chatrian. Adapted by W. P. Fuller, M.A.

M. DE BEAUFORT À VINCENNES. By A. Dumas. Adapted by P. B. Ingham, M.A.

L'EQUIPAGE DE LA BELLE-NIVERNAISE. By Alphonse Daudet. Adapted by T. R. N. Crofts, M.A.

L'HISTOIRE D'UNE TULIPE. By A. Dumas. Adapted by T. R. N. Crofts, M.A. *Second Edition.*

L'HISTOIRE DE PIERRE ET CAMILLE. By A. de Musset. Adapted by J. B. Patterson, M.A.

MÉMOIRES DE CADICHON. By Madam de Ségur. Adapted by J. F. Rhoades.

D'AJACCIO À SAINT HELÈNE. By A. Dumas. Adapted by F. W. M. DRAPER, M.A.

REMY LE CHEVRIER. By E. Souvestre. Adapted by E. E. Chottin, B-es-L.

## Simplified German Texts

Edited by T. R. G. CROFTS, M.A. *Fcap. 8vo.* *1s.*

DER MULLER AM RHEIN. By C. Brentano. Adapted by Florence A. Ryan.

DIE GESCHICHTE VON PETER SCHLEMIHL. By A. v. Chamisso. Adapted by R. C. Perry.

DIE NOTHELFER. By W. H. Riehl. Adapted by P. B. Ingham, M.A.

UNDINE UND HULDBRAND. By La Motte Fouqué. Adapted by T. R. N. Crofts, M.A.

## Six Ages of European History

Edited by A. H. JOHNSON, M.A. With Maps. *Crown 8vo.* 2s. 6d.

AGE OF THE ENLIGHTENED DESPOT, THE, 1660-1789. A. H. Johnson.
CENTRAL PERIOD OF THE MIDDLE AGE, THE, 918-1273. Beatrice A. Lees.
DAWN OF MEDIÆVAL EUROPE, THE, 476-918. J. H. B. Masterman.
END OF THE MIDDLE AGE, THE, 1273-1453. E. C. Lodge.
EUROPE IN RENAISSANCE AND REFORMATION, 1453-1659. M. A. Hollings.
REMAKING OF MODERN EUROPE, THE, 1789-1878. J. A. R. Marriott.

## Methuen's Standard Library

*Cloth*, 1s. *net; double volumes*, 1s. 6d. *net.* *Paper*, 6d. *net; double volume*, 1s. *net.*

THE MEDITATIONS OF MARCUS AURELIUS. Translated by R. Graves.
SENSE AND SENSIBILITY. Jane Austen.
ESSAYS AND COUNSELS and THE NEW ATLANTIS. Francis Bacon, Lord Verulam.
RELIGIO MEDICI and URN BURIAL. Sir Thomas Browne. The text collated by A. R. Waller.
THE PILGRIM'S PROGRESS. John Bunyan
REFLECTIONS ON THE FRENCH REVOLUTION. Edmund Burke.
THE POEMS AND SONGS OF ROBERT BURNS. Double Volume.
THE ANALOGY OF RELIGION, NATURAL AND REVEALED. Joseph Butler.
MISCELLANEOUS POEMS. T. CHATTERTON.
THE ROWLEY POEMS. T. Chatterton.
TOM JONES. Henry Fielding. Treble Vol.
CRANFORD. Mrs. Gaskell.
THE POEMS AND PLAYS OF OLIVER GOLDSMITH.
THE CASE IS ALTERED. EVERY MAN IN HIS HUMOUR. EVERY MAN OUT OF HIS HUMOUR. Ben Jonson.
CYNTHIA'S REVELS. POETASTER. Ben Jonson.
THE POEMS OF JOHN KEATS. Double volume. The Text has been collated by E. de Sélincourt.
ON THE IMITATION OF CHRIST. By Thomas à Kempis. Translation by C. Bigg.
A SERIOUS CALL TO A DEVOUT AND HOLY LIFE. W. Law.
PARADISE LOST. John Milton.
EIKONOKLASTES AND THE TENURE OF KINGS AND MAGISTRATES. John Milton.
UTOPIA AND POEMS. Sir Thomas More.
THE REPUBLIC OF PLATO. Translated by Sydenham and Taylor. Double Volume. Translation revised by W. H. D. Rouse.
THE LITTLE FLOWERS OF ST. FRANCIS. Translated by W. Heywood.
THE WORKS OF WILLIAM SHAKESPEARE. In 10 volumes.
THE POEMS OF PERCY BYSSHE SHELLEY. In 4 volumes. With Introductions by C. D. Locock.
THE LIFE OF NELSON. Robert Southey.
THE NATURAL HISTORY AND ANTIQUITIES OF SELBORNE. Gilbert White.

## Textbooks of Science

Edited by G. F. GOODCHILD, M.A., B.Sc., and G. R. MILLS, M.A.

*Fully Illustrated.*

COMPLETE SCHOOL CHEMISTRY, THE. By F. M. Oldham, B.A. With 126 Illustrations. *Third Edition. Cr. 8vo.* 4s. 6d.
ELEMENTARY SCIENCE FOR PUPIL TEACHERS. PHYSICS SECTION. By W. T. Clough, A.R.C.Sc. (Lond.), F.C.S. CHEMISTRY SECTION. By A. E. Dunstan, B.Sc. (Lond.), F.C.S. With 2 Plates and 10 Diagrams. *Cr. 8vo.* 2s.
EXAMPLES IN ELEMENTARY MECHANICS, Practical, Graphical, and Theoretical. By W. J. Dobbs, M.A. With 52 Diagrams. *Cr. 8vo.* 5s.
EXAMPLES IN PHYSICS. By C. E. Jackson, M.A. *Cr. 8vo.* 2s. 6d.
FIRST YEAR PHYSICS. By C. E. Jackson, M.A. With 51 Diagrams. *Cr. 8vo.* 1s. 6d.
OUTLINES OF PHYSICAL CHEMISTRY. By George Senter, B.Sc. (Lond.), Ph.D. With many Diagrams. *Cr. 8vo.* 3s. 6d.
ORGANIC CHEMISTRY, AN, FOR SCHOOLS AND TECHNICAL INSTITUTES. By A. E. Dunstan, B.Sc. (Lond.), F.C.S. With many Illustrations. *Cr. 8vo.* 2s. 6d.
PLANT LIFE, Studies in Garden and School. By Horace F. Jones, F.C.S. With 320 Illustrations. *Cr. 8vo.* 3s. 6d.
PRACTICAL CHEMISTRY. Part I. W. French, M.A. *Fifth Edition. Cr. 8vo.* 1s. 6d.
PRACTICAL CHEMISTRY. Part II. W. French, M.A., and T. H. Boardman, M.A. *Cr. 8vo.* 1s. 6d.
*PRACTICAL CHEMISTRY FOR SCHOOLS AND TECHNICAL INSTITUTES, A. By A. E. Dunstan, B.Sc. (Sheffield and Lond.), F.C.S *Cr. 8vo.* 3s. 6d.
PRACTICAL MECHANICS. S. H. Wells. *Fourth Edition. Cr. 8vo.* 3s. 6d.
TECHNICAL ARITHMETIC AND GEOMETRY. By C. T. Millis, M.I.M.E. *Cr. 8vo.* 3s. 6d.

## Textbooks of Technology

*Fully Illustrated.*

BUILDERS' QUANTITIES. By H. C. Grubb. *Cr. 8vo.* 4*s.* 6*d.*

CARPENTRY AND JOINERY. By F. C. Webber. *Fifth Edition. Cr. 8vo.* 3*s.* 6*d.*

ELECTRIC LIGHT AND POWER: An Introduction to the Study of Electrical Engineering. By E. E. Brooks, B.Sc. (Lond.). and W. H. N. James, A.M.I.E.E., A.R.C.Sc. *Cr. 8vo.* 4*s.* 6*d.*

ENGINEERING WORKSHOP PRACTICE. By C. C. Allen. *Cr. 8vo.* 3*s.* 6*d.*

HOW TO MAKE A DRESS. By J. A. E. Wood. *Fourth Edition. Cr. 8vo.* 1*s.* 6*d.*

INSTRUCTION IN COOKERY. A. P. THOMSON. *Cr. 8vo.* 2*s.* 6*d.*

INTRODUCTION TO THE STUDY OF TEXTILE DESIGN, AN. By Aldred F. Barker. *Demy 8vo.* 7*s.* 6*d.*

MILLINERY, THEORETICAL AND PRACTICAL. By Clare Hill. *Fifth Edition. Cr. 8vo.* 2*s.*

RÉPOUSSÉ METAL WORK. By A. C. Horth. *Cr. 8vo.* 2*s.* 6*d.*

## Handbooks of Theology

THE DOCTRINE OF THE INCARNATION. By R. L. Ottley, D.D. *Fourth Edition revised. Demy 8vo.* 12*s.* 6*d.*

A HISTORY OF EARLY CHRISTIAN DOCTRINE. By J. F. Bethune-Baker, M.A. *Demy 8vo.* 10*s.* 6*d.*

AN INTRODUCTION TO THE HISTORY OF RELIGION. By F. B. Jevons. M.A., Litt.D. *Fourth Edition. Demy 8vo.* 10*s.* 6*d.*

AN INTRODUCTION TO THE HISTORY OF THE CREEDS. By A. E. Burn, D.D. *Demy 8vo.* 10*s.* 6*d.*

THE PHILOSOPHY OF RELIGION IN ENGLAND AND AMERICA. By Alfred Caldecott, D.D. *Demy 8vo.* 10*s.* 6*d.*

THE XXXIX. ARTICLES OF THE CHURCH OF ENGLAND. Edited by E. C. S. Gibson, D.D. *Sixth Edition. Demy 8vo.* 12*s.* 6*d.*

## The Westminster Commentaries

General Editor, WALTER LOCK, D.D., Warden of Keble College, Dean Ireland's Professor of Exegesis in the University of Oxford.

THE ACTS OF THE APOSTLES. Edited by R. B. Rackham, M.A. *Demy 8vo. Fourth Edition.* 10*s.* 6*d.*

THE FIRST EPISTLE OF PAUL THE APOSTLE TO THE CORINTHIANS. Edited by H. L. Goudge, M.A. *Second Ed. Demy 8vo.* 6*s.*

A COMMENTARY ON EXODUS. By A. H. M'Neile, B.D. With a Map and 3 Plans. *Demy 8vo.* 10*s.* 6*d.*

THE BOOK OF EZEKIEL. Edited H. A. Redpath, M.A., D.Litt. *Demy 8vo.* 10*s.* 6*d.*

THE BOOK OF GENESIS. Edited with Introduction and Notes by S. R. Driver, D.D. *Seventh Edition Demy 8vo.* 10*s.* 6*d.*

Also, to be obtained separately, Additions and Corrections in the Seventh Edition of the Book of Genesis. *Demy 8vo.* 1*s.*

THE BOOK OF JOB. Edited by E. C. S. Gibson, D.D. *Second Edition. Demy 8vo.* 6*s.*

THE EPISTLE OF ST. JAMES. Edited with Introduction and Notes by R. J. Knowling, D.D. *Demy 8vo.* 6*s.*

# PART II.—FICTION

**Albanesi (E. Maria).** SUSANNAH AND ONE OTHER. *Fourth Edition. Cr. 8vo.* 6*s.*

THE BLUNDER OF AN INNOCENT. *Second Edition. Cr. 8vo.* 6*s.*

CAPRICIOUS CAROLINE. *Second Edition. Cr. 8vo.* 6*s.*

LOVE AND LOUISA. *Second Edition. Cr. 8vo.* 6*s.* Also *Medium 8vo.* 6*d.*

PETER, A PARASITE. *Cr. 8vo.* 6*s.*

THE BROWN EYES OF MARY. *Third Edition. Cr. 8vo.* 6*s.*

I KNOW A MAIDEN. *Third Edition. Cr. 8vo.* 6*s.* Also *Medium 8vo.* 6*d.*

THE INVINCIBLE AMELIA: THE POLITE ADVENTURESS. *Third Edition. Cr. 8vo.* 3*s.* 6*d.*

**Annesley (Maude).** THIS DAY'S MADNESS. *Second Edition. Cr. 8vo.* 6*s.*

**Anstey (F.).** A BAYARD FROM BENGAL. *Medium 8vo.* 6*d.*

**Austen (Jane).** PRIDE AND PREJUDICE. *Medium 8vo.* 6*d.*

**Aveling (Francis).** ARNOUL THE ENGLISHMAN. *Cr. 8vo.* 6*s.*

**Bagot (Richard).** A ROMAN MYSTERY. *Third Edition. Cr. 8vo.* 6*s.* Also *Medium 8vo.* 6*d.*

THE PASSPORT. *Fourth Edition. Cr. 8vo*

TEMPTATION. *Fifth Edition. Cr. 8vo.* 6*s.*

ANTHONY CUTHBERT. *Fourth Edition Cr. 8vo.* 6*s.*

LOVE'S PROXY. *A New Edition. Cr. 8vo.* 6*s.*

DONNA DIANA. *Second Edition. Cr. 8vo.* 6*s.* Also *Medium 8vo.* 6*d.*

CASTING OF NETS. *Twelfth Edition. Cr. 8vo.* 6*s.* Also *Medium 8vo.* 6*d.*

**Balfour (Andrew).** BY STROKE OF SWORD. *Medium 8vo.* 6*d.*

**Ball (Oona H.)** (Barbara Burke). THEIR OXFORD YEAR. With 16 Illustrations *Cr. 8vo.* 6*s.*

BARBARA GOES TO OXFORD. With 16 Illustrations. *Third Edition. Cr. 8vo.* 6*s.*

**Baring-Gould (S.).** ARMINELL. *Fifth Edition. Cr. 8vo.* 6*s.*
Also *Medium 8vo.* 6*d.*

URITH. *Fifth Edition. Cr. 8vo.* 6*s.*
Also *Medium 8vo.* 6*d.*

IN THE ROAR OF THE SEA. *Seventh Edition. Cr. 8vo.* 6*s.*
Also *Medium 8vo.* 6*d.*

CHEAP JACK ZITA. *Medium 8vo.* 6*d.*

MARGERY OF QUETHER. *Third Edition. Cr. 8vo.* 6*s.*

THE QUEEN OF LOVE. *Fifth Edition. Cr. 8vo.* 6*s.* Also *Medium 8vo.* 6*d.*

JACQUETTA. *Third Edition. Cr. 8vo.* 6*s.*

KITTY ALONE. *Fifth Edition. Cr. 8vo.* 6*s.*
Also *Medium 8vo.* 6*d.*

NOÉMI. Illustrated. *Fourth Edition. Cr. 8vo.* 6*s.* Also *Medium 8vo.* 6*d.*

THE BROOM-SQUIRE. Illustrated. *Fifth Edition. Cr. 8vo.* 6*s.*
Also *Medium 8vo.* 6*d.*

DARTMOOR IDYLLS. *Cr. 8vo.* 6*s.*

GUAVAS THE TINNER. Illustrated. *Second Edition. Cr. 8vo.* 6*s.*

BLADYS OF THE STEWPONEY. Illustrated. *Second Edition. Cr. 8vo.* 6*s.*

PABO THE PRIEST. *Cr. 8vo.* 6*s.*

WINEFRED. Illustrated. *Second Edition. Cr. 8vo.* 6*s.* Also *Medium 8vo.* 6*d.*

ROYAL GEORGIE. Illustrated. *Cr. 8vo.* 6*s.*

CHRIS OF ALL SORTS. *Cr. 8vo.* 6*s.*

IN DEWISLAND. *Second Ed. Cr. 8vo.* 6*s.*

THE FROBISHERS. *Crown 8vo.* 6*s.*
Also *Medium 8vo.* 6*d.*

DOMITIA. Illus. *Second Ed. Cr. 8vo.* 6*s.*

MRS. CURGENVEN OF CURGENVEN. *Crown 8vo.* 6*s.*

LITTLE TU'PENNY. *Medium 8vo.* 6*d.*

FURZE BLOOM. *Medium 8vo.* 6*d.*

**Barnett (Edith A.).** A WILDERNESS WINNER. *Second Edition. Cr. 8vo.* 6*s.*

**Barr (James).** LAUGHING THROUGH A WILDERNESS. *Cr. 8vo.* 6*s.*

**Barr (Robert).** IN THE MIDST OF ALARMS. *Third Edition. Cr. 8vo.* 6*s.*
Also *Medium 8vo.* 6*d.*

THE COUNTESS TEKLA. *Fifth Edition. Cr. 8vo.* 6*s.*
Also *Medium 8vo.* 6*d.*

THE MUTABLE MANY. *Third Edition. Cr. 8vo.* 6*s.* Also *Medium 8vo.* 6*d.*

THE TEMPESTUOUS PETTICOAT. Illustrated. *Third Edition. Cr. 8vo.* 6*s.*

JENNIE BAXTER JOURNALIST. *Medium 8vo.* 6*d.*

**Begbie (Harold).** THE CURIOUS AND DIVERTING ADVENTURES OF SIR JOHN SPARROW; or, THE PROGRESS OF AN OPEN MIND. With a Frontispiece. *Second Edition. Cr. 8vo.* 6*s.*

**Belloc (H.).** EMMANUEL BURDEN, MERCHANT. With 36 Illustrations by G. K. CHESTERTON. *Second Ed. Cr. 8vo.* 6*s.*

A CHANGE IN THE CABINET. *Third Edition. Cr. 8vo.* 6*s.*

**Benson (E. F.)** DODO: A DETAIL OF THE DAY. *Fifteenth Edition. Cr. 8vo.* 6*s.*
Also *Medium 8vo.* 6*d.*

THE VINTAGE. *Medium 8vo.* 6*d.*

**Benson (Margaret).** SUBJECT TO VANITY. *Cr. 8vo.* 3*s.* 6*d.*

**Birmingham (George A.).** THE BAD TIMES. *Second Edition. Cr. 8vo.* 6*s.*

SPANISH GOLD. *Fourth Edition. Cr. 8vo.* 6*s.*

THE SEARCH PARTY. *Third Edition. Cr. 8vo.* 6*s.*

**Bowles (G. Stewart).** A GUN-ROOM DITTY BOX. *Second Ed. Cr. 8vo.* 1*s.* 6*d.*

**Bretherton (Ralph Harold).** THE MILL. *Cr. 8vo.* 6*s.*

AN HONEST MAN. *Second Edition. Cr. 8vo.* 6*s.*

**Brontë (Charlotte).** SHIRLEY. *Medium 8vo.* 6*d.*

**Burton (J. Bloundelle).** ACROSS THE SALT SEAS. *Medium 8vo.* 6*d.*

**Caffyn (Mrs.) ('Iota').** ANNE MAULEVERER. *Medium 8vo.* 6*d.*

**Campbell (Mrs. Vere).** FERRIBY. *Second Edition. Cr. 8vo.* 6*s.*

**Capes (Bernard).** THE EXTRAORDINARY CONFESSIONS OF DIANA PLEASE. *Third Edition. Cr. 8vo.* 6*s.*

A JAY OF ITALY. *Fourth Ed. Cr. 8vo.* 6*s.*

LOAVES AND FISHES. *Second Edition. Cr. 8vo.* 6*s.*

A ROGUE'S TRAGEDY. *Second Edition. Cr. 8vo.* 6*s.*

THE GREAT SKENE MYSTERY. *Second Edition. Cr. 8vo.* 6*s.*

THE LOVE STORY OF ST. BEL. *Second Edition. Cr. 8vo.* 6*s.*

THE LAKE OF WINE. *Medium* 8*vo.* 6*d.*

**Carey (Wymond).** LOVE THE JUDGE. *Second Edition. Cr.* 8*vo.* 6*s.*

**Castle (Agnes and Egerton).** FLOWER O' THE ORANGE, and Other Tales. With a Frontispiece in Colour by A. H. Buckland. *Third Edition. Cr.* 8*vo.* 6*s.*

**Charlton (Randal).** MAVE. *Second Edition. Cr.* 8*vo.* 6*s.*

THE VIRGIN WIDOW. *Cr.* 8*vo.* 6*s.*

**Chesney (Weatherby).** THE MYSTERY OF A BUNGALOW. *Second Edition. Cr.* 8*vo.* 6*s.*

**Clifford (Mrs. W. K.).** THE GETTING WELL OF DOROTHY. Illustrated by GORDON BROWNE. *Second Edition. Cr.* 8*vo.* 3*s.* 6*d.*

A FLASH OF SUMMER. *Medium* 8*vo.* 6*d.*

MRS. KEITH'S CRIME. *Medium* 8*vo.* 6*d.*

**Conrad (Joseph).** THE SECRET AGENT: A Simple Tale. *Fourth Ed. Cr.* 8*vo.* 6*s.*

A SET OF SIX. *Fourth Edition. Cr.* 8*vo.* 6*s.*

**Corbett (Julian).** A BUSINESS IN GREAT WATERS. *Third Edition. Cr.* 8*vo.* 6*s.* Also *Medium* 8*vo.* 6*d.*

**Corelli (Marie).** A ROMANCE OF TWO WORLDS. *Twenty-Ninth Ed. Cr.* 8*vo.* 6*s.*

VENDETTA. *Twenty-Seventh Edition. Cr.* 8*vo.* 6*s.*

THELMA. *Thirty-Ninth Ed. Cr.* 8*vo.* 6*s.*

ARDATH: THE STORY OF A DEAD SELF. *Nineteenth Edition. Cr.* 8*vo.* 6*s.*

THE SOUL OF LILITH. *Sixteenth Edition. Cr.* 8*vo.* 6*s.*

WORMWOOD. *Sixteenth Ed. Cr.* 8*vo.* 6*s.*

BARABBAS: A DREAM OF THE WORLD'S TRAGEDY. *Forty-Fourth Edition. Cr.* 8*vo.* 6*s.*

THE SORROWS OF SATAN. *Fifty-Fifth Edition. Cr.* 8*vo.* 6*s.*

THE MASTER CHRISTIAN. *Twelfth Edition.* 177*th Thousand. Cr.* 8*vo.* 6*s.*

TEMPORAL POWER: A STUDY IN SUPREMACY. *Second Edition.* 150*th Thousand. Cr.* 8*vo.* 6*s.*

GOD'S GOOD MAN: A SIMPLE LOVE STORY. *Thirteenth Edition.* 150th Thousand. *Cr.* 8*vo.* 6*s.*

HOLY ORDERS: THE TRAGEDY OF A QUIET LIFE. *Second Edition.* 120*th Thousand. Crown* 8*vo.* 6*s.*

THE MIGHTY ATOM. *Twenty-seventh Edition. Cr.* 8*vo.* 6*s.*

BOY: a Sketch. *Eleventh Edition. Cr.* 8*vo.* 6*s.*

CAMEOS. *Thirteenth Edition. Cr.* 8*vo.* 6*s.*

**Cotes (Mrs. Everard).** See Duncan (Sara Jeannette).

**Cotterell (Constance).** THE VIRGIN AND THE SCALES. Illustrated. *Second Edition. Cr.* 8*vo.* 6*s.*

**Crockett (S. R.).** LOCHINVAR. Illustrated. *Third Edition. Cr.* 8*vo.* 6*s.* *Also Medium* 8*vo.* 6*d.*

THE STANDARD BEARER. *Cr.* 8*vo.* 6*s.*

**Croker (Mrs. B. M.).** THE OLD CANTONMENT. *Cr.* 8*vo.* 6*s.*

JOHANNA. *Second Edition. Cr.* 8*vo.* 6*s.* Also *Medium* 8*vo.* 6*d.*

THE HAPPY VALLEY. *Fourth Edition. Cr.* 8*vo.* 6*s.*

A NINE DAYS' WONDER. *Third Edition. Cr.* 8*vo.* 6*s.*

PEGGY OF THE BARTONS. *Seventh Ed. Cr.* 8*vo.* 6*s.* Also *Medium* 8*vo.* 6*d.*

ANGEL. *Fifth Edition. Cr.* 8*vo.* 6*s.* Also *Medium* 8*vo.* 6*d.*

A STATE SECRET. *Third Edition. Cr.* 8*vo.* 3*s.* 6*d.* Also *Medium* 8*vo.* 6*d.*

KATHERINE THE ARROGANT. *Fifth Edition. Cr.* 8*vo.* 6*s.*

**Crosbie (Mary).** DISCIPLES. *Second Ed. Cr.* 8*vo.* 6*s.*

**Cuthell (Edith E.).** ONLY A GUARD-ROOM DOG. Illustrated by W. PARKINSON. *Crown* 8*vo.* 3*s.* 6*d.*

**Dawson (Warrington).** THE SCAR. *Second Edition. Cr.* 8*vo.* 6*s.*

THE SCOURGE. *Cr.* 8*vo.* 6*s.*

**Deakin (Dorothea).** THE YOUNG COLUMBINE. With a Frontispiece by LEWIS BAUMER. *Cr.* 8*vo.* 6*s.*

**Deane (Mary).** THE OTHER PAWN. *Cr.* 8*vo.* 6*s.*

**Doyle (A. Conan).** ROUND THE RED LAMP. *Eleventh Edition. Cr.* 8*vo.* 6*s.* Also *Medium* 8*vo.* 6*d.*

**Dumas (Alexandre).** See page 46.

**Duncan (Sara Jeannette)** (Mrs. Everard Cotes). THOSE DELIGHTFUL AMERICANS. *Medium* 8*vo.* 6*d.*

A VOYAGE OF CONSOLATION. Illustrated. *Third Edition. Cr* 8*vo.* 6*s.* Also *Medium* 8*vo.* 6*d.*

COUSIN CINDERELLA. *Second Edition. Cr.* 8*vo.* 6*s.*

THE BURNT OFFERING. *Second Edition. Cr.* 8*vo.* 6*s.*

**Eldridge (George D.).** IN THE POTTER'S HOUSE. *Cr.* 8*vo.* 6*s.*

**Eliot (George).** THE MILL ON THE FLOSS. *Medium* 8*vo.* 6*d.*

**Erskine (Mrs. Steuart).** THE MAGIC PLUMES. *Cr.* 8*vo.* 6*s.*

**Fenn (G. Manville).** SYD BELTON; or, The Boy who would not go to Sea. Illustrated by GORDON BROWNE. *Second Ed. Cr.* 8*vo.* 3*s.* 6*d.*

**Findlater (J. H.).** THE GREEN GRAVES OF BALGOWRIE. *Fifth Edition. Cr.* 8*vo.* 6*s.* Also *Medium* 8*vo.* 6*d.*

THE LADDER TO THE STARS. *Second Edition. Cr.* 8*vo.* 6*s.*

**Findlater (Mary).** A NARROW WAY. *Third Edition. Cr. 8vo.* 6s.

OVER THE HILLS. *Second Edition. Cr. 8vo.* 6s.

THE ROSE OF JOY. *Third Edition. Cr. 8vo.* 6s.

A BLIND BIRD'S NEST. With 8 Illustrations. *Second Edition. Cr. 8vo.* 6s.

**Fitzpatrick (K.)** THE WEANS AT ROWALLAN. Illustrated. *Second Edition. Cr. 8vo.* 6s.

**Francis (M. E.).** (Mrs. Francis Blundell). STEPPING WESTWARD. *Second Edition. Cr. 8vo.* 6s.

MARGERY O' THE MILL. *Third Edition. Cr. 8vo.* 6s.

HARDY-ON-THE-HILL. *Third Edition. Cr. 8vo.* 6s.

GALATEA OF THE WHEATFIELD. *Second Edition. Cr. 8vo.* 6s.

**Fraser (Mrs. Hugh).** THE SLAKING OF THE SWORD. *Second Edition. Cr. 8vo.* 6s.

IN THE SHADOW OF THE LORD. *Third Edition. Crown 8vo.* 6s.

GIANNELLA. *Second Edition. Cr. 8vo.* 6s.

**Fry (B. and C. B.).** A MOTHER'S SON. *Fifth Edition. Cr. 8vo.* 6s.

**Fuller-Maitland (Ella).** BLANCHE ESMEAD. *Second Edition. Cr. 8vo.* 6s.

**Gallon (Tom).** RICKERBY'S FOLLY. *Medium 8vo.* 6d.

**Gaskell (Mrs.).** CRANFORD. *Medium 8vo.* 6d.

MARY BARTON. *Medium 8vo.* 6d.

NORTH AND SOUTH. *Medium 8vo.* 6d.

**Gates (Eleanor).** THE PLOW-WOMAN. *Cr. 8vo.* 6s.

**Gerard (Dorothea).** HOLY MATRIMONY. *Medium 8vo.* 6d.

MADE OF MONEY. *Medium 8vo.* 6d.

THE IMPROBABLE IDYL. *Third Edition. Cr. 8vo.* 6s.

THE BRIDGE OF LIFE. *Cr. 8vo.* 6s.

THE CONQUEST OF LONDON. *Medium 8vo.* 6d.

**Gibbs (Philip).** THE SPIRIT OF REVOLT. *Second Edition. Cr. 8vo.* 6s.

**Gissing (George).** THE TOWN TRAVELLER. *Medium 8vo.* 6d.

THE CROWN OF LIFE. *Cr. 8vo.* 6s.
Also *Medium 8vo.* 6d.

**Glanville (Ernest).** THE INCA'S TREASURE. Illustrated. *Cr. 8vo.* 3s. 6d.
Also *Medium 8vo.* 6d.

THE KLOOF BRIDE. *Medium 8vo.* 6d.

**Gleig (Charles).** BUNTER'S CRUISE. Illustrated. *Cr. 8vo.* 3s. 6d.
Also *Medium 8vo.* 6d.

**Grimm (The Brothers).** GRIMM'S FAIRY TALES. Illustrated. *Medium 8vo.* 6d.

**Haig (J. C.).** IN THE GRIP OF THE TRUSTS: A STORY OF 1914. *Cr. 8vo.* 1s. *net.*

**Hamilton (M.).** THE FIRST CLAIM. *Second Edition. Cr. 8vo.* 6s.

**Harraden (Beatrice).** IN VARYING MOODS. *Fourteenth Edition. Cr. 8vo.* 6s.

THE SCHOLAR'S DAUGHTER. *Fourth Edition. Cr. 8vo.* 6s.

HILDA STRAFFORD and THE REMITTANCE MAN. *Twelfth Ed. Cr. 8vo.* 6s.

INTERPLAY. *Fifth Edition. Cr. 8vo.* 6s.

**Harrod (F.) (Frances Forbes Robertson).** THE TAMING OF THE BRUTE. *Cr. 8vo.* 6s.

**Hart (Mabel).** SISTER K. *Second Edition. Cr. 8vo.* 6s.

**Hichens (Robert).** THE PROPHET OF BERKELEY SQUARE. *Second Edition. Cr. 8vo.* 6s.

TONGUES OF CONSCIENCE. *Third Edition. Cr. 8vo.* 6s.

FELIX. *Sixth Edition. Cr. 8vo.* 6s.

THE WOMAN WITH THE FAN. *Seventh Edition. Cr. 8vo.* 6s.

BYEWAYS. *Cr. 8vo.* 6s.

THE GARDEN OF ALLAH. *Eighteenth Edition. Cr. 8vo.* 6s.

THE BLACK SPANIEL. *Cr. 8vo.* 6s.

THE CALL OF THE BLOOD. *Seventh Edition. Cr. 8vo.* 6s.

BARBARY SHEEP. *Second Edition. Cr. 8vo.* 3s. 6d.

**Hope (Anthony).** THE GOD IN THE CAR. *Eleventh Edition. Cr. 8vo.* 6s.

A CHANGE OF AIR. *Sixth Ed. Cr. 8vo.* 6s.
Also *Medium 8vo.* 6d.

A MAN OF MARK. *Sixth Ed. Cr. 8vo.* 6s.
Also *Medium 8vo.* 6d.

THE CHRONICLES OF COUNT ANTONIO. *Sixth Edition. Cr. 8vo.* 6s.
Also *Medium 8vo.* 6d.

PHROSO. Illustrated by H. R. MILLAR. *Eighth Edition. Cr. 8vo.* 6s.
Also *Medium 8vo.* 6d.

SIMON DALE. Illustrated. *Eighth Edition. Cr. 8vo.* 6s.

THE KING'S MIRROR. *Fourth Edition. Cr. 8vo.* 6s.

QUISANTE. *Fourth Edition. Cr. 8vo.* 6s.

THE DOLLY DIALOGUES. *Cr. 8vo.* 6s.
Also *Medium 8vo.* 6d.

A SERVANT OF THE PUBLIC. Illustrated. *Fourth Edition. Cr. 8vo.* 6s.

TALES OF TWO PEOPLE. With a Frontispiece by A. H. BUCKLAND. *Third Ed. Cr. 8vo.* 6s.

THE GREAT MISS DRIVER. With a Frontispiece by A. H. BUCKLAND. *Fourth Edition. Cr. 8vo.* 6s.

**Hornung (E. W.).** DEAD MEN TELL NO TALES. *Medium* 8*vo.* 6*d.*

**Housman (Clemence).** THE LIFE OF SIR AGLOVALE DE GALIS. *Cr.* 8*vo.* 6*s.*

**Hueffer (Ford Madox).** AN ENGLISH GIRL: A ROMANCE. *Second Edition. Cr.* 8*vo.* 6*s.*

MR. APOLLO: A JUST POSSIBLE STORY. *Second Edition. Cr.* 8*vo.* 6*s.*

**Hutten (Baroness von).** THE HALO. *Fifth Edition. Cr.* 8*vo.* 6*s.*

**Hyne (C. J. Cutcliffe).** MR. HORROCKS, PURSER. *Fifth Edition. Cr.* 8*vo.* 6*s.*

PRINCE RUPERT, THE BUCCANEER. Illustrated. *Third Edition. Cr.* 8*vo.* 6*s.*

**Ingraham (J. H.).** THE THRONE OF DAVID. *Medium* 8*vo.* 6*d.*

**Jacobs (W. W.).** MANY CARGOES. *Thirty-first Edition. Cr.* 8*vo.* 3*s.* 6*d.*

SEA URCHINS. *Fifteenth Edition.. Cr.* 8*vo.* 3*s.* 6*d.*

A MASTER OF CRAFT. Illustrated by WILL OWEN. *Ninth Edition. Cr.* 8*vo.* 3*s.* 6*d.*

LIGHT FREIGHTS. Illustrated by WILL OWEN and Others. *Eighth Edition. Cr.* 8*vo.* 3*s.* 6*d.*

THE SKIPPER'S WOOING. *Ninth Edition. Cr.* 8*vo.* 3*s.* 6*d.*

AT SUNWICH PORT. Illustrated by WILL OWEN. *Ninth Edition. Cr.* 8*vo.* 3*s.* 6*d.*

DIALSTONE LANE. Illustrated by WILL OWEN. *Seventh Edition. Cr.* 8*vo.* 3*s.* 6*d.*

ODD CRAFT. Illustrated by WILL OWEN. *Third Edition. Cr.* 8*vo.* 3*s.* 6*d.*

THE LADY OF THE BARGE. Illustrated. *Eighth Edition. Cr.* 8*vo.* 3*s.* 6*d.*

SALTHAVEN. Illustrated by WILL OWEN. *Second Edition. Cr.* 8*vo.* 3*s.* 6*d.*

SAILORS' KNOTS. Illustrated by WILL OWEN. *Second Edition. Cr.* 8*vo.* 3*s.* 6*d.*

**James (Henry).** THE SOFT SIDE. *Second Edition. Cr.* 8*vo.* 6*s.*

THE BETTER SORT. *Cr.* 8*vo.* 6*s.*

THE GOLDEN BOWL. *Third Edition. Cr.* 8*vo.* 6*s.*

**Keays (H. A. Mitchell).** HE THAT EATETH BREAD WITH ME. *Cr.* 8*vo.* 6*s.*

**Kester (Vaughan).** THE FORTUNES OF THE LANDRAYS. *Cr.* 8*vo.* 6*s.*

**Lawless (Hon. Emily).** WITH ESSEX IN IRELAND. *Cr.* 8*vo.* 6*s.*

**Le Queux (William).** THE HUNCHBACK OF WESTMINSTER. *Third Ed. Cr.* 8*vo.* 6*s.* Also *Medium* 8*vo.* 6*d.*

THE CLOSED BOOK. *Third Edition. Cr.* 8*vo.* 6*s.*

THE VALLEY OF THE SHADOW. Illustrated. *Third Edition. Cr.* 8*vo.* 6*s.*

BEHIND THE THRONE. *Third Edition. Cr.* 8*vo.* 6*s.*

THE CROOKED WAY. *Second Edition. Cr.* 8*vo.* 6*s.*

**Levett-Yeats (S. K.).** ORRAIN. *Second Edition. Cr.* 8*vo.* 6*s.* Also *Medium* 8*vo.* 6*d.*

THE TRAITOR'S WAY. *Medium* 8*vo.* 6*d.*

**Linton (E. Lynn).** THE TRUE HISTORY OF JOSHUA DAVIDSON. *Medium* 8*vo.* 6*d.*

**London (Jack).** WHITE FANG. With a Frontispiece by CHARLES RIVINGSTON BULL. *Seventh Edition. Cr.* 8*vo.* 6*s.*

**Lubbock (Basil).** DEEP SEA WARRIORS. With 4 Illustrations. *Third Edition. Cr.* 8*vo.* 6*s.*

**Lucas (St. John).** THE FIRST ROUND. *Second Edition. Cr.* 8*vo.* 6*s.*

**Lyall (Edna).** DERRICK VAUGHAN, NOVELIST. 43*rd Thousand. Cr.* 8*vo.* 3*s.* 6*d.* Also *Medium* 8*vo.* 6*d.*

**Maartens (Maarten).** THE NEW RELIGION: A MODERN NOVEL. *Third Edition. Cr.* 8*vo.* 6*s.*

THE PRICE OF LIS DORIS. *Second Edition. Cr.* 8*vo.* 6*s.*

BROTHERS ALL; MORE STORIES OF DUTCH PEASANT LIFE. *Third Edition. Cr.* 8*vo.* 6*s.*

**M'Carthy (Justin H.).** THE LADY OF LOYALTY HOUSE. Illustrated. *Third Edition. Cr.* 8*vo.* 6*s.*

THE DRYAD. *Second Edition. Cr.* 8*vo.* 6*s.*

THE DUKE'S MOTTO. *Third Edition. Cr.* 8*vo.* 6*s.*

**Macdonald (Ronald).** A HUMAN TRINITY. *Second Edition. Cr.* 8*vo.* 6*s.*

**Macnaughtan (S.).** THE FORTUNE OF CHRISTINA M'NAB. *Fifth Edition. Cr.* 8*vo.* 6*s.*

**Malet (Lucas).** COLONEL ENDERBY'S WIFE. *Fourth Edition. Cr.* 8*vo.* 6*s.*

A COUNSEL OF PERFECTION. *Second Edition. Cr.* 8*vo.* 6*s.*
Also *Medium* 8*vo.* 6*d.*

THE WAGES OF SIN. *Sixteenth Edition. Cr.* 8*vo.* 6*s.*

THE CARISSIMA. *Fifth Ed. Cr.* 8*vo.* 6*s.*
Also *Medium* 8*vo.* 6*d.*

THE GATELESS BARRIER. *Fifth Edition. Cr.* 8*vo.* 6*s.*

THE HISTORY OF SIR RICHARD CALMADY. *Seventh Edition. Cr.* 8*vo.* 6*s.*

**Mann (Mrs. M. E.).** OLIVIA'S SUMMER. *Second Edition. Cr.* 8*vo.* 6*s.*

A LOST ESTATE. *A New Ed. Cr.* 8*vo.* 6*s.*
Also *Medium* 8*vo.* 6*d.*

THE PARISH OF HILBY. *A New Edition. Cr.* 8*vo.* 6*s.*

THE PARISH NURSE. *Fourth Edition. Cr.* 8*vo.* 6*s.*

GRAN'MA'S JANE. *Cr.* 8*vo.* 6*s.*

MRS. PETER HOWARD. *Second Edition. Cr. 8vo.* 6*s*. Also *Medium* 8*vo*. 6*d*.
A WINTER'S TALE. *A New Edition. Cr.* 8*vo*. 6*s*. Also *Medium* 8*vo*. 6*d*.
ONE ANOTHER'S BURDENS. *A New Edition. Cr.* 8*vo*. 6*s*.
Also *Medium* 8*vo*. 6*d*.
ROSE AT HONEYPOT. *Third Ed. Cr.* 8*vo*. 6*s*.
THERE WAS ONCE A PRINCE. Illustrated by M. B. MANN. *Cr.* 8*vo*. 3*s*. 6*d*.
WHEN ARNOLD COMES HOME. Illustrated by M. B. MANN. *Cr.* 8*vo*. 3*s*. 6*d*.
THE EGLAMORE PORTRAITS. *Third Edition. Cr.* 8*vo*. 6*s*.
THE MEMORIES OF RONALD LOVE. *Cr.* 8*vo*. 6*s*.
THE SHEEP AND THE GOATS. *Third Edition. Cr.* 8*vo*. 6*s*.
A SHEAF OF CORN. *Second Edition. Cr.* 8*vo*. 6*s*.
THE HEART-SMITER. *Second Edition. Cr.* 8*vo*. 6*s*.
AVENGING CHILDREN. *Second Edition. Cr.* 8*vo*. 6*s*.
THE PATTEN EXPERIMENT. *Medium* 8*vo*. 6*d*.
THE CEDAR STAR. *Medium* 8*vo*. 6*d*.
**Marchmont (A. W.).** MISER HOADLEY'S SECRET. *Medium* 8*vo*. 6*d*.
A MOMENT'S ERROR. *Medium* 8*vo*. 6*d*.
**Marriott (Charles).** GENEVRA. *Second Edition. Cr.* 8*vo*. 6*s*.
**Marryat (Captain).** PETER SIMPLE *Medium* 8*vo*. 6*d*.
JACOB FAITHFUL. *Medium* 8*vo*. 6*d*.
**Marsh (Richard).** THE TWICKENHAM PEERAGE. *Second Edition. Cr.* 8*vo*. 6*s*. Also *Medium* 8*vo*. 6*d*.
THE MARQUIS OF PUTNEY. *Second Edition. Cr.* 8*vo*. 6*s*.
IN THE SERVICE OF LOVE. *Third. Edition. Cr.* 8*vo*. 6*s*.
THE GIRL AND THE MIRACLE. *Third Edition. Cr.* 8*vo*. 6*s*.
THE COWARD BEHIND THE CURTAIN. *Cr.* 8*vo*. 6*s*.
THE SURPRISING HUSBAND. *Second Edition. Cr.* 8*vo*. 6*s*.
A ROYAL INDISCRETION. *Second Edition. Cr.* 8*vo*. 6*s*.
A METAMORPHOSIS. *Medium* 8*vo*. 6*d*.
THE GODDESS. *Medium* 8*vo*. 6*d*.
THE JOSS. *Medium* 8*vo*. 6*d*.
**Marshall (Archibald).** MANY JUNES. *Second Edition. Cr.* 8*vo*. 6*s*.
THE SQUIRE'S DAUGHTER. *Second Edition. Cr.* 8*vo*. 6*s*.
**Mason (A. E. W.).** CLEMENTINA. Illustrated. *Third Edition. Cr.* 8*vo*. 6*s*. Also *Medium* 8*vo*. 6*d*.
**Mathers (Helen).** HONEY. *Fourth Ed. Cr.* 8*vo*. 6*s*. Also *Medium* 8*vo*. 6*d*.
GRIFF OF GRIFFITHSCOURT. *Second Edition. Cr.* 8*vo*. 6*s*.
Also *Medium* 8*vo*. 6*d*.
THE FERRYMAN *Second Edition. Cr.* 8*vo*. 6*s*.
TALLY-HO! *Fourth Edition. Cr.* 8*vo*. 6*s*.
SAM'S SWEETHEART. *Medium* 8*vo*. 6*d*.
**Maud (Constance).** A DAUGHTER OF FRANCE. With a Frontispiece. *Second Edition. Cr.* 8*vo*. 6*s*.
**Maxwell (W. B.).** VIVIEN. *Ninth Edition. Cr.* 8*vo*. 6*s*.
THE RAGGED MESSENGER. *Third Edition. Cr.* 8*vo*. 6*s*.
FABULOUS FANCIES. *Cr.* 8*vo*. 6*s*.
THE GUARDED FLAME. *Seventh Edition. Cr.* 8*vo*. 6*s*.
ODD LENGTHS. *Second Ed. Cr.* 8*vo*. 6*s*.
HILL RISE. *Fourth Edition. Cr.* 8*vo*. 6*s*.
THE COUNTESS OF MAYBURY: BETWEEN YOU AND I. *Fourth Edition. Cr.* 8*vo*. 6*s*.
**Meade (L. T.).** DRIFT. *Second Edition. Cr.* 8*vo*. 6*s*. Also *Medium* 8*vo*. 6*d*.
RESURGAM. *Second Edition. Cr.* 8*vo*. 6*s*.
VICTORY. *Cr.* 8*vo*. 6*s*.
A GIRL OF THE PEOPLE. Illustrated. *Fourth Edition. Cr.* 8*vo*. 3*s*. 6*d*.
HEPSY GIPSY. Illustrated. *Cr.* 8*vo*. 2*s*. 6*d*.
THE HONOURABLE MISS: A STORY OF AN OLD-FASHIONED TOWN. Illustrated. *Second Edition. Cr.* 8*vo*. 3*s*. 6*d*.
**Melton (R.).** CÆSAR'S WIFE. *Second Edition. Cr.* 8*vo*. 6*s*.
**Meredith (Ellis).** HEART OF MY HEART. *Cr.* 8*vo*. 6*s*.
**Miller (Esther).** LIVING LIES. *Third Edition. Cr.* 8*vo*. 6*s*.
Also *Medium* 8*vo*. 6*d*.
**Mitford (Bertram).** THE SIGN OF THE SPIDER. Illustrated. *Sixth Edition. Cr.* 8*vo*. 3*s*. 6*d*. Also *Medium* 8*vo*. 6*d*.
IN THE WHIRL OF THE RISING. *Third Edition. Cr.* 8*vo*. 6*s*.
THE RED DERELICT. *Second Edition. Cr.* 8*vo*. 6*s*.
**Molesworth (Mrs.).** THE RED GRANGE. Illustrated. *Second Edition. Cr.* 8*vo*. 3*s*. 6*d*.
**Montgomery (K. L.).** COLONEL KATE. *Second Edition. Cr.* 8*vo*. 6*s*.
**Montresor (F. F.).** THE ALIEN. *Third Edition. Cr.* 8*vo*. 6*s*.
Also *Medium* 8*vo*. 6*d*.
**Morrison (Arthur).** TALES OF MEAN STREETS. *Seventh Edition. Cr.* 8*vo*. 6*s*.
A CHILD OF THE JAGO. *Fifth Edition. Cr.* 8*vo*. 6*s*.
THE HOLE IN THE WALL. *Fourth Edition. Cr.* 8*vo*. 6*s*. Also *Medium* 8*vo* 6*d*.

TO LONDON TOWN. *Second Ed. Cr. 8vo.* 6*s*.

DIVERS VANITIES. *Cr. 8vo.* 6*s*.

**Nesbit (E.).** (Mrs. H. Bland). THE RED HOUSE. Illustrated. *Fourth Edition. Cr. 8vo.* 6*s*. Also *Medium 8vo.* 6*d*.

**Noble (Edward).** LORDS OF THE SEA. *Second Edition. Cr. 8vo.* 6*s*.

**Norris (W. E.).** HARRY AND URSULA: A STORY WITH TWO SIDES TO IT. *Second Edition. Cr. 8vo.* 6*s*.

HIS GRACE. *Medium 8vo.* 6*d*.

GILES INGILBY. *Medium 8vo.* 6*d*.

THE CREDIT OF THE COUNTY. *Medium 8vo.* 6*d*.

LORD LEONARD THE LUCKLESS. *Medium 8vo.* 6*d*.

MATTHEW AUSTIN. *Medium 8vo.* 6*d*.

CLARISSA FURIOSA. *Medium 8vo.* 6*d*.

**Oliphant (Mrs.).** THE LADY'S WALK. *Medium 8vo.* 6*d*.

SIR ROBERT'S FORTUNE. *Medium 8vo.* 6*d*.

THE PRODIGALS. *Medium 8vo.* 6*d*.

THE TWO MARYS. *Medium 8vo.* 6*d*.

**Ollivant (Alfred).** OWD BOB, THE GREY DOG OF KENMUIR. With a Frontispiece. *Eleventh Ed. Cr. 8vo.* 6*s*.

**Oppenheim (E. Phillips).** MASTER OF MEN. *Fourth Edition. Cr. 8vo.* 6*s*.
Also *Medium 8vo.* 6*d*.

**Oxenham (John).** A WEAVER OF WEBS. With 8 Illustrations by MAURICE GREIFFENHAGEN. *Fourth Edition. Cr. 8vo.* 6*s*.

THE GATE OF THE DESERT. With a Frontispiece in Photogravure by HAROLD COPPING. *Fifth Edition. Cr. 8vo.* 6*s*.

PROFIT AND LOSS. With a Frontispiece in photogravure by HAROLD COPPING. *Fourth Edition. Cr. 8vo.* 6*s*.

THE LONG ROAD. With a Frontispiece in Photogravure by HAROLD COPPING. *Fourth Edition. Cr. 8vo.* 6*s*.

THE SONG OF HYACINTH, AND OTHER STORIES. *Second Edition. Cr. 8vo.* 6*s*.

MY LADY OF SHADOWS. *Fourth Edition. Cr. 8vo.* 6*s*.

**Pain (Barry).** LINDLEY KAYS. *Third Edition. Cr. 8vo.* 6*s*.

**Parker (Gilbert).** PIERRE AND HIS PEOPLE. *Sixth Edition. Cr. 8vo.* 6*s*.

MRS. FALCHION. *Fifth Edition. Cr. 8vo.* 6*s*.

THE TRANSLATION OF A SAVAGE. *Third Edition. Cr. 8vo.* 6*s*.

THE TRAIL OF THE SWORD. Illustrated. *Tenth Edition. Cr. 8vo.* 6*s*.
Also *Medium 8vo.* 6*d*.

WHEN VALMOND CAME TO PONTIAC: The Story of a Lost Napoleon. *Sixth Edition. Cr. 8vo.* 6*s*.
Also *Medium 8vo.* 6*d*.

AN ADVENTURER OF THE NORTH. The Last Adventures of 'Pretty Pierre.' *Fourth Edition. Cr. 8vo.* 6*s*.

THE SEATS OF THE MIGHTY. Illustrated. *Sixteenth Edition. Cr. 8vo.* 6*s*.

THE BATTLE OF THE STRONG: a Romance of Two Kingdoms. Illustrated. *Sixth Edition. Cr. 8vo.* 6*s*.

THE POMP OF THE LAVILETTES. *Third Edition. Cr. 8vo.* 3*s*. 6*d*.
Also *Medium 8vo.* 6*d*.

NORTHERN LIGHTS. *Third Edition. Cr. vo.* 6*s*.

**Pasture (Mrs. Henry de la).** THE TYRANT. *Second Edition. Cr. 8vo.* 6*s*.

**Patterson (J. E.).** WATCHERS BY THE SHORE. *Third Edition. Cr. 8vo.* 6*s*.

**Pemberton (Max).** THE FOOTSTEPS OF A THRONE. Illustrated. *Third Edition. Cr. 8vo.* 6*s*.
Also *Medium 8vo.* 6*d*.

I CROWN THEE KING. With Illustrations by Frank Dadd and A. Forrestier. *Cr. 8vo.* 6*s*.
Also *Medium 8vo.* 6*d*.

LOVE THE HARVESTER: A STORY OF THE SHIRES. Illustrated. *Third Edition. Cr. 8vo.* 3*s*. 6*d*.

**Phillpotts (Eden).** LYING PROPHETS. *Third Edition. Cr. 8vo.* 6*s*.

CHILDREN OF THE MIST. *Fifth Edition. Cr. 8vo.* 6*s*.
Also *Medium 8vo.* 6*d*.

THE HUMAN BOY. With a Frontispiece. *Sixth Edition. Cr. 8vo.* 6*s*.
Also *Medium 8vo.* 6*d*.

SONS OF THE MORNING. *Second Edition. Cr. 8vo.* 6*s*.

THE RIVER. *Third Edition. Cr. 8vo.* 6*s*.
Also *Medium 8vo.* 6*d*.

THE AMERICAN PRISONER. *Fourth Edition. Cr. 8vo.* 6*s*.

THE SECRET WOMAN. *Fourth Edition. Cr. 8vo.* 6*s*.

KNOCK AT A VENTURE. With a Frontispiece. *Third Edition. Cr. 8vo.* 6*s*.

THE PORTREEVE. *Fourth Ed. Cr. 8vo.* 6*s*.

THE POACHER'S WIFE. *Second Edition. Cr. 8vo.* 6*s*. Also *Medium 8vo.* 6*d*.

THE STRIKING HOURS. *Second Edition. Crown 8vo.* 6*s*.

THE FOLK AFIELD. *Crown 8vo.* 6*s*.

**Pickthall (Marmaduke).** SAÏD THE FISHERMAN. *Seventh Ed. Cr. 8vo.* 6*s*.

BRENDLE. *Second Edition. Cr. 8vo.* 6*s*.

THE HOUSE OF ISLAM. *Third Edition. Cr. 8vo.* 6*s*.

**'Q' (A. T. Quiller Couch).** THE WHITE WOLF. *Second Edition. Cr. 8vo.* 6s. Also *Medium 8vo.* 6d.

THE MAYOR OF TROY. *Fourth Edition. Cr. 8vo.* 6s.

MERRY-GARDEN, AND OTHER STORIES. *Cr. 8vo.* 6s.

MAJOR VIGOUREUX. *Third Edition. Cr. 8vo.* 6s.

**Querido (Israel).** TOIL OF MEN. Translated by F. S. ARNOLD. *Cr. 8vo.* 6s.

**Rawson (Maud Stepney).** THE ENCHANTED GARDEN. *Fourth Edition. Cr. 8vo.* 6s.

THE EASY GO LUCKIES: OR, ONE WAY OF LIVING. *Second Edition. Cr. 8vo.* 6s.

HAPPINESS. *Second Edition. Cr. 8vo.* 6s.

**Rhys (Grace).** THE WOOING OF SHEILA. *Second Edition. Cr. 8vo.* 6s.

THE BRIDE. *Cr. 8vo.* 6s.

**Ridge (W. Pett).** LOST PROPERTY. *Second Edition. Cr. 8vo.* 6s. Also *Medium 8vo.* 6d.

ERB. *Second Edition. Cr. 8vo.* 6s. Also *Medium 8vo.* 6d.

A SON OF THE STATE. *Second Edition. Cr. 8vo.* 3s. 6d. Also *Medium 8vo.* 6d.

A BREAKER OF LAWS. *A New Edition. Cr. 8vo.* 3s. 6d.

MRS. GALER'S BUSINESS. Illustrated. *Second Edition. Cr. 8vo.* 6s.

THE WICKHAMSES. *Fourth Edition. Cr. 8vo.* 6s.

NAME OF GARLAND. *Third Edition. Cr. 8vo.* 6s.

SPLENDID BROTHER. *Third Edition. Cr. 8vo.* 6s.

GEORGE and THE GENERAL. *Medium 8vo.* 6d.

**Ritchie (Mrs. David G.).** MAN AND THE CASSOCK. *Second Edition. Cr. 8vo.* 6s.

**Roberts (C. G. D.).** THE HEART OF THE ANCIENT WOOD. *Cr. 8vo.* 3s. 6d.

**Robins (Elizabeth).** THE CONVERT. *Third Edition. Cr. 8vo.* 6s.

**Rosenkrantz (Baron Palle).** THE MAGISTRATE'S OWN CASE. *Cr. 8vo.* 6s.

**Russell (W. Clark).** MY DANISH SWEETHEART. Illustrated. *Fifth Edition. Cr. 8vo.* 6s. Also *Medium 8vo.* 6d.

HIS ISLAND PRINCESS. Illustrated. *Second Edition. Cr. 8vo.* 6s. Also *Medium 8vo.* 6d.

ABANDONED. *Second Edition. Cr. 8vo.* 6s. Also *Medium 8vo.* 6d.

MASTER ROCKAFELLAR'S VOYAGE. Illustrated by GORDON BROWNE. *Fourth Edition. Cr. 8vo.* 3s. 6d.

A MARRIAGE AT SEA. *Medium 8vo.* 6d.

**Ryan (Marah Ellis).** FOR THE SOUL OF RAFAEL. *Cr. 8vo.* 6s.

**Sandys (Sydney).** JACK CARSTAIRS OF THE POWER HOUSE. With 4 Illustrations by STANLEY L. WOOD. *Cr. 8vo.* 6s.

**Sergeant (Adeline).** THE PASSION OF PAUL MARILLIER. *Crown 8vo.* 6s.

THE QUEST OF GEOFFREY DARRELL. *Cr. 8vo.* 6s.

THE COMING OF THE RANDOLPHS. *Cr. 8vo.* 6s.

THE PROGRESS OF RACHAEL. *Cr. 8vo.* 6s.

BARBARA'S MONEY. *Medium 8vo.* 6d.

THE MASTER OF BEECHWOOD. *Medium 8vo.* 6d.

THE YELLOW DIAMOND. *Second Ed. Cr. 8vo.* 6s. Also *Medium 8vo.* 6d.

THE LOVE THAT OVERCAME. *Medium 8vo.* 6d.

**Shelley (Bertha).** ENDERBY. *Third Ed. Cr. 8vo.* 6s.

**Sidgwick (Mrs. Alfred).** THE KINSMAN. With 8 Illustrations by C. E. BROCK. *Third Edition. Cr. 8vo.* 6s.

THE SEVERINS. *Second Ed. Cr. 8vo.* 6s.

**Smith (Dorothy V. Horace).** MISS MONA. *Cr. 8vo.* 3s. 6d.

**Sonnichsen (Albert).** DEEP-SEA VAGABONDS. *Cr. 8vo.* 6s.

**Stewart (Newton V.).** A SON OF THE EMPEROR: BEING PASSAGES FROM THE LIFE OF ENZIO, KING OF SARDINIA AND CORSICA. *Cr. 8vo.* 6s.

**Sunbury (George).** THE HA'PENNY MILLIONAIRE. *Cr. 8vo.* 3s. 6d.

**Surtees (R. S.).** HANDLEY CROSS. Illustrated. *Medium 8vo.* 6d.

MR. SPONGE'S SPORTING TOUR. Illustrated. *Medium 8vo.* 6d.

ASK MAMMA. Illus. *Medium 8vo.* 6d.

**Swayne (Martin Lutrell).** THE BISHOP AND THE LADY. *Second Edition. Cr. 8vo.* 6s.

**Thurston (E. Temple).** MIRAGE. *Fourth Edition. Cr. 8vo.* 6s.

**Underhill (Evelyn).** THE COLUMN OF DUST. *Cr. 8vo.* 6s.

**Urquhart (M.).** A TRAGEDY IN COMMONPLACE. *Second Ed. Cr. 8vo.* 6s.

**Vorst (Marie Van).** THE SENTIMENTAL ADVENTURES OF JIMMY BULSTRODE. *Cr. 8vo.* 6s.

IN AMBUSH. *Second Ed. Cr. 8vo.* 6s.

**Waineman (Paul).** THE BAY OF LILACS: A Romance from Finland. *Second Edition. Cr. 8vo.* 6s.

THE SONG OF THE FOREST. *Cr. 8vo.* 6s.

**Walford (Mrs. L. B.).** MR SMITH. *Medium 8vo. 6d.*

THE BABY'S GRANDMOTHER. *Medium 8vo. 6d.*

COUSINS. *Medium 8vo. 6d.*

TROUBLESOME DAUGHTERS. *Medium 8vo. 6d.*

**Wallace (General Lew).** BEN-HUR. *Medium 8vo. 6d.*

THE FAIR GOD. *Medium 8vo. 6d.*

**Waltz (Elizabeth C.).** THE ANCIENT LANDMARK: A KENTUCKY ROMANCE. *Cr. 8vo. 6s.*

**Watson (H. B. Marriott).** TWISTED EGLANTINE Illustrated. *Third Edition. Cr. 8vo. 6s.*

THE HIGH TOBY: Being further Chapters in the Life and Fortunes of Dick Ryder, otherwise Galloping Dick. With a Frontispiece. *Third Edition. Cr. 8vo. 6s.*

A MIDSUMMER DAY'S DREAM. *Third Edition. Crown 8vo. 6s.*

THE PRIVATEERS. Illustrated. *Second Edition. Cr. 8vo. 6s.*

A POPPY SHOW: BEING DIVERS AND DIVERSE TALES. *Cr. 8vo. 6s.*

THE FLOWER OF THE HEART. *Third Edition. Cr. 8vo. 6s.*

THE CASTLE BY THE SEA. *Third Edition. Cr. 8vo. 6s.*

THE ADVENTURERS. *Medium 8vo. 6d.*

**Webling (Peggy).** THE STORY OF VIRGINIA PERFECT. *Third Edition. Cr. 8vo. 6s.*

**Weekes (A. B.).** THE PRISONERS OF WAR. *Medium 8vo. 6d.*

**Wells (H. G.).** THE SEA LADY. *Cr. 8vo. 6s.* Also *Medium 8vo. 6d.*

**Weyman (Stanley).** UNDER THE RED ROBE. With Illustrations by R. C. WOODVILLE. *Twenty-Second Ed. Cr. 8vo. 6s.*

**Whitby (Beatrice).** THE RESULT OF AN ACCIDENT. *Second Edition. Cr. 8vo. 6s.*

**White (Percy).** THE SYSTEM. *Third Edition. Cr. 8vo. 6s.*

A PASSIONATE PILGRIM. *Medium 8vo. 6d.*

LOVE AND THE WISE MEN. *Second Edition. Cr. 8vo. 6s.*

**Williams (Margery).** THE BAR. *Cr. 8vo. 6s.*

**Williamson (Mrs. C. N.).** THE ADVENTURE OF PRINCESS SYLVIA. *Second Edition. Cr. 8vo. 6s.*

THE WOMAN WHO DARED. *Cr. 8vo. 6s.*

THE SEA COULD TELL. *Second Edition. Cr. 8vo. 6s.*

THE CASTLE OF THE SHADOWS. *Third Edition. Cr. 8vo. 6s.*

PAPA. *Cr. 8vo. 6s.*

**Williamson (C. N. and A. M.).** THE LIGHTNING CONDUCTOR: The Strange Adventures of a Motor Car. With 16 Illustrations. *Seventeenth Edition. Cr. 8vo. 6s.* Also *Cr. 8vo. 1s. net.*

THE PRINCESS PASSES: A Romance of a Motor. With 16 Illustrations. *Ninth Edition. Cr. 8vo. 6s.*

MY FRIEND THE CHAUFFEUR. With 16 Illustrations. *Tenth Edit. Cr. 8vo. 6s.*

LADY BETTY ACROSS THE WATER. *Tenth Edition. Cr. 8vo. 6s.*

THE CAR OF DESTINY AND ITS ERRAND IN SPAIN. With 17 Illustrations. *Fourth Edition. Cr. 8vo. 6s.*

THE BOTOR CHAPERON. With a Frontispiece in Colour by A. H. BUCKLAND, 16 other Illustrations, and a Map. *Fifth Edition. Cr. 8vo. 6s.*

SCARLET RUNNER. With a Frontispiece in Colour by A. H. BUCKLAND, and 8 other Illustrations. *Third Ed. Cr. 8vo. 6s.*

SET IN SILVER. With a Frontispiece. *Second Edition. Cr. 8vo. 6s.*

**Wyllarde (Dolf).** THE PATHWAY OF THE PIONEER (Nous Autres). *Fourth Edition. Cr. 8vo. 6s.*

**Yeldham (C. C.).** DURHAM'S FARM. *Cr. 8vo. 6s.*

## Books for Boys and Girls

*Illustrated. Crown 8vo. 3s. 6d.*

THE GETTING WELL OF DOROTHY. By Mrs. W. K. Clifford. *Second Edition.*

ONLY A GUARD-ROOM DOG. By Edith E. Cuthell.

MASTER ROCKAFELLAR'S VOYAGE. By W. Clark Russell. *Fourth Edition.*

SYD BELTON: Or, the Boy who would not go to Sea. By G. Manville Fenn. *Second Ed.*

THE RED GRANGE. By Mrs. Molesworth.

A GIRL OF THE PEOPLE. By L. T. Meade. *Fourth Edition.*

HEPSY GIPSY. By L. T. Meade. *2s. 6d.*

THE HONOURABLE MISS. By L. T. Meade. *Second Edition.*

THERE WAS ONCE A PRINCE. By Mrs. M. E. Mann.

WHEN ARNOLD COMES HOME. By Mrs. M. E. Mann.

## The Novels of Alexandre Dumas

*Medium 8vo. Price 6d. Double Volumes, 1s.*

ACTÉ.
THE ADVENTURES OF CAPTAIN PAMPHILE.
AMAURY.
THE BIRD OF FATE.
THE BLACK TULIP.
THE CASTLE OF EPPSTEIN.
CATHERINE BLUM.
CECILE.
THE CHEVALIER D'HARMENTAL. (Double volume.) 1*s.*
CHICOT THE JESTER.
CONSCIENCE.
THE CONVICT'S SON.
THE CORSICAN BROTHERS; and OTHO THE ARCHER.
CROP-EARED JACQUOT.
DOM GORENFLOT.
THE FATAL COMBAT.
THE FENCING MASTER.
FERNANDE.
GABRIEL LAMBERT.
GEORGES.
THE GREAT MASSACRE.
HENRI DE NAVARRE.
HÉLÈNE DE CHAVERNY.
THE HOROSCOPE.
LOUISE DE LA VALLIÈRE. (Double volume.) 1*s.*
THE MAN IN THE IRON MASK. (Double volume.) 1*s.*
MAÎTRE ADAM.
THE MOUTH OF HELL.
NANON. (Double volume.) 1*s.*
PAULINE; PASCAL BRUNO; and BONTEKOE.
PÈRE LA RUINE.
THE PRINCE OF THIEVES.
THE REMINISCENCES OF ANTONY.
ROBIN HOOD.
THE SNOWBALL AND SULTANETTA.
SYLVANDIRE.
TALES OF THE SUPERNATURAL.
TALES OF STRANGE ADVENTURE.
THE THREE MUSKETEERS. (Double volume.) 1*s.*
THE TRAGEDY OF NANTES.
TWENTY YEARS AFTER. (Double volume.) 1*s.*
THE WILD-DUCK SHOOTER.
THE WOLF-LEADER.

## Methuen's Sixpenny Books

*Medium 8vo.*

**Albanesi (E. Maria).** LOVE AND LOUISA.
I KNOW A MAIDEN.

**Anstey (F.).** A BAYARD OF BENGAL.

**Austen (J.).** PRIDE AND PREJUDICE.

**Bagot (Richard).** A ROMAN MYSTERY.
CASTING OF NETS.
DONNA DIANA.

**Balfour (Andrew).** BY STROKE OF SWORD.

**Baring-Gould (S.).** FURZE BLOOM.
CHEAP JACK ZITA.
KITTY ALONE.
URITH.
THE BROOM SQUIRE.
IN THE ROAR OF THE SEA.
NOÉMI.
A BOOK OF FAIRY TALES. Illustrated.
LITTLE TU'PENNY.
WINEFRED.
THE FROBISHERS.
THE QUEEN OF LOVE.
ARMINELL.

**Barr (Robert).** JENNIE BAXTER.
IN THE MIDST OF ALARMS.
THE COUNTESS TEKLA.
THE MUTABLE MANY.

**Benson (E. F.).** DODO.
THE VINTAGE.

**Brontë (Charlotte).** SHIRLEY.

**Brownell (C. L.).** THE HEART OF JAPAN.

**Burton (J. Bloundelle).** ACROSS THE SALT SEAS.

**Caffyn (Mrs.).** ANNE MAULEVERER.

**Capes (Bernard).** THE LAKE OF WINE.

**Clifford (Mrs. W. K.).** A FLASH OF SUMMER.
MRS. KEITH'S CRIME.

**Corbett (Julian).** A BUSINESS IN GREAT WATERS.

**Croker (Mrs. B. M.).** ANGEL.
A STATE SECRET.
PEGGY OF THE BARTONS.
JOHANNA.

**Dante (Alighieri).** THE DIVINE COMEDY (Cary).

**Doyle (A. Conan).** ROUND THE RED LAMP.

**Duncan (Sara Jeannette).** A VOYAGE OF CONSOLATION.
THOSE DELIGHTFUL AMERICANS.

**Eliot (George).** THE MILL ON THE FLOSS.

**Findlater (Jane H.).** THE GREEN GRAVES OF BALGOWRIE.

**Gallon (Tom).** RICKERBY'S FOLLY.

**Gaskell (Mrs.).** CRANFORD.
MARY BARTON.
NORTH AND SOUTH.

**Gerard (Dorothea).** HOLY MATRIMONY.
THE CONQUEST OF LONDON.
MADE OF MONEY.

**Gissing (G).** THE TOWN TRAVELLER.
THE CROWN OF LIFE.

**Glanville (Ernest).** THE INCA'S TREASURE.
THE KLOOF BRIDE.

**Gleig (Charles).** BUNTER'S CRUISE.

**Grimm (The Brothers).** GRIMM'S FAIRY TALES.

**Hope (Anthony).** A MAN OF MARK.
A CHANGE OF AIR.
THE CHRONICLES OF COUNT ANTONIO.
PHROSO.
THE DOLLY DIALOGUES.

**Hornung (E. W.).** DEAD MEN TELL NO TALES.

**Ingraham (J. H.).** THE THRONE OF DAVID.

**Le Queux (W.).** THE HUNCHBACK OF WESTMINSTER.

**Levett-Yeats (S. K.).** THE TRAITOR'S WAY.
ORRAIN.

**Linton (E. Lynn).** THE TRUE HISTORY OF JOSHUA DAVIDSON.

**Lyall (Edna).** DERRICK VAUGHAN.

**Malet (Lucas).** THE CARISSIMA.
A COUNSEL OF PERFECTION.

**Mann (Mrs. M. E.).** MRS. PETER HOWARD.
A LOST ESTATE.
THE CEDAR STAR.
ONE ANOTHER'S BURDENS.
THE PATTEN EXPERIMENT.
A WINTER'S TALE.

**Marchmont (A. W.).** MISER HOADLEY'S SECRET.
A MOMENT'S ERROR.

**Marryat (Captain).** PETER SIMPLE.
JACOB FAITHFUL.

**Marsh (Richard).** A METAMORPHOSIS.
THE TWICKENHAM PEERAGE.
THE GODDESS.
THE JOSS.

**Mason (A. E. W.).** CLEMENTINA.

**Mathers (Helen).** HONEY.
GRIFF OF GRIFFITHSCOURT.
SAM'S SWEETHEART.

**Meade (Mrs. L. T.).** DRIFT.

**Miller (Esther).** LIVING LIES.

**Mitford (Bertram).** THE SIGN OF THE SPIDER.

**Montresor (F. F.).** THE ALIEN.

**Morrison (Arthur).** THE HOLE IN THE WALL.

**Nesbit (E.)** THE RED HOUSE.

**Norris (W. E.).** HIS GRACE.
GILES INGILBY.
THE CREDIT OF THE COUNTY.
LORD LEONARD THE LUCKLESS.
MATTHEW AUSTIN.
CLARISSA FURIOSA.

**Oliphant (Mrs.).** THE LADY'S WALK.
SIR ROBERT'S FORTUNE.
THE PRODIGALS.
THE TWO MARYS.

**Oppenheim (E. P.).** MASTER OF MEN.

**Parker (Gilbert).** THE POMP OF THE LAVILETTES.
WHEN VALMOND CAME TO PONTIAC.
THE TRAIL OF THE SWORD.

**Pemberton (Max).** THE FOOTSTEPS OF A THRONE.
I CROWN THEE KING.

**Phillpotts (Eden).** THE HUMAN BOY.
CHILDREN OF THE MIST.
THE POACHER'S WIFE.
THE RIVER.

**'Q' (A. T. Quiller Couch).** THE WHITE WOLF.

**Ridge (W. Pett).** A SON OF THE STATE.
LOST PROPERTY.
GEORGE and THE GENERAL.
ERB.

**Russell (W. Clark).** ABANDONED.
A MARRIAGE AT SEA.
MY DANISH SWEETHEART.
HIS ISLAND PRINCESS.

**Sergeant (Adeline).** THE MASTER OF BEECHWOOD.
BARBARA'S MONEY.
THE YELLOW DIAMOND.
THE LOVE THAT OVERCAME.

**Sidgwick (Mrs. Alfred).** THE KINSMAN.

**Surtees (R. S.).** HANDLEY CROSS.
MR. SPONGE'S SPORTING TOUR.
ASK MAMMA.

**Walford (Mrs. L. B.).** MR. SMITH.
COUSINS.
THE BABY'S GRANDMOTHER.
TROUBLESOME DAUGHTERS.

**Wallace (General Lew).** BEN-HUR.
THE FAIR GOD.

**Watson (H. B. Marriott).** THE ADVENTURERS.

**Weekes (A. B.).** PRISONERS OF WAR.

**Wells (H. G.).** THE SEA LADY.

**White (Percy).** A PASSIONATE PILGRIM.

CPSIA information can be obtained at www.ICGtesting.com
Printed in the USA
LVOW01s2122230614

391293LV00034B/610/P